First World War FOR DUMMIES®
A Wiley Brand

by Dr Seán Lang

FOR DUMMIES® A Wiley Brand   IWM IMPERIAL WAR MUSEUMS

First World War For Dummies®

Published by: **John Wiley & Sons, Ltd.,** The Atrium, Southern Gate, Chichester (www.wiley.com) in association with Imperial War Museums

This edition first published 2014

© 2014 John Wiley & Sons, Ltd, Chichester, West Sussex.

Registered office

John Wiley & Sons Ltd, The Atrium, Southern Gate, Chichester, West Sussex, PO19 8SQ, United Kingdom

For details of our global editorial offices, for customer services and for information about how to apply for permission to reuse the copyright material in this book please see our website at www.wiley.com.

Wiley publishes in a variety of print and electronic formats and by print-on-demand. Some material included with standard print versions of this book may not be included in e-books or in print-on-demand. If this book refers to media such as a CD or DVD that is not included in the version you purchased, you may download this material at www.dummies.com. For more information about Wiley products, visit www.wiley.com.

Designations used by companies to distinguish their products are often claimed as trademarks. All brand names and product names used in this book are trade names, service marks, trademarks or registered trademarks of their respective owners. The publisher is not associated with any product or vendor mentioned in this book.

LIMIT OF LIABILITY/DISCLAIMER OF WARRANTY: WHILE THE PUBLISHER AND AUTHOR HAVE USED THEIR BEST EFFORTS IN PREPARING THIS BOOK, THEY MAKE NO REPRESENTATIONS OR WARRANTIES WITH THE RESPECT TO THE ACCURACY OR COMPLETENESS OF THE CONTENTS OF THIS BOOK AND SPECIFICALLY DISCLAIM ANY IMPLIED WARRANTIES OF MERCHANTABILITY OR FITNESS FOR A PARTICULAR PURPOSE. IT IS SOLD ON THE UNDERSTANDING THAT THE PUBLISHER IS NOT ENGAGED IN RENDERING PROFESSIONAL SERVICES AND NEITHER THE PUBLISHER NOR THE AUTHOR SHALL BE LIABLE FOR DAMAGES ARISING HEREFROM. IF PROFESSIONAL ADVICE OR OTHER EXPERT ASSISTANCE IS REQUIRED, THE SERVICES OF A COMPETENT PROFESSIONAL SHOULD BE SOUGHT.

For general information on our other products and services, please contact our Customer Care Department within the U.S. at 877-762-2974, outside the U.S. at (001) 317-572-3993, or fax 317-572-4002. For technical support, please visit www.wiley.com/techsupport.

A catalogue record for this book is available from the British Library.

ISBN 978-1-118-67999-9 (paperback); ISBN 978-1-118-67996-8 (ebk); ISBN 978-1-118-67997-5 (ebk)

10 9 8 7 6 5 4 3 2 1

MIX
Paper from
responsible sources
FSC® C013604

Contents at a Glance

Table of Contents

Introduction

. . . .

Some years ago I had a job at Exeter University training student teachers to teach history in secondary schools. One day we were talking about the First World War and how to teach children about it, and one of them said, 'Why don't we just go there?' So we hired a minibus, took the ferry and spent a few days visiting the battlefields around the area of the Battle of the Somme in northern France. We visited cemeteries and museums; we looked at maps and traced where the lines of trenches had run, and worked out where this advance had taken place and where that machine gun had been positioned: all very useful experience. The most useful lesson of the trip, however, was entirely unexpected.

During our trip, we visited the memorial park that commemorates the men from Newfoundland who fought on the Somme. It has an impressive memorial, a cemetery and a large area where the trenches and shell holes have been preserved. By the entrance we found a group from an English boys' school. The boys were sitting on the ground and their history teacher was telling them about the war. I caught words like 'Sarajevo' and 'invaded Belgium', so I guessed he was taking them through the events of 1914. They didn't look very gripped. We went on and visited the monument, explored the trenches and worked out what had happened where. One student even found her grandfather's grave in the cemetery, which was a poignant moment. And then we headed back to the minibus.

When we got to the entrance, the school party was still there. They'd advanced four or five yards, but the boys were still sitting on the ground and the teacher was still talking. This time I heard the words 'Loos' and 'Ypres' and I realised that in all the time we'd been exploring, these poor boys had been sitting down while their teacher talked his way through the history of the war – *and he'd only reached 1915!* When we reached the minibus I told my group, 'That's a perfect example of how you should never, *ever* teach children – or anyone – about the First World War'.

And I promise not to do it to you.

About This Book

Like all the *For Dummies* books, you can read this one how you like. You can read it cover to cover, you can dip into it, you can go straight to the bit you want or you can hop about. Wherever you start reading, I try to make sure you know where you are and what's been happening while you've been away.

This book is called *First World War For Dummies*. That doesn't mean you're a dummy, but you might feel like one when you run into someone who appears to know all there is to know about the war. And such people undoubtedly exist. They spend their lives studying the war in minute detail, and they can tell you exactly which battalion was based where and who commanded whom and what the soldiers on each side wore and when they wore it. Don't get me wrong: I'm full of admiration for these people. I just try not to get stuck with them at parties.

Most people tend to have a rather less precise idea of the First World War. You may well have studied some aspects of the war at school, either in history or possibly in your English lessons. The war produced some very powerful poetry that pupils often study at school, and modern writers such as Pat Barker and Sebastian Faulks have written successful novels set in the war. But even if you've looked at the war before, you may not have a full picture of what was going on. You may well know that life in the trenches could be appalling, but why were the men sitting in trenches in the first place? And how did they plan to get out of them? Even more importantly: what did they think the war was actually *for*?

I've designed this book to give you an overview of the way the war developed and how it changed the world. I take you through the causes of the war and who the men and women were who got caught up in it. I do take you through various battles – you can't really avoid that – but I try to explain why people felt the need to fight them in the first place. (No, they weren't doing so just for fun or to give future generations lots of historical details to learn.) My aim isn't to fill you with more pieces of information than you can take in – that's what our fact-collecting friends are for – but to *explain* what happened, why it happened and what the people at the time hoped (often wrongly) would follow from their actions.

Having an understanding of the First World War is crucial for being able to understand the modern world. The war marks the point when the old certainties of the Victorian age ended and the 20th century really got going. It was the first war of mass production – and mass destruction. It was the first war in history to be fought on land, on sea, under the sea, in the air and even in the home. And it was truly a *world* war. In the west, awareness of the war tends to be dominated by the trenches of the Western Front, but the war was fought across eastern and southern Europe, in the Middle East, the Pacific, in the Atlantic and across Africa. It brought in countries from every continent. The war led to a huge range of major developments in world history, including the Russian Revolution, the rise of fascism and of the Nazis, the Second World War, the Cold War, the Arab–Israeli conflict and even the British love affair with irony.

Like any historical topic, historians have sharply differing views on the First World War. For many years they saw it essentially as a tragedy, in which a whole generation of young men paid a terrible price for the self-indulgent follies of their leaders. Writers and filmmakers were haunted by the image of troops going 'over the top' (that's a phrase from the First World War), only to be mown down in 'no-man's-land' (and that's another one) by machine guns, while their generals sat sipping brandy in comfortable chateaux located miles behind the lines. 'Lions led by donkeys' was how one German general is said to have described his British opponents – brave Tommies let down by their own uncaring and inept generals. It's a powerful narrative and you can find it in many books and films about the war.

More recently, historians have challenged that stereotype. They've shown that these generals were far from inept, and that they actually showed consider-able ingenuity and imagination in coping with a type of warfare that was completely new to them – and to everyone else. Perhaps even more importantly, more historians have made a powerful case that the First World War, like the Second, was a war worth fighting, that it was about important issues and that it did achieve something important. You're not convinced? Well, I look at the question from both sides in the book so keep an open mind for now.

Foolish Assumptions

Like any author I have to make certain assumptions about you, the reader, and these assumptions may be right or they may be wrong.

Firstly, I'm assuming that you've heard a bit about the war but don't know much about it in any detail. Secondly, I'm assuming that you've probably gathered, from TV, from films or from what you did at school, that the war was a pretty grim affair from which no one, and certainly no one in charge, emerges with much credit. You may very well know of one of your family who fought, and possibly died, in the war and you may wonder what, if anything, that person fought and died for. And, of course, I'm assuming you've picked up this book to try to find out more, to get a better grasp on the war and what it all meant. If even some of those assumptions are right then you've come to the right place.

I'm also making another assumption, and this one may not be quite so secure. I'm assuming that you're ready to have your eyes opened, your own assumptions challenged and, if need be, your ideas changed. History isn't about confirming people's stories, however important these stories might be to them. History is about looking at the past as objectively as possible and working out what happened, how it happened, why it happened and what it led to. Along the way those who consider history tend to overturn many cherished versions of the past, many legends and many comforting stories. I'm assuming you're ready for that. If not, brace yourself now.

Icons Used in This Book

History isn't the same as the past. *The past* is what you're trying to find out about; *history* is what you make of the past and how you communicate your thoughts about it. This means that at various points I want to highlight for you my own – and it is only my own – view of some of the details. Most of the time you'll be able to pick that up from the way I write about them, but at some points I highlight what I think is important for you to realise with one of these symbols:

Or, alternatively, 'Who you gonna call? Mythbusters!' History is full of famous stories that people hand down and repeat without anyone really checking whether they happened. Some did, but a lot didn't. The First World War has its fair share of such stories. But did they actually happen? When you see this sign, you can find out.

The First World War involved millions of people in all areas of life, but certain people were at the very centre of events. When you spot this icon, you're introduced to some of the people who, for better or worse, made a difference.

I don't know why people complain about history being rewritten. History is *always* being rewritten: that's what history *is*. You can view almost any event or development in more than one way, and different historians view some events in very different ways. This sign indicates some of the biggest areas of disagreement and debate.

Sometimes keeping a detail in mind is important because it explains something that you'll come across later. When you see this sign, make a mental note of it.

War often helps speed up technological change and the First World War is a good example. From aircraft design to medicine, big technological changes happened during the war. Stop at this sign to find them.

Not to be confused with Technological Innovation. Technical Stuff is where you need to get your head round some of the detail. Okay, maybe some of the boring detail, but important boring detail. Don't worry: I guide you through it, it'll be over soon and you'll feel better for it afterwards.

Beyond the Book

You never know when you may need to check your knowledge of the First World War. You're watching TV and a documentary on the war comes up, or you're on holiday and you come across a striking war memorial. At times like these, you find yourself thinking, 'Wait a minute. Where did that battle fit into the picture? Why were they fighting there? I didn't realise those countries were in the war: which side were they on?' and so on. That's where you can whip out your trusty smart phone and check the online features that accompany this book.

The online content has two main parts. First, you can find the cheat sheet (at www.dummies.com/cheatsheet/firstworldwar), which gives you a timeline of the key events and battles, so you can fit your discovery into the overall picture of the war and see how it relates to everything else. The second part is a set of four short articles that look at four big questions about the war: who was to blame for it, how bad were those generals, did the First World War really mark the end of a golden age and, very importantly, did the First World War cause the Second World War? These articles and a bonus Part of Tens chapter (which you can find at www.dummies.com/extras/firstworldwar) give you my own thoughts on these questions. You're under no obligation to agree with me, but I hope you find them a good place to start developing your own ideas about the significance of the First World War.

Where to Go from Here

Where to go from here? Over the page, of course! You want to get started, don't you? But where *exactly* to go depends on what you already know and what you want to find out.

If you want to get an idea of the whole war then start with Chapter 1, because that gives you an overview of the war, who fought in it and where, and what some of the big issues were that they had to face up to. After you've got that, you can then head off to whichever part of the story you want to find out more about. You may find that way of reading the book particularly useful if you already know a bit about some part of the war but you're not sure how it fits into the whole.

Alternatively, if you want to go through the story from the start, you'll find I begin by giving you a picture of the world before 1914, and I then take you through the thorny question of how the war began. Of course, you may prefer to browse through the book, dipping in and out to get a flavour of the war and to see which aspects particularly engage your attention.

But one thing to bear in mind: this is history, yes, but it's also about what real people went through only a few generations ago. The last surviving people who fought in the war only died in the 2000s. It might seem as if the war took place an age ago, and in a way it did, but in historical terms these events took place only yesterday, almost within living memory. Treat the war with respect. And the greatest respect you can show is to find out more about it. Start right here.

Part I
Origins of War

For Dummies can help you get started with lots of subjects. Visit www.dummies.com to learn more and do more with *For Dummies*.

In this part...

- Find out why the assassination of one European statesman caused the nations of Europe to throw themselves at each other's throats.

- Understand the background to the outbreak of war in 1914, the Great Powers of Europe and their people, and how Europeans dominated the world.

- Discover how Europe, the continent that prided itself on its sophisticated culture and civilisation, plunged the world into the most destructive and ghastly war in world history.

Chapter 1

The First World War: An Overview

*Y*ou can find plenty of battles and generals and details in this book, and they're all important to know about, but plunging straight into the events of the war can be a bit disorientating, especially if you're not quite sure of what else was happening in the period. So, in this chapter I try to give you a roadmap of the war, to explain who was fighting whom, where the fighting took place and to give you an overall shape of the way the war developed.

Thinking of the war having a 'shape' might seem a bit strange if your picture of the war is essentially one in which soldiers spent their whole time sitting in the trenches, launching occasional suicidal attacks on the enemy lines. However, although it might not have seemed like it to the ordinary soldiers at the time, or to many people since, the war did have a shape and a direction: each side did try various ways to break through the enemy lines and to win. The generals and political leaders learned many hard lessons along the way and, believe it or not, they did try to avoid repeating their most disastrous mistakes. Of course, they didn't always succeed, but this chapter gives you an overview of what they were *trying* to do.

I Name This War . . . Er, What Should We Call the War?

How about starting with the basics, like what exactly the war should be called? This might sound like a silly question, but it's not. Wars don't come ready-packaged with a name on top: they usually get named after they've happened and people often disagree – sometimes quite sharply – on what to call them. For example, what the Russians call 'the Great Patriotic War' is, to the rest of the world, a little thing called 'the Second World War'. The Russian name suggests that the war on the Eastern Front was the most important area of conflict and that the rest was just a sideshow. Seeing why some other countries may disagree isn't hard!

Even the dates of wars can be problematic. Most of the countries involved in the First World War went to war in 1914, but not all of them: Italy only entered in 1915, Romania in 1916 and the United States not until 1917. Most people think the war ended in 1918, but it didn't: the *fighting* ended then, but the war itself wasn't over (and it could have been renewed at any time) until the peace treaty was signed, which was in 1919. Some war memorials do carry the dates 1914–1919 and people often think it's a mistake, but in fact those memorials are the ones that get it right!

While it was going on, people usually referred to the war as the European War or the Great War – a name that people often still use today. (Of course, no one called it the First World War at the time for the very good reason that there hadn't been a second one then!) Towards the end, people sometimes referred to it as the War to End All Wars: the war had been so costly and so terrible that it had to have been fought for *something*. (Not surprisingly, after the Second World War, this phrase became something of a bad joke.) With similar optimism, US President Wilson sometimes called it a War to Make the World Safe for Democracy, though that certainly wasn't what anyone had in mind when they started it. Years later, after the Second World War, some people did refer for a while to the First and Second German Wars, which suggested that the Germans had been entirely responsible for them both, but the names haven't lasted and were never entirely accurate anyway.

More recently, and especially in the non-western world, some historians have questioned the use of the term 'world war'. The far-away quarrels between Austria-Hungary and Serbia or between Britain and Germany were of no interest to people in Africa or Asia, and they only got dragged into them by their European colonial masters. What was really happening, these scholars say, was a 'European Civil War' – the first of two. It's not difficult to see where this idea comes from, but it rather ignores the role played by non-European countries such as Japan, China, the United States and some of the South American states, which weren't European colonies and which came into the war very much following their own agenda.

Strictly speaking, the First World War wasn't even the *first* world war! The religious wars between Protestants and Catholics that ravaged Europe in the 16th and 17th centuries also saw fighting in Central America, India and the Pacific. The first wars to be *planned* on a global scale were the European wars of the 18th century, which were fought in North America, in India and on the all the world's oceans as well as in Europe. The French Revolutionary and Napoleonic Wars involved serious fighting in India, the West Indies, North Africa, the Middle East, Canada and the United States. So what people call the

'First' World War was actually the fourth or fifth! On the other hand, all these 'world' wars were really European wars that spread around the world, so maybe they're better off with the names they have.

All things considered, I'm going to stick to 'First World War' in this book, because at least everyone knows what you're referring to by that name, even if they don't like it.

Analysing the Causes

The war was so destructive and its consequences were so far-reaching that it's hardly surprising that many people – and not just historians – have asked how on earth it started in the first place. This question hasn't been without its controversy.

Historians at war

When the war ended the political leaders on the winning side thought it was quite easy to work out how the war began: it was all Germany's fault. They even wrote that claim into the peace treaty and made the Germans sign it (see Chapter 17). Then, after the war, historians started ploughing their way through thousands and thousands of diplomatic memos and telegrams and papers and letters in the archives to *prove* who caused the war. And the answer was: Germany! Or maybe Austria. Or maybe the British Foreign Secretary. Or else the Russians. It all depended on which documents you read.

These disagreements may come as a surprise to you, but this is how history works. Very seldom do you find a piece of evidence that definitely *proves* something; usually, a document's significance depends on the different ways historians interpret it. All too often historians – like anyone else – can read into the evidence what they want to see, rather than what's actually there!

An accident waiting to happen . . .

In the years after the war, some historians liked to argue that no one *caused* the war. They argued that the outbreak of war was inevitable and that the countries all just somehow slid into it. Or, if you prefer, they were all equally self-interested and therefore equally to blame.

The trouble with this argument is that nothing in history is inevitable until it happens (otherwise, you might as well blame fate or the stars and have done with it). What makes history so interesting is precisely that people often *don't* act in their own best interests. Every country stood to lose heavily from the war, and they all did. So maybe the 'accident waiting to happen' idea raises more questions than it answers. Let's try Plan B.

. . . or was villainy afoot?

When the *Second* World War started in 1939 some people began asking: what is it with the Germans and their invading-the-neighbours addiction? Other people said that starting the Second World War didn't prove that Germany had started the First World War as well. And then in the 1960s a German (yes, German) historian called Fritz Fischer started producing what appeared to be documentary proof that the Germans had definitely been planning the First World War. Ever since then the debate has raged, though generally scholars accept the broad outline of Fischer's argument nowadays – except, understandably, in Germany. (I say more about how and why the war started in Chapter 3.)

Reviewing the Combatants

The war involved a huge range of countries from all parts of the world, from the *Great Powers* – the strongest and most powerful countries of all – to the most humble of colonial territories. Allow me to introduce you to some of them. (I look at them in greater detail in Chapters 2 and 3.)

The Central Powers

Germany and its allies dominated the centre of the continent and, after the war had started, they came to be known as the *Central Powers*.

Germany – nation most likely to succeed

Germany was the one to watch. The German army was highly organised and it was run by a sort of military ministry called the General Staff, in which hundreds of highly professional officers studied all the possible permutations for war and worked out how to win them all. It was also building up a powerful fleet. Germany's erratic Kaiser (emperor), Wilhelm II, declared that Germany wanted its 'place in the sun', but the other Great Powers wanted to know just what that meant in practice.

Austria-Hungary – one state, two kingdoms

Once Austria had been one of the great titans of Europe, but it had been crushed by Napoleon and then badly shaken by a series of revolutions, from which it had never recovered. The proud Hungarians, who had been merely a province of the old Austrian Empire, demanded and got equal status with the Austrians, and so in 1867 the curious *dual monarchy* of 'Austria-Hungary' was born. This dual monarchy idea is complex, but woe betide anyone who got it wrong! Within the dual monarchy, Austria was an *empire,* with an emperor, but Hungary was a *kingdom,* with a king. Since the emperor and the king were the same person, it meant he held two different titles, had two different crowns and two different coronations. When anything was done purely within Austria it was *imperial;* when it was done within Hungary it was *royal;* and when it was done by Austria-Hungary together, it was *imperial and royal.*

As well as Austrians and Hungarians, Austria-Hungary included a huge range of other national groups – Czechs, Slovaks, Slovenes, Poles, Croats and, most importantly, Serbs – which were, in effect, subject peoples of an empire, although to complicate things further some were ruled just by Austria and some just by Hungary.

The two halves of the empire shared the same monarch, the Habsburg Emperor Franz Josef, and they were to follow the same foreign and military policy, but for all other things they would operate as separate states. This was to prove crucial in 1914.

Turkey – the Ottoman Empire

The Turkish Empire was officially called the Ottoman Empire. The *Ottomans* were originally a tribe of the Turkish people who took their name from their founder, Sultan Osman. The Ottomans took over the leadership of the Turks back in the middle ages and the Turkish empire had been known as the Ottoman Empire ever since.

By 1909 the Ottoman Empire was in a very sorry state. Its government was weak and corrupt, it had lost control of Egypt, Greece, Serbia, Romania, Bulgaria and Bosnia-Herzegovina, and no one expected it to keep hold of the rest of the empire for long. But although the Empire may have been weak, the Turks had shown themselves to be utterly ruthless when it came to crushing revolts and had twice defended themselves against Russian invasion with impressive determination. Turkey had been a British ally, but the Germans were wooing the new, nationalist Turkish government with friendship, investment and top-notch German military advisers. And the Turks were very interested in what the Germans were offering.

The Allied and Associated Powers

Opposing Germany and its allies was a sort of alliance (but not actually an alliance – don't worry: I explain in this section) of France, Britain, Russia and Italy, and their respective empires, later joined by the United States. Not forgetting Belgium and Serbia.

France – hungry for revenge

France had been the military giant of Europe back in Napoleon's day, but since then the country had been torn apart by revolutions and in 1870–1 it had lost a catastrophic war with the German states. First, the Germans had paraded through Paris and staged a great ceremony in the Hall of Mirrors in the Palace of Versailles to celebrate the creation of a united Germany. (Don't forget this.) The

Germans had also annexed two of France's most important industrial provinces, Alsace and Lorraine. The French could only dream of getting revenge, because they were too deeply divided between left and right to start launching wars on their own. But give them an ally and that situation might change . . . .

Britain – feeling slightly nervous

Britain had been the most powerful state in the world but by 1900 other countries were catching up, including the United States and, more worryingly, Germany. Maybe it was time for Britain to look around for a friend or two. Doing so wasn't easy: the other Europeans didn't much like Britain and the only alliance the British could sign was an admittedly very useful deal with Japan. But in 1904 Britain signed an agreement with the French to patch up their differences, and in 1907 a second one with Russia. These agreements were known as *ententes* (that's French for *agreements,* folks) and they weren't alliances: they didn't tie Britain down to intervening in any war that might break out. Or did they?

Russia – the friendless giant

No one much liked Russia. It was a huge, oppressive state with an all-powerful ruler, and it was expanding everywhere – in the Baltic, in eastern Europe, in the Balkans, in Central Asia, in the Far East: nowhere seemed to be beyond Russia's grasp.

But Russia had serious problems. It was way behind the rest of Europe in industrial development, it had a serious internal security problem (one group of revolutionaries blew up Tsar Alexander II, and no Russian minister was safe from assassination) and in 1904 it went to war with Japan – and lost. Russia had been a German ally and some people in both countries thought it still should be, but the Russians didn't trust Germany's other ally, Austria-Hungary. With three people in the marriage, something had to give. Russia and Germany split up and, on the rebound, as it were, Russia signed an alliance with France in 1894. Which meant that if Germany ever went to war with France, it would be at war with Russia too.

Italy – open to offers

Italy was allied to Germany and Austria-Hungary, but it wasn't very happy about it. The Austrians were the Italians' old enemies; the Germans had helped the Italians unify their country and wouldn't let them forget it. The pope was sulking in the Vatican because Italy had taken nearly all his lands without asking, and when the Italians tried to cheer themselves up by doing what other Great Powers did – grabbing hold of some part of Africa – they invaded Ethiopia. And lost. So Italy was in a strange position in 1914: it was allied to Germany but open to a better offer.

The United States of America – keeping out of things

The United States was home to thousands of European immigrants who'd gone there to escape all those kings, generals and wars (see Chapter 11). The USA had just a small army, though that didn't stop the country from expanding: it fought a war with Spain and took over territories in the Pacific and the Caribbean. The Americans were content to establish themselves as the world's greatest economy and let the Europeans fight their own wars.

Japan – east is west

The Japanese had spent 40 years successfully turning themselves into a modern western-style country, with western-style industry and administration and western-style armed forces. They had an alliance with Britain and in 1904 they took on the Russians and won. They had their eyes on expanding in China and the Pacific, and a European war might give the Japanese just the opportunity they were looking for.

Serbia – a little country with big ideas

Serbia was a small Balkan state with ambitions to be a big Balkan state. In particular, it wanted to take over the ethnically mixed region of Bosnia-Herzegovina (see Chapter 3). What made Serbia a worrying country was its tendency for political violence. In 1903 Serbian army officers had launched a coup and hacked the King and Queen to death. Some of those conspirators were still powerful in 1914 and they hadn't lost their taste for royal blood.

Belgium – sitting in the way

If people thought of the Belgians before 1914, it was as the pretty ruthless rulers of a huge African colony in Congo. Belgium itself seemed a quiet, peaceful country, but appearances are deceptive. The Belgian coastline faces the southern coast of England, and for anyone wanting to invade France, Belgium provided an easy way round the back of the French frontier defences. If war came, Belgium would be in the front line.

The rulers

The early 20th century was a good time for designers of crowns and coronation robes because most of Europe was ruled by monarchs. Only one of these monarchs was an *autocrat* (that's a monarch who can rule pretty much as he likes) – Tsar Nicholas II of Russia. That, at any rate was the theory: in reality Nicholas depended heavily on his ministers, his general, his wife and even on the mystic monk Rasputin.

Other rulers were more open about the limits on their powers. The British monarchy, with Queen Victoria still on the throne when the 20th century opened, was a *constitutional monarchy* in which the monarch had to respect the wishes of parliament and accept the prime minister's advice. The Italian monarchy was broadly based on the British model. Emperor Franz Josef was both Emperor of Austria and King of Hungary, so he, poor man, had two governments to listen to. France was a *republic,* so in theory power lay with the elected president, though in practice French politics were based on ever-changing coalitions, so the president had to keep a very wary eye on everyone in the French national assembly.

The big question mark was over Germany: who really ruled that powerful military state? The Kaiser liked to think he did, but the German constitution said otherwise: the Kaiser had to work with the *Reichstag* (parliament) and above all with the *Chancellor* (Prime Minister). But the Chancellor, in turn, had to carry the military with him. This meant that in Germany the military had far more political power than in any other European country. This was going to matter.

Mapping the Conflict

Countries fought over particular parts of the world in the First World War. Most people think of wars in terms of arrows and symbols stuck on maps of the world, so here I have a look at the theatres of war.

Viewing the different theatres of war

Here I list the main areas of the world where fighting took place, but first, I need to explain a few terms:

- ✔ **Theatres of war:** Historians use this term to denote a whole geographical area where fighting took place. So the Western and Eastern Fronts were both parts of the *European theatre;* the fighting in Kenya, German South West Africa, Portuguese East Africa, Togo and the Cameroons all made up the *African theatre,* and so on.

- ✔ **Fronts:** *Front* refers to the area where the fighting was happening: The term is linked to 'front line'. Fronts can move, sometimes very rapidly, or they can be stuck in more or less the same place, as happened with the Western Front.

- ✔ **Campaigns:** A *campaign* is a big military plan, with a set of objectives which, you hope, either win the war or at least badly hurt the enemy. Campaigns often involve many battles.

- ✔ **Battles:** *Battle* took a change of meaning in the First World War. The word used to mean a single fight at a specific place, such as the Battle of Waterloo or the Battle of Hastings. However, First World War battles were much bigger than battles had been in the past: the British attack on the Somme in 1916, for example, was so huge that generals in previous wars would've called it a whole campaign.

The Western Front

The Western Front is, for many people, the *only* part of the First World War they know about. The war in the west began with a German invasion of Belgium and France, and when this was pushed back, both sides dug in and took shelter in trenches (see Chapter 7). This line of trenches ran in an unbroken line from the Swiss border, where Swiss border guards could watch both sides and kept a careful eye to make sure they stayed on their own sides of the frontier, to the Belgian coast, where it petered out before hitting the sand dunes (see Figure 1-1). Although each side did make some advances, this line of trenches remained fairly static, despite some huge battles, until 1918.

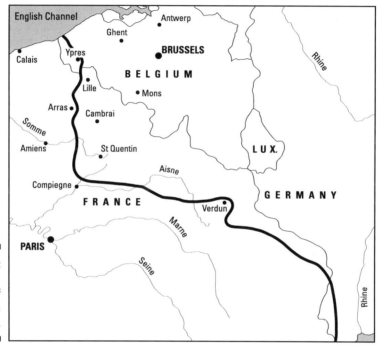

Figure 1-1:
The stabilised line of the Western Front.

The Eastern Front

Although trenches were dug on the Eastern Front, they never dominated the scene in quite the way they did in the west. The Eastern Front was more of a war of *movement* (see Figure 1-2). Like the Western Front, though, it was huge. In the north it ran through Poland and western Russia, where the Germans and Russians faced up to each other. Then the Front ran south through southern Poland and into Czech and Slovak territory, into the area where the Russians faced the Austro-Hungarians. Romania entered the war in 1916, thus extending the Eastern Front even farther south.

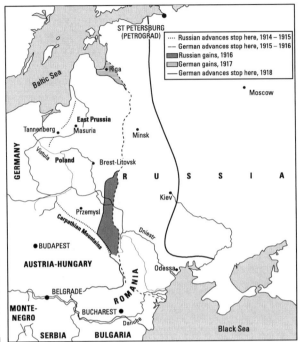

Figure 1-2:
The area of
the Eastern
Front.

The southern theatre

The war was fought in various parts of southern Europe (see Figure 1-3). In 1915 Italy joined in the war on the Allied side and a front opened up along its Alpine border with Austria. This Alpine war was extremely dangerous and costly but it often gets overshadowed by the Western Front. Bulgaria joined in the war on Germany's side, so fighting took place along its borders too. Austria's border with Serbia was where the fighting actually began, but after Serbia was overrun in 1915, the British and French opened another front against the Austria, at Salonika in northern Greece.

The Turkish theatre

Turkey's entry into the war sparked off fighting over a very wide area (see Figure 1-4, and check Chapter 9 for the details). First, Turkey fought against the Russians in the Caucasus region of central Asia. British forces from India then invaded Turkish-held Mesopotamia (modern-day Iraq) and in 1915 Allied troops landed at Gallipoli on the Turkish coast. A major anti-Turkish rebellion started up in Arabia and the British launched an offensive from Egypt that moved northwards through Palestine and Syria.

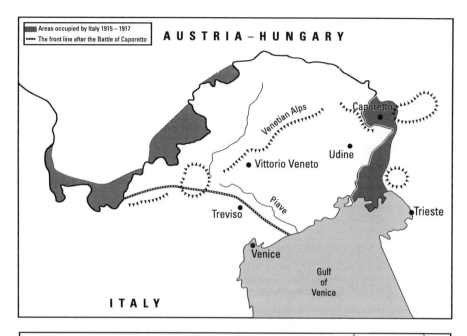

Figure 1-3: The Italian (left) and Salonika (right) fronts of the southern theatre.

Figure 1-4:
The wide area of the Turkish theatre.

The African theatre

Britain, France, Belgium and Germany all had colonies in Africa and the outbreak of war in Europe set the Allied colonies up against the German ones. The Germans were outnumbered but their commander in east Africa conducted a guerrilla campaign that led the British a merry dance. Fighting in Africa stretched from German South-West Africa, through the centre of the continent to Kenya and East Africa (see Figure 1-5). (Chapter 10 contains all you need to know about how the war dragged in the African colonies.)

The Pacific theatre

The Australians and New Zealanders attacked Germany's Pacific colonies. The Japanese were keen to contribute their bit to the Allied war effort by attacking German possessions in China and the Pacific (see Figure 1-6 and Chapter 10). They also took the opportunity to start taking Chinese territory until China came into the war on the same side and the Allied leaders asked the Japanese to refrain from attacking their ally.

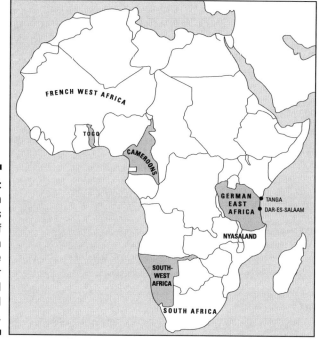

Figure 1-5:
German colonies (in grey) of the African theatre where war was waged (shaded areas).

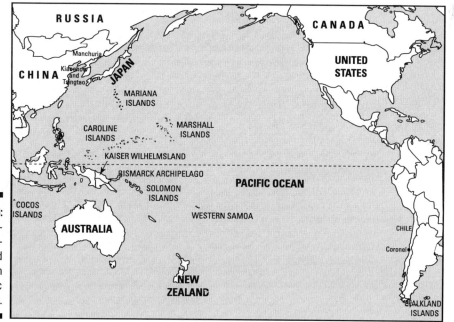

Figure 1-6:
Key locations of conflict at land and sea in the Pacific theatre.

The naval war

Navies can fight anywhere in the world and the First World War is a good example. The British and German fleets squared up to each other in the North Sea and the English Channel (the biggest naval battle, Jutland in 1916, was fought off the coast of Denmark) and clashed at Coronel, off the coast of Chile, and then again off the coast of the Falkland Islands in the south Atlantic (see Figure 1-6). German U-boats (submarines) operated all round the British Isles and far out across the Atlantic. German surface raiders operated even farther afield: one of the most famous and successful, the *Emden,* attacked shipping in both the Pacific and the Indian Oceans (see Chapter 8).

Making the struggle global: Other areas of war

As well as the areas where the actual fighting took place, the war also had a great impact on other places.

A home front

The First World War has a good claim to be the first war with a concept of a *home front.* Of course, all wars affect those people who stay at home, but the First World War was the first to turn everyone's ordinary lives into a front of the war. The most obvious example was in the factories, where both sides employed large numbers of women to replace the men who'd been conscripted into the army. Both sides had to introduce strict controls on food consumption too, and both used poster campaigns to put psychological pressure on everyone to get involved in the war effort.

In fact, the home front angle means that, whether or not you accept that this was the first *world* war (you can see in the first section of this chapter why some people quibble over that), a very good case exists for saying it was the first *total* war. (You can read more about the home front in Chapters 12 to 14.)

Neutral countries

Some countries managed to stay neutral in the war, such as Spain, Switzerland, the Netherlands and Sweden. Neutral countries were important areas for espionage and for attempts to find a peace settlement to end the war, but neutrality didn't save countries from the effects of the fighting. Some countries came under pressure to join in the war, and all found their trade seriously disrupted by the blockades and U-boat campaigns that the belligerents were throwing at each other.

Forging Ahead with the Technology and Science of War

Many soldiers went into battle in 1914 still wearing the colourful uniforms of a century earlier, and commanders still placed enormous hopes in cavalry charges to scatter the massed ranks of enemy infantry. However, the early 20th century was a time of enormous technological change, which meant that these antiquated styles of warfare were on their way out. This was going to be a scientist's war.

Open fire! Inspecting the new weaponry

Soldiers still used their familiar rifles and pistols in the First World War; in hand-to-hand fighting in the trenches they even used weapons like spikes and maces that would've been familiar to medieval knights. But they also had to get used to some very new types of weaponry:

- **Aircraft:** The world's first powered, controlled flight, made by the Wright brothers, took place in December 1903, and a decade later aircraft were being used to fight wars. The First World War was the first conflict to be fought in the air. Planes conducted reconnaissance and attacked each other, first with pistols and rifles, and later with machine guns. Airships carried out bombing raids, and by the end of the war special bombing aircraft were doing the same.

- **Barbed wire:** One of the most deadly weapons of the war wasn't designed as a weapon at all. Barbed wire was first developed as cattle fencing on the American prairie but it proved a very effective defensive measure in the First World War. Troops who got caught on the wire – and it was very easy to do so – were sitting targets for enemy marksmen.

- **Gas:** Huge advances in the chemical industry meant that militaries now had the use of poison gas. Not all gas was intended to kill, but plenty of gases did.

- **Machine guns:** Machine guns had been developed 40 years earlier, but they'd been large affairs, mounted on big wheels like cannon, and they were prone to jam. Machine guns in the First World War became much lighter and more portable – and more accurate.

- **Submarines:** Submarine plans were first drawn up in the Napoleonic Wars of the early 19th century and the first use of submarines in combat was in the American Civil War of the 1860s. But the First World War saw submarines used for the first time in large numbers and with the capacity to operate far from base. And to fire torpedoes: a deadly new development.

> ✔ **Tanks:** Tanks were originally to be called 'landships'. 'Tank' was a code-name, used to make it seem to any enemy agents who may hear of them as if they were large watertanks. The earliest tanks often broke down, but designs quickly improved. Tanks would revolutionise warfare and they certainly meant the end of cavalry.

Making advances in medicine

Many of the war's scientific advances were channelled into weaponry, but important advances were made in medicine too.

Trialling triage

Medical officers first applied *triage*, the system of prioritising casualties into those who'll definitely live, those who'll definitely die and those who'll live with immediate medical intervention, on a wide scale and systematic basis in the First World War. Ambulances took casualties to *clearing stations* just behind the front line where the exhausted doctors made their decisions. You just had to hope they got it right.

Sharpening surgery

The war produced a constant stream of casualties needing surgery. Some disagreement exists over whether this led to advances in military surgery or not. On the one hand, army surgeons gained a lot of experience and they certainly made advances in restorative surgery. On the other hand, many surgeons were so overwhelmed by the numbers of casualties they had to cope with that they went back to amputating limbs as the easiest way of dealing with the problem – just as surgeons had done in centuries past.

Minding mental health

Mental health was the area of medicine that saw the most obvious advances during the First World War. The effects of constant shelling on men's nerves was so shattering that many went through complete mental collapse. This was the first war where doctors began to treat shattered nerves and the effects of *shellshock* – what nowadays is called *post-traumatic stress disorder* – with sympathy and a much greater understanding of the symptoms and their underlying causes.

The First World War in a Nutshell

The First World War went through three distinct phases. I outline them for you here, to give you an overall feel for the shape of the war. If you want to know more – well, the rest of book is just over the page.

1914–15: The best-laid plans go wrong

Both sides went into the war in 1914 with plans of how they'd run rings around the enemy and be back home in time for Christmas. To general consternation, these well-laid plans all went wrong. The Germans *didn't* swing round and take Paris, the French *didn't* march straight into the heart of Germany, the Russians *didn't* steamroller their way into Berlin and the Austrians *didn't* march all over Serbia.

These failures (which I tell you about in Chapter 4) meant that military commanders on both sides had to spend the winter of 1914–15 going back to their drawing boards and rethinking their war-winning strategies from scratch. Nineteen fifteen was a sort of 'Plan B' year, with attacks in Belgium, in Turkey and in Poland, none of which broke through. It was also the year when the Germans tried to force Britain out of the war through submarine warfare, which was a different sort of Plan B. It didn't work either. (You can read about 1915 in Chapter 5.)

1916–17: The big battles

If Phase 1 was about trying to find the cleverest strategy, Phase 2 was about much less subtle and ever more desperate attempts to break through the stalemate on all sides by launching massive offensives. The Allies co-ordinated their plans for big attacks in both the west and the east, but the Germans struck first with a massive offensive against the French at Verdun. The British then launched their own massive offensive on the Somme. When those attacks failed, the French planned yet another massive offensive under General Nivelle. That failed. Then the British launched yet another one, at Ypres. That failed too. The only successful attack made in 1916 was by the Russian General Brusilov, who broke through the Austrian lines but wasn't able to keep his attack going, and in 1917 by the Austrians, who broke through the Italian lines at Caporetto.

By the end of 1917 the Allies were exhausted: revolution broke out in Russia, and although the United States entered the war in April, American troops wouldn't be arriving in large numbers for another year. (Chapters 6 and 15 take you through the ups and downs of 1916 and 1917.) Nineteen eighteen started with all the advantages very much on the German side.

1918–19: Endgames

In the spring of 1918 the German launched their massive offensive, the *Kaiser battle,* which broke through the Western Front and sent the British and French spinning back to their separate bases. The Germans headed towards Paris and it looked as if they might snatch victory. But the Allied troops rallied and started to fight back. American troops started arriving in large numbers and went straight into battle, the Allies pushed the Germans right back to their frontier and the German army collapsed.

Meanwhile the Italians had got their breath back and defeated the Austrians. And as the war collapsed, so did the governments of Germany and Austria-Hungary: socialists staged a revolution in Berlin that toppled the Kaiser, and the different nationalities of the Austro-Hungarian Empire finally made their bids for independence, with the result that Austria-Hungary imploded.

US President Wilson offered Germany and its allies what sounded like very reasonable peace terms and they agreed to a ceasefire. However, the peace treaties that the Allies drew up in 1919 were anything but reasonable, and are generally regarded as an important root cause for the outbreak of a Second World War barely 20 years later. (Chapters 16 and 17 guide you through the final dark days of war and the peace negotiations and settlements that followed.)

The Legacy: Why the First World War Still Matters

The years from 1914 to 1919 may seem like ancient history, and you may wonder whether the First World War still matters.

One important result of the First World War was the creation of thousands of war memorials and war cemeteries in all the countries touched by the conflict. These tributes to the dead of the war started off a whole culture of remembrance that people still keep going to this day. Even though many years have passed since the First World War and many other wars have happened, people still commemorate the dead of all wars in November, in memory of the First World War (see Chapter 18).

The war also had a knock-on effect on world events that has carried through to today. It helped bring about the Russian Revolution and the Second World War, both of which led to the Cold War, which continues to affect relations between Russia and China and the west to this day. But the impact of the First World War on recent history has been even more direct than that:

- The modern problems in the Middle East have their roots directly in the Allied campaigns in Arabia and Palestine and the policy the British followed about who should be allowed to settle where.

- The Northern Ireland conflict grew directly out of the Irish settlement brought about by the First World War.

✔ The bloody civil war that tore former Yugoslavia apart in the 1990s was a *direct* response to the settlement that the Allied leaders imposed on the region at the end of the First World War.

✔ The First World War provided the first major cracks in the bonds that held Britain's overseas empire together, and started the process that led to Britain's withdrawal from India, its most important colonial possession.

✔ The First World War marked the first time when the United States played a central role on the world stage. After the war – and despite their own preferences to keep out of world affairs – the Americans would go on to play a dominant world role for the rest of the century.

The First World War set the tone for the whole of the 20th century that followed, which in turn shaped the 21st. Think the First World War is ancient history and has nothing to do with you? Dream on, my friend. Or better still – read on.

Chapter 2

The World in 1900

*P*eople often get excited as one century ends and another begins. You may enjoy a good knees-up on New Year's Eve yourself. That excitement, however, was more marked than ever in 1900 as the 19th century drew to its close. The old century had seen so many changes in technology and in the way people lived that the world of 1900 would've been almost unrecognisable to anyone who'd been around a century earlier. The changes were most obvious in the technologically developed western countries of Europe, North America and Australasia, but other parts of the world had changed too, thanks to the westerners who went over and changed them – whether they liked it or not.

By 1900 railways and steamships could connect even the most distant places more quickly and easily than ever before; the electric telegraph could take messages over thousands of miles in a matter of seconds; engineers were developing ever-more efficient automobiles and would soon be sending aircraft into the skies. Medical knowledge was advancing rapidly: antiseptics, X-rays and vaccinations against a whole range of diseases were all well established by 1900. Surely this new century could only get even better? That was certainly how it seemed to many people.

Looking back from today, however, it can seem as if the people of the 1900s were still living in the Victorian age. In many ways they were: societies and cultures don't change overnight just because a new date arrives on the calendar. But it wasn't a static, unchanging time. Theirs was a changing, challenging, boundary-stretching, rule-breaking rollercoaster of a world, and a whole range of people, including politicians, artists, scientists, writers, and sportsmen and -women, were working to make the world a much better place than anyone had lived in – ever. But things were about to take a turn for the worse. In a big way.

When the First World War began, it ended abruptly the 19th-century world and gave birth to the unsettlingly Brave New World of the 20th century. So in this chapter, I look at the world that both spawned the war and was destroyed by it: the world of the new century, the world of 1900.

The State We're In: Taking a Tour of the World in 1900

In the world of 1900, massive contrasts existed between the developed world of the industrial countries and their under-developed overseas colonies. Tensions between countries are nothing new in history, and they certainly existed at the start of the 20th century. Here, I look at what exactly these tensions were and how they threatened the world of 1900.

Everybody wants to rule the world – well, the Europeans do, anyway

The world before 1914 was so dominated by Europeans that you can forget that the rest of the world existed. That was how the Europeans themselves tended to see the world. The major European powers ruled colonies in every continent; thanks to their presence, European languages were spoken around the globe, European dress was becoming the normal clothing for serious people to wear while other forms of dress were becoming thought of as 'traditional', 'exotic' or 'native dress'. European domination meant that the whole world needed to keep an eye on how these over-mighty European states got on with each other. The outlook was very worrying.

The disunited states of Europe

In the 19th century the political landscape of Europe had changed thanks to some important new ideas. Two of the most important of these ideas were

- ✔ **Nationalism:** This idea said that the ethnic identity and culture of a people (that is, a *nation*) mattered and that each nation ought to have its own state. Some nations, such as the French or the Spanish, had had their own states for a long time; nationalism led to others, like the Italians and Germans, creating their own states and changing borders within Europe during the 19th century – though only after a lot of fighting. But some peoples, such as the Serbs of south-eastern Europe, the Irish, the Jews and – farther afield – some of the peoples of India, had a sense of national identity but no nation state. Yet. (You can read more about nationalism in Chapter 3.)

✔ **Socialism:** This idea was based on the writings of Karl Marx and said that people's main identity should not be their nationality but their social class. Marx held that working people in different countries had more in common with each other than they had with the middle and upper classes in their own countries.

Europe by 1900 was dominated by the industrial middle classes, who owned the continent's factories and mills, and who enjoyed increasing wealth and power. Marx preached that working people should join together in a great worldwide revolution to overthrow these middle classes and take control of industrial production from the hands of the wealthy industrialists who got all the profits. Marx's ultimate dream was that the workers of the world would set up an equal society that would be run by the ordinary people *for* the ordinary people. By 1900 socialism had already helped to create an extensive trade union movement across Europe.

Not surprisingly, the ruling classes of Europe regarded these ideas as highly dangerous and subversive, and had a fear of working-class revolution. Maybe a bit of flag waving and a successful war might be a way of taking the workers' minds off these new socialist ideas? Some European leaders thought this idea was certainly worth trying.

The empire-building states

Owning overseas territory wasn't an optional extra for 19th-century European states: it was a sort of must-have, almost a definition of what it meant to be a Great Power, and the major powers ruled colonies in every continent on Earth. Some states, such as Britain and France, had possessed colonies overseas for centuries, but others, such as Germany and Italy, came to empire-building relatively late, in the 19th century. Even a small country like Belgium believed that it had to own an overseas empire if it was to be taken seriously. Accordingly, it took over the Congo, a huge land area in central Africa much larger than Belgium itself.

Almost the whole of Africa, a vast land mass much bigger than Europe, fell under European control within 20 years at the end of the century, and the Europeans set about reshaping it, redrawing its boundaries, taking hold of its raw materials and, all too often, forcing the local people to do the hard work for them. Even countries that appeared to be independent were in fact under European domination. For example, China was an independent state but was dominated by the western powers, and some republics of South America were so dependent on British investment that historians have referred to them as being part of Britain's 'informal' empire – not technically ruled by the British or coloured in red on the maps, but effectively British colonies nonetheless.

This list gives you an idea of how much overseas territory the Europeans controlled in 1900. And this list isn't exhaustive!

- ✔ **Britain** ruled a vast global empire that included India; Ceylon; Burma; Singapore; Hong Kong; most of southern Africa; Kenya, Uganda; Egypt; Sudan and part of Somaliland; Nigeria; Gambia and the Gold Coast; West Indian islands including Jamaica, Trinidad, Tobago, St Kitts, Grenada and Bermuda; Pacific islands including Tonga, the Solomon and Ellis Islands, New Guinea and North Borneo; Gibraltar; Malta; Cyprus; and a group of large self-governing dominions: Canada, Newfoundland, South Africa, Australia and New Zealand.

- ✔ **France** ruled another huge global empire, which covered Algeria; Tunisia; Morocco; a vast area of West Africa including Senegal, Ivory Coast, Chad and the French Congo and Madagascar; the Seychelles; Polynesia; New Caledonia; Guadeloupe; Martinique; and Indo-China (modern-day Vietnam, Laos and Cambodia).

- ✔ **Germany** held territory in Africa including Togo, Cameroon, South West Africa, Rwanda and Tanganyika, as well as land in the Pacific including the Marshall, Mariana and Caroline Islands and Samoa, and Kiaochow in China.

- ✔ **Italy** had conquered Tripoli, Italian Somaliland, Eritrea and the Dodecanese Islands.

- ✔ **Belgium** ran the huge area of the Congo.

- ✔ **The Spanish, Portuguese and Dutch** still held overseas territories they'd conquered many years earlier.

The United States, too, was building its own empire in the Pacific and the Caribbean.

Empire enemies, empire ententes

You may wonder what the Europeans wanted all these territories for. In most cases they were interested in the financial profits these colonies could fetch: for example, as the new century dawned, Britain was fighting the Anglo–Boer War in South Africa mainly to gain control of the region's fabulously wealthy gold mines (the Brits didn't say that's what they wanted, but don't let that fool you). But these western states also believed that because their culture was more technologically advanced than that of other parts of the world (which it was), western rule would be more beneficial for the people they ruled (which is more debatable).

In some cases, European states took over areas simply to stop other European powers from getting them, even if the territory itself wasn't worth very much. Empire-building was very closely linked to the Europeans' own national rivalries. For example, Britain and France nearly went to war in 1898 over a dispute in a small town in Sudan (see 'Annoy the French! Annoy them again!' later in the chapter). That war scare prompted the 1904 *Anglo–French Entente,* an agreement between both governments about how they'd decide who got what land in Africa. In 1907, the British signed a similar entente with Russia about who should get what land in Central Asia. These ententes showed how closely colonial and European affairs were linked.

Budge up – Germany wants a place in the sun

The great German Chancellor Otto von Bismarck had never been very interested in overseas colonies. He thought Germany should concentrate on getting territory in Europe. But even he couldn't withstand the pressure from German investors and the German public to start taking over land in Africa and the Pacific. He even got an archipelago in the Pacific named after him, though he probably wasn't very impressed.

When Kaiser Wilhelm II came to the throne, he made gaining colonial territory Germany's top priority. Germany, he said, wanted its place in the sun, alongside the British and the French. Germany's drive for colonial territory overseas meant that it would need a large navy, which provided the excuse for Admiral Tirpitz's big naval expansion programme that sparked off the Anglo–German naval race (see Chapter 8).

Empires in trouble

Not all Europe's empires were confidently extending their hold over the globe in 1900. Some were facing serious problems:

- **Austria-Hungary:** The Austro-Hungarian Empire had a difficult job keeping all its different ethnic groups together. It was painfully aware that its days of military glory were long gone, and knew that if it wanted to fight any major European state, it would need the support of its ally, Germany.

- **The Ottoman Empire (Turkey):** The Turkish Empire covered Syria, Palestine, Transjordan, Arabia (Hejaz), Mesopotamia, Armenia, north Africa and south-eastern Europe, but by 1900 it had had to give independence to some of its European subject peoples, while the French, Italians, Russians and British were all manoeuvring to take over Turkish territory in north Africa and the Caucasus. (Chapter 9 looks at the Ottoman Empire in detail.)

- **Russia:** Russia was vast but very backward compared with its rival empires. It was much less heavily industrialised and although the Russian army was huge, everyone knew that it was badly organised and hopelessly inefficient.

REMEMBER

The nations without states

In 1900 some peoples had a strong sense of national identity but didn't have their own state. That didn't stop them wanting one, badly. Here are some examples:

- ✔ **The Czechs:** The Czechs inhabited Bohemia and Moravia, regions within the Austro-Hungarian Empire. Bohemia had a long history as a kingdom in its own right and the Czechs didn't see why they shouldn't be a nation on their own once again. The problem was that neither the Austrians nor the Hungarians saw things that way, and as long as the Austrians and Hungarians ran the Empire, the Czechs were going to have put their dreams of nationhood on hold. Of course, if one day the Austro-Hungarian Empire were to collapse. . . .

- ✔ **The Irish:** Ireland had been united with Great Britain a century earlier, but some Irish nationalists never accepted this union and were fighting a guerrilla war to set up a separate Irish state. The complication was that many nationalists were Catholics, and Ireland's Protestant population wasn't sure that it wanted to live in a Catholic-dominated Ireland – actually, they were adamant that they didn't. The divisions between Catholics and Protestants in Ireland were so serious that by 1914 it looked as if Ireland might sink into civil war at any moment.

Next year in Jerusalem – okay, maybe the year after

For centuries Jewish communities around the world had marked the annual Jewish feast of Passover with the words 'Next year in Jerusalem', meaning that they hoped they'd be back in Jerusalem by the time the next Passover came round. No chance of that happening seemed to arise until well into the 19th century, when a young Austrian journalist called Theodore Herzl, inspired by the success of other European nationalist movements such as those of the Italians and Germans, wrote a book putting the case for a national home in Palestine for the world's Jews.

Herzl's nationalist movement was known as *Zionism*, from *Zion*, the old name for Jerusalem. The trouble for Herzl and the Zionists was that Palestine was part of the Turkish Ottoman Empire, and even though the Empire always seemed to be about to collapse and the European Great Powers were always drawing up fantasy-league lists of which bits of it they were hoping to get hold of when it did, no one in any position of power or influence was giving any thought to handing over part of the Ottoman Empire to the Zionist movement for a Jewish homeland. Herzl's dream was going to need a long time, a lot of lobbying and, ideally, a very different European situation before it could become reality.

✔ **The Jews:** The Jews had been expelled from Judaea back in Roman times and over the centuries that followed they'd spread all over the world. Large Jewish communities were to be found in places as far apart and as diverse as Russia, England, southern Africa, Syria, France, Egypt and the United States. Wherever they lived, Jewish people never gave up hope that one day they might return to their ancient homeland.

✔ **The Poles:** Poland had completely disappeared from the map of Europe at the end of the 18th century: it had been swallowed up by its neighbours, Germany, Austria-Hungary and especially Russia. But the Poles never forgot that their homeland had once been a great and powerful nation, and they hoped and believed it would be so again.

✔ **The Serbs:** Of all the nationalist dreams in Europe in the 1900s, the Serbs' was to prove the most important. The *Serbs* are one of the Slavic peoples of the Balkan region and, like their neighbours the Greeks, the Bulgarians and the Romanians, they'd spent centuries under Turkish domination. Also like their neighbours, the Serbs had won their independence from the Turks, but that wasn't enough for them. They dreamed of creating a much larger Slavic state, to include the peoples who lived in Bosnia, Herzegovina, Croatia and Slovenia – a huge area of south-eastern Europe going up the Adriatic coast. The Serbs' problem was that some of the area they had their eyes on was ruled by the Turks and the rest was part of the Austro-Hungarian Empire (see the sidebar 'Whose land is it anyway? Bosnia-Herzegovina').

Whose land is it anyway? Bosnia-Herzegovina

Bosnia and *Herzegovina* are two conjoined regions. In 1900 they were in the border area where the Ottoman Empire and the Austro-Hungarian Empire met. Other Europeans tended to regard Bosnia-Herzegovina as a remote and insignificant area, definitely in the 'crazy name, crazy people' category, but that view was seriously mistaken: the fate of Bosnia and Herzegovina proved to be of the highest political importance to everyone in Europe.

The population of Bosnia-Herzegovina was very mixed: it had Serbs (who belonged to the Greek Orthodox Church), Croats (who were Catholics) and Bosniaks (who were Muslims). For centuries the region had been controlled by the Turks – hence the Muslim population – and in 1900 it was still officially part of the Ottoman Empire. But under an international deal hammered out in 1878 it was run by officials of the Austro-Hungarian Empire. This compromise seemed to keep everyone happy – except the Serbs. The Serbs wanted Bosnia-Herzegovina, and they wanted it now.

Down, but not out: The dragons and tigers of Asia

Europe's influence spread all over the globe, but that didn't prevent some of the peoples of Asia from asserting their own identity and trying to control their own futures. The results were a bit mixed.

The defeated dragon: China

Napoleon is supposed to have said that when China woke up it would shake the world. What he meant was that 19th-century China was vast, with a population to dwarf anything Europe could throw at it, yet it seemed to have fallen asleep some time in the Middle Ages and never woken up.

China was ruled by an imperial dynasty that hardly ever moved outside the Forbidden City in Beijing (or Peking, as it was generally known in the west) and only vaguely believed in the existence of the world outside China itself. China's vast population of peasants was kept in poverty and its armies were huge but still fought largely with spears and bows and arrows as they'd always done. As a result, the Europeans spent the 19th century humiliating the Chinese, forcing the Emperor to sign treaties giving them control of China's seaports and, above all, forcing the Chinese to accept huge imports of opium from British India. Thousands of Chinese became dependent on the drug, and when the Chinese government tried to crack down on the opium trade, the British and French launched wars to stop them.

By 1900, to patriotic Chinese it seemed as if China was helpless before these westerners. So they decided to do something about it. A secret society took shape, dedicated to driving the foreigners out of China. It was called the Society of Harmonious Fists, though westerners nicknamed it the Boxers.

In 1900 the Boxers struck, killing foreigners and besieging foreign legations (a *legation* is a kind of embassy in a country that isn't thought to be important enough to have proper embassies – which in itself tells you how the west regarded China). The Europeans, Americans and Japanese (see the later 'Thoroughly modern Meiji: Japan' section to find out why the Japanese were fighting alongside the westerners) organised a multinational force to defeat the Boxers. The westerners imposed heavy *reparations payments* – a sort of compensation – on the Chinese government and the western troops occupied huge areas of China, burning villages and confiscating goods.

The Boxer Rebellion created a deep sense of injustice and anger against the west amongst many Chinese, which lasted until the very end of the century.

The tamed tiger: India

India had been the seat of the mighty Mughal Empire, but in 1900 the imperial throne of India was occupied by Queen Victoria, who held the title of Empress of India alongside her British crown.

The British had invested heavily in India, building railways, founding schools and hospitals, and providing India with all the infrastructure of a modern state. By 1900 increasing numbers of Indians were being educated along western lines and working in administration or the law.

Each December, Indian nationalists would meet at a gathering known as the Indian National Congress and call for Indians to have more of a say in the running of the country. They were still very loyal to the British Empire – the Congress wasn't calling for independence – but they knew about the advances made by the different nationalist groups in Europe and they reckoned that they could achieve the same. The British weren't against giving Indians a bit more of a role in government, especially in the provinces, but they weren't thinking in terms of handing power over to Indians. The British regarded India as an essential part of their Empire: in fact, many British thought that it was holding India that made Britain a Great Power in the first place, and some historians have agreed with them. (See Chapter 3 for more about the Great Powers.)

Thoroughly modern Meiji: Japan

Nineteenth-century Japan had seemed poised to fall under western domination, as all its Asian neighbours had. Like China (see the earlier 'The defeated dragon: China' section), Japan was a medieval country. It was in the grip of powerful warlords known as Shoguns who could square up to each other but would be powerless against the Americans or Europeans. In 1853 an American fleet under Commodore Matthew Perry had anchored near Tokyo to open Japan up to western trade, just as the British and French had done to China: it looked as if Japan was going to go the same way as all the rest of Asia. Some Japanese, however, were determined not to end up as a western colony.

In 1867 Emperor Meiji staged a coup in Tokyo and took power away from the Shoguns and back into his own hands. He used his new power to put Japan on a sort of crash course in western industry and culture. Japanese representatives travelled all over the western world, learning about western industry, society and, above all, western ways of waging war. The Japanese set about adopting as much of the western way of life as they could without entirely losing touch with their own culture. By 1900 Japan was a unique example of an Asian country that had westernised itself without being taken over by the western powers. So, when the Boxer Rebellion broke out in China in 1900, the Japanese sent troops to fight alongside the westerners.

Taking the Mikado

In 1885 that famous operetta-writing duo Gilbert and Sullivan produced their famous skit on Japan and the Japanese, *The Mikado*. Gilbert got his idea for the show from a major exhibition of Japanese culture that had been held recently in London, and he presented the Japanese in much the way everyone in the west thought of them – a feudal, rather barbaric people (the show has lots of talk of cutting people's heads off) with just enough western culture to make them figures of fun. Everyone enjoyed the show hugely except the Japanese ambassador, who was most put out that the Mikado – the Emperor of Japan himself – was made into a figure of fun: it was as if a Tokyo show had turned Queen Victoria into a pantomime dame. The ambassador issued a protest against the show – and no one took the slightest notice, which shows what little respect westerners felt for the Japanese. Twenty years later the Japanese fought a war against the Russians and beat them soundly. *The Mikado* still played in theatres all over the world but the joke had worn rather thin.

You can see what the Japanese were hoping to achieve by this modernisation programme: they wanted Japan to be accepted as a Great Power alongside the western powers. And because the westerners all seemed to think that a Great Power ought to have an empire, the Japanese – who did after all have an emperor – decided that they'd quite like an empire too.

They had their eyes on China. It was just across the sea from Japan and it was rich in raw materials that the Japanese islands lacked. The only problem was whether or not the western powers would allow the Japanese to build their own empire, and that in turn depended on whether or not the westerners accepted the Japanese as equals. Many of them, particularly the Russians, didn't – essentially on racial grounds: Europeans simply didn't believe that Asians were equal to them. But in 1902 the Japanese scored a major coup: Britain signed an alliance with Japan. With a major power such as Britain onside, the Japanese reckoned they could beat any other western power that felt hard enough to take them on. They were right too.

The new empire of the west: The United States of America

In 1900 the British writer Rudyard Kipling wrote his famous poem 'The White Man's Burden', which conjured up an image of an old, tired empire – that is, Britain – handing over the task of ruling the less advanced people of the world (that's Kipling's view, not mine!) to the new, young, strong power of the west – the United States of America. But was that the role the United States saw for itself?

To the New World

The key to understanding the United States in this period is to remember that the country was *different*. The Americans might speak English (with some funny spellings, but hey, English nonetheless), they might dress in the latest European fashions and they might read European literature, but they lived in the New World, not the Old one.

Of course, 'New World' is just a phrase: America is just as old as any other part of the world. But the Europeans who settled on the American continent in the years after Columbus landed liked to think they were creating a new, improved version of the world. They firmly believed that theirs was a purer, happier, freer and more equal society than the ones they'd left behind. The slaves of the American South had a rather different perspective and, even by 1900, for many black Americans the talk of America as a land of liberty and equality rang very hollow indeed, but they still believed in making their life in the United States rather than looking for greater freedom elsewhere.

The end of the frontier

The Americans had spent much of the 19th century exploring the interior of the continent, and then settling down and farming it, all the time fighting wars with the native tribes who lived on what the Americans called the frontier. *The frontier* was a rough place where you needed to be tough and resourceful to survive, where the law was in the hands of gun-toting sheriffs and marshals, fighting off bandits and gunmen. Through the 19th century writers and artists were conjuring up the myth of the western frontier. Until 1890, that is, because in 1890 the frontier closed down. Officially. The US Census Bureau said so. The native tribes had been rounded up into reservations and the American land mass from sea to sea had been settled and organised, so there literally was no 'frontier': all the land belonged to the United States.

After a 19th century taken up with its internal problems, exploring and settling the west, arguing over slavery and fighting the Civil War, 20th-century America would be seeking a role for itself in the world. Just as soon as it had worked what that proper place should be.

The huddled masses

High on its pedestal at the entrance to New York harbour stands the Statue of Liberty, holding aloft a flaming torch as a light for the world. On its base are these words:

> *Give me your tired, your poor, Your huddled masses yearning to breathe free, The wretched refuse of your teeming shore. Send these, the homeless, tempest-tost to me, I lift my lamp beside the golden door!*

And to her they came, in their thousands.

As the old century moved to its close, poor people from all over Europe scraped together what money they could, gathered their possessions in bundles and bags, and made their way, often in dangerously overcrowded and leaky ships, to start a new life in America: Italians and Poles escaping grinding poverty; Russian Jews escaping persecution; others simply seeking greater opportunities in life than they'd have at home. They passed through the immigration centre on Ellis Island and out into New York, which soon became a bustling, multi-lingual, multicultural city quite unlike the rather refined British-style city it had been. The new arrivals had to put up with dirty, overcrowded tenements, unscrupulous landlords and hard manual work. In some ways they were no better off than they'd been in their old countries, but America offered one thing that Europe didn't: a Dream.

Striking it rich . . .

In America – so the Dream went – anyone, if they worked hard enough, could rise up even to the very top. Americans could point to examples of people who had struck it very rich indeed, such as Andrew Carnegie (a penniless Scottish immigrant who became a fabulously wealthy industrialist and philanthropist) and Henry Ford (the son of immigrants who revolutionised car manufacture, and was soon rolling in it too).

. . . and striking it poor

Not everyone who came to America was able to live the American Dream. The great majority of first-generation immigrants lived in poverty, working for low wages and living in squalor. Much the same was true for third- or fourth-generation black Americans.

American workers did organise labour unions to protect their rights and interests, but these never achieved the sort of power and influence that unions enjoyed in Europe. Many employers, such as Henry Ford, refused to recognise unions, and some even employed company spies to report on union meetings and company heavies to break them up. Sometimes the American Dream could turn very sour.

An American empire?

Modern Americans don't always realise it, and President Theodore Roosevelt argued otherwise, but the United States in 1900 was an imperial power. It had conquered the Midwest (you might not think of the story of the frontier as one of conquest and expansion but that's what it was), annexed the Hawaiian islands, fought a war with Spain and taken over most of Spain's remaining colonies, including the Philippines, Puerto Rico, Guam and Cuba. And other imperialist and expansionist powers thought that a Very Good Thing Too.

American historians nowadays tend to take the view that America was actually an anti-imperial power and that its possessions weren't colonies in the sense that the Europeans' overseas possessions were. European historians, however, tend to take the view that they know an empire when they see one and that the United States in the 1900s ticked all the boxes. It's probably impossible to reconcile these points of view: you just have to accept that different perspectives exist. What matters is that the United States in the 1900s was in a strange position: it was profoundly suspicious of those imperialist Europeans but, as a global power itself, it couldn't ignore them either.

KEY PEOPLE

Theodore Roosevelt: World police

You've got to hand it to Theodore ('Teddy') Roosevelt. This is the man who, as Assistant Secretary of the Navy, had the job of getting the US Navy ready for the war with Spain, and who then resigned so he could go off and fight in it. He was a dashing – some would say foolhardy – cavalry commander in the war with Spain who then came home and plunged back into politics, first as governor of New York and then as President McKinley's running-mate in the 1900 presidential election. Following McKinley's assassination, the tough-talking, rough-riding Roosevelt became president. After he was elected in his own right in 1904, Roosevelt started to assert himself in foreign policy. He once said that his approach was to 'talk softly and carry a big stick', like a sort of global policeman with his truncheon. Roosevelt asserted the United States' role as an active player in world affairs.

Meet the new neighbours: Canada, Newfoundland, Australia, New Zealand and South Africa

The Europeans justified their empires by saying that they were only looking after all these peoples around the world until they were grown-up enough to leave home and look after themselves (I leave aside the point that these peoples had been happily ruling themselves for hundreds of years before the Europeans arrived, or I'll never get to Chapter 3). If you'd asked these Europeans for examples of people who'd grown up enough to rule themselves, they'd have pointed with great pride to a growing number of British colonies that were morphing into self-governing colonies known as *dominions*:

- **Australia's** separate colonies joined together and formed the self-governing Commonwealth (that is, dominion) of Australia in 1901.

- **Canada** became a self-governing dominion in 1867.

- **Newfoundland** remained separate from Canada and became a self-governing dominion in 1907.

- **New Zealand** became a self-governing dominion in 1907.

- **South Africa,** including both English-speaking and Afrikaaner areas, became a self-governing dominion in 1910.

You might be detecting a pattern here. These colonies all had substantial settler populations of white European descent. Does it look to you as if only white people were judged to be grown-up enough to rule themselves? Yes, that's how it seemed at the time to nationalists in India and Africa.

These nations were proud of their new nationhood, with national flags, capital cities and elected parliaments, yet at the same time they considered themselves as British as people in Liverpool or Edinburgh, for example, and they were proud of being British, too: in fact, for many purposes the British still counted Canadians, Newfoundlanders, Australians and New Zealanders *as* British. And that meant that Britain's quarrels and wars were their quarrels and wars too. Units from all these colonies and dominions were serving alongside the British in the Anglo–Boer War, which was going on as the century started. But for how long could the British regard these new nations essentially as an extension of their own country?

Scrambled Africa

In 1884 Berlin became, in effect, the capital city of the whole African continent. In that year representatives of the major powers of Europe met to divide Africa up between them so that everyone who wanted African territory could get it without annoying any of their European neighbours. You can probably guess: not a single African was present at the conference.

What followed was a mad land-grab, nicknamed the *Scramble for Africa,* by Europeans hoping to get their hands on all the best bits of Africa, though some of them were happy to make do with any bit of Africa, even the Sahara Desert, as long as they could plant their flag on it and colour it in on their wall maps. By 1900 only two states in the entire African continent had escaped the clutches of the Europeans: Liberia, which was under American protection anyway, and Ethiopia (also known as Abyssinia), which had managed to defeat an Italian invasion force.

The Scramble for Africa threw up some dangerous clashes and rivalries among the European colonial powers that would have important consequences when war broke out in 1914.

Annoy the French! Annoy them again!

The Scramble for Africa is often dated from the British invasion of Egypt in 1882. That invasion seriously annoyed the French (it didn't exactly please all the Egyptians either), who'd regarded Egypt as their special territory ever since the days of the Crusades. Annoying the French always added to the fun of any enterprise for the British, and in 1898 that invasion of Egypt gave them a chance to drive the French to absolute fury. Egypt had lost control of Sudan, and in 1898 an Anglo-Egyptian army under General Kitchener marched into Sudan and retook the country. Because Egypt was run by Britain, this meant that the British now ruled Sudan too.

The Europeans: Liberators or oppressors?

The Europeans liked to claim that they were liberating the Africans from oppression and slavery, and in some cases that was true. However, many Africans suffered terribly at the hands of their new masters. For example, soldiers working for King Leopold II of Belgium employed wide scale mutilation and rape to force the Congolese people to work for them, and in German South-West Africa the colonial masters put down a Herero uprising by driving them into the desert, where thousands died from thirst.

Just then, a small French expedition arrived in Sudan and confronted Kitchener at a tiny place in the middle of nowhere called Fashoda. The French tried to claim that the British were intruding on French territory, and for a time the French press called for all-out war against the 'perfidious English' until they had to calm down and see sense: it wasn't worth launching a full-scale war over who controlled the Sudanese desert.

The war scare over Fashoda forced the British and French to rethink their relationship in Africa. The result was an understanding – the French word was *entente* – between the two powers that looked very like an alliance. The entente was a major factor in bringing about war in 1914.

Here come the Germans: Muscling in

At first the major players in the African land-grab were the British, French, Italians and Belgians. The German government hadn't seemed interested. That changed in the 1890s, though, and the Germans started muscling in with everyone else, taking territory in West Africa (Togo and the Cameroons), East Africa (Tanganyika) and South-West Africa. This sudden change of policy by the Germans had other Europeans worried: why had it happened and where might the Germans be looking to expand next?

Here come the Italians: All right, we'll have a bit of north Africa, then

The Italians had only finished creating their new nation state in 1870 (actually they hadn't quite finished – they didn't control the Vatican, but I won't quibble for now) and they wanted to show the rest of the world that Italy was a Great Power and could play with the big boys. And because the big boys all seemed to have colonies in Africa, the Italians decided to get one of their own.

They began by taking part of Somaliland and Eritrea, and in 1896 they launched an invasion of the ancient kingdom of Ethiopia. It didn't go to plan: the Ethiopians cut the Italians to pieces at the Battle of Adowa. So they gave up the idea of conquering Ethiopia, and looked at Tripoli in north Africa instead. Tripoli belonged to the Ottoman Empire, and after losing to the Ethiopians, the Italians were nervous about taking on the Turks – not to mention the French, who ruled Algeria and had their eyes on Tunisia and Morocco. Would France welcome an Italian takeover in Tripoli?

This international rivalry in north Africa added to the suspicions and tensions that led to war in 1914.

The British and the Boers

When the new century started a major war was already going on, between the British and the two Boer (that is, Dutch) republics in South Africa. The war began very well for the Boers and disastrously for the British, but by 1900 the British had got their breath back and had defeated the Boer armies in the field. British forces marched into the two republics' capitals and it seemed as though the Brits could proclaim, 'Mission accomplished'. They even started sending most of their troops home. But the mission wasn't accomplished, not by a long chalk.

Some Boer commanders started a guerrilla campaign, launching raids, ambushing British patrols and keeping the resistance going. What followed is still controversial and was to be of enormous importance for the First World War and for the whole of the 20th century. The British commander, Lord Kitchener, faced a problem: the Boer guerrilla units knew the countryside far better than the British, so it was pointless to try to go into the hills to hunt them down. On the other hand, the guerrillas depended on support from civilians who provided them with food, medicine and money for weapons and ammunition. So Kitchener devised a three-pronged plan to bring the commandos to their knees. Be warned: it was ruthless.

- ✔ **Barbed wire:** Developed for the North American prairie but just as effective spread across the South African veldt, where it seriously hindered the guerillas' ability to manoeuvre.

- ✔ **Scorched earth:** To stop the guerillas getting hold of food supplies, the British simply burned down all the farms in the *veldt* and destroyed all the crops they could find. Simple, effective – and ruthless.

- ✔ **Concentration camps:** The people whose farms had been destroyed had to go somewhere, so the British concentrated them together into hastily built *concentration camps* – not prison camps like Nazi concentration camps, but deadly nonetheless. No one gave a thought to basic health sanitation, and the death rate, especially among children, averaged over 2,000 – a month.

Kitchener's ruthless methods worked, but victory came at a horrific price.

To the ends of the Earth

As if carving up Africa and conquering Asia were not enough, the Europeans and Americans were also engaged in exploring and claiming the Arctic region and the Antarctic continent. Just like the Scramble for Africa, polar exploration had a strong tinge of patriotic rivalry, especially the urge to be first at one or other of the poles. In 1912 two of the leading nations, Britain and Norway, squared up to each other for a race for the biggest prize: to be the first to arrive at the South Pole. The Norwegian team won; the British team, led by Captain Scott, arrived too late and perished on the return journey. Polar exploration provided plenty of stories of courage and endurance, but it was also about imperial expansion and international rivalry.

The Anglo–Boer War taught some important lessons for when the First World War broke out. It showed the importance of good communications and the effectiveness of accurate rifle fire; it showed the deadly potential of simple barbed wire; above all, it showed that sometimes victory came to those who were prepared to pay any price, however inhuman, to win.

How People Lived: A World of Extremes

In many ways the pre-1914 world didn't look that different from the current one, especially when a few more motor cars started appearing. But if you were able to travel back to it, you'd find that it contained some more extreme contrasts than you might have been expecting.

Urban warriors: The cities of the world

The world of 1800 had been a rural one, outside of some areas of industrial Britain, but by 1900 the major cities in Europe and the Americas were large, industrial metropolises linked by railway and telegraph lines. They had large, ornate railway stations (by 1900 some of them had underground railways too) and steel frames allowed builders to construct much higher buildings than in the past. Down at street level, roads could be just as congested with horse-drawn traffic as they'd later be with motor cars, but cities were becoming better planned, with parks and open spaces where people could get some fresh air and exercise. Hospitals were being built, and medical officers appointed. People could also go window-shopping: the early 20th century saw the arrival of big department stores, such as Selfridge's in London and La Samaritaine in Paris. Apart from the horse-drawn traffic and the ladies' fashions, much of city life would look pretty familiar today.

What would look less familiar would be the huge contrast between the rich and the poor areas. To get an idea, forget modern-day London or New York and think instead of cities such as Mumbai or Rio de Janeiro, with their mix of flashy buildings and huge slums and shanty towns. The Russian leader Vladimir Ilyich Lenin wrote how, when he was living in London, he and his wife would go for evening strolls. They'd look at the beautiful houses of the rich, where they could see opulent dinner parties going on, and then they'd turn maybe only one corner and find themselves in another world: the dark and filthy back alleys where people lived in rags, often with no shoes, and with a life expectancy far below that of their rich neighbours around the corner. The British statesmen Benjamin Disraeli had described the rich and the poor as two nations, with virtually nothing in common with each other, and Lenin and his wife could see exactly what he meant.

The terribly respectable middle classes

Spotting the *middle classes* was easy: they were the ones taking the train or tram to work in the morning rush hour, or going to church on Sunday morning and for a walk on Sunday afternoon. The *upper middle classes* were the professionals – the lawyers, civil servants, bankers and stockbrokers – who kept national economies buoyant and national governments going. The *lower middle classes* were the middle managers, cashiers and counter clerks who implemented their seniors' decisions.

Making fun of the middle classes, with their obsession with respectability and appearances, is an easy thing to do, but without them the huge changes of the 20th century could never have happened.

Urban slums can seriously damage your health – and your national military efficiency

In 1899, when the Anglo–Boer War broke out, the British came in for a terrible shock. Thousands of patriotic young men came forward to volunteer to go to South Africa and fight, but when they went for their standard army medical check-up, something like a third of them – in some areas it was over half – were medically unfit to fight. These men were the products of the unhealthy slums areas of urban Britain. It was a sharp lesson in the importance of improving living conditions in the big industrial cities – for everyone's sake.

Workers of the world

Industry had produced a whole new type of people: *industrial workers,* who lived in the crowded, filthy slums, and who worked in the dirty and dangerous factories and mines that drove the industry that made western countries so rich. By 1900 these people were beginning to organise themselves into trade and labour unions and into political parties. Socialists called on workers around the world to unite and work together to win better wages and conditions for themselves; some called on them to rise up in revolution and overturn the system that had forced them into such appalling poverty. In some countries, such as Russia and the United States, unions encountered strong opposition from employers and the authorities, but in all western European countries the socialist parties were advancing. In 1913 the socialists became the largest single party in the *Reichstag,* the German parliament.

According to the socialist doctrine of Karl Marx, workers should identify themselves entirely with their class: their nationality was irrelevant. In other words, Italian workers should feel a common identity with workers in Russia or Argentina or Wales or wherever, and should feel hostility towards the middle and upper classes of their own country. The test of whether this idea worked in practice would come when countries went to war with each other. Would workers refuse to fight against their fellow workers from other countries, or would patriotism come first and workers' solidarity second? Until a major war broke out, no one quite knew the answer to that question.

Country folk: Living on the land

Not everyone lived in cities in 1900: even the industrial countries depended on the countryside to keep their cities fed. Cities demanded a constant supply of food, cloth, tobacco, coffee, rubber and a whole host of other products that had to be grown on farms and plantations. So underneath the urban life was a vast global infrastructure of farms and plantations. New refrigerated ships meant that meat could be slaughtered in Argentina or New Zealand and end up on dinner plates in Paris or Vienna. Rubber could be tapped in Congo or Malaya and turned into tyres or fan belts for motor factories in Detroit or Birmingham.

Despite the huge demand for produce, fields were still ploughed and reaped in much the same way that medieval peasants would've recognised. However, some changes were happening in America that looked useful: farmers in the Midwest had pioneered the use of barbed wire fences to protect their crops from cattle and they were also trying out motorised tractors with caterpillar tracks for crossing rough ground. Both of these ideas would be put to military use in the First World War.

Uptown girls at Downton Abbey

The pre-1914 world is well captured in the British TV series *Downton Abbey*, which shows the intrigues going on upstairs and downstairs in the grand house where the fictional Earl of Grantham lives with his family and his staff. This is a male world, where even a distant relation (and a middle-class one too!) takes precedence over the earl's decidedly upper-class daughters.

Before 1914 domestic service was indeed one of the major forms of employment for ordinary people across Europe, but don't be fooled by the smart clothes and beautiful décor: the hours were very long and the work could be exhausting. Try carrying heavy jugs of hot water (no spilling, mind) up three or four flights of stairs, just to fill a bath for whoever might want one – not just once but several times a day. And that's just one of your daily duties. Domestic service could be steady and reasonably secure employment (though you could still be sacked at a moment's notice, don't forget), but don't think of it as an easy option.

How (Some) People Thought: Brave New Ideas for a Brave New World

Historians use the French term *fin de siècle* to refer to the last decade of the 19th century. Literally, it just means 'end of the century', but it also has the sense of the end of the old order, of a world coming to its close. That's partly because historians know, of course, that the First World War was on the horizon, but equally it refers to some of the radical – and, to the established order, unsettling – new ideas that were developing as the old world drew towards its end.

It's art and music, Jim, but not as we know it

In the rapidly changing world of the 19th century people could at least rely on some certainties: if you looked at a painting, for example, you knew what it was meant to be, and music comprised tunes you could hum, such as Franz Lehár's jolly little operetta *The Merry Widow* or the stirring, patriotic tunes of Edward Elgar.

But other artists and musicians seemed determined to turn all that certainty on its head. For example, Henri Matisse, the French painter, pioneered a trend for bright, unnaturally garish colours that prompted one art critic to call him and his colleagues *les fauves* – the wild beasts. Spanish artist Pablo

Picasso alarmed the art world in 1905 with a painting of a group of nude prostitutes called *Les Demoiselles d'Avignon* (The, er, Ladies of Avignon). What raised eyebrows wasn't the subject matter but the way he painted them: they start naturalistic enough on the left, but get steadily more abstract, until the one on the right is more of a set of shapes topped off by what appears to be an African tribal mask (I bet she never sat for him again). Russian composer Igor Stravinsky provoked a riot with his ballet *The Rite of Spring* when it premiered in Paris in 1913. It's set in pagan Russia and shows a young girl dancing herself to death to an increasingly frenzied, savage rhythm, to appease the gods and feed the crops of her tribe.

These writers and artists were disturbing Europe's feelings of superiority by seeking ideas and inspiration from non-western art and traditions – in other words, from cultures that most Europeans thought barbaric and inferior. To some, these new artistic movements were an exciting way out of the boring, predictable styles they'd grown up with; but to others these radical new styles were dangerous – a rejection of European civilisation itself.

The windmills of your mind – Freud, Jung and psychoanalysis

In 1901 an Austrian doctor called Sigmund Freud published a book with the intriguing title *The Interpretation of Dreams*. Interpreting people's dreams is as old as the Bible, but Freud had some startlingly new things to say about what's going on in your sleep. Based on interviews with hundreds of patients, whom he encouraged to lie out on a comfy couch so they could open up while he sat taking notes behind them, Freud said that dreams reflect the subconscious, and that the subconscious spends most of its time thinking about sex. Not just adolescent fantasies, but deeply suppressed sexual desires for mothers and fathers. Freud said that even apparently harmless objects that appeared in people's dreams had sexual meanings. It was all most shocking and disturbing, and very good news for booksellers.

Meanwhile another doctor, Carl Jung, was working with mental patients in a Zurich mental hospital and developing the study of the subconscious even further. Jung thought that people have two levels of subconsciousness – their own individual one and a sort of collective subconscious, common to all people within a particular culture.

To many people these new sciences of *psychology* and *psychoanalysis* was exciting and disturbing at the same time. People often like the idea of being decoded or explained, but Freud's work also suggested that beneath the civilised and cultured surface of *fin de siècle* Europe were some savage and primitive desires and emotions. This too would be a major theme in trying to understand the First World War when it came.

The intriguing world of physics

As if deconstructing art and music and unpicking the mind weren't enough, by the turn of the century scientists were even examining and changing the make-up of the universe itself. The exciting science to be involved in by 1900 was *physics* – the story of the physical world itself. The happening part of physics was the study of atoms and electrons and molecules – the building blocks of life and matter. Key figures included Pierre and Marie Curie, who were exploring the nature of radiation, and Ernest Rutherford, who was investigating the structure of the atom and would later oversee the splitting of the atom and the development of atomic power.

Even more far-reaching was the publication in 1905 of Albert Einstein's theory about the structure of the universe and its relationship to the light through which people perceive it. Einstein put forward the idea that in some circumstances, such as those that might exist in space, the rules of gravity and motion (which had seemed rock solid since Newton drew them up 200 years earlier) weren't fixed at all, but relative. Energy, he declared, equals mass times the speed of light squared. Or $E = mc^2$, as relativists say.

God is dead! (Nietzsche). That's what you think! (God)

Frederick Nietzsche was a rather intense character, a writer and philosopher and an admirer of the German nationalist composer Richard Wagner, with a passionate interest in religion in all its forms. Nietzsche quite frequently declared in his writings that 'God is dead', by which he meant that organised religion was increasingly irrelevant in the modern world. The churches spent far too much time preaching the virtues of pity, he thought, whereas modern man should be strong, self-made and ruthless. Nietzsche developed the idea that the world should be led by what he termed the *superhuman,* the man who had been bred and brought up to be perfect physically and intellectually (and probably racially too – like most Europeans, Nietzsche believed that white Europeans were best suited to lead the world). Impressionable young Europeans who could work their way through Nietzsche's dense writings – I'm not talking a little light reading before bedtime here – could find some exciting ideas in Nietzsche: the Nazis later looked on him as the father of their ideas. He was wrong to write off the power and influence of religion, though. The 20th century would show religious belief to be as strong and powerful as it ever had been.

Don't worry if all this science has you a bit lost: not many people outside the scientific world understood these developments at the time (except for X-rays, which did begin to pass into general use). However, these advances in science would have a huge impact on the 20th century in due course, and they certainly showed that the world of the 1900s was one in which absolutely nothing, not even the very structure of matter itself, was taken for granted: *everything* was open to question.

When the revolution comes . . .

With so many new ideas around at the time, it might not come as a great surprise to hear that numerous revolutionary groups were operating in the Europe of the 1900s. Some were socialists, wanting to pull down society and rebuild it along Marxist lines; some were nationalists, wanting to set up their own nation states; some were anarchists, who didn't believe in rules and wanted to destroy states, not set them up. Apart from a revolution in Russia in 1905 (and that didn't achieve much), these revolutionaries had few opportunities to put their ideas into action in the years before the First World War broke out, so they threw their energies into writing endless pamphlets and bitter in-fighting. But they knew their day would come.

Working with What We've Got: Building a Better World

While some groups were hoping to pull down the old world order and construct a new one (see the preceding sections), others were more interested in trying to improve the existing system.

The Red Cross

The Red Cross was the brainchild of a Swiss, Henry Dunant, who was appalled at the lack of facilities for the wounded when he witnessed a battle between the French and Austrians in 1859. The Red Cross was originally intended to provide a battlefield ambulance service, but in 1864 its International Committee drew up the first Geneva Convention, laying down certain humane rules to be observed when fighting a war, and persuading governments to sign up to it. The Geneva Convention was extended in 1907, laying down rules for the treatment of prisoners of war and establishing the Red Cross as a neutral humanitarian organisation to be respected by all sides, even in the thick of the fighting.

The Hague Conventions

In 1899 governments from around the world sent representatives to The Hague to draw up an international agreement on the waging of war. They agreed rules for the proper treatment of prisoners of war and they banned certain types of weapon that they thought were inhumane, such as:

- **Aerial bombing:** At a time when aircraft had only just started to fly, it was remarkably fore-sighted of the Convention-signers to consider the dropping of explosives from balloons or aircraft. Like gas, it was thought to be an inhumane way of fighting, not least because it was so indiscriminate in whom it could kill.

- **The dum-dum bullet:** This bullet expanded after it penetrated a body, so that a single bullet could tear a person's guts out. Both sides used it in the Anglo–Boer War.

- **Poison gas:** As the chemicals industry developed, the potential for using chemicals as weapons became much clearer. The general view was that this was an insidious and inhumane way of fighting, though others disagreed. When war broke out in 1914, the others got their way.

In 1907, representatives of the leading nations added a few more clauses, covering warfare at sea, steps to take to rescue the crews of sunken merchant ships and so on.

The Hague Conventions represent a remarkable attempt by the Great Powers to try to avert the full force of the industrial and military capacity they were uneasily aware that they possessed. Unfortunately, as you've probably guessed, they had very little influence over the way the First World War would be fought, especially after its early stages. Of the three types of weaponry banned, countries respected only the ban on the dum-dum bullet.

The 1900 Paris Universal Exhibition – come and see the future!

All the hope and vision of these exciting years was visible at the Universal Exhibition held in 1900 in Paris. People flocked to see how the marvels of technology were transforming the modern world: a world in which you could buy soup in a metal tin, move up and down buildings on travelling staircases and watch films with recorded sound to go with them. To emphasise the vision of a future of international harmony and aspiration, the Exhibition even included the games of the Second Olympiad (see the following section). The future seemed very bright. How very appropriate, then, that the Exhibition was brought to an early and unexpected close by an assassination: US President McKinley was shot, in his own country, by an anarchist in 1901. It wouldn't be the last time an assassin ruined hopes of world peace.

Nobel – dynamite for peace

The Nobel Prizes have a curious history. They're named after Alfred Nobel, a Swedish dynamite tycoon who left money in his will to fund prizes for the most eminent contributions to physics, chemistry, medicine, literature and world peace (later a Nobel Prize for Economics was added to the list). The idea was to honour human achievement, at a time when most honours and awards went to politicians and military figures. In 1901, as if to set the new century off on the right note, the first Nobel Prize for Peace was awarded. It went jointly to a French pacifist writer and to Henry Dunant, founder of the Red Cross.

Anyone who thought this a good omen for a century of international peace and humanity was going to be very disappointed.

The Olympic Vision

A world without war, in which rivalry would be channelled into healthy competitive sport – that was the vision of the French Baron Pierre de Coubertin. Inspired by the spirit of sportsmanship at British public schools and the 'Olympian Games' held at the country town of Much Wenlock, he decided to revive the ancient Greek Olympic Games. The first modern Olympiad was held at Athens in 1896, and had it not been for the Paris Universal Exhibition in 1900 the Games might have stayed in Greece as the original ones did.

Alas for Baron de Coubertin, the familiar themes of politics and trickery soon began to spoil his dream. At the 1908 London Olympics, for example, the Americans accused the host team of cheating in the tug-of-war by fielding a team of burly policemen who planted their heavy boots in the mud and proved impossible to shift. And the Italian winner of the marathon was disqualified for being inadvertently helped over the finish line by overenthusiastic spectators. But somehow the Games survived, and not even the First World War could kill them off or the ideals that underpinned them.

Chapter 3

Crisis Mismanagement: Unpicking the Causes of the First World War

In This Chapter

▶ Watching Europeans go to war with each other – and quite enjoying it

▶ Arranging alliances and planning for war

▶ Arguing – fiercely – about just who started the war

*T*he First World War was so destructive that after the war was over people began to ask exactly why it broke out in the first place. People have been asking that question ever since.

The outbreak of the First World War wasn't inevitable: that the pre-1914 world had plenty of problems is certainly true, but it doesn't follow that the only way to solve those problems was by a huge war. On the other hand, plenty of people, including some in the governments and military high commands of Europe's Great Powers, thought that a *short* war might be just the thing to give their countries a bit of healthy exercise. That helps to explain why some statesmen were so ready to resort to warfare to solve problems that could easily have been resolved around a table.

This chapter explains why the Europeans ended up going to war with each other in 1914 – and why so many of them were so pleased about it.

Heigh-Ho, Heigh-Ho, It's Off to War We Go

The last time all of Europe had gone to war was during the Napoleonic Wars (1803–15), which had been fought to break Napoleon's stranglehold on the continent and had lasted 12 years. Since then, wars had tended to be shorter and smaller, but the idea of fighting to stop one country dominating the continent persisted. In Napoleon's day, France was the country to keep a nervous eye on. Next came Russia, which was spreading its influence across eastern and southern Europe and extending its frontiers south towards India. By 1900 if any country was likely to dominate and spread its influence across Europe, that country was Germany.

To understand why European countries went to war with each other again in 1914, but on a larger scale than ever before, it helps to know why nations in the 19th century had so often turned to war to solve their problems.

Real men make war

European states, especially new ones like Italy and Germany (which had only been united in 1860 and 1871), saw war as a test of their national manliness, a way of demonstrating that they were real nations, worthy of respect.

Statesmen and writers sometimes compared nations with individuals, with every citizen contributing to the health and fitness of the people as a whole. Just as individuals need to keep fit and healthy – and the late 19th century saw a veritable craze for sport and exercise – so nations needed to maintain their physical fitness. Many Europeans saw their overseas colonies as a testing ground for character and manliness. The best test of a nation's manliness, however, was a war. Europeans still thought of war in terms of colourful uniforms and exciting cavalry charges. War was like a glorified sporting match: short, sharp and decisive. Or so they thought.

God is on our side! No, he's on ours!

Most religions teach about spreading peace and harmony, but they also talk of a cosmic battle between Good and Evil. Religion wasn't usually a direct cause of war in the 19th century, but combatants often genuinely believed that God was on their side. Likewise, both sides in the First World War claimed that God was supporting them against an evil enemy. The Germans went a step further and tried to stir up the Muslim world into a holy war to topple British rule in India.

Your problems solved – you need a war!

Normally, countries declare war on each other only in the last resort, if diplomacy has failed. However, in 1832, a German military analyst called Carl von Clausewitz argued that war could be the *first* resort, a normal part of policy. If you wanted something from your neighbour, just launch a quick war, take it and move on. Simple! Of course, Clausewitz's ideas made sense only if you could be certain that you'd win quickly, and that meant careful planning for war, making use of the latest technology.

Worrying wars from the recent past

Even short wars gave worrying lessons. For example, in 1859 the French and Italians fought a short war against the Austrians that was so bloody that one battle, Magenta, lent its name to a dye the colour of dried blood, and the other, Solferino, so horrified a Swiss onlooker called Henry Dunant that he founded the International Red Cross (see Chapter 2).

So a short war wasn't necessarily a cheap or easy war, but long wars had even more serious lessons for the planners of 1914:

✔ **The Crimean War, 1854–6:** British, French and Turkish troops besieged the southern Russian naval base of Sevastopol. Incompetent leadership meant that the war dragged on for some two years longer than it need have done.

Lesson for 1914: Avoid elderly commanders who don't know how to run a modern army.

✔ **The American Civil War, 1861–5:** European military leaders tended to think of themselves as the professionals and the Americans as amateurs, but the American Civil War showed how amateurs could turn into experienced professionals. It was also the first war to make effective use of iron warships and of submarines.

Lessons for 1914: a) Volunteers can be as good as professionals. b) European admiralties would need to completely rethink naval warfare.

✔ **The Boer War, 1899–1902:** The British were confident they'd be able give their enemies, the southern African republics of Transvaal and the Orange Free State, a good, sound thrashing, but at first it was the Boers who thrashed the British, and then they launched a long guerrilla campaign. The British made very effective use of an American farming invention – barbed wire – as a way of impeding the enemy's movement.

Lessons for 1914: a) Accurate, rapid rifle fire is deadly. b) British soldiers are as vulnerable to it as anyone else. c) Stock up on barbed wire.

In 1904 a war broke out between Russia and Japan that seemed to provide a most surprising lesson (aside from the fact that Japan inflicted stunning defeats on Russia, which no one expected). Every officer cadet in every military academy in the world learned the maxim: 'The attacker always has the advantage'. But in the Russo–Japanese War, when one side was securely dug into a trench, the other side found it extremely difficult to dislodge them if the defenders had machine guns. Most observers thought this was just an interesting exception to the general rule; the First World War would show how wrong they were.

The Germans were good at planning, and liked von Clausewitz's way of thinking. And, as it happened, they did want a few things from their neighbours:

✔ **The Schleswig-Holstein War (1864):** The Germans and Austrians crushed Denmark in a short, sharp campaign to take control of two Danish duchies.

- ✔ **The Seven Weeks' War (1866):** The Prussians (North Germans) crushed Austria in a matter of weeks to establish just who should lead Germany.

- ✔ **The Franco–Prussian War (1870–1):** The Germans crushed the French and took two valuable border provinces off them – Alsace and Lorraine.

In the run-up to 1914 the Germans gave their planning skills a serious workout and came up with the *Schlieffen Plan* (see Chapter 4) – their scheme for successfully dealing with a war on two fronts, a situation which they feared more than anything. What the Germans forgot, though, was that by 1914 other countries had learnt from their successes and knew how to use railways, rifles, heavy artillery and machine guns too. When the enemy is just as well prepared as you are, Clausewitz's idea of winning a short and decisive victory falls down.

Understanding How (and Why) the First World War Started

How the First World War broke out is one of the biggest and most controversial historical questions around. After the war, many people blamed the Germans, but other explanations are on the table:

- ✔ **Was it inevitable?** This idea is tempting, but it doesn't stand up to investigation. Nothing in history is inevitable until it happens: events can always take an alternative path. People before 1914 did often talk of a big war coming, but that doesn't mean that it was bound to happen.

- ✔ **Was it just one crisis too many?** This idea is easy to understand, and the years before 1914 certainly saw a series of international crises. But you could say that of almost any period. Crises don't have to lead to a huge war. Even these crises didn't *have* to lead to a big European war.

- ✔ **Was it no one's fault?** This argument went down well in Germany after the war, when everyone was blaming the Germans, and it may be what you conclude. The trouble is, if you decide no one was to blame, you still have to explain how war broke out. *Something* must have caused it.

One problem with searching for that *something* is talk of 'the First World War' breaking out. It makes more sense to say that a series of different wars broke out: Austria-Hungary went to war with Serbia; Russia went to war with Austria-Hungary and Germany; Germany went to war with France, Belgium and Britain – and all for different reasons. To understand the outbreak of the war, you need to look at these different conflicts and the different causes that lay behind them.

Get off our land! Nationalism

Nationalism was the big new idea of the 19th century. It defined the people who make up a nation in terms of their history, language and culture, and talked of a special bond between the people of a nation and its territory.

Nationalism was becoming an ever-bigger issue in the run-up to 1914; tensions between peoples were running high and certain areas were looking more and more like potential flashpoints. Different peoples across Europe were latching onto the idea of *self-determination* – that nations should have the right to throw off their foreign masters and determine their own destiny for themselves.

The most dangerous problems of nationalism before 1914 were

- ✔ **Slavs:** Among these people of southern and eastern Europe, the biggest Slav state was Russia. Other Slav populations lived in southern Europe. Slav nationalists dreamed of a big Slav state to which all southern Slavs then ruled by the Turks or the Austro-Hungarians could belong, to be led by the biggest southern Slav group, the Serbs.

- ✔ **The Austro-Hungarian Empire:** As well as Austrians and Hungarians, this empire included Italians, Czechs, Slovaks, Poles, Romanians, Slovenes, Serbs, Bosniac Muslims and Croats. Many of these groups dreamed of breaking free from the empire and having their own nation states. Running this empire was a complex game of divide and rule among the rival nationalities.

- ✔ **Alsace-Lorraine:** The Germans took these two coal-rich border regions from France in 1871, and French nationalists had been itching to get them back ever since. By 1914 most French people accepted that they weren't likely to get them back any time soon (rather as many Germans during the Cold War came to accept the existence of the Berlin Wall while hoping that one day it would come down), but they still dreamed of reclaiming them one day.

Love me, love my ally – the Great Power rivals

The most powerful nations were known as *Great Powers*. The theory was that Great Powers were strong enough to stand up for themselves, but by 1914 the European Great Powers had linked up in a series of alliances for their own protection (see Figure 3-1).

Figure 3-1:
The
European
Great
Powers and
alliance
networks in
1914.

An *alliance* is like a lifeboat on a ship –reassuring, but you don't expect
to have to use it. The alliances in Europe before 1914 were meant to be
deterrents, to scare the other side off from launching a war. Alliances didn't
just say, 'Whatever you get into, we'll support you'. Each alliance laid down
specifically in what circumstances one ally would help another. For example,
the Franco–Russian alliance said that Russia would help France if the French
were attacked by Germany or by Italy supported by Germany, but it didn't
say anything about an attack by Austria-Hungary or by Italy on its own.
France was to help Russia against Germany or Austria-Hungary supported
by Germany, but not necessarily against Austria-Hungary on its own.

War didn't have to break out for an alliance to gear into action. The Franco–
Russian alliance said that both countries should mobilise their armies if
any of the Triple Alliance partners mobilised theirs. Mobilising an army is a
massive undertaking, but it doesn't *have* to result in war. It's just that in 1914
it did.

I'll have a Dual Alliance, barman. No, make that a Triple

The *Dual Alliance* was an alliance between Germany and Austria-Hungary, signed in 1879, but it became the *Triple Alliance* when the Italians joined in 1882. These apparently testosterone-filled bullies were, in fact, very aware of their own weaknesses and nervous – afraid, even – of their neighbours:

- ✔ **Germany:** Germany was strong. It had a military power that was second to none and had beaten both the Austrians and the French. However, Germany's Chancellor, Otto von Bismarck, knew that France would recover and want revenge for its defeat in 1871. His solution was an alliance with Austria-Hungary and Russia known as the *Dreikaiserbund* or 'Three Emperors' League' to warn the French off. Unfortunately for Bismarck, the Austrians and Russians distrusted each other so deeply that he couldn't keep the league together. Bismarck reckoned, reluctantly, that Germany had to stick with its fellow Germans, the Austrians, and say goodbye to the Russians.

- ✔ **Austria-Hungary:** The Austrians' two main worries were that their multi-ethnic empire would fall apart and that they'd have to fight a war on their own against Russia. The Austrians and Russians didn't get on. Some of the reasons went back a long way, but the final breach happened in 1908 with a quarrel over what was to happen to the Balkan provinces of Bosnia and Herzegovina (see the later section 'Crisis in Bosnia-Herzegovina'). The Austrians knew that they couldn't defeat Russia on their own, so they signed the Dual Alliance with Germany. Bismarck was sacked in 1890 and Germany's new leaders were much more anti-Russian, so the Austrians assumed they'd welcome a war with Russia.

- ✔ **Italy:** Italy joined the Dual Alliance, turning it into the Triple Alliance, in 1882. The Italians didn't particularly like either the Germans or the Austrians, but they wanted an empire in north Africa and they were angry because the French had beaten them to it. So, on the basis of 'my enemy's enemy is my friend', it made sense to the Italians to team up with France's greatest rival, Germany. Confused? It gets better. When the war came, Italy declared war on its own allies and joined its enemies!

European Great Power seeks ally with GSOH for long-term relationship. Must be anti-German

The other alliance network was designed to counter the Triple Alliance. However, it consisted of two countries that had little in common and could hardly have been farther apart if they'd tried: Russia in the east and France in the west:

- ✔ **Russia:** The Russians had got on well with Bismarck, but since he'd left the scene the Germans had broken off their alliance with Russia and, under Kaiser Wilhelm II, had been sounding ever more hostile to Russia. The Russians worried that the Germans and Austro-Hungarians might have plans to take some of Russia's lands in Poland and they worried about Austria-Hungary's intentions in the Balkans. The Russians knew that

Germany was strong, so they were on the lookout for an ally in case things came to war. It took time, because the other Great Powers were more worried about the Russians than they were about the Germans at first, but soon the rest of Europe grew increasingly worried about Germany's ambitions and the Russians found they did have a friend after all – France.

✔ **France:** The French had been dreaming of revenge after the Germans humiliated them in the Franco–Prussian War of 1870–1, but as long as Germany had both Austria-Hungary and Russia on its side, the French couldn't do anything. When the Russians split from the Germans and Austro-Hungarians in 1887, though, the French saw their chance, and in 1894 the two countries signed an anti-German alliance. This alliance meant that if it came to war, the Germans would now have a fight on their hands on two fronts – in both the east and the west.

Splendidly isolated: Britain

Britain didn't join either of the two alliance networks. That might come as a surprise, because Britain did fight in the war when it came, but Britain wasn't allied to any of the European Great Powers and it was very important to the British that they shouldn't be. The British were ambivalent about being part of Europe (they still are) and they didn't like the idea of being tied into an alliance that could force them to fight someone else's war for them. They had considered an alliance with Germany, but the idea fell through, and an alliance with Russia or France was impossible because both countries threatened Britain's overseas colonies. So the British played a sort of fox-and-the-grapes game, saying they didn't want one of those smelly old alliances anyway, so there: they would live in what they called *splendid isolation,* feeling very smug and superior but with no friends.

The British changed their mind after the Fashoda crisis in 1898 and when they found themselves without any European friends during the Boer War of 1899–1902 (you can read about both in Chapter 2). They still didn't want a European alliance, though: instead they signed three separate agreements:

✔ **Anglo–French Entente (1904):** *Entente* is a French word for an understanding – not an alliance. This particular understanding sorted out the two countries' differences in Africa. But was this understanding also an alliance? No one was quite sure. The Anglo–French Entente had secret clauses that said the British and French military high commands should start working together, jointly planning for war and generally operating just like – well, just like allies.

✔ **Anglo–Japanese Alliance (1902):** The Japanese would keep an eye on Britain's Asian possessions so the Royal Navy could concentrate on keeping an eye on the Germans closer to home.

✔ **Anglo–Russian Entente (1907):** This entente wasn't an alliance: it was an agreement about colonial territory, this time in Central Asia. Signing it didn't in any way commit Britain to support Russia in war.

Very cordial, this entente

At the time the British and French signed the entente in 1904, the French were still very anti-British after the Boer War. Some of the credit for changing that situation belongs to the British king, Edward VII, who in 1903 visited Paris and set about winning over French public opinion. Edward's visit showed him to be friendly and approachable, as different from a stuffy Englishman as it was possible to imagine. By the time he left, the French had been completely won round, and so warm were Anglo–French relations that the entente signed the following year came to be called the *Entente Cordiale* – something more like an international friendship. But did this mean it was an alliance really? That was what the Germans were determined to find out.

One international crisis after another

The years before 1914 saw a number of major international crises. These crises increased the tension between the Great Powers, though this doesn't mean they had to lead to a full European war.

The Russo–Japanese War

Japan was the Asian country that had been steadily turning itself into a modern western-style state (see Chapter 2 to find out why). In 1904 Japan and Russia went to war over control of Korea (which borders Russia and points towards Japan). To everyone's surprise, the Japanese inflicted a humiliating defeat on the Russians. The Russians had even sent their Baltic Sea fleet all the way to the China Sea, where it was sunk by the Japanese at the Battle of Tsushima. The general consensus after the war was that although Russia was big, it wasn't quite as powerful as it looked. (See also the earlier sidebar, 'Worrying wars from the recent past'.) On the other hand, the Russians would also be keen to restore their international prestige – if the right war came along.

Britain v. Germany: The great naval race

In the years between 1905 and 1914 the British and Germans tried desperately to outbuild each other in dreadnoughts (see Chapter 8). Their building programmes were horribly expensive, and the Germans had to give up and let the British win, because the army was demanding its fair share of Germany's military budget and the naval spending had to stop. But by the time war broke out, each fleet was just itching to meet the other in battle.

He said WHAT? The Kaiser in The Daily Telegraph

It seemed such a good idea at the time. In 1908 the Kaiser gave an interview to the British newspaper *The Daily Telegraph*. He hadn't cleared it with the German government beforehand, and when German ministers read it, their hair must have stood on end. The Kaiser told the English they were 'mad, mad, mad as March hares' to believe Germany was hostile to them. Then he said he had saved the British from disaster by refusing a Russian and French request for Germany to intervene in the Boer War (which caused spluttering over breakfast in St Petersburg and Paris when the Russian and French governments read it!). For good measure, he said the German navy was aimed against Japan, not Britain. The Kaiser's interview caused outrage in Britain, Japan and around the world. German ministers tried (not entirely successfully) to keep the Kaiser out of foreign policy after that.

Into Africa

One of the centres of serious trouble before 1914 was north Africa. Most of north Africa belonged nominally to the Turkish Ottoman Empire, but the Turks had largely lost control of it by 1900 and the European Great Powers all had their eyes on the prize.

Morocco 1905: Not-So-Cunning Plan No. 1

The real trouble in north Africa was in Morocco. And the people who caused it weren't the French or the Italians (and certainly not the Moroccans) – they were the Germans.

No one quite knew whether the 1904 entente between Britain and France (see the earlier section 'Love me, love my ally – the Great Power rivals') was an alliance or just an agreement about land in Africa. So the Kaiser decided to find out. The terms of the entente suggested that if the French wanted to take Morocco (they already had Algeria and Tunisia), that was all right by London. So in 1905 the Kaiser went to Morocco – in person – rode through the streets, and declared that if the Sultan of Morocco needed a friend to warn off the French, well, here was the Kaiser's card and contact details: just get in touch. The French were hopping mad about it, but Wilhelm was more interested in the reaction in London. It wasn't long in coming.

The British strongly denounced this German interference in north Africa and demanded an international conference to sort the issue once and for all. It met in 1906 at the very pleasant Spanish resort of Algeciras, where the delegates spent a lot of time debating details like whether French or Spanish policemen should operate in this or that Moroccan town. The real issue at Algeciras, though, was the Kaiser's cunning plan to isolate Britain. The Kaiser tried (without telling his own government, by the way) to tempt the French and the Turks into a huge anti-British alliance. Sneaky, eh? But the plan didn't work. The French didn't trust him, and neither did anyone else. France and Britain were now closer than ever. So much for *that* plan.

Morocco 1911: Not-So-Cunning Plan No. 2

In 1911 a rebellion broke out in Morocco against the French, and Paris sent in reinforcements. Some hawkish members of the German government decided that this action was an intolerable threat to Germany's (not-very-extensive) economic interests in Morocco, and they sent a German gunboat, the *Panther,* to the Moroccan port of Agadir. The French weren't too worried by the *Panther*'s arrival, and they struck a deal with the Germans: the French would take over Morocco completely and in return the French would give the Germans some land in the Cameroons and Congo. But the British went ballistic. David Lloyd George, normally a pro-German voice in the British Cabinet, made a speech warning that Britain wouldn't tolerate German expansion in Africa and the British fleet was put on standby for war.

War breaking out between Britain and Germany over the fate of Morocco wasn't *very* likely, but it did show how strongly the British were standing by their French 'not allies just very good friends' and how deeply suspicious they were of German intentions.

Let's take a trip to Tripoli

In 1911 the Italians launched an invasion of Tripoli – modern-day Libya – essentially, to make up for failing to conquer Ethiopia (see Chapter 2). The Italians took Tripoli without much trouble, partly thanks to their use of aeroplanes, and the war seemed to confirm that the Turkish army wasn't up to much – a point that Turkey's enemies in the Balkans took note of. This might be their chance to get rid of Turkish rule once and for all. (This Italian attack on Tripoli did have consequences for British rule in India, though; see Chapter 9.) The Balkan states' bid to push the Turks out of Europe started the train of events that led to the outbreak of war in 1914.

The deadly battle for the Balkans

The war that broke out in 1914 started in the Balkans. This area comprises the countries of south-eastern Europe, including Greece, Bulgaria, Romania and Serbia. The different nationalist groups of the region, when they could take a break from fighting each other, had two main enemies in their sights: the Turks and the Austro-Hungarians. The Turks still ruled a large part of the Balkans, and in 1908 the Austro-Hungarians took over an important part of the Balkans: Bosnia-Herzegovina.

War in the Balkans

In 1900 Serbia, Bulgaria, Greece, Montenegro and Romania were just waiting for the chance to drive the Turks out of the Balkans. When the Italians defeated the Turks so easily in Tripoli in 1911–2 (see 'Let's take a trip to Tripoli', earlier in the chapter), it seemed to these Balkan states that the time had come. So in 1912 all of them, except Romania (which had its own plan for expanding its frontiers), formed a 'Balkan League' and launched a devastating attack on the Turks.

This *First Balkan War* went very well for the Balkan League: they took all of Turkey's lands in Europe, except for a small parcel of land around the Turkish capital, Constantinople. Even so, some states were left unsatisfied:

- ✔ **Serbia** gained territory but didn't get what Serb nationalists really wanted: a port on the Adriatic coast. Austria-Hungary didn't want them to have one so the Great Powers insisted on creating the coastal state of Albania specifically to keep Serbia back from the coast.

- ✔ **Bulgaria** wanted Salonika but couldn't have it because the Greeks had got it. Bulgaria also wanted to keep the city of Adrianople that it had taken from the Turks; however, the peace treaty said Bulgaria had to give it back. The Bulgarians said they wouldn't, so in 1913 the Balkan states plunged into a *Second Balkan War.*

- ✔ **Turkey** felt humiliated: it had been defeated first by the Italians in Tripoli and now by the Balkan states. The Turks were keen for a re-match, and the Second Balkan War gave them just what they wanted.

This time everyone attacked Bulgaria. The Turks retook Adrianople and the Greeks held Salonika and took southern Macedonia, all of which the Bulgarians wanted. All in all, a bad year for Bulgaria.

As a result of all this, Bulgaria and Turkey both felt hard done by (each state thought the others had ganged up on them and, of course, they were right!), while the Greeks, Macedonians and Serbs felt rather pleased with themselves. The Serbs still wanted that port, though, and they blamed Austria-Hungary for stopping them from getting it. This matters because the really dangerous rivalry that in the end provoked war was between Austria-Hungary and Serbia.

Crisis in Bosnia-Herzegovina

The provinces of Bosnia and Herzegovina belonged to the Ottoman Empire but were run by Austria-Hungary (it's a long story; you can find it in Chapter 2). That suited the Austrians and Hungarians but not the Serb nationalists, who wanted the whole region for themselves (see Chapter 2). The Austro-Hungarians reckoned they could ignore the Serbs, but they couldn't ignore the Turks. In 1908 the nationalist Young Turks staged a palace revolution and seized power in Constantinople. Austria-Hungary worried that the Turks might take back the government of Bosnia-Herzegovina, and began to consider annexing the provinces outright. They knew that the Serbs wouldn't like it and that they'd go to the Russians for help. So if Austria-Hungary wanted to avoid a war – and it did – it was going to have to sweeten the Russians.

Count Aerenthal, the Austro-Hungarian Foreign Minister, knew just how to do it. He met his Russian opposite number, Alexander Izvolsky, and the two men did a deal: the Russians would let Austria-Hungary take the provinces over, and in return Austria-Hungary would help the Russians send their warships through the Dardanelles and out into the Mediterranean. This was very much a secret, never-to-be-written-down deal, and here's why:

✔ The Russians were supposed to be on the Serbs' side, and that did *not* involve allowing the Austro-Hungarians to annex Bosnia-Herzegovina.

✔ Sending Russian ships through the Dardanelles was strictly forbidden by international agreement.

✔ Izvolsky hadn't cleared this agreement with the Russian Prime Minister – in fact, he hadn't even *told* him, for the simple reason that the Prime Minister was bound to disown what Izvolsky had done.

What happened next would've been predicable to anyone brighter than Izvolsky. First, Aerenthal announced that Austria-Hungary was annexing Bosnia-Herzegovina. The Serbs protested and called on the Russians to back them up. But the Russians didn't, because of Izvolsky's deal (though he was now trying to wriggle out of trouble, claiming that no deal existed). Moreover, Aerenthal said nothing about the Russians sending their ships through the Dardanelles – after all, how could he when it was forbidden? Slowly, the penny dropped and Izvolsky realised he'd been tricked: Austria-Hungary had got the provinces and Russia had got nothing. And Izvolsky couldn't say anything because it had all been done with his agreement.

Count Aerenthal could feel very pleased with himself. His photo was no doubt decorating dartboards in St Petersburg and Belgrade, but he'd run rings around the Russians and denied the Serbs the one thing they really, really wanted. He'd even pre-empted the Turks. But there were good reasons that Aerenthal shouldn't have been quite so smug:

✔ The Russians had been humiliated. They wouldn't let Austria-Hungary get away with anything a second time – especially if it involved Bosnia or Serbia.

✔ Humiliating the Serbs undermined those in the Serbian government – including the Prime Minister, Nikola Pasič – who in fact hoped for good relations with Vienna. By the same token, it massively strengthened those Serb nationalists who wanted nothing better than a showdown with Austria-Hungary.

Aerenthal had certainly been very clever, but he'd also given Austria-Hungary a lot of very bitter enemies.

Warring neighbours – Austria-Hungary and Serbia

Serbia was a small country with big ideas. Since winning their independence from the Turks back in 1835, Serb nationalists had dreamed of setting up a large Slav state under Serbian leadership – a sort of Greater Serbia. Doing that would mean taking over its neighbour, Bosnia-Herzegovina, which had the largest Serb population in Europe outside Serbia itself. But in 1908 Austria-Hungary took over Bosnia-Herzegovina. The Austro-Hungarian government thought there was nothing the Serbs could do about the annexation. Boy, were they wrong.

Bleeding Serbia

Until 1903 the King of Serbia was Alexander I. Alexander wanted good relations with Austria-Hungary, but that didn't suit the Serb nationalists and it didn't suit the Russians either, who had their own quarrels with the Austro-Hungarians (check out the earlier sections 'Love me, love my ally' and 'Crisis in Bosnia-Herzegovina'). So in May 1903 a group of Serb nationalist army officers, led by one Colonel Dimitrijevic (codename: 'Apis') and with secret Russian backing, staged a violent coup d'état in the Serb capital, Belgrade. They seized the King and Queen, shot them and hacked their bodies to pieces. Then they put in place a new, aggressively nationalist and anti-Austro-Hungarian regime under King Peter I. But make no mistake (the Austro-Hungarians certainly didn't): the real power in this new Serbia was Colonel Apis and his pals.

Killing Franz Ferdinand – the shot heard around the world

Colonel Apis's aim was simple: take Bosnia-Herzegovina from Austria-Hungary. His problem was that the Bosnians, even the Bosnian Serbs, might not want to go. The Austro-Hungarians weren't oppressing the Bosnians; they were giving them control over their own affairs and generally making them feel welcome. (The Austro-Hungarians weren't just being nice. They wanted a strong ally who'd support them against the Hungarians, and they thought the Bosnians fitted the bill.) Leading this school of 'be nice to Bosnians' thinking was none other than the heir to the Habsburg throne, his Imperial and Royal Highness the Archduke Franz Ferdinand (see Figure 3-2). Which, from the point of view of Colonel Apis in Serbia, made Franz Ferdinand a serious nuisance. And Apis knew how to deal with serious nuisances: he killed them.

Figure 3-2: Archduke Franz Ferdinand, his wife Sophie and their three children.

© Imperial War Museums (Q 81810)

Colonel Apis was head of Serbian Military Intelligence, but he also ran an assassination and terrorist group called the Black Hand. In 1914 he recruited a group of assassins and supplied them with weapons from Serbian government stores. On 28 June Franz Ferdinand would be inspecting troops in the Bosnian capital, Sarajevo, with his wife, Sophie. That day was also the anniversary of the 1389 Battle of Kosovo – the Serbs' national day. Apis's men would mark the day by blowing the Archduke to smithereens.

The plan nearly failed. The bomb bounced off the car and exploded behind, wounding some of the escort. The bomber leapt into the river, found it came only up to his knees and was dragged out by the police. Fiasco! The Archduke was furious and insisted on visiting the wounded men in hospital. Unfortunately, no one remembered to tell the driver of the change of plan, so he turned a corner according to the original route. When he stopped to reverse, the car stalled outside a cafe where one of the plotters, Gavrilo Princip, was sitting wondering what to do next. With the Archduke and his wife sitting in a stationary open-top car just in front of him, Princip walked up to the car and fired at point-blank range. He claimed later he was trying to kill the Archduke and the governor of Bosnia, who was also in the car. If so, he was a poor shot: he killed the Archduke and his wife. Princip was immediately arrested. And no, war didn't immediately break out.

The July crisis

Q: Did the assassination have to provoke a war? A: Probably, yes.

Q: Did the assassination have to provoke a world war? A: Probably not.

History has known plenty of assassinations of famous people, but they don't usually spark off major wars. The Sarajevo assassination in 1914, however, was the spark that finally set off the First World War. Part of the reason was that the Archduke Franz Ferdinand was far from the first prominent figure to be assassinated. Recent victims included three American Presidents, a Tsar of Russia, a President of France, a Viceroy of India, the King of Portugal (and the Prince), a Japanese Prime Minister, a Russian Prime Minister, and from Greece, the Minister of the Interior, and the King as well as the Empress Elizabeth, wife of Emperor Franz Josef. Not surprisingly, any country that took a tough line with assassins, as Austria-Hungary did in 1914, was likely to gain a lot of international support. And yet, the Austrians quickly lost that support and ended up with a war that no one expected.

Viennese in a whirl

The Austro-Hungarian government was outraged by the assassination of the Archduke Franz Ferdinand, especially because it reckoned it had been the work of the Serbian government. (The Serbian government did know what Apis was up to and even sent a guarded warning note to Vienna, but they didn't try to stop the assassination.) General Conrad, in charge of the Austro-Hungarian army, wanted an immediate military strike against Serbia: he reckoned – and he may have been right – that no one, not even the Russians, would've stopped them. But the Austrians couldn't act that quickly even if they wanted to; they had to persuade the Emperor and the Hungarians to agree. Franz Josef was weary of war, and the Hungarian Prime Minister, Count Tisza, thought this quarrel with Serbia was a cunning Austrian plan to bring more Serbs into the empire and weaken Hungary's position. And, as he pointed out, they still had to face the nagging question: what would the Russians do?

Germany promises to pay the bearer . . . anything he wants

The Austro-Hungarian Foreign Minister, Count Berchtold, sent an envoy to Berlin to get a guarantee that the Germans would support it in a war with Serbia. The envoy saw the Kaiser personally – the Foreign Minister was on honeymoon and others were mostly off on holiday – and the Kaiser gave his personal guarantee that Germany would support Austria-Hungary in whatever the Austro-Hungarian government decided to do. This went far beyond the terms of the Triple Alliance; in fact, historians have called it the *blank cheque*. The Kaiser hoped this would warn off the Russians and leave Vienna free to deal with Serbia as it liked. In effect, the Kaiser was handing control of events over to the Austro-Hungarians.

The Germans were growing increasingly scared of Russia. Russia was modernising its railways and communications and getting its armed forces into shape; soon Germany would be caught between a strong Russia in the east and a vengeful France in the west. The Germans believed the Russians would be ready by about 1917 or so. If they *had* to fight the Russians, they reckoned that it would be better to do it now, in 1914, before the Russians had finished getting their military act together, rather than waiting until it was too late.

Keep calm and carry on talking

What's striking about the outbreak of the war is how long the countries spent trying to avoid war. A month elapsed between the assassination and the outbreak of war.

Three weeks after the assassination the Austro-Hungarian government sent a harsh ultimatum to the Serbs demanding the right to send Austro-Hungarian police into Serbia to hunt down the assassins and giving the Serbs only 48 hours to reply. The British Foreign Secretary, Sir Edward Grey, proposed an international conference to stop the problem getting out of hand, but the Germans rejected the proposal. The Serbs accepted nearly all the Austro-Hungarian ultimatum and suggested the rest could be discussed at Sir Edward's conference. Even at this point, at the end of July, a war could've been avoided. But the Austro-Hungarians said the Serbs hadn't met their demands, and on 28 July, exactly a month after the assassination, Austria-Hungary declared war on Serbia.

And even then it didn't have to be a European war.

As far as historians can tell, the Austro-Hungarian government genuinely believed it could have its war just against Serbia (which it reckoned – probably rightly – was about as big a war as it could take on with any reasonable hope of winning). The Russians would no doubt protest loudly, but they'd be too scared of the Germans to do anything. And by the time someone proposed the inevitable international conference to settle the dispute, the Austro-Hungarian army would be in the Serb capital, Belgrade, and the war would be over. That, at any rate, was the theory.

Mobilising men

To understand how a full-scale European war arose out of this crisis (especially when no one wanted one) you need to get to grips with mobilisation. *Mobilisation* means calling up your army and navy, getting men back from leave, sobering them up, equipping them with uniforms, food and everything else they'll need, and getting them into position for war – not just in barracks or port, but in position to attack a specific enemy. In other words, you mobilise *against someone.* Some countries, such as Austria-Hungary, could order a *partial mobilisation,* which meant mobilising against one country (in this case Serbia) but not against another (Russia). But most countries could only order a *general mobilisation,* which meant mobilising against all the countries they were expecting to fight.

On 29 July the nagging question over what Russia would do was answered when it mobilised its army in solidarity with the Serbs. It only needed to mobilise against Austria-Hungary, and the Tsar did try to change the mobilisation plan accordingly, but it couldn't be done: the mobilisation plan was aimed at Austria-Hungary and Germany, so Russian troops started to mass along the German border too. On 31 July the Germans sent an ultimatum to the Russians: stand your troops down or we fight you. Without really waiting for an answer, on 1 August the Germans mobilised their own forces and declared war on Russia (which might suggest that the Germans were just waiting for a chance to fight Russia and that the Russians' mobilisation was just an excuse).

Now it was the Germans' turn to find they couldn't change their mobilisation plans even if they wanted to (and, briefly, the Kaiser did). Implementing the Schlieffen Plan (see Chapter 4) meant amassing troops along the border with Belgium and France too, even though neither country had mobilised yet, and demanding the Belgians allow their friendly German neighbours to send a huge army through their country to attack Paris. The Belgians refused. On 2 August the Germans invaded Luxemburg and France, and the following day they got round to declaring war on France. Two days later, following Count von Schlieffen's famous plan, German troops swept into Belgium. All eyes were now on London: what would Britain do?

Britain decides

The British had made clear that they had no alliance in Europe and weren't committed to going to war, but they had signed a treaty guaranteeing the independence of Belgium (and so had the Germans). The Germans couldn't quite believe the British threat was serious: they called the treaty a mere 'scrap of paper' and the Kaiser convinced himself that he had the word of his cousin, King George V, that Britain would stay neutral (he hadn't: George had said Britain would try to stay out of it, which is a very different thing). But on 3 August Sir Edward Grey spoke in the House of Commons and made an important commitment: Britain would protect the French coast from attack, according to the spirit of the Entente Cordiale. This meant that the entente was now an alliance.

The next day, the Germans moved into Belgium. The British sent an ultimatum to the Germans telling them to get out, and when they didn't, Britain declared war. A week later, Britain and France declared war on Austria-Hungary (with whom they had absolutely no quarrel) almost as a way of tidying things up. And, because Britain, France and Germany all had overseas colonies in Africa and Asia, as soon as their 'mother' countries had declared war in Europe, these overseas colonies were at war too.

Within three weeks most of the world had gone to war, without anyone having ever intended it.

Countdown to war

Here's the outline of the main events of what's often called the 'July crisis':

28 June	Archduke Franz Ferdinand is assassinated.	1 August	Germany mobilises and declares war on Russia. France mobilises.
5 July	Kaiser Wilhelm issues the 'blank cheque' to Austria-Hungary.	2 August	Germany invades Luxembourg and France. Britain guarantees to protect the French coast.
23 July	Austria-Hungary sends an ultimatum to Serbia.		
24 July	Sir Edward Grey proposes an international conference.	3 August	Britain guarantees to support Belgium. Britain mobilises.
28 July	Austria-Hungary declares war on Serbia.	4 August	Germans invade Belgium. Britain declares war on Germany.
29 July	Russia mobilises against Austria-Hungary, but against Germany too.	6 August	Austria-Hungary declares war on Russia. Serbia declares war on Germany.
3 July	Germany sends an ultimatum to Russia.	12 August	Britain and France declare war on Austria-Hungary.

So What Did Cause the War?

You can blame many factors for causing the war. The intense national rivalries all played their part. The suspicion between Serbia and Austria-Hungary was crucial in producing war between those two countries, but it doesn't explain how it then spread to the rest of Europe. The alliances help to explain it – they certainly helped to create the two 'armed camps' in Europe – and the idea that the Europeans were so closely tied that as soon as one country went to war the others all got dragged in is tempting to believe, but it doesn't fit the facts of what happened, and it doesn't quite explain why countries mobilised their troops so readily. The rigid mobilisation plans, with their strict timings, explain why it was difficult to stop the process of mobilising after it had begun, but they don't explain why countries gave the order to mobilise in the first place.

Some historians have blamed individuals. Was it the Kaiser's fault? Or Sir Edward Grey's for not being tough enough with the Germans? Or Tsar Nicholas's for allowing the Russians to mobilise? Was it Colonel Apis's or Gavrilo Princip's? (Princip said that if he hadn't shot the Archduke, the Germans would've found some other excuse for the war. Historians have tended to agree with him.) You can say that the assassination of Franz Ferdinand caused a crisis; it didn't *on its own* cause the war.

One German historian, Fritz Fischer, said that Germany had indeed been planning for a war so it could dominate Europe. German historians found that idea pretty hard to swallow, but most historians now accept that Fischer was broadly right. Certainly, that blank cheque suggests that the Germans weren't too worried if things did come to a war – though that doesn't mean they were planning to have the war they actually got.

We'll probably never know exactly who wanted what in 1914, or what they all thought they were doing – they probably didn't fully know themselves. But whether the Great Powers wanted a general European war in August 1914 or whether they just welcomed it when it arrived, that was what they had got. Now they'd have to win it.

Part II
Europe at War, 1914–1916

© Imperial War Museums (Q 70032)

For a great bonus article that assesses the competency of the First World War generals, head online and take a look at www.dummies.com/extras/firstworldwar.

In this part...

- ✔ Unravel the story of how a war that began almost in a party atmosphere, with cheering crowds and brightly coloured uniforms, went sour very quickly as soldiers discovered the reality of modern warfare.

- ✔ See why Christmas 1914 passed without the quick victory that everyone was expecting, and how the war dragged on and quickly reached stalemate in 1915. Understand how the growing frustrations of that year in turn led to bigger and bigger offensives – and ever bigger disappointments – throughout 1916.

- ✔ Appreciate how these first years of the war were dominated by the war in Europe – the Western Front that ran through Belgium and France, the even longer Eastern Front that extended all the way from the Baltic Sea to the Black Sea, and the smaller fronts that opened up in Turkey and Italy – and how non-Europeans from India, Canada, Australia, New Zealand, China, Indo-China and the Caribbean were soon brought into the Europeans' war.

Chapter 4

1914: The First World War Starts Here

In This Chapter

▶ Watching the excitement – and the reticence – over going to war

▶ Getting up close and personal with the armies of 1914

▶ Reaching stalemate in the west

▶ Meeting triumph and tragedy in the east

*T*he First World War started the way wars usually do – with young men forming up in smart new uniforms and marching off through cheering crowds.

By the end of 1914 the war had become something that no one had anticipated. It had cost every combatant country thousands more casualties than they'd ever expected – the French had lost over half a million men; the British nearly 90,000 (in fact, the British Expeditionary Force had virtually ceased to exist) – and on both fronts the war was deadlocked. In the west both sides were stuck in an immense line of trenches that ran without a break from the Belgian coast to the borders of Switzerland, and they had no clear idea of how to get out. Absolutely key was heavy artillery, for blasting a way through the enemy lines, but by the end of the year the armies on both sides were beginning to run out of shells.

The war was definitely not going according to plan and would certainly not be over by Christmas, as many people had expected. This chapter looks at how the first months of the war unfolded, and how this situation came to be.

The War You've All Been Waiting for – Must End by Christmas!

Before 1914 Europeans talked about a war breaking out – and the international tensions of those years (Chapter 3 outlines them) made some people think that a war would be like a welcome storm breaking up a spell of particularly heavy weather – but they hadn't necessarily given much thought to what sort of war it would be. Most people expected a sort of massive international boxing final, where the two sides would spar for a while before one side knocked the other one out; it was just a question of which side it would be. The whole thing, most people thought, might last three months and be over by Christmas.

Hurrah, lads, we're off to war!

In 1914 every European Great Power except Great Britain operated a system of military *conscription* (where ordinary people are compulsorily enlisted in military service): all young men had to serve for two or three years in the army, followed by a longer period in the reserve. Military training was about getting physically fit and learning to march, to scale a wall, to fire a rifle and to use the bayonet, and to these young men across Europe the chance to go off and do it all for real felt like an exciting adventure.

The situation was slightly different in Britain, which only had a small regular army plus the *Territorial Army* – part-time soldiers who combined some weekend military training with their day jobs. But Britons were as keen as anyone else to put on a soldier's uniform and prove their manliness on the

We'll just overlook that you're underage, shall we?

Such was the enthusiasm for volunteering to join the British army that many men attempted to join underage. The lower age limit for joining was 18, but recruiting sergeants didn't always enforce it. Many soldiers later told how they'd tried to join when they were 16 or 17, or younger. When a recruiting sergeant realised that a volunteer was underage he might send him home, but the youth could always try another recruiting office. Years later, one soldier remembered how he'd told the recruiting sergeant that he was 16. The sergeant told him to go outside, come back in again and say that he was 19. The boy did so, and was immediately enlisted!

battlefield. That's why the photos from Britain show huge crowds outside recruiting offices (see Figure 1 in the insert section): in Britain, if you wanted to be part of the war, you needed to join the army first, and fast – or you'd miss your chance. Or so everyone thought.

But was everyone really so happy?

One of the most puzzling things to modern minds about the outbreak of the First World War is that so many people seemed so *happy* about it (see Figure 4-1). Usually, nowadays people regard the outbreak of war as a tragedy, but if you look at photos taken in 1914 in the major European capitals, you see huge, excited crowds and soldiers marching off to war with a smile and a wave. But not everyone was as happy about going to war as the photos suggest.

The people who gathered in town squares (see Figure 2 in the insert section) to cheer at the news were the ones who were excited about it, but elsewhere, especially in the countryside, reactions were mixed. In the French country-side, for example, older people gloomily recalled the last time the French had fought the Germans, back in 1870, and that it hadn't gone well at all. Those photos of cheering crowds aren't wrong: they just don't tell the whole story.

Join up! Bring your friends! The Pals' Battalions

Soldiers often forge strong bonds of friendship. The volunteers of 1914 went one better: they joined up in ready-made friendship groups. These groups started in Liverpool, where the authorities wanted to make a special contribution to the war effort by presenting the army with units of local men. The idea quickly spread. Volunteer groups became known as *Pals' Battalions*. Some units, such as the Accrington Pals, the Barnsley Pals or the Grimsby Chums, came from close-knit communities in industrial towns; others had been to school together, like the Public Schools battalion, or else they were all in the same profession, such as the Glasgow Tramways, the Hull Commercials or the Artists' Rifles. Groups of friends would join up from the factory where they all worked, the football club they all belonged to or the town – even the street – where they all lived.

The thinking behind the Pals' Battalions seemed very sensible: joining up with your friends was a good way to calm men's nerves and give them a strong sense of comradeship that would get them through the ordeals they'd face at the front. Pals' Battalions had one major problem, though, that no one apparently thought of at the outset: just imagine the effect that very heavy casualties within a Pals' Battalion could have on the men's communities. That was the fate that awaited many of them when they went into action in the Battle of the Somme (see Chapter 6).

Figure 4-1: German crowds cheering the Kaiser as Germany mobilises against Russia.

Haven't We Met Before? The European Armies of 1914

The European states called themselves Great Powers because of their military strength, which, for most of them, meant their armies. Here, I look at just how strong those armies were. (Chapter 5 looks at how the navies and nascent air forces steamed in on the action.)

Austria-Hungary: Divided state, divided army

The army of the Dual Monarchy was the most ethnically mixed of all the combatants. This made for problems.

- ✔ **In charge:** General Conrad von Hötzendorf – the man who had been so keen to crush Serbia when the Archduke Franz Ferdinand was assassinated back in June. A competent general, but no military genius.

- ✔ **Major strengths:** The Austro-Hungarian army was perfectly competent but it was short of men and hampered by some serious weaknesses.

- ✔ **Major weaknesses:** The Austro-Hungarians couldn't be sure how many fronts they'd need to fight on aside from Serbia in the south and Russia in the east; they worried that they might have to fight the Italians and the Romanians too. The second problem was that their army included

Germans, Hungarians, Czechs, Poles, Italians, Slovenes, Bosniaks, Croats and so on, some of whom hated each other and couldn't be trusted to co-operate. Some national groups, such as the Poles and Italians, would be fighting against their fellow countrymen in the enemy armies. So Austro-Hungarian commanders had to work out which troops they could safely place next to which, and opposite which enemies.

France: The state wary of its own army

The French army's problem was politics: socialists saw it as a dangerously right-wing, anti-socialist and anti-semitic organisation whose generals would seize power unless they were very carefully watched. So the French would only come together for a defensive war or a war to liberate French territory, such as Alsace-Lorraine.

KEY PEOPLE

✔ **In charge:** General Joseph Joffre – a capable leader, shrewd and calm; a man who didn't like to miss lunch and enjoyed long snoozes (see Figure 4-2). He wouldn't panic, but he didn't have the killer instinct either.

Figure 4-2:
French Commander-in-Chief General Joffre decorating a soldier.

© Imperial War Museums (Q 70069)

✔ **Major strengths:** The French had a very good 75 millimetre field gun that could do a lot of damage when they deployed it properly. They also had some strong forts along the frontier with Germany.

✔ **Major weaknesses:** They didn't have enough heavy artillery to back up their field gun. They also depended too heavily on those fortresses, which were going to prove deathtraps – for the men inside them.

Germany: The military state

Nowhere else in Europe did the military have the sort of decisive political influence they enjoyed in Germany.

- ✔ **In charge:** Chief of the General Staff Helmuth von Moltke. Although he was an intelligent man and had a good grasp of modern warfare, von Moltke was a worrier and inclined to panic in a crisis. Soon replaced by the more decisive Erich von Falkenhayn.

- ✔ **Major strengths:** The German army was well equipped with machine guns, *howitzers* (short-nozzled artillery guns that could lob shells high in the air – very good for dealing with fortifications) and spades for digging in. The German railway system had lines leading from east to west so the Germans could easily transfer troops from one front to the other.

- ✔ **Major weaknesses:** The Germans had long thought that a war on two fronts would be a disaster for Germany; they were right.

Great Britain: Professional, but small

Britain was the only European Great Power not to have conscription (Chapter 12 explains why), which made its situation rather different. The army on the Western Front, known simply as the British Expeditionary Force (BEF), was highly professional but much smaller than the armies of the other Great Powers. The BEF in 1914 (see the sidebar, 'Who are you calling contemptible?') had two main sorts of soldiers:

- ✔ **Regulars** were the men of Britain's famous and ancient regiments, such as the Grenadier Guards or the Royal Fusiliers, and of the regiments recruited from, and named after, the different counties of Britain.

- ✔ **Territorials** were volunteer, part-time soldiers. The Regulars were rather scornful of them, but Territorials proved very tough fighters in battle.

These soldiers were soon joined by the *citizen soldiers* of Kitchener's New Army (see the sidebar, 'A little moral blackmail goes a very long way') – men who were only intending to serve in the army until the war was over, when they could go back to civilian life, and a very different type of soldier from the experienced Tommies of the professional British army. The citizen soldiers would greatly swell the army's size. Britain could also call on the considerable military forces of its colonies and dominions – and it did.

- ✔ **In charge:** The commander of the BEF was Sir John French (see Figure 4-3), who had made a name for himself as an aggressive cavalry commander in the Anglo–Boer War. He hadn't commanded a whole army before, though, and despite his name he didn't speak French and didn't like the French much either. Which was a bit of a shame because the French were his allies.

Figure 4-3:
Sir John
French
reviewing
army
volunteers
in Hyde
Park,
London,
in 1914.

© Imperial War Museums (Q 70032)

- ✔ **Major strengths:** The BEF was highly professional. It was expert at using the terrain, and with a firing rate of 15 rounds a minute, the British were the best marksmen of all the armies of 1914. They also deployed their highly experienced Indian troops in France and other troops from the British Empire. Troops from Britain's overseas dominions, Canada, South Africa, Australia and New Zealand, proved some of the toughest troops the Germans encountered.

- ✔ **Major weaknesses:** The BEF was small. Bismarck joked that if the British army ever landed in Germany, he would send the local police force to arrest it. The British were recruiting fast (see the sidebar, 'A little moral blackmail goes a very long way'), but they'd need at least a year to get the new recruits trained and ready for combat.

Who are you calling contemptible?

When Britain declared war on Germany, the Kaiser, who should have known better, dismissed the small BEF as 'a contemptible little army'. He meant it was contemptibly small, but the British took it to mean that he was calling the soldiers contemptible. To tell the Kaiser where he could stick his words, the BEF soldiers used the tag as their nickname for themselves, and after the war the survivors of the original BEF of 1914 were very proud to be known as the Old Contemptibles.

A little moral blackmail goes a very long way

When everyone else was talking of a short, sharp spat that would be over by Christmas, one influential voice in Britain disagreed. Lord Kitchener, the Secretary of State for war, told the British Cabinet members (much to their surprise and dismay) that this was going to be a long war of two or three years, and that Britain would need a huge army in order to fight it. He talked of recruiting a million men for starters. His proposed solution was a huge recruiting drive, and within a couple of weeks of the outbreak of the war posters went up all over Britain calling for volunteers.

Someone once said that Kitchener might or might not have been a great general (opinions differ) but he made a great poster. Although it came out in different versions, the famous Kitchener recruitment poster showed just his face, without anything else to say who he was (everyone knew who Kitchener was), his finger pointing directly at you, wherever you were standing and, of course, the slogan 'Your Country needs YOU!'. It was cleverly designed to make people feel guilty if they didn't answer his call to join up and fight for king and country. The design has been copied many times all over the world: it's a reminder that this war was going to use the latest knowledge and expertise – even psychological warfare.

Kitchener's recruiting drive didn't entirely rely on people's patriotism: it also indulged in a bit of moral blackmail. One famous poster showed a young father, who had obviously remained a civilian, looking guilty and ashamed as his children ask, 'What did YOU do in the Great War, Daddy?' Some people took an even more direct approach. Young women would go up to any young man wearing civilian clothes and give him a white feather – the sign of a coward. Not everyone agreed with this practice: sometimes the young man would be engaged in vital civilian war work, and often white feathers were mistakenly given to soldiers home on leave.

Russia: Huge army, huge problems

The Russian army had broken Napoleon a hundred years earlier, but it had been disastrously led and heavily defeated in the war with Japan in 1904–5.

- ✔ **In charge:** The Grand Duke Nicholas, the Tsar's uncle. In reality, the military headquarters (the *Stavka*) were too far away to control events and key Russian commanders were the generals in charge on each front.

- ✔ **Major strengths:** The Russians' biggest advantage was the sheer number of men they had: more than the German and Austro-Hungarian armies combined. After their defeat against the Japanese, the Russians had started reorganising their army, and although the programme was far from finished in 1914, the Russian army was already much better organised and equipped than it had been ten years earlier.

- ✔ **Major weaknesses:** The Russian railway and communications system was chaotic, and that would affect the troops' supplies of essentials such as food, warm clothing and ammunition – not to mention moving troops around and bringing in reinforcements. They also lacked a decent system for sending messages in code.

Wrestling for the West

The war began with movements on both the Western and Eastern Fronts. However, all hopes for a quick victory were centred on the Western Front.

Germany's dilemma, and the not-so-clever Schlieffen Plan

The Germans were pretty sure that they couldn't win a war on two fronts, against France in the west and Russia in the east. Bismarck had devoted all his diplomatic skill to avoiding that situation, and now his successors had blundered into exactly what he'd tried to avoid. They needed to keep one front on hold while they concentrated on the other one. But which?

'Westerners' within the German high command argued that France and especially Britain were Germany's most dangerous enemies and that Germany should concentrate on crushing them. They argued that war with Russia wasn't strictly necessary. 'Easterners', on the other hand, thought that Russia was a dangerous enemy that would crush Germany if it could, so Germany should concentrate its forces in the east.

The solution to the Germans' dilemma seemed to lie in the *Schlieffen Plan* – the plan devised by Count von Schlieffen, the former head of the German General Staff, to knock France out of the war hard and fast by going around French border defences and sweeping down through Belgium and around the west of Paris, so the Germans could then concentrate their efforts on fighting the Russians before the Russians had time to get themselves ready.

For some reason, you can still meet people who speak in awe of the Schlieffen Plan, as if it was one of the best military plans in history. It wasn't. It was riddled with flaws, so much so that the Germans themselves had been tinkering with it ever since it was drawn up. The big problems with Count Schlieffen's famous plan were as follows:

> ✔ **Keeping troops in line as they wheeled in huge numbers through Belgium and around the west of Paris was almost impossible.** You try it with a line of people – and that's without a hostile army trying to stop you. Schlieffen was always going on about how important it was to keep the right wing of the attack strong, but this was easier said than done: the troops on the extreme right had so far to go that it would be difficult to keep in touch with them and keep them supplied. Moreover, von Moltke was worried about leaving the left wing too weak, so he altered the plan to take troops from the right wing and position them on the left. But without enough troops on the right, would the Germans be able to get around the west of Paris at all?

✔ **Forgetting about Paris was an error.** Paris was a major military centre, yet Schlieffen seems to have thought that the French troops stationed there would simply sit still and let the Germans move around them. Not very likely!

The most vulnerable parts of an army are the two ends of the line – the *flanks*. If you think of an army marching past you, you see that the troops nearest you are facing the wrong way to be able to fire back if you attack them, and when they do turn to face you, they can't deploy anything like as many men as they could if you were attacking from the front. For that reason, officers all around the world were taught *never* to present their flank to the enemy. Yet that is exactly what the Schlieffen Plan did: as the Germans swept past Paris, they'd be presenting their flank to the troops stationed in Paris. Maybe the Germans thought the French wouldn't notice. If so, they were wrong.

✔ **Overlooking Britain was a mistake.** Schlieffen had talked airily of invading Belgium even though it was common knowledge that Britain would never allow a major power to occupy Belgium. Even if France was beaten, Britain's navy could blockade the German coast, cut off supplies and sink German shipping, and Britain could gather its own army and its formidable colonial troops to launch an attack on Germans in Belgium or France whenever it chose. The Schlieffen Plan was meant to resolve the problem of a war on two fronts, but by bringing Britain into the war, it actually made a war on two fronts virtually certain.

✔ **Underestimating Russia was fatal.** Schlieffen considered Russia to be so disorganised that it would take weeks or months to get its army into position. That meant the Germans could deal quickly with the French in the west and then turn east, to the Russians. (The Germans were vague on how they would beat the Russians, but figured no doubt they'd think of something.) This was a crazy scheme even when Schlieffen came up with it. After all, if your enemy is disorganised, that's the time to attack him. You don't wait around until he's ready for you! But in any case, in the time since Schlieffen had drawn up his plans the Russians had made major improvements in their military organisation and would be ready more quickly than Schlieffen had thought possible.

Ultimately, the Russians invaded German territory first, not vice versa, which from the word go deprived the Germans of their hopes of beating France before heading east and made them revise their plans – again.

Apart from all that, the Schlieffen Plan was a really good idea.

Any idea how to win this war by Christmas?

The biggest problem with Germany's Schlieffen Plan was that it wasn't a plan to win the war; it was a plan to win part of the war. Much the same was true of the plans of the other combatants:

- **Belgium:** The Belgians didn't really have a plan except to stop the Germans taking over their country, or at least slow them down. Somehow.

- **Britain:** The British war plan was to send the BEF to France to fit in with the French plans, whatever they might be. Because the French hadn't included the BEF in their plans and were planning to invade Germany, not Belgium, fitting in with the French plans while pushing the Germans out of Belgium wasn't going to be easy.

- **France:** Plan XVII. The French were the only ones on the Allied side who had a war plan as such and theirs was quite simple: gather along the border with Germany, move into Alsace and Lorraine (the two former French regions the Germans had annexed in 1871) and liberate them. The French hoped the Germans would then give up and go home. No, it wasn't a realistic hope.

Soldiers of France, charge!

When the war began, the French launched Plan XVII. They wanted revenge for what the Germans had done to them back in 1871, and they'd do it wearing similar uniforms and using similar tactics as in 1871 too. Unfortunately for them, the Germans were living in 1914, not 1871. The French in their colourful uniforms made easy targets for German rifles and machine guns. The French charged at the German lines – and were slaughtered. By the end of August, the French had lost 260,000 casualties in the Battle of the Frontiers. Just a few weeks earlier these same men had been marching off to war through cheering crowds. What a difference a month makes in wartime.

The Battle of the Frontiers was a disaster for the French. Just to make it even worse, while they were charging to their deaths in front of German machine guns in Alsace-Lorraine, the German invasion of Belgium was going ominously well.

What *are* casualties?

From a commander's point of view, the *casualty figure* means the number of men he had at the start of the battle but no longer has, because they're either dead or wounded. As a very rough rule, you can divide any casualty figure into three: roughly a third will have been killed, another third so badly wounded that they won't fight again (that is, men who've lost a limb or an eye or whatever) and the final third injured badly enough to have to go home for treatment, but who'll probably be able to return to the front when their wounds have healed. Even by that measure, with 260,000 casualties, nearly 90,000 French men had been killed in the very first month of the war. How long could any country keep going with that rate of loss?

Ruthless justice

Soldiers in all armies at the start of the war imagined themselves charging gloriously against the enemy, who'd then obligingly turn tail and run away. They weren't prepared for what they encountered – rifle and machine gun fire so thick that no one could even stand up in it, never mind advance. It's no surprise to learn that many soldiers simply turned and fled in terror, but doing that was almost as dangerous as staying under enemy fire because armies dealt ruthlessly with deserters. The French government, for example, gave orders that anyone caught running away from the enemy was to be shot within 24 hours. Something like 400 French soldiers were executed in this way in 1914 alone. This was to be a war with no mercy for your own side, never mind the enemy.

The Battle for Belgium

The Belgians were deeply shocked by the German invasion of their country. They knew that if war ever came, the Germans might come through Belgium, but they didn't expect it to happen. On 2 August, though, the Germans invaded Luxembourg and sent the Belgians an ultimatum demanding free passage for their army or they'd occupy the whole country. King Albert rejected their demand and declared that Belgium would resist. The Belgian plan was quite simple:

1. **Hold the German advance up as long as possible.**

   This meant holding out in the strong border fortresses in Liège and Namur. It also meant ordinary Belgians should feel free to sabotage as they liked: destroying bridges and railway lines, or just letting the tyres down on German lorries.

2. **The Belgian army would then fall back on the port of Antwerp, up near the Dutch border.**

   Antwerp was strongly defended, and from there the Belgians could move out to wherever the army was needed.

Bravo, Belgium!

The sight of little Belgium standing up to the Germans struck a chord with many people in Britain. A famous cartoon showed Belgium as a young country lad, armed only with a thin stick, standing his ground against a large German, his pockets full of sausages and a German meerschaum pipe in his mouth, advancing on him and brandishing a great big club. Many British people didn't understand the ins and outs of European diplomacy, but they did understand the idea of small country standing up to a big bully. The German invasion of Belgium undoubtedly helped encourage recruitment in Britain (see Figure 3 in the insert section).

The killing grounds of Belgium

The Germans were surprisingly nervous about the Belgians. They had very uncomfortable memories of when they'd invaded France back in 1870 and encountered what the French called *franc-tireurs,* which means 'free firers' – ordinary people, not in uniform, who would suddenly produce rifles and open fire on German patrols. The Germans thought this sort of fighting broke all the laws of war and that they were entitled to take savage reprisals.

In 1914 their worry was that the Belgians would operate as *franc-tireurs.* The Germans didn't bother checking: if they got reports that their patrols had been shot at, they went to the nearest town or village, rounded up the local civilians and shot them – men, women and children. Anyone not killed outright was bayoneted: 200 killed here, 600 somewhere else and so on. In the worst cases, the Germans rounded up civilians and shot them even though there hadn't been any *franc-tireur* activity, just as a warning. It doesn't seem to have occurred to them that this sort of atrocity would encourage people to fight back.

German atrocities in Belgium made very good news stories. When the Germans burned down the library of the ancient University of Leuven (to get an idea of what this meant, imagine an invading army burning down the Bodleian Library in Oxford), it seemed as if the Germans were setting out to destroy civilisation itself. Belgian refugees (see the photograph below) told pitiful tales of wholesale murder in their towns and villages by the invading Germans. The British began to refer to the Germans as Huns, after the savage tribesmen of Attila who'd swept into Europe in ancient times, killing and destroying everything in their path.

Atrocity stories helped to strengthen support for the war among the British and French people, and to win over neutral countries that might yet join in the war on the Allied side, such as Italy, Romania and the United States. Unfortunately, some atrocity stories were so heavily exaggerated that in time people didn't know what to believe. Only in more recent years have historians looked again at the very real savagery of the German occupation of Belgium in 1914.

© *Imperial War Museums (Q 53383)*

Bring up Big Bertha!

The Germans' first obstacle in Belgium was the city of Liège, which was surrounded by a ring of thick concrete forts. The Germans needed to take Liège quickly if they were to keep to the timetable of the Schlieffen Plan, but the forts were too strong. So the Germans brought up their big guns, huge howitzers known as *Big Berthas,* which were mounted on railway tracks. Big Berthas smashed through the concrete forts and blew them to bits. The Germans carried on into Belgium, taking Brussels, sending a force up towards Antwerp and then heading south towards the French frontier. Everything seemed to be going to plan.

General von Kluck has problems . . .

General von Kluck was the man in command of the German first army. His job was to sweep through Belgium and northern France and go round the far side of Paris. But he wasn't happy because he didn't have enough men for it: he had to set up garrisons in Belgium, and then he had to detach a large number of men to go up and threaten Antwerp, not to mention the men he was losing in battle. To make things worse, von Moltke had transferred two whole corps (that's like two whole armies) from the Western Front over to the east because he was worried the Russians were going to break through. All these problems would only get worse the farther von Kluck went.

And then, on Sunday 23 August, near the Belgian town of Mons, von Kluck's men ran into deadly accurate rifle fire from an enemy they just couldn't see. The Germans lost 5,000 men that day, three times as many casualties as they were able to inflict on the unseen enemy. The unseen enemy was the BEF (see Figure 4-4).

Figure 4-4: Well-concealed British troops firing at advancing Germans. The BEF was small but highly professional.

© Imperial War Museums (Q 53320)

. . . and so has Sir John French

Sir John French, the leader of the BEF, also had problems. His instructions were to co-operate with the French but not to take orders from them: the BEF was an independent command and his orders would come from London. Moreover, because the BEF was so small, Sir John was under strict instructions to avoid heavy casualties. This was easier said than done.

The French commander in northern France and Belgium was General Charles Lanrezac. Lanrezac didn't have enough troops in his sector because Joffre didn't believe the Germans would attack through Belgium and wouldn't send him any. So when Sir John sent the BEF forward into Belgium, Lanrezac wasn't able to send many French troops with them. When the Germans started pouring through Belgium, Lanrezac was worried his men would be cut off and he gave the order to withdraw, which meant that the BEF would have to pull out too. That was when the problems began.

The man leading the BEF troops in Belgium was a fiery veteran of the Zulu and Boer Wars, Sir Horace Smith-Dorrien. He couldn't stand Sir John French (the feeling was mutual) and he didn't think much of being ordered to retreat, especially after his men had done so well at Mons. He fell back to the town of Le Cateau where he turned and fought, in defiance of Sir John's orders. It was probably the right thing to do: it certainly held the Germans up and gave some of the BEF a chance to get away. But it cost the British nearly 8,000 men. And afterwards Smith-Dorrien had to retreat again.

The British had to retreat a long way from Mons, back through northern France and down to the River Marne, east of Paris. One regiment had to cover over 200 miles on foot in just 13 days. To make things worse, the weather was boiling hot. And, of course, the Germans were hard on their heels. By September, as the exhausted BEF drew close to Paris, Sir John French reckoned the time had come to pull them out of the line and give them a rest. Unfortunately for him, General Joffre had other ideas.

Honest, guv, I know a bloke who saw them! The angels of Mons

The Battle of Mons produced one of the oddest myths of the entire war. The story goes that as the British were busy aiming their rapid fire at the advancing Germans, some ghostly figures appeared on the battlefield in front of them dressed in the fighting gear of King Henry V's archers from the Battle of Agincourt and fired ghostly arrows into the German line. The story was widely repeated (for some reason 'archers' became 'angels') and the British took it as a sign that God was on their side. It was either that or a newspaper publicist with an overactive imagination.

The battle for Paris

By September 1914 everyone seemed to be converging on Paris. General Joffre was gathering troops to defend the French capital, while the Germans were moving in from Belgium in the north. Joffre wanted to put the BEF into the defensive line he was preparing along the River Marne, but Sir John French thought they needed rest after the long retreat from Mons (see the preceding section). Joffre appealed to the British government and Lord Kitchener came over to Paris and gave Sir John a dressing down: Sir John would have to do what the French wanted him to do. So the British took their place alongside the French and waited for the Germans to arrive. Meanwhile, the French government packed up and headed for the distant safety of Bordeaux. It seemed nothing could save Paris from disaster. And then something very strange happened: the Germans went the wrong way.

It says 'No Left Turns', General von Kluck!

General von Kluck was supposed to take his men around the back (that is, the west side) of Paris, but the closer he got to the city, the more convinced he was that he just didn't have enough men to do it. So he changed the plan. Instead, he gave the order to turn left and pass to the east – that is, in front of Paris. Which meant he was presenting his flank to the enemy, the one thing generals were supposed never to do (see the earlier section 'Germany's dilemma, and the not-so-clever Schlieffen Plan' to find out why). This was the French army's chance to attack.

The mystery of the Battle of the Marne

Two French generals saw their chance when von Kluck turned left: General Joffre, in charge of the whole French army, and General Galliéni, who was in charge of the garrison in Paris. They had to move quickly: Galliéni even requisitioned a fleet of 500 Parisian taxis to rush some of his troops out to the front along the River Marne. The resulting *Battle of the Marne* was crucial: if the Allies lost, the Germans would take Paris and the war in the west would be over. The French put up a fierce fight, but so did the Germans. And then another strange thing happened: the Germans suddenly gave up and retreated. Why? It was all very mysterious.

What happened was that the German commander, von Moltke, got cold feet. He was already nervous about the war Germany had taken on and appalled at the heavy German losses; he didn't like the sound of the way things were going in France one bit. So he sent a staff officer, Colonel Hentsch, to the Marne to have a look at what was happening and report back. Hentsch reckoned that if the British crossed the Marne, the Germans would be in danger of being cut in two and surrounded, and they'd need to get out quickly. German aerial reconnaissance confirmed that the British had indeed crossed the river (and met no resistance), and so von Moltke gave the order to retreat. The French could breathe again: Paris was saved.

The taxis of the Marne

The taxis that General Galliéni sent out from Paris to the Marne became legendary. French children still learn how Galliéni's taxis were all that stood between France and defeat, rather like the pilots of fighter command in the Battle of Britain. The truth isn't quite so romantic: only some of Galliéni's men travelled by taxi (and the drivers wanted to be paid too), and although they certainly held the Germans up, they didn't exactly defeat them: the battle was actually going the Germans' way when von Moltke gave the order to retreat. But the story certainly made the French people feel much better about the war.

Dig in for victory – the trenches

The Germans didn't retreat in disorder from the Marne; far from it. They headed for carefully prepared positions above the River Aisne, which runs parallel to the Marne a few miles to the north. The Germans had dug some strong trenches in the high, chalky ground from where they could fire at anyone coming at them from the south. The British tried to dislodge them but found it harder than it looked. The key to success in this sort of fighting was heavy artillery and the British didn't have enough of it. Never mind, they thought; they could always work their way around the Germans' flank.

Working your way around the enemy's flank was a bit like attacking your enemy's flank (see 'Germany's dilemma, and the not-so-clever Schlieffen Plan' for more on this manoeuvre): it put your enemy at a serious disadvantage and meant you could attack him from both sides at once. The trick was to get into position to do it, but if you could manage that, the battle – possibly even the war – was as good as yours.

Unfortunately, when the British tried to work their way around the German flank, they found that the Germans were now trying to do the same to them.

Head them off at the pass!

Before long, the British found that they were needed elsewhere – in Belgium – so they slipped away and left the French and German armies to work their way around each others' flanks. But every time one side made a move, the other side blocked it. As each attempt at flanking failed, each side dug themselves into trenches, so as not to lose the ground they did hold. And so, bit by bit, each side was building a line of trenches along the whole length of the Western Front.

No one was expecting to spend the war in these trenches. Trenches were temporary shelters where troops could get a breather in relative safety before emerging in a great wave to overwhelm the enemy. Each side thought they would spend a short time in their trenches and then get moving again. They were quite dumbfounded when they found that doing so wasn't going to be so easy.

Head for the coast!

As the line of trenches grew, the Allies had a new worry: if the Germans reached the coast and took the Channel Ports, such as Calais and Dunkirk, they could make it very difficult for Britain to send supplies and troops back and forth across the Channel. So the two sides embarked on what became known as the *race to the sea,* building trenches as they went. Now, all eyes were on Belgium again:

- ✔ **Antwerp:** The Belgians held out, helped by a British naval brigade, but the Germans destroyed the Belgian forts one by one and the British and Belgians had to evacuate the town. The Belgians headed south; the British were mostly interned in Holland.

- ✔ **Ostend:** The Germans took this important Channel port. But would they be able to take the others – Dunkirk and Calais?

- ✔ **The sluices:** The Belgians stopped the Germans taking the coastal area of Flanders, south of Ostend, by opening the sluice gates and flooding the whole area. The Germans had to dig in farther north.

  Flooding the land in Flanders was a good way to stop the Germans taking it, but it was a reminder of how wet the area is. It only takes a bit of heavy rain to start a flood, and if the ground is churned up by shelling, it can become a quagmire. As both sides would find out.

- ✔ **Ypres:** Everything now depended on this medieval market town in southern Belgium that stood between the Germans and the Channel ports. The British held it. The Germans had to take it.

The bloody First Battle of Ypres

Ypres was very difficult for the British to hold because it was located in a *salient,* which means that the front line bulged out in front of the town: not a comfortable place to be, because the enemy can fire at you from three sides. The 1914 Battle of Ypres (the first of three before the war was over, though they didn't know that then) was very bloody on both sides. The Germans poured troops in, including a regiment of freshly trained college students, 25,000 of whom were slaughtered in front of the village of Langemarck by the deadly rifle fire the British were getting a reputation for. The Germans called this disaster the 'Massacre of the Innocents at Ypres'.

In many ways the British might have been better off letting the Germans take the town and falling back to a strong, entrenched position without having to sit in a dangerous salient. But holding on to Ypres had become a matter of honour for the British: they felt that if they lost Ypres, it meant they'd lost the war. It was also about the only corner of Belgium they still held – and after all, they'd come into the war to liberate Belgium. So the Brits held on to Ypres for dear life and they managed to stop the Germans taking the town. Just. But the Germans would be back.

Tragedy on the Eastern Front

In the east the Russian army was so vast it was nicknamed 'the Russian Steamroller', meaning that, in theory, it just needed to move forward and it would crush everything in its path. And, at first, it did. Before the Germans could invade Russian territory in Poland, two Russian armies moved into East Prussia, and when the Germans tried to stop them at a town called Gumbinnen, the Russians beat them. This was definitely not in the German war plan.

Behold the titans of Tannenberg

Von Moltke sacked the German general who lost at Gumbinnen and replaced him with one of the most successful double acts in military history. Paul von Hindenburg was a decorated veteran brought out of retirement (he'd put on a bit of weight, so his old uniform didn't quite fit him any more). He was experienced, shrewd and calm. His Chief of Staff and right-hand man was General Erich Ludendorff, a much more excitable character – hysterical, even – but a very able commander, with ruthless drive and energy. The two men were very different, which is probably why they worked so well together. They would need to, because two Russian armies were now steadily advancing into eastern Germany towards the Baltic coast.

The two Russian commanders were General von Rennenkampf (in the north) and General Samsonov (in the south). Unlike Hindenburg and Ludendorff, they didn't make a good double act. In fact, they couldn't stand each other. They didn't communicate with each other much, and even when they did, the Russians sent their messages by ordinary radio without any attempt to put them in code, so the Germans just listened in and took notes.

Instead of moving against both Russian armies, Hindenburg concentrated all his forces against Samsonov in the south and left Rennenkampf alone for the moment. Of course, Rennenkampf could've come to Samsonov's rescue, but the Germans reckoned he'd leave Samsonov to stew in his own juice – and they were right. Samsonov's men were cut off in small groups, no one knew what was happening or what they should be doing, and General Samsonov was so devastated by his defeat that he shot himself.

Next, Hindenburg and Ludendorff turned against Rennenkampf and trapped his army against the Masurian Lakes. The Russians suffered terrible losses, including many who drowned trying to get away across the lakes. The Russian invasion of Germany had started in triumph but ended in disaster.

Teutons at Tannenberg

Near the site of Samsonov's defeat was a little village called Tannenberg. For the Germans, this was too good to be true: Tannenberg was where their ancestors, the Teutonic Knights, had been defeated by the Russians back in the Middle Ages. Now they could portray this battle as the revenge of the modern-day Teutons (that's a rather archaic word for Germans) against the invading Slavic hordes. Perfect propaganda.

The defeats at Tannenberg and the Masurian Lakes didn't spell the end of the Russian army, though. As the Germans started to push the Russians back out of Germany and into Poland, the Russians fought back, and by the end of the year both sides were back more or less where they'd started.

The news wasn't all bad for the Russians in 1914: farther south, against the Austro-Hungarians, they were doing very well.

New man, new priorities

By September 1914 the Chief of the German General Staff, General von Moltke, was convinced that the war would be a disaster for Germany. The Schlieffen Plan had failed (see Figure 4-5) and now, von Moltke thought, Germany was trapped in a long war that it couldn't win. He couldn't face it and he suffered a mental breakdown. The man who took over was Erich von Falkenhayn. Falkenhayn had a very clear understanding of the war:

- ✔ Germany's most deadly enemy was not France or Russia, but Britain.

- ✔ Therefore, the priority should be the Western Front, not the Eastern.

- ✔ Germany should try to make a separate peace with one or more of Britain's allies.

- ✔ Of all Britain's allies, the one most likely to make a separate peace (and possibly even become a German ally in due course) was Russia.

Falkenhayn didn't want to send too many troops to the Eastern Front (and he refused to send any there from the Western Front), and he certainly didn't want to launch the sort of full-scale invasion of Russia that General Ludendorff talked about. Falkenhayn's attitude was infuriating for Hindenburg and Ludendorff, who thought the Eastern Front should have priority over the Western one. It was even worse news for the Austro-Hungarians.

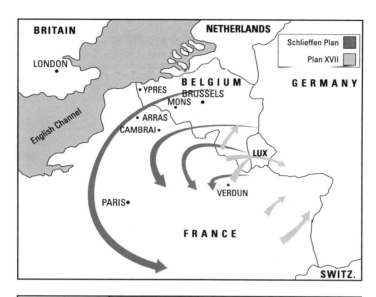

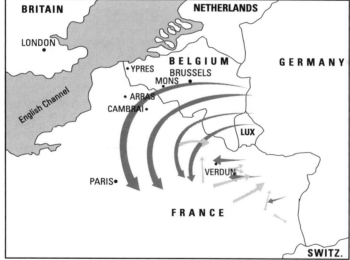

Figure 4-5:
(a)
Germany's
Schlieffen
Plan, and
France's
Plan XVII,
and (b) what
actually
happened.

General Conrad's dilemma

The Austro-Hungarian commander, General Conrad, had wanted a war against Serbia as soon as Franz Ferdinand was shot (see Chapter 3). Conrad talked with von Moltke and they agreed that the Germans and the Austro-Hungarians would each invade Russian territory in Poland. Conrad's war with the Serbs would have to wait. But then everything started going wrong. The

Russians invaded East Prussia and beat the Germans at Gumbinnen, and von Moltke had to pull out of the joint attack on Russia. If Conrad decided to go ahead with the attack on Russia, he'd be on his own.

Conrad now found himself facing a difficult dilemma. The Austro-Hungarian army ought to be able to beat the Serbs, but it couldn't take the Russians on without German help. His options were:

- ✔ **Attack Serbia and forget about the Russians.** Not a good idea, unless Conrad wanted the Russian steamroller moving unopposed into Austria-Hungary (he didn't).

- ✔ **Attack the Russians and forget about the Serbs.** This option made more military sense, but little political sense: the whole point of going to war in the first place had been to teach the Serbs a lesson, after all.

- ✔ **Attack the Russians *and* the Serbs.** Attacking both was possible in theory, but because it would mean splitting the Austro-Hungarian forces between two fronts, it would probably mean losing on both fronts too.

Conrad decided that the Austro-Hungarians would go it alone and invade Russian Poland and attack Serbia as well, without German help. So there. But he didn't have enough men to defeat either foe. The war in the east had hardly started and already Austria-Hungary seemed to have lost it.

You mean you can't even beat the Serbs?

Conrad gave General Potiorek the job of leading the Austro-Hungarian invasion of Serbia. Unfortunately, he didn't give Potiorek anything like enough men to do the job (partly because Conrad needed men for his campaign in Russian Poland). As a result Potiorek was driven back, and instead of the Austro-Hungarians invading Serbia, the Serbs invaded Bosnia-Herzegovina. Potiorek had another go later in December and he did briefly take the Serbian capital, Belgrade. But he had to give it up again. Potiorek had lost 24,000 men and he still hadn't beaten the Serbs.

Bosnian atrocities, part one . . . to be continued

General Potiorek was afraid that the Serbs would encourage the Bosnian Serbs to start attacking his troops, so he decided to act first by rounding up the populations of whole villages and shooting them. So began the cycle of systematic massacre in Bosnia-Herzegovina that would reach its ghastly conclusion in the massacres and 'ethnic cleansing' (a.k.a. mass murder) of the 1990s.

The epic Siege of Przemysl

General Conrad decided to press ahead with his invasion of Russian Poland without German help. He gathered his troops and headed for the city of Lemberg (the German name for the city of Lvov). He didn't have enough men to take it, and the Russians completely defeated him. Conrad was furious with the Germans for not helping him (and they were furious with him for losing) and he fell back to his headquarters in the town of Przemysl. The Russians moved in to besiege the town.

The Siege of Przemysl was an epic. It lasted all through the winter of 1914 and into the spring of 1915. Both sides suffered terribly: the Russians were in rags by the end of it and hardly in better condition than their enemy.

War comes to Warsaw

Even a 'westerner' like Chief of the German General Staff Falkenhayn couldn't entirely ignore the Eastern Front. So after the German victory at Tannenberg and the Masurian Lakes (see 'Behold the titans of Tannenberg'), he agreed that Hindenburg and Ludendorff should join the Austro-Hungarians in a joint attack on Warsaw. Unfortunately for them, the Russians attacked first, the Austro-Hungarians messed up their part of the counter-attack and they all had to turn around and go home.

The Germans weren't impressed with their Austro-Hungarian allies.

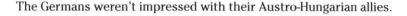

Peace on Earth – the Christmas Truce

On Christmas Eve 1914 British soldiers in their trenches in Belgium were surprised to hear the sound of the Germans singing a Christmas carol. Even more unexpected was what happened on Christmas Day: soldiers from both sides climbed out of the trenches and greeted each other in the middle. No one started shooting. Instead they had a game of football and exchanged gifts. Some soldiers had their photos taken with their enemies. When it was all over, they had to say goodbye, go back to their trenches and start killing each other again.

The British and German high commands were aghast at the news of the Christmas Truce. If soldiers got to know each other

– maybe even made friends with each other – who knew what might happen? They might even stop fighting. Stern orders came down that the 1914 Christmas Truce was *not* to be repeated, and it wasn't.

But perhaps those British and German soldiers had recognised something important: that even in wartime all people are human, and they would all rather be kicking footballs around than shooting each other. And what better time to make that point than at Christmas?

Chapter 5

1915: Cunning Plans to Win the War

In This Chapter

▶ Planning for a breakthrough

▶ Learning trench warfare the hard way on the Western Front

▶ Rolling back the Russians on the Eastern Front

▶ Widening the war

The year 1914 had been a disappointing one all round. Both sides hoped for greater success in 1915, but with deadlock in the west and no clear dominant side in the east, reality was sinking in. By the time 1915 rolled around, no one had any illusions about the scale of the challenge ahead. Everyone knew that they needed to do some major rethinking about the war and how to fight it in the coming year.

Some countries felt they had reason to think positively – Britain, for example. The British naval blockade of Germany would start to take effect in 1915 and many thousands of volunteers would soon be finishing their training and be ready to fight, swelling the numbers of men that the British could send to the field. Other countries would be joining in the war too, on each side, providing yet more men and munitions on more fronts. So although Christmas 1914 had proved to be a false hope, may be there was a chance that the war would be wrapped up by Christmas 1915.

Hopes such as these were dashed, one by one, on both sides as the year progressed. By the end of 1915, stalemate was as firmly entrenched as ever on the Western Front. The Allies hadn't broken through, and neither had the Germans. On the Eastern Front, the Germans might have rolled them back but the Russians were determinedly hanging on. On other fronts, the Allied efforts at Gallipoli had been a disaster; the Italians had failed to break through in the Alps; the Germans, Austro-Hungarians and Bulgarians *had* managed to beat Serbia; and the French and British were stuck at Salonika, achieving little. This chapter looks at how, and why, 1915 turned out the way it did.

Winning Wheezes in the West

Despite some countries' hopes of turning the war around to their advantage in 1915, plenty of doubts still remained. What about that unbroken line of trenches on the western front, for example? Should armies keep trying to break through there, or should they try to break through somewhere else?

Some people, such as Lord Kitchener, the British Secretary of State for war, and Falkenhayn, the Chief of the German General Staff, thought it was best to keep trying to break the deadlock on the Western Front whilst attempting to achieve a breakthrough somewhere else. Falkenhayn did succeed in refocusing German efforts eastwards in 1915 (see 'Rolling Back the Russians; Seeing Off the Serbs', later in this chapter), but the Allied commanders on the Western Front, such as Sir John French and General Joffre, reckoned that the west was the only front that mattered. They thought that sending troops and materials to other fronts – 'sideshows', as they called them – was a complete waste of time. And the biggest waste of time, money and lives, they reckoned, was an idea that Winston Churchill (Britain's First Lord of the Admiralty) had to help the Russians by invading the Ottoman Empire at a place called Gallipoli, in modern-day Turkey. The invasion went disastrously wrong (check out Chapter 9 to find out what happened), and the Allied governments realised that if attacking Turkey wasn't going to end the war then they'd *have* to find a way to break through and win on the Western Front. Doing that would require two things: men and artillery shells.

It's training, men!

You have to pity the drill sergeants who were tasked with the job of training the volunteers of Kitchener's New Army. They were used to taking rough farm boys through their paces and turning them into soldiers; now they had to deal with huge numbers of city-dwelling clerks and shop assistants who'd never done anything violent but had a lot more education than the recruits the drill sergeants were used to. Sometimes the volunteers came from the same social background as their officers, so they'd talk to them as equals. Sergeants found that when they told the men to shoulder arms and march, some of the men would step out of line to ask whether there was any point to all this marching – not that they wanted to be a nuisance, but it did seem a bit unnecessary and rather old fashioned. The sergeants had to take a deep breath and explain that learning to obey orders without question and to operate as a unit was still very important, even in modern warfare.

To start with, volunteers had to do lots of physical exercise to get their bodies into shape. Then they learned to fire a rifle without doing themselves an injury, and how to use their bayonets. Above all, they had to learn to take pride in themselves and in their regiments, so they could hold their heads high alongside the Regulars. Most Regulars still rather looked down on the New Army, but it was impossible to miss the New Army's enthusiasm. They couldn't wait to be sent to France to 'have a crack at the Hun'.

Come in, men! Your time is up!

Thanks to the recruitment campaign in Britain, thousands of young men, almost all with zero military experience, were in training by the end of 1914 (to give you an idea of the numbers, 33,204 men joined up on 3 September alone!). (See the nearby sidebar, 'It's training, men!' for the lowdown on military training.) These men would be ready for frontline fighting by the spring or summer of 1915, just in time to replenish the seriously-thinned out ranks in the trenches and to launch the long-awaited breakthrough attack.

The increasing numbers of British soldiers on the Western Front were bolstered by large numbers of Indian troops. The Indians were experienced soldiers who were very proud to be standing by Britain in its hour of need, and they soon showed their worth in battle. The French army, too, was being reinforced by similarly professional troops from France's north African colonies.

The situation on the shells front wasn't quite so good.

She sells HE shells . . . and we need more

The Western Front was a long unbroken line of trenches (see Chapter 4 to find out how it had taken this quite unexpected form). The armies needed constant supplies of sandbags, barbed wire and wooden planks for maintaining their trenches, as well as flare pistols, which could light up the sky during night attacks, and trench mortars – specially designed guns for lobbing bombs from one trench to another. Above all, they needed high explosive (HE) artillery shells. Attacking an enemy's trench was suicidal unless you'd destroyed his defences first, and the only way to do that seemed to be for artillery to blow them to smithereens. The problem was that by the start of 1915, the armies had fired so many thousands of shells that they were beginning to run out.

Easterners on the Western Front

Britain's armies in India had made Britain a military Great Power in the first place, so it made perfect sense to deploy Indian troops on the Western Front. Indian soldiers proved formidable fighters, and they played a key role in the British success at Neuve-Chapelle in March 1915. But these Indians, used to rather warmer conditions, soon grew tired of the cold and the mud of Flanders and France. The British authorities did their best to keep their Indian troops happy. The King even handed over the Royal Pavilion in Brighton as a hospital for Indian troops because he thought its oriental decoration might help them feel at home. But in the end the British realised that serving in the trenches in France wasn't good for the troops' morale, and Indian troops were redeployed to fight in the Middle East against the Turks.

In France, the 'shell shortage' crisis brought the government down. In Britain the shell scandal forced the Liberal government to form a coalition with the Conservative (Unionist) and Labour parties. As a result, the government reorganised the munitions factories, with young women replacing the male workforce, and the newly-created Ministry of Munitions made better checks to ensure that commanders were getting the sort of shells that they actually required. Getting supplies right was essential if the Allies were ever going to achieve their planned breakthrough in the west.

Germany's way to win

Like the Allies, who hoped to win the war by attacking at Gallipoli, the German high command was also thinking much more broadly about how to win the war. The Chief of the General Staff, General Falkenhayn, was convinced that victory would only come from a breakthrough in the west, but it didn't seem very likely that that would happen in 1915. Falkenhayn did authorise one major offensive against the British at Ypres (see 'The deadly second Battle of Ypres', later in the chapter), but it didn't break through and the Western Front reverted to deadlock. So Falkenhayn decided to leave the Western Front on hold and concentrate Germany's efforts on defeating Russia in the east (see 'Rolling Back the Russians; Seeing Off the Serbs').

The Germans were also keen to use their fleet of submarines (U-boats) to cut off Britain's food supplies. Admiral Tirpitz, the German naval commander, pressed for unrestricted U-boat warfare, sinking any vessel, of any nationality, heading to or from the British Isles. The German government was nervous about this idea: they feared it would alienate public opinion in the United States – and they were right. Americans were particularly outraged when a U-boat sank the British passenger liner *Lusitania*, killing over a thousand people, including 128 Americans. (I look in more detail at the war at sea in Chapter 8.)

How to Break Through in the West and Win the War in a Year

General Joffre and Sir John French, the Allied commanders on the Western Front, were certain that they could break through the German lines on the Western Front and win the war by the end of 1915. The only question was, where? They had three main potential jumping-off bases:

- ✔ **Artois:** In northern France. Good, firm farmland, ideal for fighting. British commander: Sir Douglas Haig.

- ✔ **Champagne:** Yes, the area where the wine comes from. Champagne was much farther along the line of trenches, well into the French sector. French commander: General Joffre.

✔ **Ypres:** Farther north than Artois, this Belgian town was in a *salient* (a bulge) in the Allied line, which meant the Germans could shell it on three sides. British commander: Sir Horace Smith-Dorrien.

The original idea was to launch simultaneous British and French attacks, but when Sir John French asked for reinforcements, instead of Regulars he got *Territorials* (that is, volunteer part-timers). Sir John was furious, especially as the Regulars he'd been hoping for had been sent off to Salonika, of all places (see the later sidebar 'Salonika?' to find out why). This substitution prompted Joffre to cancel the French part of the attack: the British would be on their own. Sir John decided the attack would be at Neuve Chapelle, in Artois, and General Haig's men would launch it. (By the way, the Territorials proved just as good in battle as the Regulars, so Sir John and Joffre had had nothing to worry about.)

The battle of nerves at Neuve Chapelle

The British offensive of March 1915 at Neuve Chapelle illustrates many of the things that can go wrong in trench warfare.

Sir Douglas Haig gave the job of planning the attack on Neuve Chapelle to General Sir Henry Rawlinson (you also meet this Haig–Rawlinson partnership in Chapter 6). Contrary to what you may have heard about British generals in the First World War, Rawlinson prepared the battle in meticulous detail. He had a clear, limited objective, he had sufficient heavy artillery and huge numbers of shells, and he had enough men, including a large contingent of experienced Indian troops. And everything went according to plan: the Germans were pulverised by the shelling, and the first wave of the attack took the town and nearly the whole of the German line of trenches. And yet the attack was – not a failure, exactly, but definitely a disappointment. Instead of breaking through the German lines, the British and Indians advanced only about 1,000 yards.

The British encountered four problems at Neuve Chapelle that would recur time and time again throughout the war:

✔ **Advancing too far:** The farther the attackers went forward, the *farther* they went from ammunition, medical help, orders from headquarters and so on. On the other hand, the farther the defenders were pushed back, the *closer* they were to their supplies, ammunition and reinforcements, and the easier they found it to resist the attack.

✔ **Communications:** As soon as troops climbed out of their trenches, communication with them was almost impossible. Without field telephones they could tell HQ what was happening only by waving flags (which HQ might not see), or by sending pigeons or runners (both easily shot by the enemy).

✔ **Following through:** Attacking the enemy lines was pointless if you couldn't follow through and drive the enemy back before he had time to counter-attack. But the men who'd attacked were too exhausted to follow through and fresh infantry took time to come up. (And following through wouldn't work without proper communications anyway.)

✔ **Machine guns:** The small section of the German trenches the British didn't manage to capture happened to contain two machine guns, and these alone caused 1,000 British casualties.

The Allies would need to learn the lessons of Neuve Chapelle quickly, because they'd be fighting plenty more battles like it on the Western Front.

The deadly second Battle of Ypres

The German commander on the Western Front, General Falkenhayn, had a political problem. He was a firm believer that the war would be won or lost on the Western Front, but Germany's 'star' generals, Ludendorff and Hindenburg, were 'easterners' and they were using their friends in the German government to undermine him. Falkenhayn badly needed a victory in the west. He decided to get it at Ypres: he launched his attack in April 1915. He also decided to use gas.

No one had thought to issue troops with gas masks, and so when the Allies at Ypres saw German gas heading towards them, most of them ran, except for a remarkably tough Canadian unit that somehow managed to hang on.

The Germans made good progress at Ypres and took a lot of ground, flattening out the salient around the town. The British commander, General Smith-Dorrien, thought this German advance was actually no bad thing: it made the British line much more compact and easier to defend. He even proposed falling back to an even shorter line. But Sir John French didn't want to hear this sort of talk (he wanted a victory and he didn't like Smith-Dorrien anyway), so he sacked him and appointed General Plumer instead. Who immediately fell back to a shorter line, just as Smith-Dorrien had suggested. The town was still in British hands, but the Germans were now dug in much closer.

The horrors of gas

Chemicals have been used in warfare ever since the first tribal warrior dipped his arrowhead in poison, but the modern chemicals industry presented military commanders with a wider range of poisons to choose from than ever before. The Hague Convention banned using gas, and it still fills people with a particular horror today. Yet gas was originally intended to be a more *humane* way of fighting: it would incapacitate the enemy without causing any permanent damage, just as police forces nowadays use CS gas or pepper spray. The gas used in the First World War, however, blinded and choked and burned men's lungs. Worse: because armies began to issue their men with gas masks, the type of gas used had to get deadlier, through phosgene right up to the worst and deadliest – mustard gas.

Remember, men, you're fighting for king, country – and for me to keep my job: Aubers Ridge

Just like Falkenhayn, Sir John French had to watch his back: his enemies in London and Paris wanted him sacked. The best way to see off his critics would be for him to win a battle and break through, and so in April, he ordered an attack by British and Indian troops at Aubers Ridge, just beyond the site of the disappointing attack at Neuve Chapelle (see the earlier section 'The battle of nerves at Neuve Chapelle'). It achieved nothing.

Sir John told *The Times* newspaper that this failure was because the army hadn't had enough shells (in fact, the Germans had learned their lesson from Neuve Chapelle – see 'The battle of nerves at Neuve Chapelle' – and had simply improved their defences and positioned more machine guns). The stink this allegation caused in the press forced the Prime Minister to bring the opposition parties into a new coalition government and to appoint the dynamic and ambitious David Lloyd George as Minister of Munitions, responsible for providing the army with enough shells. Even so, Sir John French's reputation was on the line, and he knew it. He needed a victory and he needed one fast, or he'd be on the next boat home.

Sir John French – setting the record straight

Sir John French has had a bad press and it's not entirely fair. He was a brave soldier and had shown himself a very capable commander in the Anglo–Boer War. Historians have sometimes said he couldn't understand modern war because he was a cavalryman, though that never stopped Churchill (who was also a cavalryman) seizing the latest developments in weapons and strategy. French was far from the only general who found trench warfare frustrating and difficult to solve.

French's biggest problem, perhaps, was that he wasn't an easy man to get to know or like. He made enemies easily and he never enjoyed a very warm relationship with his men. Charisma and popularity are no substitute for winning battles, but they can help you overcome setbacks. Sir John lost his battles and he had no real friends to fall back on.

Fight at Loos, lose at Loos

Nineteen fifteen wasn't turning out the way the Allies had confidently predicted at the start of the year. They hadn't so far broken through the German lines and they'd suffered enormous casualties. By September, General Joffre was ready to launch the big attack postponed from the spring (see the earlier section 'How to Break Through in the West and Win the War in a Year' for why he'd cancelled the spring offensive). He would attack in the Champagne region, supported by a British attack at a French town with the not-very-promising name of Loos, farther north, in Artois. The Loos attack would be Sir John French's last chance to rescue his reputation, or his enemies at home would get him recalled.

The British attacked at Loos on 25 September. This time, they used gas, though the wind was so low that it hung in the air and even drifted back into the British lines. The British did manage to take the German front-line trenches and the town, but when reinforcements moved up, they were mown down by German machine-gun fire. Once again, the British hadn't had enough shells to destroy the German defences. And once again the British had lost thousands of men for a few feet of ground.

The Battle of Loos finally convinced the British government that Sir John French would have to go. The obvious man to replace him was Sir Douglas Haig, who had commanded the successful (well, as successful as any attack could be in 1915) attack on Neuve Chapelle.

How not to win the Battle of Champagne

General Joffre had never been particularly impressed with the efforts of the British Expeditionary Force (and he was decidedly unimpressed with its commander, Sir John French). He hoped his attack in Champagne in September 1915 would show the *Tommies* (that is, the British soldiers) how to fight a battle properly. Unfortunately for Joffre, the only people teaching anyone how to fight in the Battle of Champagne were the Germans. The French had several problems:

✔ They didn't have anything like enough artillery to flatten the German defences.

✔ They attacked on a fairly narrow front. That meant the Germans knew exactly where the French would be coming from, which gave them a pretty good idea of where the French were heading for.

✔ When the French took the German front line, the Germans simply fell back to a second line of trenches that they'd prepared earlier. These trenches were on higher ground and in pristine condition; the French were on the lower ground and utterly exhausted.

Tommies, Huns and hairy Frenchmen

Back in the days of the Duke of Wellington someone, no one knows who, described a typical British soldier as a tough, solid son of the countryside with a good, solid name like Thomas Atkins. Soon *Tommy* became the universal nickname for the British soldier, just like *GI Joe* for Americans in the Second World War (though in the First World War American soldiers were known as *doughboys*). The French also thought of their soldiers as tough peasants from the depths of the countryside, with thick peasant moustaches, so they called their soldiers *poilus,* which literally means *hairy ones* (it works better in French). The French referred to the Germans as the *Boche,* a term the British picked up too, though the Tommies usually called German soldiers *Fritz* or *Jerry.* (German soldiers referred to themselves as *Landser,* which is a bit like the grizzled old peasant image of the Tommy or the poilu.) As stories of German atrocities in Belgium and attacks by German U-boats began to spread, however, the British began to use a new name for their German opposite numbers: *Huns.*

Just like the British at the Battle of Loos, the French had lost thousands of men just so they could move their front line forwards a few hundred yards. Meanwhile, the Germans were nicely dug in at new defensive positions that were much stronger than the ones the French had taken. This situation wasn't what Joffre had had in mind when he talked about breaking through the German lines.

How to win the war next year

The Allied commanders' general verdict on 1915 was that the attacks on the Western Front hadn't been big enough and, above all, hadn't been supported by enough artillery bombardment. The solution, clearly, was to launch much bigger attacks that would completely overwhelm the German defences and give the Allies complete superiority. It would be Haig's job to prepare for these super-offensives to be launched in the new year.

Rolling Back the Russians; Seeing Off the Serbs

Because it looked clear that no one was going to break through on the Western Front any time soon (and the whole first half of this chapter tells you why), Chief of the German General Staff Falkenhayn decided to go all out for a major victory against the Russians in the east. The Germans had crushed the Russians at Tannenberg the year before, but the Russians had regrouped and done very well farther south against the Austro-Hungarians (see Chapter 4).

In the spring of 1915, after an epic siege in freezing conditions, the Russians finally took the Polish fortress town of Przemysl from the Austro-Hungarians. Defeating Russia in 1915 was going to take careful planning.

Falkenhayn's priority was the Western Front. Ideally, he wanted to make peace with Russia and then turn on Germany's main enemy, Britain. That meant Falkenhayn needed a victory in the east that was heavy enough to make the Russians pull out but not so humiliating that they'd fight on to the death or resent the Germans for years. Getting such a victory was likely to prove tricky. It was.

Polishing off Poland

Falkenhayn prepared very carefully for the 1915 eastern offensive. He transferred men from the Western Front (he gave the troops in France and Belgium extra machine guns to make up for the loss) and he identified clear and limited targets. Hindenburg and Ludendorff wanted to lead an invasion right into the heart of Russia, but Falkenhayn had read his history and knew how previous invaders of Russia, such as Charles XII of Sweden and Napoleon I of France, had come to grief attempting that very thing. With help from their Austro-Hungarian allies, the Germans would launch hammer-blow attacks on the Russian positions in Poland and the Baltic, driving the Russians back but not charging ahead towards Moscow.

Falkenhayn's Polish campaign, which he launched in April in the Gorlice-Tarnow region, was a triumphant success. The Russians weren't expecting it, and when they did finally wake up to what was happening, their rail connections were far too slow to get reinforcements where they were needed. This lack of organisation may have been part of the reason for the Russian commanders' not-very-original response to the German assault: they just told their men to stand fast and not retreat an inch (this, incidentally, was Hitler's tactic in Russia during the Second World War. It didn't work then either). The Russians put their trust in the line of fortresses they'd built in Poland, but the Germans knew just how to deal with these: they brought up their heavy artillery and smashed them to pieces.

On 4 June the Germans took Przemysl, the fortress the Russians had spent so long taking from the Austro-Hungarians, and on 22 June they took the Polish city of Lvov. Finally, on 4 August the Germans took Warsaw. The Russians fell back in confusion. They lost over a million casualties and another million were taken prisoner. It was the worst defeat in Russian military history.

The Russians didn't know what had hit them. The Germans and Austro-Hungarians had hammered them with artillery and the Russians simply hadn't had enough shells to hit back. To make things worse, they *had* had huge stockpiles of shells in Przemysl and Lvov, but those were now in German hands. The Russians simply had no way of hitting back. They had no choice: they'd have to retreat.

Er, we seem to have mislaid Poland

In this chapter you see a lot of mention of fighting in Poland but if you look at maps of the Eastern Front you won't find a country bearing any such name.

Poland had been a powerful state in its day, but its day had been the 17th century. Poland's powerful neighbours, the Prussians, Austrians and Russians, had gradually taken over more and more Polish territory so that by the end of the 18th century they'd completely swallowed the country up. Some alterations of boundaries followed in the 19th century but by 1914 most of Poland was still ruled by Russia, while significant parts lay in Austria-Hungary and Germany. The Poles remained determined to get rid of their foreign rulers and re-establish a Polish state; in the meantime, Poles from different parts of Poland found themselves fighting on opposite sides of the battlefields of the Eastern Front, serving in the German, Austro-Hungarian and Russian armies.

Oh, those retreating Russians

Retreating may sound like an admission of defeat, but the Russians had long experience of using retreat to their advantage. The trick was to destroy everything that might be useful to the enemy: houses, bridges and, above all, food. That way, the enemy has to advance into a complete wasteland with no food or water: imagine advancing into a vast desert and you get the idea. This tactic is known as a *scorched earth policy,* because it usually involves burning everything. It had worked against Napoleon and now it worked against Falkenhayn. The Russians retreated over 300 miles and the Germans realised, sensibly, that they couldn't follow.

A scorched earth policy can be a very useful way of fighting an invader but it creates appalling suffering for the people who live in the area. The hardship the Russian people suffered due to the actions of their own leaders would be a big factor in the Russian revolution two years later.

Curb your victorious enthusiasm!

Despite its success, Falkenhayn knew how costly the Polish campaign had been: the Germans and Austro-Hungarians had lost nearly a million men. He didn't think Germany could afford to lose such large numbers of troops and he badly wanted to bring the war with Russia to an end. He was in a strong position to impose terms on the Russians, as long as the Russians were prepared to listen. His problem was that some people in the German government and high command wanted him to crush Russia even more.

General Ludendorff wanted to push ahead towards Moscow itself. Falkenhayn, on the other hand, thought Ludendorff had underestimated the Russians' ability to fight, especially on their home ground, and that invading Russia would be a massive waste of money and lives. Others thought that Germany should annex Poland: after all, they'd just conquered it. But Falkenhayn was still hoping to negotiate some sort of deal with Tsar Nicholas II. He didn't want to crush irrevocably or humiliate the Russians; he just wanted to beat them, have a chat with the Tsar about how to conclude the war in the east to the winner's advantage, and turn his attention back to the Western Front, which he saw as priority number one. The Tsar, however, wouldn't be able even to consider talks if Germany took over such a huge amount of Russian territory. It would be like France and Alsace-Lorraine all over again. (The Germans had taken Alsace-Lorraine off France in 1871 and the French had never forgiven them.)

All the signs were that Falkenhayn's fears were right. Far from offering to talk with the Germans, in September 1915 Tsar Nicholas II took personal command of the Russian armies. He would carry on the fight against Germany into 1916 and on to the bitter end. So much for Falkenhayn's hopes of a deal with the Russians.

Things must be bad – the Tsar of Russia's in charge

Nicholas II was a kind man, a loving father – and a hopeless tsar. He believed firmly in his right to rule as an autocrat, but he didn't have the nous or the strength of character to do so successfully. In 1905 he'd ordered his troops to open fire on demonstrators outside his palace in St Petersburg, and then couldn't understand why more and more Russians turned against their 'little father'. He insisted that power in Russia belonged to him alone and that no one else had a right to share it, but in 1906 he gave in to pressure and allowed the Russians to have an elected parliament (*duma* in Russian). Then, when he didn't like what the duma did, he dismissed it and changed the electoral rules so he could get a duma he did like. Then he closed that down too. You really knew where you were with Nicholas II – he *always* changed his mind.

Nicholas had hoped that a quick victory over the Germans would win the Russian people over and help them forget the poverty and hunger that so many of them faced each day. That meant that Russia's defeats in 1914 and 1915 weren't just military disasters: they were political disasters for Nicholas too. Nicholas took his duties very seriously and he decided that in Russia's hour of need his place was at very top – of the army. In September, as the Russians were still reeling from their defeats in Poland, Nicholas announced that he was taking over as Commander-in-Chief of the Russian armies in the field. He was hoping, of course, that his presence alone would inspire the officers and men to greater efforts, and that he'd lead them to a great victory. It doesn't seem to have occurred to him that taking command also meant that if anything went wrong – and on current form that was quite likely – he'd get the blame.

Swansong for Serbia

Austria-Hungary had wanted to crush Serbia ever since Franz Ferdinand was assassinated (see Chapter 3 for more on this momentous murder). They'd made good progress against the Serbs at the start of the war, but then they'd had to divide their forces in order to fight the Russians as well, and the Serbs had been able to recover. Now that the Russians had been pushed back in Poland, Falkenhayn reckoned it was time to deal with the Serbs once and for all.

Falkenhayn decided on a two-pronged attack on Serbia: the Germans and Austro-Hungarians would attack from the north, and their new allies, the Bulgarians (see the later section, 'Bulgaria – picking a winner'), could attack from the east. The commander Falkenhayn chose for this campaign was a tough old boot who'd distinguished himself in the campaign in Poland earlier in the year, Field Marshal August von Mackensen. Unfortunately for the Serbs, von Mackensen proved just the man for the job.

The Serbs (see Figure 5-1) were in a very bad way. They'd gained themselves a breathing space by beating the Austro-Hungarians back in 1914, but they'd achieved nothing since then and by the autumn of 1915 their troops were tired, demoralised and wracked with typhus. They were in no state to stand up to the onslaught von Mackensen was about to unleash.

Figure 5-1:
Serbian troops moving to a forward area on the Balkan front.

© *Imperial War Museums (Q 32447)*

In October 1915 the Germans, Austro-Hungarians and Bulgarians descended on Serbia and the Serbs crumbled. The French did what they could to help the Serbs from their base in Salonika (see the nearby sidebar 'Salonika?'), some 280 miles from the Serbian front. At one point von Mackensen nearly had the Serbian army completely surrounded; the Serbs managed to escape but they could do nothing to stop the conquest of their country. In blinding snow the Serbs were forced onto what they called the Great Retreat through the mountains to the Albanian coast, where British and French ships were waiting to transfer them to Salonika.

Serbian nationalists had hoped that assassinating Franz Ferdinand in Sarajevo would lead to a great future and a greater Serbia. Little more than a year later, their dreams, and their country, lay in ruins.

Salonika?

You might be wondering why Salonika (nowadays called Thessaloniki) has suddenly started featuring in the story. So did the Salonikans. Salonika is a town in northeastern Greece, and in 1914 it had a direct rail link with Belgrade, the Serbian capital: that's why the French identified Salonika as a useful base for sending help to the Serbs. The French thought that by doing so they could divert German and Austro-Hungarian attention to that front, and so away from the Western Front, which could only help France's attempts to break through there.

After Serbia fell, the French fortified their base at Salonika and called in British and French reinforcements. They had a problem, though: the Greek Prime Minister, Venizelos, was happy for them to be there, but the pro-German King Constantine wasn't. Constantine sacked Venizelos and soon the French commander in Salonika, General Sarrail, found himself facing a Greek threat as well as the combined force of Germans, Austro-Hungarians and Bulgarians.

As things turned out, the Germans preferred to leave the Allies more or less alone in Salonika: they weren't going anywhere, and if they surrendered, the Germans would only have the expense of looking after them. People joked that Salonika was Germany's biggest internment camp. The French managed to drive the Bulgarians back from Salonika in 1918, but otherwise, the Salonika front was a massive waste of Allied time and effort.

This Looks Fun – Can We Play? Italy and Bulgaria Join the War

However difficult the war was proving to be for its combatants, other countries still saw it as a not-to-be-missed opportunity to advance their own interests while they still had time. Two countries – Italy and Bulgaria – were looking to do just that when they joined the war in 1915.

From 1915 onwards, after these countries joined the war on their side, Britain, France and Russia began to refer to themselves – officially – as the *Allied Nations*, or *Allies* for short. Being allied meant that none of them would make a separate peace with the Germans: they'd all see this war through to its bitter end.

Italy – looking after numero uno

Italy was allied to Germany and Austria-Hungary, so you might think that deciding which side to support in the war was a no-brainer for the Italians. If so, you'd be wrong. During their long 19th-century struggle to unify Italy, their implacable enemy had been Austria, and the Italians hadn't forgotten. They weren't comfortable with being allied to Austria-Hungary.

More importantly, the Italians had started to talk about what they called *Italia Irredenta,* which means something like 'Italy with all the recovered bits included'. The policy, called *irredentism,* meant that Italian nationalists got out their historical atlases and identified all sorts of areas that had once belonged to the various Italian states in ages past and decided to reclaim them. Most of these territories were in Austria-Hungary, either in the Alps or along the Croatian coast. The fact that no Italians lived there any more was neither here nor there: as far as nationalists were concerned, these territories should be reunited with Italy whether the people living in them wanted it or not.

The Italian Prime Minister, Antonio Salandra, called his foreign policy 'sacred self-interest'. Full marks for candour, then. The Allies were quick to take advantage of it. The British and French put a tempting package before Salandra's eyes: if Italy joined the war on the Allied side, the Italians could reclaim all the Austro-Hungarian and Turkish land they wanted (the Italians also thought they really ought to have a bit more land in Africa). The plan worked. In April 1915 Italy signed the Treaty of London, declaring itself allied to its enemies and declaring war on its allies. If you see what I mean. However, the war didn't bring the Italians the quick gains they were hoping for. They opened a difficult front line against the Austro-Hungarians high up in the mountains – think trench warfare with crampons (see Figure 5-2) – which quickly settled into stalemate. Just like all the other fronts.

Figure 5-2:
Austrian troops manning trenches on the Italian front.

© Imperial War Museums (Q 60442)

Bulgaria – picking a winner

The war put the Bulgarians (see Figure 5-3) in a dilemma:

- They got on well with the Russians, so they ought to join the Allies. But Russia was supporting the Serbs, and the Bulgarians had very serious issues with Serbia. So maybe they shouldn't join the Allies.

✔ The Turks were Bulgaria's old enemies, so Bulgaria should join the Allies. But Bulgaria depended very heavily on Germany and Austria-Hungary for its imports. So perhaps Bulgaria shouldn't join the Allies.

Figure 5-3:
Bulgarian troops manning trenches in a mountain position.

© Imperial War Museums (Q 60367)

The Allies and the Central Powers (Germany, Austria-Hungary and Turkey) all tried to persuade Bulgaria to join the war on their side, and Tsar Ferdinand of Bulgaria, sensible chap, decided to see which side made him the better offer.

In the end, Bulgaria decided to join the Central Powers. The reason? Easy: it looked as if they'd win. The British and French clearly weren't winning on the Western Front and were being heavily defeated at Gallipoli; Russia had just lost to the Germans in Poland. Moreover, if Bulgaria joined the German side, it could join in the attack on Serbia that Falkenhayn had planned for the autumn of 1915 (see the earlier section, 'Swansong for Serbia'). Joining the (apparently) winning side and getting revenge on Serbia for the Balkan Wars (see Chapter 3 for details of Bulgaria's beef about these conflicts) . . . what was not to like?

Chapter 6

1916: The Big Battles

In This Chapter

▶ Planning for the Big Push

▶ Struggling for victory in Verdun

▶ Battling for a breakthrough on the Somme

▶ Breaking through in the east

*Y*ou may be thinking, '1916. I'm about halfway through the war here, aren't I?' (though, of course, no one at the time knew that!). But as the new year dawned, generals on both sides were thinking along a very different line: they intended 1916 to be the *last* year of the war.

The Allied powers all agreed that 1915 had been a very bad year. They hadn't been able to break through the German lines on the Western Front and the Gallipoli campaign had been a complete failure (check out Chapter 9 for details). The fighting had got even more vicious, with both sides making regular use of poison gas. But the year hadn't been a success for the Germans either: they'd pushed the Russians back but Russia was still in the war, and it was starting to look as if America might enter the war on the Allied side as a consequence of the German U-boat campaign. So both sides went into 1916 determined to find the solution to winning the war before the end of the year. They both reached the same conclusion: attack – and attack big.

Just like 1914 and 1915, however, 1916 ultimately proved to be another disappointing year for both sides. The massive German attack at Verdun turned into a nightmare for both sides; the British-led attack on the Somme was a disaster; the long-awaited showdown between the British and German fleets produced an indecisive battle at Jutland (Chapter 8 has the details); and an offensive by the Russian General Brusilov, which started as a spectacular success, petered out. Even the Americans, who weren't yet in the war, were disappointed by the way 1916 turned out. In this chapter, you find out why.

BIG Plans: BIG Push

By the time 1916 arrived, both sides felt that the time had come to get serious about winning the war. The Allies and the Central Powers would both have to raise their game and they were under no illusions: the enemy would be doing exactly the same. Both sides were heading, they reckoned, for the showdown. Or, to use the phrase they used at the time, the *Big Push*.

Woodrow Wilson – desperately seeking solutions

So far, the United States of America had remained firmly out of the war, and so it remained in 1916. But the German U-boat campaign (see Chapter 8) was systematically sinking American merchant ships, and the American public was growing increasingly angry about it. President Woodrow Wilson was keenly observing the war in Europe and considering what role, if any, America should play. He was a strongly idealistic man who didn't see why the war had to carry on until one side had won completely and felt that it could be possible to get the two sides to agree to some sort of compromise settlement.

The United States was neutral in the war. In fact, many Americans were *isolationist:* they didn't want to be entangled in any European wars. Wilson himself wasn't against taking military action if it proved necessary – he was deeply angered by the German U-boat campaign – but many people in the US didn't share his feelings and remained opposed to intervention on either side.

To Wilson it seemed that reaching some sort of peace deal in 1916 was a no-brainer. Did the Europeans *want* to keep losing thousands of their young men? He gave the task of negotiating a settlement to Colonel Edward House, his special adviser and envoy on foreign affairs. Colonel House wrote to the British Foreign Secretary, Sir Edward Grey, and together they worked out peace terms that would be broadly acceptable to the Allies:

- ✔ Germany to hand back Alsace-Lorraine to France
- ✔ Germany to get some colonial land in Africa or Asia as compensation for losing Alsace-Lorraine
- ✔ Russia to be allowed to send its warships through the Dardanelles

Wilson planned to table these proposals at a peace conference. If Germany refused to attend, or if the Germans were so stubborn that the conference broke down, then the United States would declare war. However, his plan came to nothing. The British and French expected to win the war soon, so the British weren't as committed to the conference idea as Wilson was and the French weren't interested at all, so the proposal was never put forward to the Germans. In any case, since the Germans wanted land in Europe more than compensation in the colonies, they would almost certainly have turned Wilson's proposals down.

Later in 1916, Wilson tried again to achieve a negotiated peace. President Theodore Roosevelt had negotiated a peace deal between the Russians and Japanese back in 1905, and Wilson attempted to do the same thing with the warring Europeans. The British and French gave a not-very-precise response. The Germans didn't respond at all. Wilson was trying to stay neutral, but it was becoming clear that his sympathies lay with the Allies. This was bad news for the Germans but mixed news for the Allies. They wanted to win the war on their terms: they didn't want to have to accept terms laid down by the American President, which seemed likely if America did come into the war. All the more reason, they thought, to get a quick victory before the United States got involved.

Chantilly – leaders and lace

In December 1915 the Allied leaders met at the spectacular Chateau de Chantilly, home of a famous race track for horses and of the celebrated Chantilly lace. The plans they drew up for 1916 ultimately proved to be full of holes too.

The Allied leaders decided to stage a series of massive co-ordinated attacks on the Central Powers in the spring of 1916, in the west, the east, Italy and Salonika. These offensives would be the biggest yet seen: the leaders agreed that the reason the attacks in 1915 hadn't worked was because they hadn't been anything like big enough. The Allies decided that they needed to blast the enemy with the sheer scale of their forces: vast armies in both the east and west and artillery bombardments so big the mind could hardly take it in. The Russians would attack the Austro-Hungarians in the east, and the French and British would hit the Germans near the River Somme in the west. In particular, the Somme attack would be so big, they thought, that the Germans wouldn't know what had hit them.

In many ways the Chantilly agreement was a very good plan. It was just a pity the Germans had their own ideas.

Falkenhayn rains on the Allies' parade

While the Allied leaders were meeting in comfort at Chantilly to plan the following year's campaigns, the German commander, Falkenhayn, was drawing up his own plan for 1916 and it didn't involve sitting around waiting for the Allies to attack him.

Nineteen fifteen had been a frustrating year for Falkenhayn. He'd had great success against Russia in the east, but he hadn't broken through in the west, where he reckoned Germany's real enemies lay (if you're not sure about all this, see Chapter 5). The Germans hadn't come up with a solution to the problem of breaking through the trenches of the Western Front any more than the Allies had. So Falkenhayn decided to play for big stakes: to launch a high-profile attack that might not break through the enemy line, but would be so costly in human life it would break a whole enemy country's will to carry on the war. The enemy country he had in his sights was France. His target: Verdun.

Historians disagree about Falkenhayn's plans for Verdun. After the battle, Falkenhayn said that he'd wanted to bleed France white, killing as many of the French as possible, so that Verdun would become a sort of mincing machine, crushing the youth of France. That is certainly what happened (though of course it drained the German army too), but was it really what he wanted? After all, the Germans didn't just try to kill French soldiers: they also tried very hard to break through the French line. Some historians think Falkenhayn was only trying to divert the French from their own planned attack on the German lines at the Somme and to force them to fight on ground of his choosing. Whatever his real intention, Falkenhayn thought the French were bound to fight hard for Verdun for their sense of prestige – and he was right.

A Struggle for Life and Death: The Battle of Verdun

The French were rather proud of their historic tradition of building military fortifications, and in 1916 Verdun – a medieval town, important in French history back to the days of Charlemagne – was defended by a number of huge concrete fortresses. Fortresses looked strong, but the campaigns in Belgium at the start of the war (see Chapter 4) had shown that really heavy artillery could blast even the strongest concrete fortresses to pieces. For this reason, most military commanders now thought the days of great fortresses were over and the French had started pulling their men out of the Verdun forts. At the start of 1916 the whole area was more lightly defended than usual. The local commander appealed to General Joffre for more men, but Joffre was more interested in the big Allied offensive planned for the Somme. He didn't reckon that a battle was likely at Verdun. He was wrong.

The German assault

First World War offensives usually began with a huge artillery barrage and Verdun was no exception: the Germans fired a *million* shells at the French positions. The Germans were going to pound the French into the dust.

The Germans' first targets were the forts that were supposed to protect Verdun but that were more vulnerable than they looked. They opened up with their heavy guns to pound the fortresses to pieces, while German infantry advanced across no-man's-land towards the French lines. On 25 February 1916 a German patrol was very cautiously approaching the mighty French Fort Douaumont when a German shell exploded nearby and their sergeant was blown into Fort Douaumont's moat. He decided he might as well have a closer look at the fort, so he found a way in and to his surprise, he found it deserted. He wandered up and down the empty corridors until he eventually stumbled upon a group of French soldiers. They were so surprised to see him that they surrendered the fort there and then!

The fall of Fort Douaumont was a terrible shock to the French – especially the way it fell – and they soon started fighting back. Even so, the Battle of Verdun had started so badly for the French that General Joffre decided to send in a tough new commander to take charge: General Philippe Pétain.

General Philippe Pétain

Pétain was regarded as a rather unfashionable general when the war started. Most French generals were firm believers in attacking the enemy relentlessly, whatever the cost in men. (They were following in the tradition set by Napoleon, who never let high casualties worry him too much.) Pétain was much more cautious: he thought the artillery should do most of the work and the infantry should only go in when the enemy had been properly hammered. This approach didn't win him many friends among his fellow generals, but it was just the sort of attitude that might suit the defence of Verdun (it was popular with his men too).

Pétain was a man with his own sense of priorities. When the call to go to Verdun came, he was in a small hotel meeting a lady friend. His aide de camp brought the message and Pétain decided that he had time to finish things with the lady first before heading for the front first thing in the morning. After his arrival there, his determined and successful defence of Verdun made him a national hero: at the end of the war he was made a Marshal of France – the highest honour a soldier can receive.

Unfortunately, Pétain's story has a sad ending. In 1940, when the Germans invaded France again, Pétain did a deal with the Germans and set up an 'independent' French government based at the spa town of Vichy. In reality it collaborated wholeheartedly with the Nazis. After the war, Pétain was sentenced to death for treason, though the sentence was commuted to life imprisonment. After he died, Pétain was considered a hero by some and a traitor by others. It was a tragic end for a man who had come to embody all that was best about the fighting spirit of France.

They shall not pass!

Right from the start it was clear that Verdun was going to be much bigger and more fiercely fought than other battles. Not only was it the flagship German offensive for 1916, but Verdun was in a large *salient* (that is, a bulge) in the French line. This meant the Germans could bombard the French – and their vulnerable forts – from three sides.

Perhaps the main reason that Verdun was destined to be such a huge battle was that it wasn't really about gaining military advantage: it was a political battle. Militarily, the French would've been sensible to let the Germans take Verdun and fall back to a much stronger position in the rear, where the Germans wouldn't be able to shell them from three sides. But the French hated the idea that the Germans had invaded their country and they didn't like the idea of giving up another inch of French soil. The French Prime Minister, Aristide Briand, knew that letting the Germans take Verdun would be politically disastrous. It might even spark off a revolution (the French had known military defeat to do this before in their history). So he instructed Pétain to hold Verdun at all costs. Pétain's battle cry was, *'Ils ne passeront pas!'* – 'They shall not pass!' It might not have made military sense, but it was the only message France's politicians and generals wanted to hear.

Although the French had determination by the bucketload at Verdun, the Germans seemed to have all the practical advantages. They had a whole railway network that they could use for moving their troops up to the front line. The French, meanwhile, had to use a single road for all their troops, supplies, wounded, messages and everything else they needed. It became known as the 'Sacred Way', partly because it was such a vital lifeline to the troops but mainly because so many soldiers followed it to their deaths (see Figure 6-1).

Figure 6-1:
A dead French soldier lies in the mud next to a German soldier at Verdun.

© Imperial War Museums (Q 23760)

Flamethrowers

The fighting at Verdun saw the Germans making extensive use of a particularly horrifying new weapon: the flamethrower. A *flamethrower* consists of a couple of heavy gas cylinders, carried on the soldier's back, that shoot a flammable liquid out of the nozzle. The liquid is lit, so it looks as if the soldier is literally shooting flames at the enemy. You can probably imagine what happens to anyone who gets caught by a flamethrower: it's a horrible way to die.

Flamethrowers were used to attack fortifications, because the liquid would go through gaps and loopholes and incinerate everyone inside. The soldiers who carried flamethrowers, though, were very vulnerable. They had to get much closer to their targets than they needed to do with a rifle, and enemy soldiers would always try to kill anyone armed with a flamethrower. This was partly because the weapon was so horrible that soldiers always hated enemy flamethrower men, and it was partly because you needed to shoot the flamethrowing soldier before he could turn his attention to you. Getting too indignant about the use of flamethrowers is probably pointless, though, because both sides used them and they're still in use today.

Pétain operated a system of rotating troops on two-week placements at Verdun, so that just about every unit and every soldier in the French army came up the Sacred Way and served at Verdun at some point. In that way Verdun really did become a sort of national epic: all of France was fighting there and all of France was determined to win.

Bleeding France white

The Battle of Verdun was terrible, probably the worst battle of the war on any front so far. It became an exercise in *attrition* – fighting so as to kill as many of the enemy as possible. The Germans hurled men and shells at the French, killing thousands. The Germans also used a new type of poison gas: *phosgene.* They reckoned it was more effective at killing people than the chlorine gas they'd been using so far. Here's why:

- **Chlorine gas** made men vomit and gag, so they knew to get their gas masks on a.s.a.p. If you were too slow, you'd probably die, but those who got their gas masks on before they'd breathed in too much chlorine gas were usually all right.

- **Phosgene gas** wasn't as noticeable as chlorine, so it was less likely to cause coughing or vomiting. That meant men could breathe a lot more of it in before they even realised the gas was in the air. Phosgene could also kill with delayed action – men could die from phosgene poisoning a day or more after a gas attack.

The French certainly inflicted heavy losses on the Germans, but Falkenhayn's tactics still gave the Germans the upper hand for most of the battle. Historians can't know how close the French came to losing, though it certainly looked at points as if the Germans were about to break through the French lines. More forts fell to the Germans (though after putting up a huge resistance, unlike Fort Douaumont – see 'The German assault', earlier in the chapter), so now the French were determined to take them back, which meant the battle dragged on still further. Casualties on both sides were mounting higher and higher. How long could either side possibly keep the battle going?

The fighting at Verdun was so costly to the French that Joffre had to completely change his war plans for the rest of 1916. The Allies had agreed the previous year to launch a big French and British attack on the German positions along the River Somme (see the earlier section 'Chantilly – leaders and lace'). With the battle still raging at Verdun, however, it would be impossible for the French to send so many troops for the attack on the Somme. The British would have to take it over.

At the end of June, the British launched their own massive artillery attack on the German lines on the Somme (see 'Britain's End of Innocence: The Battle of the Somme', later in the chapter). Falkenhayn knew this Allied Big Push was coming, so he stopped sending reinforcements to Verdun and started strengthening his defences against the British farther north. The French retook the Verdun forts, and shortly before Christmas the Battle of Verdun finally petered out. It had lasted almost the whole year.

It is impossible to overstate the impact that the horror of Verdun had on the French: it was almost as if the country had been crucified. Not only did the losses severely weaken the French army, but the conditions had been so terrible that at times the French soldiers came close to breaking point. They were pleased that they'd stopped the Germans, but their morale wouldn't take too much more.

Farewell, Falkenhayn. Hello, Hindenburg!

Falkenhayn had enemies in politics and at court, and he knew that many in the German government would prefer to see Hindenburg in charge. He'd staked a lot on winning at Verdun, and was hoping that a victory in France would see off his critics, but Pétain defeated that plan. Then, in the summer, the Russians launched their own very successful offensive that completely broke through the Austro-Hungarian lines in the east. It looked as if Falkenhayn's plans had failed and his enemies closed in. On 29 August he bowed to the inevitable and resigned as Chief of the German General Staff. His arch-rival Hindenburg took over.

Erich von Falkenhayn

Falkenhayn's problem was that he was too clever. He was often able to analyse a problem in much greater depth than those around him; unfortunately, he never learned the knack of how to deal with people tactfully. He made powerful enemies, especially Hindenburg and Ludendorff, who just happened to be national heroes.

Falkenhayn was probably right to recognise Britain as Germany's most deadly enemy and to see that it might be possible to reach a deal with the Russians. In fact, in the end that's exactly what happened. But Falkenhayn never produced the breakthrough victory he kept promising, and the appalling losses at Verdun were too much for the German Chancellor, Bethmann Hollweg. Falkenhayn was replaced by Hindenburg and had to settle for commanding the armies fighting down in Romania (he actually did very well there, but Romania was a sideshow and Falkenhayn knew it – and so did everyone else).

Falkenhayn's fate illustrates an important point in any war: being intelligent, or even being right, isn't enough for success in war: you've got to have friends in high places – and you've got to win.

Britain's End of Innocence: The Battle of the Somme

To this day, the attack on the Somme, which began on 1 July 1916, remains one of the most controversial battles in British military history. Like Verdun, the Battle of the Somme is important for its symbolism as much as for its military value. People accuse the British generals of this battle of being butchers, throwing away their men's lives for no gain.

The overall British commander was General Sir Douglas Haig. It was he who agreed to take over responsibility for the Somme offensive when Joffre announced that, thanks to the German attack at Verdun, the French would no longer be able to lead it (see the earlier section, 'Bleeding France white'). A contingent of French troops still took part in the battle (and did very well), and the Allied lines also included troops from Newfoundland, Canada, New Zealand, Australia and South Africa, but the bulk of the Allied offensive was to be made up of those keen, excited British volunteers who'd responded to Kitchener's famous appeal for men back in 1914 (see Chapter 4 for details).

KEY PEOPLE

Sir Douglas Haig

Field Marshal Sir Douglas Haig is one of the most controversial British figures of the entire war. His critics (and he has a lot of critics) accuse him of sitting in his comfy chateau, throwing thousands of his own men's lives away in suicidal attacks. You can see some bitterly satirical attacks on Haig in the 1969 film *Oh! What a Lovely War* and the BBC TV series *Blackadder Goes Forth*. Some historians have called Haig a butcher and share the view of the German general at the time who's said to have described British troops as 'lions led by donkeys'. But is this fair?

Haig was surprisingly popular with his men (and soldiers tend not to like 'butcher' generals), and after the war he led the huge operation to raise money for wounded ex-servicemen by selling poppies. Many historians now defend Haig's tactics, pointing out the enormous difficulties he was working under and that he had good reasons for his decisions, even when some of them proved to be bad mistakes. When the Germans broke through the Allied lines in 1918, Haig proved an inspiring figure: he halted the German attack and went on to win one of the most crushing victories in British military history.

Reaching a conclusion about Haig that everyone agrees with is probably impossible, but we can agree that the caricature version is far too simplistic for understanding this complex and controversial man.

The Big Push begins

Recapturing the spirit of innocent excitement in which British soldiers went off to fight in the First World War isn't easy nowadays. Many of them thought of war as the sort of thrilling adventure they'd read about in the popular children's magazine, *The Boys' Own Paper*. They firmly believed that Britons were worth more than people of other countries and that all it needed was for plucky British lads to pull together in one 'Big Push' and the whole German war machine would come crashing down. The Biggest Push of all was to be the huge British attack on the Somme that, the British soldiers firmly believed, would soon wipe the smile off the Kaiser's face. From the generals in charge down to the ordinary Tommies in the army, everyone just *knew* that the battle would be a huge success. The idea that it might not be just didn't seem possible.

Kitchener's Army is on its way

By the time of the attack on the Somme, Britain's army had grown dramatically in numbers as a result of volunteers coming forward in response to Lord Kitchener's recruitment campaign (see Chapters 4 and 12). Many of these volunteers would still be going through their training in 1915, but by 1916 the men of this *New Army*, as it was called, were trained and ready to 'have a crack at the Hun'.

The soldiers of the New Army had tremendous enthusiasm. They came from all social classes, and many of them had enrolled with their friends and colleagues from work in what were known as *Pals' Battalions* (you can find more details about them in Chapter 4). Many of them had enjoyed their training, which was like a longer-than-usual gym class at school. Now they were looking forward to showing the Germans, and the world, just what good, stout-hearted Britons could do.

From their generals' point of view, however, the trouble with the New Army was that it was almost entirely inexperienced. Some professional units were stationed in the battle line, and a couple of experienced French units were on the extreme right wing, but otherwise almost the entire British line consisted of men going into battle for the very first time. That was a major headache for the British high command, because inexperienced troops were notorious for losing discipline on the battlefield: either they got overexcited and started running ahead of their units or, worse, they got scared and panicked. The best way to deal with this problem was to have a balance of old and new units, so the old timers could help steady the nerves of the rookies. But, unfortunately, the attack on the Somme was going to consist almost entirely of rookies. Taking this fact into account called for some very careful planning.

The best laid plans go awry: Heading for disaster

The British commander in charge of planning the attack on the Somme was General Sir Henry Rawlinson. Rawlinson originally wanted to launch a relatively small attack on a narrow front, but Haig insisted on a much bigger assault. It was going to be the biggest attack in the history of the British army.

Haig's insistence on launching such a huge attack wasn't necessarily a bad idea (the Russians did exactly the same later in the year and their attack worked very well indeed) but it created problems. It would mean co-ordinating attacks taking place over a very large area, and it also meant that, in order to break through such a long section of the German defences, the Allies would need many more shells and heavy guns than Haig had first realised.

Haig and Rawlinson *seemed* to have thought of everything for the attack on the Somme:

- ✔ **Artillery bombardment:** The British would flatten the German trenches with a massive artillery bombardment lasting a whole week. No one would be able to survive it: the Germans would all be dead long before the attack came.

- ✔ **Shrapnel:** The artillery would fire thousands of shrapnel shells that would cut the German barbed wire into shreds.

- ✔ **Mines:** The British would explode huge mines under the German lines just as the attack started, to kill any Germans who might have survived the bombardment.

- ✔ **Walk, don't run:** To guard against New Army troops getting too excited and running ahead, all troops would walk at a steady pace towards the German lines. This would be quite safe because the Germans would all be dead.

What, the British wondered, could possibly go wrong? Well, these things for a start:

- ✔ **The artillery bombardment was devastating, but it couldn't destroy the very deepest German dugouts.** Moreover, vast though it was (the sound of the big guns – see Figure 6-2 – could be heard as far away as London), it wasn't big enough for the huge area the Allies were attacking. In addition, because the British were shelling the German trenches, they didn't aim their shells at the German guns, so they would be ready and waiting to fire at the British as soon as the attack started.

Figure 6-2:
A British 15-inch howitzer ready for action on the first day of the Battle of the Somme. Howitzers fired shells high, so they were ideal for bombarding enemy positions.

© Imperial War Museums (Q 37)

- ✔ **Artillery, even firing shrapnel, can't destroy barbed wire.** Shrapnel can tangle up barbed wire even more, however, making it totally impenetrable. On the morning of the attack the British would find the German wire thick and uncut, and they hadn't prepared any way of dealing with that.

- **The massive artillery bombardment was a very good way of announcing to the Germans that the British were about to attack and showing them exactly where.** This attack might be a Big Push but it could hardly claim to be a surprise attack!

- **The artillery bombardment even told the Germans the exact time of the attack.** When the guns stopped, the Germans knew the attack would start soon afterwards, so that was when the Germans ran into position. One of the huge underground mines provided another clue: the British exploded it ten minutes before the attack so it could be filmed for the newsreels. The Germans had ten minutes to get ready.

- **When the Germans took to their deepest dugouts during the bombardment, they had their machine guns with them.** These machine guns survived the bombardment and would be ready and waiting for the British when the attack came.

The blackest day of the British army

The first day of the Battle of the Somme was a disaster and a tragedy. The British had massively miscalculated: the bombardment hadn't destroyed the Germans at all. As the British climbed out of their trenches and started to walk towards the German lines, the Germans got their machine guns into position and opened fire. The British, who were walking in long, stretched-out lines, just started falling like flies. The Germans couldn't quite believe what they were seeing. But they kept firing. The British were being cut down before they got anywhere near the German lines. Opposite the village of Beaumont Hamel, the Newfoundlanders were so keen to get into action they climbed out of their trenches even before they'd reached the British front line. The Germans machine-gunned them even before they made it into no-man's-land.

Some Allied troops did reach their objectives that day. The British Regulars (that is, the professional soldiers) on the Allied right wing managed to take German trenches, and the French took all their objectives. The South Africans managed to take and hold on to Delville Wood, despite being heavily out-gunned by the Germans and suffering appalling casualties. One of the most heroic actions of the day came from the Ulster division, which took a formidable German position called the Schwaben Redoubt. This success could have turned the day into a victory, but the British commanders stuck rigidly to the original plan and didn't send any reinforcements, so the Germans counter-attacked and took the position back again.

The Allied successes were too small to outweigh the appalling losses the British suffered across the rest of the battlefield. By the end of that first day, the British had suffered *60,000* casualties, including some 20,000 killed. The first day of the Battle of the Somme still remains the blackest day in the history of the British army.

Footballs at the front

One story often gets repeated about the attack on the Somme: how some British troops were kicking a football between them as they advanced. Can this be true? It can, and it is.

Captain Nevill of the East Surrey Regiment thought it would help calm his men's nerves if they had some footballs to kick. Unlike the generals, he knew the Germans' barbed wire was still intact and he didn't want his men to panic when they found out. He thought a bit of homely football would take the men's minds off what awaited them at the other side of no-man's-land. Believe it or not, the East Surreys somehow managed to get through the uncut wire and they took German trenches. At least one of the footballs survived the battle and is now in the regimental museum. Captain Nevill wasn't so lucky: he was killed trying to tackle that uncut German barbed wire he'd (rightly) been so worried about.

The British loved the story of the footballs and told it as an example of British pluck and courage under fire. The Germans told it too, but as an example of 'an English absurdity'. You could probably say that both sides had a point.

Learning the lessons

Despite the immense tragedy of the first day of the battle, Haig couldn't call the attack off: the French still desperately needed it to take some of the pressure off them at Verdun. However, some of the follow-up attacks were almost as disastrous as the 1 July attack. Later in July, British and Australian troops attacked farther north, opposite the town of Fromelles, to take the pressure off the Somme and, ideally, break through the German lines (you might be spotting a theme here) and head towards the city of Lille. The attack didn't break through and didn't get anywhere near Lille, but it still cost the Australians 5,500 men in just two days.

However, the British did start learning lessons from these disastrous attacks. In September, British troops launched a much more successful attack on the German lines and took the village of Thiepval, one of the original objectives of the 1 July attack. The British were applying some of the lessons they'd learned with so much difficulty in the summer:

- ✔ Use artillery to fire a creeping barrage ahead of the men so they can advance safely against the German lines (a *creeping barrage* was a line of shell burst carefully aimed to stay just ahead of the advancing infantry).

- ✔ Give more authority to the officers at the front; don't make them wait for orders from generals behind the lines.

- ✔ Use aircraft to keep commanders informed of how the attack is progressing.

These new tactics proved very successful, and the British would apply them in future battles too.

Fighting a war of attrition

Taking Thiepval was a major success for the British, but it still meant that, three months into the battle, they were only just taking the positions they'd been supposed to seize on the first day. Moreover, as the British took the German positions, the Germans just fell back to stronger positions they'd prepared. Instead of a Big Push that would break the German army, the British were losing thousands of lives just so they could capture a few hundred yards of land. So the generals started talking about the battle in a new way: as a battle of attrition.

If you've read 'A Struggle for Life and Death: The Battle of Verdun', earlier in the chapter, you've met this word *attrition* before. It was a new idea about how to fight a war. Instead of performing clever feats on the battlefield, outflanking the enemy or surrounding him and cutting him off from his base (you know, the sort of phrases you find in military history books), with attrition the idea was simply to kill as many of the enemy as possible. Inflicting the highest casualty rates usually meant shelling the enemy positions as heavily and unceasingly as possible. So the guns kept firing, until men on both sides began to go mad with the never-ending noise.

Up to a certain level, in wartime people accept heavy losses as the price they have to pay for victory. But at some point the losses get so great that the civilians, the politicians and even the generals start asking whether winning the war is worth losing so many men. When one side loses the will to win, it usually loses. Attrition was about trying to break the enemy's will to win. But it didn't work at Verdun and it didn't work on the Somme either.

Blood and mud

On 15 September 1916 the Germans on the Somme must have thought their worst nightmares had come true. Heading straight towards them were enormous monsters, crushing everything in their path and firing machine guns at the Germans. Two and a half months into the battle, the British desperately needed something to help them gain the upper hand, so they introduced the world to the tank. Unfortunately, they also introduced the world to the mechanical fault: although they helped in the successful attack on Thiepval (see the earlier section, 'Learning the lessons' above) most of the tanks broke down and made easy targets for German artillery. The first tank assault in history was a failure, but others would undoubtedly follow.

The idea for tanks came from the caterpillar tracks that American farmers used on their tractors to help them deal with muddy and uneven ground. Winston Churchill took up the idea and commissioned a fleet of what he called 'land ships' (he was First Lord of the Admiralty, so he thought in naval terms at this point). The word *tanks,* as in water tanks, was used to keep the new weapon secret, though it became the word that was eventually used for them. The earliest tanks had machine guns and small cannons at their sides, they sometimes carried large bundles of rods to fill any really deep ditches, and they could reach a top speed – on a good day – of about 7 miles per hour. Although their first outing, on the Somme, was a failure, the British soon learned to use them properly, in force and in full working order, and the Germans were quick to copy with tanks of their own.

By the autumn of 1916 the British and French had moved the German line back about five miles, but they still hadn't taken the towns like Bapaume and Peronne that they'd originally hoped to re-take on the first day in July, and so the battle continued. And then, in the autumn, it rained. The ground was already so thickly churned up by the shelling that the terrain quickly turned to thick, liquid mud, deep enough to drown in. But still the British kept launching attacks, gaining no more than a few hundred yards here or there, until finally, in November, with snow on the way, the battle petered out. The attacks stopped and the sector finally fell quiet. The Allies had succeeded in pushing the Germans back some 7 miles but at a fearsome cost. By the time the battle ended, the British had lost 400,000 men, the French 200,000 and the Germans at least 500,000.

Some historians argue that the British never really recovered from the shock of the Somme. It wasn't just that the losses on the first day were so appalling: the British began to lose faith in the leaders and even in the society that had sent them into such a nightmare in the first place. It could even be said that Victorian Britain died on the Somme and a more cynical, less idealistic modern Britain was born there.

In the more immediate term, though, the losses on the Somme showed that the British rethink of their army recruitment and training procedures had been necessary. Recruiting men from the same communities to form Pals' Battalions (see Chapter 7) might have seemed a good idea at first, but it had a terrible effect on the communities at home when they learned that all their young men had been killed in one disastrous attack. In March 1916 Britain had finally bitten the bullet and introduced conscription for the first time in British history: New Zealand did the same and Australia only just decided against it. The Germans had some rethinking to do, too – the battle had cost them huge numbers of experienced men that they needed to train and lead their new recruits.

Italy's slow snowy slog

The Italian contribution to the Allied offensives of 1916 was an assault on the Austro-Hungarian positions along the River Isonzo. Time and again the Italians hurled themselves against the enemy, but the Austrians beat them back each time. The Italian high command took out their frustrations on their men: any Italian who even looked as if he wasn't pulling his weight was liable to be shot. It did no good – by the end of the year the Italians had still not broken through and they'd lost thousands of men in a series of disastrous avalanches too.

The Eastern Front: Hopes Raised, then Dashed

If the Allies' plans in the west were coming unstuck, the picture looked much more hopeful for them on the Eastern Front. The Russians launched a huge and very successful attack and another country – Romania – joined the Allied side. But the Germans struck back and by the end of the year the situation on the Eastern Front was even worse for the Allies than the situation in the west.

The Russians' last hurrah

Contrary to all expectations, of all the big attacks planned back in Chantilly for 1916, the only one that achieved all its aims was launched by the Russians (see Figure 4 in the insert section). In June 1916 General Alexei Brusilov (see Figure 6-3) launched a huge attack on the Austro-Hungarian army in the Carpathian Mountains that achieved the seemingly impossible: it broke through the enemy's trenches and out into the countryside beyond.

Brusilov's thinking was simple. He knew that most offensives are launched on a narrow front, so as to 'punch' through the enemy line, but they fail for two reasons:

- ✔ The artillery bombardment before an attack rather gives the game away.
- ✔ The enemy can rush fresh reinforcements up to where they're needed just when the attackers are at their most exhausted.

So Brusilov reasoned that his attack should

- ✔ Hit the enemy over a wide area, not a narrow one, so the reinforcements didn't know where to go.
- ✔ Dispense with the preliminary bombardment – just run at the enemy lines.

© Imperial War Museums (Q 54534)

Figure 6-3:
General Alexei Brusilov – one of the best generals of the war.

Brusilov's plan worked brilliantly: it was one of the most successful attacks of the war (*the* most successful when it was launched). The Austro-Hungarians were left reeling and their humiliation encouraged the different peoples of their empire to start planning to overthrow their Habsburg masters and set up their own states. Unfortunately, the Russian supply system simply couldn't keep up with Brusilov's advance and the attack petered out. So in the end, even a successful offensive achieved nothing – and cost both sides about half a million men.

Romania joins in – and gets crushed

The successful Brusilov offensive persuaded Romania to enter the war on the Allied side. The Romanians had their own 'Alsace-Lorraine' situation: Hungary had taken over Transylvania and the Romanians wanted it for themselves. Unfortunately for them, the Romanian army simply wasn't equipped or in any way ready for the storm that descended on them.

In the winter of 1916, the Germans, Austrians, Hungarians and Bulgarians – with Falkenhayn in command (see Figure 6-4), alongside von Mackensen, one of Germany's most successful generals – attacked Romania from all directions. By 6 December Bucharest, Romania's capital, fell to the Germans: apart from some sporadic fighting, Romania was out of the war. The one consolation for the Allies was that the British had managed to destroy many of Romania's oil wells before the Germans and Austro-Hungarians got hold of them.

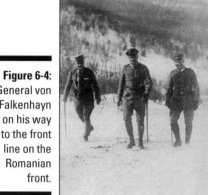

Figure 6-4:
General von Falkenhayn on his way to the front line on the Romanian front.

© Imperial War Museums (Q 24008)

Any news from Salonika? No, I thought not

A French and British force had been sitting around in Salonika in northern Greece achieving precisely nothing since 1915. Under the Chantilly Plan, they were supposed to launch an attack on Bulgaria in conjunction with the Romanians, but the Romanians launched an attack on Hungary instead. By the end of 1916 the French and British were *still* sitting around in Salonika — achieving precisely nothing.

Part III
A World at War

© Imperial War Museums (CO 2215)

For a bonus article that asks who was to blame for the world being at war, go to
www.dummies.com/extras/firstworldwar.

In this part...

- ✔ Head offshore and to the skies to see how technology transformed the war and led to it being the first to be fought both at sea and in the air.

- ✔ Go underground and get an understanding of what trench warfare was really like for the soldiers who lived, suffered, fought and died there.

- ✔ Grasp how the war was fought all over the globe, from the Indian Ocean to the South Atlantic, from the heart of Africa to the heat and dust of Iraq and Palestine, and even right out in the middle of the Atlantic.

- ✔ Watch the world change irreversibly as Europe's problems force America to come out of its shell and start playing a big role on the world stage.

Chapter 7

Welcome to the World of the Trenches

*W*hen soldiers in the First World War went home on leave, they often found that they couldn't talk about life at the front: the world of the trenches was so different from anything civilians, or even old soldiers, had experienced that it wasn't worth even trying to describe it. They could only talk about it with other people who'd been there.

The world of the trenches was what made the First World War different from any war before or since. Nothing in the men's training or experience could prepare them for the world that awaited them at the front. At its worst, trench warfare produced battered and barren landscapes that looked like the surface of the moon, or else the guns churned rain-sodden ground into thick mud deep enough to drown in. But the trenches also created a strong sense of camaraderie among the men who lived there – even between soldiers on different sides. Elsewhere in this book I concentrate on the generals and leaders who took the big decisions about who to fight and where, but in this chapter I introduce you to the ordinary men who fought in the trenches and give you a guided tour of their world.

The last survivors of the First World War trenches died as recently as the 2000s, and it's a safe bet that many people reading this book have an ancestor who served their country in the trenches. These men's story is part of your own.

Negotiating the Trenches of the Western Front

Soldiers arriving at the Western Front – on either side – usually spent a few weeks in a training camp familiarising themselves with the conditions in which they'd be fighting before being sent up the line to the Front. They needed a period of acclimatising themselves because trench warfare was so different to anything that any soldiers had seen before. Men still needed to know how to attack across a battlefield and how to shoot straight, but much of their drill sergeants' previous experience of warfare was irrelevant to conditions in the trenches.

Navigating state-of-the-art trench systems

Trenches were dug in all the European theatres of war, but they were most extensive on the Western Front. The enormous line of opposing trenches that formed the Western Front stretched all the way from Switzerland to the English Channel (see Chapter 4 to find out how this situation came about), running through farmland, woodland and villages, and even over mountains. The sector of the line manned by British, Empire and Belgian troops lay in northern France and a small corner of Belgium around the town of Ypres; the rest was in French hands. Portuguese troops also served on the Western Front. In 1918 large numbers of American troops arrived, though by then the war had moved out of the trenches and become a war of movement again (Chapter 16 explains why). Ranged against these Allied troops, for the full length of the Front, were the Germans.

The area between the two lines of trenches was known as *no-man's-land,* because no one could claim to control it. Sometimes no-man's-land was quite wide, but in some sections the two lines of trenches were so close that the troops could hear each other's conversations. In one sector the two sides actually shared a single line of barbed wire and took turns to check it for any damage!

The Western Front was more than just two continuous trenches facing each other, though; a whole trench system existed behind both (see Figure 7-1). A *trench system* usually consisted of two or three parallel lines of trenches, with communications trenches running at right angles between them. Communications trenches ran right to the rear, which was where men entered the trench system. Communications trenches could get badly crowded, especially when men were gathering for an attack.

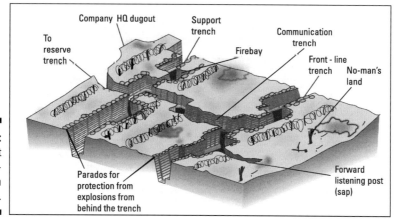

Figure 7-1:
The layout of a typical trench system.

Company HQ dugout — Support trench — Communication trench — To reserve trench — Firebay — Front-line trench — No-man's land — Parados for protection from explosions from behind the trench — Forward listening post (sap)

Trenches were built in a zigzag pattern, like the battlements of a castle, so that the men always had corners to hide around should the enemy get into the trench. Zigzag trenches were also less likely to collapse if a shell hit them. However, zigzags made it easy to get lost, so trenches usually had plenty of signs pointing the way to different parts of the front line. The soldiers used to give names to different parts of their trench system, such as Hyde Park Corner or Piccadilly Circus, which helped them to orientate themselves and gave them a little touch of home.

The trenches also had to be deep enough to protect the men in them, so you needed to stand on a *firestep* if you wanted to fire your rifle at the enemy. Deeper down into the earth were the *dugouts,* which were like underground rooms where the troops could spend their time when they weren't on duty. The best trenches (which tended to be the German ones) were lined with wooden planks and had solid wooden floors; most British trenches had to make do with wooden *duckboards* (slatted wooden boards) to walk on.

In front of the trenches lay a long line of barbed wire – not just a few strands, as you might see today around a sheep pen: First World War barbed wire was made up of several strands, held up by long metal pegs stuck into the ground. The idea was that any attacker would have a real job trying to cut through the wire and might easily get stuck on it, making him an easy target for the defenders to fire at. Barbed wire was supposed to hinder the enemy, but it could also be fatal to its own side. When troops gathered for an attack, they had to get through their own barbed wire first, so they'd cut a passage through it. But that meant that the enemy machine gunners just needed to aim at any gap they spotted in the wire to decimate the attacking force before it even left its own lines.

Special Delivery – the army postal service

If you're tempted to think the British military authorities in the First World War couldn't organise their way out of a paper bag, spare a thought for one of the most important services an army can provide: the postal service. Soldiers were always desperate for news from home and not receiving letters from their families and sweethearts could have a very bad effect on morale, so the army went to great pains to ensure an efficient postal service. Letters and parcels were delivered regularly even to men in the front-line trenches, within one or at most two days of being posted from any part of the British Isles. The British First World War postal service was every bit as good as the postal and delivery service today.

Keeping the trench lines supplied was a major operation. Electricity supplies were needed for lights and telephones, as was a constant supply of food, equipment and ammunition for the soldiers. Getting supplies through to where they were needed wasn't the most glamorous job in the army, but it was absolutely vital. The men who supplied and supported the front-line troops came from all over Britain's Empire, including many from the British West Indies and a Chinese Labour Corps. Their essential contribution to the war needs to be remembered.

Smoking can seriously damage your health. No, seriously

When in their trenches, the soldiers were below ground level, so they were protected from rifle and machine gun fire, if not from shells. But to attack the enemy and advance, soldiers had to show themselves above the parapet (going 'over the top', as it was called). Even just putting your head above the trench parapet, however, whether to fire your rifle or just to have a look at what was going on, was extremely dangerous: a sniper could hit you within a split second. It was much safer to use a periscope; some rifles even had clever devices so you could fire them from down in the trench using a periscope to aim them and a complicated bit of mechanism to pull the trigger.

From the outset of the war, so many men suffered head injuries from being shot when putting their heads above the parapet that in 1915 the French authorities issued their soldiers with steel helmets; the British followed suit in 1916. In the same year, the Germans dropped their decorative pointed *Pickelhaube* helmets in favour of the more practical 'coal scuttle' helmets that were to become very familiar in the Second World War. Steel helmets offered protection against the effects of artillery, but unless they were heavily reinforced (which made them very heavy to wear) they offered little protection against a direct hit from a sniper.

It's a Long Way to Tipperary

Some of the songs the soldiers sang as they marched are still familiar today, such as 'It's a Long Way to Tipperary' and 'Pack Up Your Troubles in Your Old Kit Bag'. The military authorities liked to see images of the men marching along smiling and singing cheerful songs like these: it made very good copy for the newspapers back home. These songs also became very popular with the French and even the Germans! Equally, British Tommies picked up some French songs, such as 'Alouette', and took them back home.

Not all the Tommies' songs were quite so cheerful, however. As the war dragged on, the men would take popular tunes or hymns and give them more cynical words, such as 'Far Far from Wipers I Long to Be' and 'I Don't Want to Be a Soldier'. Of course, some of the most popular songs weren't about the war at all, but concerned the men's imaginative plans for various young ladies of their acquaintance, which couldn't be printed at the time and can't be printed here either.

Going over the top was dangerous enough, but soldiers usually had to carry heavy packs on their backs as well as their weapons. Imagine running a cross-country race with a heavy rucksack on your back and you have an idea of what these men had to do (and that's without people firing at you!). Enemy snipers often used to aim first at the officers: they were easy to spot because they tended to carry pistols rather than rifles and usually didn't have a heavy pack to carry.

Even after darkness fell on a battlefield, the trenches were a dangerous place to be. The enemy might send up a flare that would light up the whole area, allowing his snipers to pick off men who'd been hidden in the dark. Even smoking in your own trench could be dangerous.

Smoking was fashionable at the time and many men found it calmed their nerves. (In those days many doctors even recommended smoking, saying it was good for the lungs!) However, soldiers who lit up after dark had to be very careful: at the first drag on the cigarette the enemy sniper might see you; when you took a second drag, he'd take aim; when you took a third, he'd fire. For years afterwards men who'd been in the trenches would only take two drags on a cigarette before throwing it away.

The dangers of rain and mud

One of the most deadly enemies the men in the trenches faced was rain. If trenches weren't properly drained – and most of them weren't – the men found themselves standing for months on end ankle-deep in water. They often developed a very nasty fungal condition called *trench foot*, which caused the foot to swell and blister and, if untreated, could develop into gangrene. In the worst cases, the foot had to be amputated. To try to catch cases before they became serious, officers undertook regular foot inspections, looking carefully at their men's naked feet for bad sores, blisters or signs of decay. It probably wasn't the sort of glamorous leadership role many young cadets had in mind when they joined up (and it can't have been what the men were expecting either), but it was a vital task if the troops were to be kept fit and in fighting condition.

Heavy rain – and the First World War saw some very heavy rain – could turn a battlefield into a swamp, especially when it was being churned up by constant shelling. The mud sometimes got so deep that men who fell into it drowned and the only way to cross it was on wooden duckboards. Horses couldn't move in it and guns sank into it, and even if they could fire their shells sank, which seriously reduced their effectiveness. Whole battles got bogged down in the thick mud of the Western Front, such as the later stages of the Battle of the Somme in 1916 and the Battle of Passchendaele in 1917 (see Chapters 6 and 15). Pictures of men in a wasteland of mud from battles such as these have become some of the most familiar iconic images of the war (see Figure 7-2).

Figure 7-2: Canadian stretcher-bearers coping with the thick mud at Passchendaele in 1917.

© Imperial War Museums (CO 2215)

No pets allowed – except lice and rats

A trench, even one with wooden walls and walkways, is basically a ditch in a field, and it's no surprise that the trenches were soon overrun with unwelcome wildlife. Unpleasant as it was for them at first, the men soon got used to having lice in their hair, though it came as quite a shock to civilians when the men came home on leave and inadvertently deposited their little companions on the furniture.

The trenches were home to plenty of rats too, and the men used to enjoy hunting them when they'd nothing better to do, which was often.

The bore war

Many people imagine that army life is all made up of action, and that's certainly how many volunteers imagined it when they joined up in 1914. What they found, however, was that most of the time they spent in the trenches was actually rather boring. They weren't being shelled or gassed or shot at or sent over the top *all the time*.

Unless they were sent to a hotspot such as Ypres, where the shelling was pretty much constant, most soldiers could expect to pass most of their time in a quiet sector of the line where nothing much was happening. In these sectors life might consist of long periods on duty in the trenches, waiting and watching in case anything happened. To liven things up and keep the men on their toes, the officers would often order a patrol into no-man's-land or a raid on the enemy trenches (see the later 'How to raid your enemy's trench' section for some idea of what these raids entailed).

When off duty, the men could take time out behind the lines, visiting the nearest towns that weren't in ruins, and going to cafes or bars. Ordinary life had to go on too: the men had meals to cook, clothes to wash, and letters to read and write. Life in the trenches became a strange balance between periods of danger and suffering and a sort of extended weekend away.

In quiet sectors of the front, the two sides would shout out the occasional jokes to each other, fire a few shots from time to time (often at a set time so everyone knew to take cover) and generally carry on with things until orders arrived to get ready for an attack (life quickly became a lot less boring then).

How quiet your sector of the line would be depended on which enemy troops you were up against. All armies contained some regiments that got a reputation for being fairly easy-going; others were more hard-nosed. The Allied troops were always pleased to have the Bavarians facing them from the German trenches, because the Bavarians were happy to live and let live; Prussian regiments, on the other hand, were more aggressive. At the time of the Christmas Truce in 1914 (see Chapter 4), British and German soldiers met in the middle of no-man's-land and played football, but some of the Scottish regiments were less inclined to fraternise with the men who'd been shelling them for the past four months and kept the fighting going, Christmas or no Christmas.

The Wipers Times

The British trenches around the town of Ypres (which the British Tommies used to call 'Wipers') produced one of the most remarkable pieces of writing of the war. Lieutenant Colonel 'Fred' Roberts was a highly professional soldier, who won the Military Cross for bravery, but who also possessed an acute sense of humour. When he and his men stumbled across an abandoned printing press he started up *The Wipers Times,* a light-heartedly satirical newspaper distributed among the men, with spoof adverts and articles based on the reality of trench life. Hill 60, for example, a desolate hill near Ypres that was blasted into a vast crater by a British mine, was advertised as a suitably 'bright, breezy, invigorating' destination for a daytrip, commanding 'an excellent view of the historic town of Ypres'. The paper also offered advice on how soldiers could cure themselves of the terrible scourge of Optimism.

Roberts didn't have much success as a journalist after the war, but *The Wipers Times* is a little literary masterpiece from the trenches and perhaps the most authentic voice of the First World War soldiers that exists.

Getting Out of the Trench Trap

The trench warfare of the Western Front posed some very difficult questions for the soldiers on both sides. Throughout the history of warfare armies had had to attack heavily fortified positions, and doing so often meant taking heavy losses, but it was still usually possible for the attackers to win in the end. But an unbroken line of trenches like the Western Front was simply without precedent: nothing quite like it had ever happened before. So the generals had to experiment and try out new tactics and new technology – *anything* that would allow their men to break through the enemy lines so they could all start fighting properly again.

How to raid your enemy's trench

In between the big battles (Chapter 6 tells you about some of those) the men on the Western Front sometimes launched raids on the enemy's trench, usually in order to take a few prisoners and get information from them. Here's what the men who carried out these daring raids were told to do:

1. **Launch your raid at night. And avoid moonlit nights.**

   Just be aware that raiding at night also increases the likelihood of men on your own side shooting each other by mistake in the dark.

2. **Don't take heavy packs on your backs.**

   Keep those for major offensives. On a raid, you might need to crawl under the wire.

3. **Use grenades to clear enemy dugouts and keep track of how many you've thrown.**

   Don't throw two grenades and go in after the first explosion. Remember the second one!

4. **Have some spiked clubs and knives handy – trenches may be too cramped for using your rifle and bayonet.**

   Some of the weapons you may need to use in trench fighting might not have looked out of place on a medieval battlefield, but they have their uses.

5. **Don't forget to take some prisoners.**

   It would defeat the whole point of the raid if you just shot every enemy you met!

Raids such as these could provide valuable information about how the enemy was deploying his troops and what his plans might be. Raiders might even be lucky enough to seize some enemy plans or instructions. All this information would be fed back to headquarters, where it could help the generals plan much bigger attacks on the enemy's line.

How to attack your enemy's line

The generals on both sides of the war spent most of their time trying to crack the conundrum of how to successfully attack the enemy line. The heavy casualties of the 1916 battles at Verdun and on the Somme (see Chapter 6) showed what could happen if they got this wrong.

Here are some of the most common tactics employed on the Western Front:

1. **Use aircraft spotters to pinpoint where the enemy guns and defences are.**

   Properly used, air reconnaissance could make all the difference between a successful attack and a failure. As long as your pilots didn't get shot down, of course.

2. **Begin the attack with a heavy preliminary bombardment of the enemy lines.**

   Most generals thought this was essential in order to weaken the enemy defences and give the attacking *infantry* – the soldiers advancing on foot – a chance. Unfortunately, even the heaviest bombardments had several weaknesses:

   • Shelling couldn't destroy the very deepest dugouts, which is where the enemy sheltered.

   • Shelling couldn't destroy barbed wire.

- Huge numbers of shells – perhaps as many as a third – turned out to be duds.

- Many shells landed in soft, muddy ground, where their impact was much reduced (even though the explosions looked impressive on film).

- Too many shells were *shrapnel*, which was designed to hit people, rather than *high explosives*, which would blow up enemy positions.

- Too many shells were aimed at the enemy trenches rather than at the enemy's guns, which posed the real threat to the attack.

- To be effective, *artillery* – that is, heavy guns – needed to be heavily concentrated against relatively small stretches of the enemy line. Big attacks, such as the Somme, simply didn't have enough guns for the huge area they covered.

3. **Gather your troops for the attack as quietly and discreetly as possible.**

   The most deadly enemy wasn't in fact enemy machine guns aimed at advancing troops, but enemy shelling of forward trenches that were densely packed with troops waiting to go over the top.

4. **Send the troops over the top at a precise time. And tell them to walk, not run.**

   Telling the men to walk wasn't as crazy as it might sound. If men ran, they could end up at the enemy line all at different times, and it would be easy for the enemy to pick them off individually. Going forwards at a steady pace was the best way to ensure the whole attacking line arrived together, with maximum impact.

5. **Use gas to cover your attack.**

   Just make sure the wind isn't blowing the gas back into your own trenches.

6. **As soon as your men have taken their objectives, send the second wave in fast.**

   Don't forget that the enemy might have fallen back to a much stronger position that you probably won't have shelled, so your second wave could still be as vulnerable as the first.

Going underground

Both sides sometimes used a deadly variant on the usual preliminary bombardment: they planted mines deep underneath the enemy's trenches. The British did this at the opening of the Battle of the Somme, and in 1917 mines were crucial to the successful British attack at Messines (the details are in Chapter 15).

Battlefield ghosts

Many stories circulated among the troops of the First World War of strange supernatural sights that soldiers swore they'd seen. Some reported seeing whole troops of phantom cavalry riding alongside them, while other stories told of units disappearing into mysterious clouds and never being seen again. One tale that was widely told was of a mysterious figure all in white who appeared on the battlefield and tended to wounded soldiers and, miraculously, was never hit himself, however fierce the fighting might be. Some even thought it was Jesus Christ himself, though most historians nowadays think it was more likely to be a bit of wishful thinking on the part of badly wounded men.

Digging mines under the enemy lines was nothing new: mines had been used to great effect in the American Civil War. However, the mines of the First World War were bigger and more devastating than any that had been used before.

Digging and planting these mines was the job of the *tunnellers,* men recruited from the coalfields to dig tunnels deep under no-man's-land and beneath the other side's front line. The work was difficult and dangerous and had to be carried out as quietly as possible, because each side knew what the other was up to and had listening devices to pick up the sound of digging. Sometimes British and German tunnellers were digging within a few feet of each other; sometimes their tunnels even met and the men had to fight it out underground. Even if they managed to dig their way to the correct position, they had to carry the explosives there without any going off prematurely.

The tunnellers had one of the toughest and most dangerous jobs in the entire Western Front and they knew it. They tended to be more independently minded and less respectful of authority than other soldiers, and most Tommies learned to treat them with respect – and some caution.

Dealing with Men Who Couldn't – or Wouldn't – Fight

The First World War saw a huge number of casualties: the maimed, the wounded, the psychologically scarred and the dead. Medical personnel were often overwhelmed by the numbers of casualties they were dealing with. As well as casualties of the fighting, armies also had to deal with men whose will to carry on snapped under the pressure of the trenches. Sometimes the effects of living under constant bombardment drove men mad, but sometimes they were only too sane and had simply had enough of the conditions in which they were expected to live. Armies also had to deal with soldiers from the other side who gave up and surrendered.

Tending to wounds and the wounded

When men were wounded, they were taken to a *casualty clearing station,* normally positioned near a railway station behind the front lines. The surgeons there would deal with any lightly wounded, so that they could go back to the front line quickly; more serious cases were sent by rail or road to the military hospitals farther behind the lines or else back in the home country (see Figure 5 in the insert section).

During the First World War military medical services adopted the *triage* system, dividing the wounded into three groups:

✔ Those who would be able to recover, given treatment and time

✔ Those who were permanently wounded and wouldn't be able to fight again (men who'd lost limbs, for example, fell into this category)

✔ Those who were too badly wounded to be saved

What about trenches on the other fronts?

Some people in western countries think the whole war was fought on the Western Front, but in fact men endured similarly terrible conditions of trench warfare on the other fronts, too.

Russian, Austrian and German soldiers fighting on the Eastern Front also endured long periods of trench warfare, though their trenches there were never quite as extensive or permanent as the ones in France and Belgium. The Russians suffered particularly badly because their supply system was so poor that conditions in their trenches rarely matched those enjoyed in the west. In the Alps, in what became known as *the White War* because of the extensive snow, the Italians and Austrians faced each other with each side dug into the mountainside. It was a deadly form of warfare: artillery shells killed many more people than on the Western Front, because they were exploding directly onto rock rather than burying themselves in mud, which shells fired on the Western Front often did. The fighting at Gallipoli (see Chapter 9) quickly got bogged down in trenches; the Australians and New Zealanders found themselves cooped up in trenches that were virtually dug into a cliff. The Salonika front in northern Greece was another example of static warfare: the Allies were hemmed in and not able to move out until right at the end of the war.

The only theatre of war that largely escaped the horrors of trench warfare was the fighting in the Middle East, which was much more of a war of movement.

Men in the first two categories were sent on to hospital; men in the third were quietly left on one side to die.

Many soldiers quite liked the idea of being sent home as a casualty. British soldiers used to refer to it as getting a 'blighty wound' (*blighty* was a word picked up by British soldiers in India meaning 'home', and soldiers in the trenches used it to refer to Britain). Sometimes soldiers deliberately wounded themselves, hoping to get shipped home, but this was a dangerous game: the punishment for deliberate wounding was severe (see the later section 'Dealing with mutineers and deserters'). The French, in particular, were ruthless in having anyone who deserted or tried to maim himself shot.

Those who died were buried behind the lines, often in huge pits – when their bodies were recovered, that is: thousands of men from all armies were killed but their bodies were never recovered, or else they were so blown to pieces that they couldn't be identified. These men were officially listed as 'missing', though everyone knew that usually meant 'dead'. (I deal with the way the dead were buried and the memorials that were put up to honour them in Chapter 18.)

Mending minds

One area of medicine where big advances were made in the First World War was in psychiatric care. The terrible shelling on the battlefields badly shook the nerves of many soldiers and they developed psychiatric symptoms of what nowadays is recognised as post-traumatic stress disorder but which in those days was called *shell shock*. At first many officers thought the men were just being cowards, but gradually people understood more about the psychological impact of exposure to prolonged periods of heavy shelling.

At Craiglockhart Hospital near Edinburgh a pioneering military doctor, Captain William Rivers, developed a 'talking cure' for his patients. As well as being given the opportunity for sport or hobbies, they were encouraged to talk openly about their feelings and fears as a way of overcoming them. Greater understanding of psychological trauma was one of the most important medical advances of the war.

Dealing with mutineers and deserters

It can be difficult nowadays to understand why so many young men went off to war so eagerly in 1914, but it can be even more difficult to understand how they were able to put up with conditions in the trenches for so long without doing something to protest.

Soldiers often went off to war full of belief in their country and its cause, but this sort of patriotism often changed subtly when they arrived at the front. There, they often forged strong bonds with the other men in their units, and if you asked them why they were fighting, they'd have said they were fighting mainly for their pals: you look out for your comrade-in-arms and he looks out for you. Some soldiers retained a sense of what the war was meant to be about, but many, in all armies, sat in the trenches and obeyed orders because that's where they were and what they were there to do. (As one British song put it, sung to the tune of 'Auld Lang Syne', 'We're 'ere because we're 'ere, because we're 'ere because we're 'ere . . . '.) Ultimately, though, some soldiers were driven to desert or mutiny.

I've had enough of this for a game of soldiers

Sometimes, even looking out for his pals wasn't enough to keep a soldier in his post: thousands of men *deserted* (that is, ran away). In all armies, the punishment for desertion in the face of the enemy was death, so men had to have a pretty good reason for undertaking such a risky and dangerous act. Sometimes, they'd just had enough of conditions in the trenches and wanted to go home: after all, if they stayed in the trenches they'd probably get killed anyway, so it must have seemed worth the risk. Sometimes, soldiers with impeccable records of good service simply couldn't take any more and snapped mentally.

Sometimes, men got lost on the battlefield and ended up a long distance from their units: doing this could also get you accused of being a deserter.

Mutiny!

Mutiny is an even more serious military offence than desertion. *Mutiny* is the deliberate defiance of military order and rejection of military authority, and it's almost always punishable by death.

Almost every army of the Great Powers in the war rose in mutiny at some point during the war: the major exception was the British army. (The Americans didn't face mutiny either, but they were involved in fighting only in the final months of the war.) A riot did break out at the main British transit camp at Etaples in 1917, but it was a protest about conditions at a nearby training camp, not about conditions in the trenches, and it was soon put down. But after a major offensive had gone disastrously wrong in 1917, the French army mutinied. They'd defend their trenches against the Germans, the soldiers said, but they absolutely refused to take part in any more badly-planned attacks. By the end of 1918, German and Austrian soldiers felt the same: they weren't going to risk their lives in more attacks to support what they could see by then was a lost cause.

Probably the most serious outbreaks of mutiny came in the Russian army during 1916. The Russians had suffered appallingly in the war, and much of their hardships had been the result of their own leaders' incompetence and callous attitude towards them. By 1916, the Russians were deserting in their thousands: whole units just got out of their trenches and headed home. These mutinies were very dangerous: the soldiers would simply kill any officer who tried to stop them. The mutinies in the Russian army were a symptom of the revolution that would break out in 1917.

Sentenced to death

Armies had some very severe punishments for men who broke the rules. In the British army in particular, punishments were quite antiquated. Flogging had long been abolished, but soldiers who were found guilty of minor misdemeanours, such as being drunk or asleep on duty, could be given Field Punishment No. 1, which meant being tied to an upright post or wheel for two hours a day (usually, an hour in the morning and another hour in the evening), sometimes – or so it has been alleged – within range of enemy fire. More serious offences in all armies, such as striking an officer, deliberately wounding yourself (including deliberately allowing yourself to be wounded by the enemy) or desertion, were punishable by death.

Military offences are tried by a special military court known as a *court martial.* A panel of senior officers acts as judge (there's no jury) and officers, usually with a background in the law, present the case for the prosecution and the defence. The courts martial of the First World War were supposed to judge cases by the evidence, but they were run by serving officers who also had to bear general army discipline in mind when they decided on a defendant's guilt or innocence, and on what sentence to impose. A few executions were often thought to be a good way to concentrate men's minds on their duty, something for which the French and Italian armies were particularly notorious.

Executions ordered by courts martial were usually carried out by firing squad. Soldiers never liked taking part in firing squads, especially when, as sometimes happened, the prisoner was suffering from shellshock or had just got too scared to know what he was doing. One of the firing squad rifles was always loaded with a blank, so each man could think he hadn't killed the prisoner, though a real bullet gave much more of a kickback against the shoulder, so the men usually knew.

Sometimes a death sentence was suspended, which meant that the man went back to the front line but if he committed any further offences, however minor, the death sentence would be enacted. That way he could still fight but he was unlikely to cause any more trouble. Rather than face a firing squad, many deserters preferred to try to get themselves taken prisoner by the Germans (and German deserters did the same).

No prisoners?

The *Geneva Convention,* the internationally agreed set of rules for conducting warfare, was quite clear on how prisoners should be treated: as soon as a soldier laid down his arms and gave himself up to the enemy he was a prisoner of war, and should be treated properly. That, at least, was the theory. In reality, if you surrendered on the battlefield you were quite likely to get shot: soldiers of all armies reckoned that shooting prisoners was a lot less trouble than having to keep an eye on them and get them back behind the lines in one piece. And if anyone asked awkward questions, you could always claim they'd been trying to escape.

Shooting prisoners wasn't just against international law: it may even have prolonged the war. Soldiers were much more likely to fight on when they thought they'd be shot if they surrendered: this may help to explain why no mass surrenders took place on either side even after terrible battles such as Verdun or Passchendaele (see Chapters 6 and 15). On the other hand, when the German army started to collapse at the end of the war (see Chapter 16), the fact that the first Germans to surrender were properly treated encouraged other Germans to surrender too.

Chapter 8

War at Sea, War in the Air

T he First World War was the first war in history to be fought both in the air and under the sea. It saw one of the biggest naval battles in history, the first widespread use of submarines and the first use of airpower at sea. Air technology in particular was transformed by the war, and in this chapter you meet the first men to become famous for their exploits in fighter aircraft – and see how these campaigns in the air and out at sea contributed to the final outcome of the war.

Sea Power = Great Power: Ruling the Waves

Back in 1890 the American Admiral AT Mahan wrote a book called *The Influence of Sea Power Upon History,* which considered Britain's long war with Napoleonic France, when the French had controlled all of mainland Europe but Britain had controlled all the seas around it. Mahan concluded that mastery of the sea was the key to a nation's economic and political prowess, and that a naval power like Britain would always be able to defeat any country, however powerful, that had only military power on land. Many people agreed with him.

Ever since the days of Admiral Lord Nelson and his famous 1805 victory over the French at Trafalgar in the Napoleonic wars, the British had controlled the world's oceans and prided themselves on their naval power. In the years leading up to the First World War, Britain was *the* dominant sea power and, under the dynamic First Sea Lord Sir John 'Jacky' Fisher, the British had been ditching their old wooden battleships and adopting the very latest in ironclad

Alfred von Tirpitz

Alfred von Tirpitz was a career naval officer, committed to building up Germany's sea power so that it could challenge the British. He had to be a politician too: the Germany army resented the huge sums being spent on expanding the navy and Tirpitz needed every bit of political support from the Kaiser that he could get. When the war started, however, Tirpitz switched from supporting big battleships to promoting the use of the submarine. He was determined to wage unrestricted U-boat warfare against the British and he hated the political considerations that sometimes got in the way. He stepped down as head of the German navy in 1916, convinced that Germany could've won the naval war if the high command had followed his wishes.

technology to further strengthen their position. They even maintained a *two-power standard:* they'd keep their fleet larger than the next two largest fleets in the world combined. No other country, it seemed, could possibly challenge Britain's command of the sea. Until the Germans began expanding their navy, that is.

Germany's Kaiser Wilhelm wanted a large fleet, and Admiral Alfred von Tirpitz proposed to give him one. Von Tirpitz was influenced by Mahan's book, which became required reading in the German high command. He argued that Mahan had shown that a Great Power had to have a powerful navy, and he got the German parliament – the *Reichstag* – to agree to a huge spending programme to expand the German fleet. It wasn't long before the British began to wonder exactly why the Germans were building so many ships and whom they expected to be fighting. The answer wasn't too difficult to work out: Britain.

Tirpitz knew he had no chance of building a fleet bigger or more powerful than Britain's, but he reckoned he could build one that could do the British fleet serious damage, enough to force the British to give up their two-power standard and threaten their control of the seas.

Updating and Innovating: Dreadnoughts and Destroyers

In Nelson's day ships had been built of wood and they carried cannon to blast holes in each other. By 1914, however, ship design had completely changed. Ships were now made of steel and they carried huge gun turrets that swung around to target an enemy who might be many miles away. Small vessels could damage, even sink, much bigger ships with the latest in sea warfare technology, the *torpedo* – an explosive, fast-moving missile that travels underwater. Before long, navies were developing new types of ships to meet the challenge of new hardware:

- ✔ **Destroyers** were fast, lightly armoured ships whose main task was to deal with torpedo boats. They could fire torpedoes themselves and they were also useful as fast scouts. When U-boats started to attack British shipping, destroyers were armed with depth charges to attack them.

- ✔ **Cruisers** came in different versions: light cruisers or the more heavily armoured battlecruisers. Cruisers were faster than battleships but more lightly armoured. They were useful as escorts for convoys to protect them from surface raiders, and cruisers could take on other cruisers, but they were much less useful in battle against battleships.

- ✔ **Dreadnoughts** were the state-of-the-art game-changers. The first, HMS *Dreadnought,* was launched by Britain's Royal Navy in 1906 – a full battleship that was more heavily armoured and yet faster than any other warship afloat. All navies had to scrap all their existing battleships, go back to the drawing board and start building dreadnoughts.

The history books say – rightly – that *Dreadnought* made all other ships obsolete overnight, but the bad news for Britain was that this included the rest of Britain's own vast navy, so the country needed to start building more dreadnoughts – and fast, because the Germans were building them too. From 1906 to 1913 the two countries thrust vast sums of money into a desperate race trying to out-build each other, until the Germans decided it was costing too much and that they'd never win: they had 17 dreadnoughts but the British had 29. The naval race didn't lead directly to war, but it did lead the British to see the Germans as a dangerous enemy, set on undermining them.

Raiders and Blockaders

The key to winning a war is food. No one can fight without sufficient food, so if you control your enemy's food supply, in effect you control your enemy.

As soon as war broke out in 1914, each side planned to use its fleet to starve the other into submission. The British used their fleet to blockade Germany's ports and stop any seaborne imports getting through, though the Germans could still get imports through neutral Holland. Britain, on the other hand, as an island was entirely dependent on shipping to feed its population.

Cutting off the enemy's food supply didn't mean positioning your ships or submarines just outside his ports: you could operate just as effectively at a distance. The British blockaded Germany by positioning ships far out in the North Sea, to intercept merchant ships heading for Germany. In return, German raiders attacked British merchant ships all over the world, even in the Pacific and the Indian Ocean.

Sink the Emden!

Before they sent U-boats into action in significant numbers, the Germans used *surface raiders* – small, fast naval vessels designed to sink merchant vessels – to attack Allied merchant ships and troopships. German raiders did a lot of damage and were difficult to catch, though if they were cornered by an Allied warship they were too small and lightly armoured to defend themselves very effectively.

The most successful surface raider was the *Emden,* which operated in the Indian Ocean under its captain, the daring Karl von Müller. Müller constructed a dummy fourth funnel to make his ship look from a distance like a British ship, so he could get in close before his victim realised the danger. The *Emden* sank some 16 British merchant ships, a French destroyer and a Russian cruiser at anchor in the harbour at Penang; it even bombarded the port of Madras in British India and set alight its oil tanks.

At one point 60 ships, British, Russian, Japanese and French, were all out looking for the *Emden.* Eventually, in November 1914, the *Emden* was cornered by the Australian cruiser HMAS *Sydney* at Direction Island in the Cocos Islands and battered into surrender (see Figure 8-1). Even then some of her crew managed to escape from the island in a stolen schooner and make it back to Germany.

Figure 8-1:
The *Emden,*
damaged
by HMAS
Sydney.

© Imperial War Museums (Q 22743)

The courtesies of war

Captain von Müller of the *Emden* was famous for treating his prisoners with every consideration. He allowed the crew of *merchantmen* – unarmed trading vessels – to evacuate their ships before he sank them and he took the crews onto the *Emden,* sometimes passing them on to neutral or even Allied merchant ships that he encountered. This chivalrous way of conducting war at sea would come to an end, however, when Germany started depending on U-boats rather than surface raiders. Submarines have no space for prisoners and the crews of torpedoed ships were left to fend for themselves. Naval warfare was about to become a lot nastier and more ruthless – just like the war on land.

Coronel and the Falklands

The *Emden* had been part of a German squadron under Admiral von Spee that was causing serious damage to Allied shipping in the Pacific. By October 1914, the rest of von Spee's squadron was operating off the west coast of South America with five powerful cruisers, including two light cruisers, *Scharnhorst* and *Gneisenau.*

The British were determined to catch von Spee, but their nearest force, based in the Falkland Islands under Admiral Cradock, had only one modern cruiser, HMS *Glasgow:* Cradock's other three ships were old and slow. Cradock had been told to wait for reinforcements, but he was too impatient. He took his force around Cape Horn and challenged the Germans at Coronel, off the coast of Chile, on 1 November 1914. It was a disaster. The Germans sank two of Cradock's old ships, his flagship HMS *Good Hope* and HMS *Marlborough,* and forced the others to withdraw. Admiral Cradock went down with his ship.

The British were aghast at the news of the disaster at Coronel, and sent a powerful fleet, including two large battlecruisers, to find von Spee's fleet and destroy it. In fact von Spee found the British first. Von Spee was heading to raid the British base on the Falkland Islands, thinking they were undefended, when he spotted the British ships in the harbour. They were in the middle of taking on coal and would have been defenceless if the Germans had attacked, but von Spee didn't know that. He headed back out to sea and the British gave chase. The Germans' gunnery was more accurate, but the British ships were bigger and faster. Only one of von Spee's ships escaped; the others were all sunk. It was Admiral von Spee's turn to go down with his ship.

U-boats and Q-ships

Before the war started everyone expected the war at sea to be dominated by huge battleships, but the key type of ship turned out to be the submarine.

Although rudimentary submarines had already been around for a long time, it was only in the 20th century that countries started using them on a wide scale. All navies in the First World War had them, but the Germans used submarines (or *U-boats* – from *Unterseeboot*, the German for 'submarine' – as they called them) in a particular way: to blockade the British Isles and try to force Britain out of the war.

Things aren't always what they seem

People often think of submarines as being the kings of the sea, able to sink anything on the water and impossible to detect. Submarines have some distinct advantages over surface vessels – they can move about virtually unseen and unheard, and stealthily creep up on their unsuspecting enemy before attacking them with torpedoes (see Figure 8-2). Certainly, submarines proved their worth during the war. Navies around the world built more and more of them as the war progressed in an attempt to gain the upper hand in the war beneath the waves.

Figure 8-2:
A German U-boat on the surface torpedoes a merchant vessel.

© *Imperial War Museums (a detail of Q 20343)*

One particularly sad tale illustrates only too well the devastating impact U-boats could have on the enemy. In 1914 the British admiralty gave the job of patrolling the Dutch coast to the elderly *Cressy* class of cruisers, the oldest ships in the Royal Navy. They were so vulnerable to attack that they were given their own escort of destroyers and were nicknamed the 'live bait'. By September 1914 the navy had decided to withdraw the ships, but a German U-boat managed to catch three of them, HMS *Cressy*, HMS *Aboukir* and HMS

Hogue, in the open without their destroyers, and it sank all three, killing 1,400 men. It was a terrible demonstration of what U-boats could do and a signal to the British that the U-boat was an enemy to be reckoned with.

Despite this evidence of the U-boats' advantages of stealth and surprise, waging war by submarine had some significant drawbacks:

- At the start of the war, submarines didn't carry radios (though this changed when the war got underway).

- Travelling underwater was very slow, so submarines had to spend most of their time travelling on the surface.

- Even on the surface, submarines were quite slow and most ships could easily outrun them.

- Submerging took anything up to three minutes, so a submarine caught on the surface was very vulnerable.

- Submarines had no guns with which to defend themselves. A submarine caught on the surface could be sunk by even quite small ships.

- A submarine didn't stand a chance if a ship decided to ram it – as many did.

- Ships could avoid torpedoes relatively easily by zigzagging.

- Submarines could be torpedoed by enemy submarines or by torpedo-firing ships, such as destroyers.

With these weaknesses, submarines in the First World War were actually very vulnerable.

Please observe the rules when sinking enemy ships

Many people thought it was distinctly unethical for a submarine to sink a ship, especially an unarmed merchant or passenger ship, with no regard for the safety of the people on board. After all, surface raiders such as the *Emden* would pick up survivors from the ships they sank and look after their wounded. So international law imposed a set of rules, known as *Prize Rules,* telling submarine captains how they should operate in wartime:

- **Submarines must surface before stopping merchant ships.** They might creep up underwater, but they had to show themselves before doing any harm.

- **Submarines should warn the captains of merchant ships that they must stop and allow their ships to be searched.** Only ships that refused to stop should be fired upon.

- **Ships' crews should be given time to evacuate the ship and take to the lifeboats with any necessary supplies.** Ideally, the submarine should call other ships to pick up the crew.

- **The submarine is allowed to sink the ship only after all the crew have left it.**

Following these rules further weakened the effectiveness of submarines, taking time, making them vulnerable to attack from Q-ships (see the later 'The Allies strike back' section) and rather denying the submarines the element of surprise. However, most people viewed submarine attacks in much the same way that they viewed gas attacks on land: as a dishonourable form of warfare that should be used only if absolutely necessary. So the rules stuck – for a while, at least.

Yes, but what about the neutrals?

At first the German U-boats operated according to Prize Rules. Result: the British were able to fight against the blockade and defend themselves, and could sometimes sink the U-boats. Because of this, Admiral Tirpitz, the head of the German navy, wanted to tear up the Prize Rules and declare unrestricted U-boat warfare, or *Handelskrieg* (war on trade), sinking ships on sight without coming to the surface and leaving the survivors to their fate. However, the German Chancellor, Bethmann Hollweg, opposed this idea. He realised that U-boats were bound to sink neutral ships as well as enemy ones, and doing that could seriously damage Germany's international relations. He reckoned it could even cause the neutral United States to come into the war against Germany. The decision on the U-boat war would have to rest with the Kaiser.

Kaiser Wilhelm longed to end Britain's dominance of the sea, but with Germany's battle fleet bottled up in port (see 'High Noon on the High Seas: The Battle of Jutland', later in the chapter, to find out why), he couldn't see any alternative to using U-boats. He gave his approval to Tirpitz's plan, and in 1915 Germany announced it was declaring unrestricted U-boat warfare within a defined area around the British Isles called an *exclusion zone*. Any ship entering this exclusion zone around the British Isles was now in danger of being torpedoed. Even neutral vessels. Even passenger liners.

The Lusitania

The most significant victim of the new German policy of unrestricted U-boat warfare was the huge British passenger liner the *Lusitania,* which sailed from New York in May 1915 with a large number of passengers, including many Americans, heading for Southampton. The German embassy in Washington issued a warning that the ship was heading into the exclusion zone and could be sunk, but most people took no notice. As one overconfident American told the press, 'The Germans dare not sink this ship!'

But on 7 May, off the southern coast of Ireland, it was spotted by Captain Schwieger of U-boat *U-20.* He fired a single torpedo, the ship rolled over and sank within 18 minutes, and over 1,000 people drowned, including 128 Americans. The *Lusitania* was unlucky: it was zigzagging to avoid submarines, and it had run into *U-20* quite by chance. Captain Schwieger doesn't even seem to have realised which ship he was attacking.

The Germans claimed the *Lusitania* was a legitimate military target and that it was carrying military supplies. We now know this was true: like most British ships crossing the Atlantic, the *Lusitania* was secretly carrying 4,200 cases of ammunition to help alleviate the desperate shortages the British were experiencing on the Western Front. Quite possibly the ship was carrying other forms of munitions too, which could account for a second explosion that eyewitnesses of the sinking reported.

None of the Germans' claims affected the enormous public anger, on both sides of the Atlantic, that followed the sinking. American public opinion was outraged. Americans were particularly indignant that so many of their fellow countrymen had been drowned. Posters were produced there that showed women and children drowned by the U-boat, and in Britain the press presented the sinking as another example of uncivilised German behaviour, a reminder of why the Allies were fighting and why they had to defeat Germany.

After the *Lusitania* was torpedoed, Allied propaganda picked up on a strange medal that had appeared in Germany, apparently celebrating the sinking (see Figures 6 and 7 in the insert section). On one side it showed the ship going down and on the other it showed people buying tickets for the liner from a figure of death. 'Aha!' shouted Allied posters. 'This shows how inhuman the Germans are!' The medal certainly existed, but it wasn't issued by the German government. It was produced privately as a cynical comment both on the sinking and on the attitude of Cunard, the shipping company that owned the *Lusitania* and had insisted on its sailing, despite the danger. Sometimes satire backfires: the medal was a gift to Allied propaganda.

The German government was so deeply alarmed by the impact of the *Lusitania* sinking that it called off the unrestricted U-boat campaign. Tirpitz was furious, but Bethmann Hollweg overruled him: from now on, German submarines would switch to the Mediterranean, where they could attack ships supplying the Allied troops at Gallipoli.

U-boats will win the war!

It didn't take the Germans long to change their minds and go back to using U-boats around the British Isles. With no one breaking through on land, the U-boat campaign seemed the only way the Germans might cause one of their western enemies to collapse. In fact, they seemed to be Germany's best chance of winning the war. But the Germans still couldn't entirely ignore international public opinion:

- ✔ **Spring 1916:** Germans declare unrestricted U-boat warfare once again. Huge international protests: public opinion in the United States is particularly outraged. Germans cancel unrestricted U-boat warfare. Fed up with all these changes of policy, Tirpitz resigns as head of the German navy.

- ✔ **February 1917:** Desperate to bring the war to an end, the Germans re-declare unrestricted U-boat warfare. Two months later, angry at having lost so many of its ships and seamen, the United States declares war on Germany. Many South American countries do the same.

Throughout the war and particularly during these intermittent periods of unrestricted warfare, the U-boat was a serious threat to the Allies, and especially to Britain. But the Allies were learning how to fight back against the U-boats.

The Allies strike back

At first, with U-boats operating on the surface and observing Prize Rules, the Allies had a chance to sink them. From the start of the war, the British used special decoy vessels, codenamed *Q-ships* – armed naval vessels disguised as merchant ships – to trick and sink German U-boats. When U-boats were operating according to Prize Rules, a U-boat would warn a merchant ship to stop and submit to a search. The U-boat would approach, and some of the ship's crew might even start getting into lifeboats. Then, when the U-boat was well within range, the Q-ship crew would suddenly reveal their guns and open fire on it. The Germans protested that Q-ships were unfair; the Allies retorted that they weren't as unfair as sinking unarmed merchant ships.

But as U-boat tactics changed, so did the Allies counter-tactics:

- **Laying mines:** Well-positioned mines could catch U-boats where the Allies expected them to gather.

- **Attacking surfaced U-boats:** U-boats on the surface were very vulnerable either to gunfire or, failing that, to being rammed.

- **Setting the Dover Barrage:** A line of underwater netting and mines, the *Dover Barrage* was designed to keep U-boats away from the English Channel, where they could interfere with the vital troop transport boats. The barrage needed to be repositioned and strengthened at times, but it generally did a good job and forced the U-boats to pass through the North Sea, where Royal Navy destroyers could hunt them.

- **Employing Allied submarines:** The Allies sometimes used their own submarines to attack German ones. The *Deutschland Class* U-boats the Germans deployed at the end of the war made particularly good targets because they were so big.

- **Dropping depth charges:** Towards the end of the war, the Allied navies developed explosives that they could drop off ships and time to explode at the depth of a U-boat.

- **Attacking by air:** The British used long-range airships to attack U-boats travelling on the surface. They also began using aircraft launched from the decks of ships. This use of air power against ships was a sign of the way naval warfare was changing.

The deadly Mediterranean

The Mediterranean Sea was vital for carrying Allied troops and supplies between Europe and the war fronts at Gallipoli, Salonika, Palestine and Mesopotamia, and the Japanese navy provided vital naval escorts for Allied shipping here. However, some of the most bitter U-boat fighting took place in the Mediterranean, where both Germany and Austria-Hungary deployed U-boats against Allied shipping. German U-boats even flew the Austro-Hungarian flag and sank two Italian ships at a point when Italy was at war with Austria-Hungary but not with Germany: this incident helped persuade the Italian government to declare war on Germany. In April 1915, an Austro-Hungarian U-boat captained by Count von Trapp (the same man who features in the musical, *The Sound of Music*) sank the French battleship *Leon Gambetta,* and in July of the same year an Austro-Hungarian U-boat sank the Italian cruiser *Giuseppe Garibaldi.* The last U-boat sinkings of the war, in January 1919, were a French passenger ship and a French torpedo boat, both sunk by mines laid by U boats in the Mediterranean.

The British did have some success with these new counter-tactics, but without doubt the U-boats definitely hit the British very hard, and their blockade of the British Isles in particular came closer than any of the land campaigns to causing Britain to consider pulling out of the war. U-boats sank over 5,000 Allied ships, including 104 warships, most of them British. The U-boat campaign caused serious problems of food supply in Britain. On the other hand, in some ways the campaign was self-defeating for the Germans: it was very costly in terms of U-boat losses and in propaganda terms it was a disaster, especially because it was the key issue that brought the United States into the war.

A cost–benefit analysis would probably say that the Germans had to take a gamble: the U-boat campaign *was* their best chance of winning the war. But they paid a very heavy price by bringing the United States into the conflict. They gambled – but they lost.

High Noon on the High Seas: The Battle of Jutland

When war broke out, the men of the German and British fleets could hardly wait to have a big battle that would settle once and for all which of them ruled the seas. As it turned out, though, they had to wait nearly two years for the chance to come to blows. During those two years, the Germans sent out U-boats and surface raiders to sink British merchant ships (see 'Raiders and Blockaders', earlier in this chapter) but they kept their battle fleet, the *High Seas Fleet,* in harbour.

The German High Seas Fleet stayed at home for so long for a good reason: the British *Grand Fleet* under Admiral Sir John Jellicoe was based at Rosyth in Scotland and Scapa Flow in the Orkneys, patrolling the North Sea and waiting like a cat outside a mouse hole for the moment when the Germans would venture out. Jellicoe had to keep Britain's Grand Fleet together, blockade Germany's ports and keep the German High Seas Fleet bottled up in harbour, well away from the waters around Britain.

Jellicoe's responsibility was such that Winston Churchill, Britain's First Lord of the Admiralty, called Jellicoe 'the one man who could lose the war in an afternoon'. If Jellicoe made a misjudgement and lost control of the sea, Germany would be able to sail at will around Britain's coasts and cut Britain off from all its sources of food. He took his responsibilities very seriously and knew it was more important to keep the Grand Fleet together than to go looking for big battles with the Germans. That made him appear a bit cautious and hesitant to the public, who much preferred their admirals more aggressive, such as Admiral Sir David Beatty.

Those two years weren't without their fair share of naval action close to home, though:

- ✔ **Battle of Heligoland Bight, August 1914:** A British force of destroyers and submarines under Commodores Tyrwhitt and Keyes ambushed German ships patrolling the North Sea coast. Jellicoe sent reinforcements but Tyrwhitt didn't get the message, so the British fired at them, thinking they were Germans. Eventually, the British sank four German ships and damaged many others, and the Kaiser ordered his fleet to stay safely in harbour, but the British had some serious lessons about communications and co-ordination to learn as well.

- ✔ **Battle of the Dogger Bank, January 1915:** The British intercepted a German raiding squadron. Although the British sank the German cruiser *Blücher* and badly damaged the German flagship, the Germans were able to badly damage the British flagship, HMS *Lion,* in return. With the British Admiral unable to get clear orders to his ships, most of the German squadron escaped back to port.

These two engagements, however serious, were precursors to what many people still felt was coming: the big naval showdown between Britain and Germany.

Admiral Scheer's plan

In 1916 a new commander took charge of the German High Seas Fleet, Admiral Reinhard Scheer. Scheer didn't believe in sitting around in harbour: he wanted to attack. He decided to set a trap for the British.

Scheer's thinking went like this:

1. **The British Grand Fleet is far too big and powerful for the German High Seas Fleet.** But if the Germans could defeat *part* of the British fleet, they could weaken the whole Royal Navy. Scheer's target was the British battlecruisers based at Rosyth under Beatty.

2. **Send a squadron of German battlecruisers out into the North Sea to tempt Beatty to come out in pursuit.** Beatty enjoyed a good battle: he would come (and he did).

3. **While Beatty is engaged with the German battlecruisers, the whole German High Seas Fleet will suddenly appear, surround Beatty's ships and blow them out of the water.** Then the Germans could nip back into port before the main British Grand Fleet appeared.

It was a good plan and it *nearly* worked. Beatty took the bait and set sail with his battlecruisers to attack the Germans. However, Sir John Jellicoe had also heard of the German movements and he decided to order the Grand Fleet into action straight away, steaming southwards from Orkney into the North Sea. Instead of staying in harbour, as Scheer had expected it would, Jellicoe's fleet was at sea and not very far behind Beatty. And the Germans didn't know.

The battlecruisers' battle

Beatty caught up with the German battlecruisers near Jutland, off the coast of Denmark (see Figures 8 and 9 in the insert section). He had moved so quickly that they weren't yet ready for him. Beatty gave orders to attack and the great Battle of Jutland began. And immediately began going wrong.

Beatty's men were so keen to get to grips with the Germans that they forgot to take basic safety measures, such as closing hatches and bulkheads. As a result two of his battlecruisers, HMS *Queen Mary* and HMS *Indefatigable*, blew up when German shells penetrated through to their ammunition stores. Beatty was aghast. 'There seems to be something wrong with our bloody ships today,' he exclaimed.

Beatty lures the Germans

While the battlecruisers were slogging it out, Admiral Scheer was closing in on Beatty with his dreadnoughts. But when Beatty saw the German battleships approaching he didn't stay put: he ordered his ships to disengage and head north. He knew the Germans would pursue him. What the Germans didn't know was that Beatty was drawing them right into the path of Jellicoe, who was closing in rapidly with the entire British Grand Fleet. The Germans had originally set a trap for Beatty; now Beatty was setting a trap for them.

Crossing the T and turning away

Jellicoe sent some of his battlecruisers ahead to help Beatty, so when they arrived on the scene the Germans still thought they were only up against a force of battlecruisers. But at about 6.30 in the evening the smoke cleared to reveal to Scheer's men their very worst nightmare: the *entire* British Grand Fleet lay across their path in a very long line, like the crosspiece of a capital T. All the British ships could fire at the Germans, but very few German ships could fire back.

Scheer needed to get out of there fast. He sent in his battlecruisers to keep the British occupied while he withdrew his battleships, but Jellicoe followed him and shortly afterwards the British crossed Scheer's 'T' once again. With only a short length of daylight left, each side fired torpedoes and the Germans headed for home. Jellicoe turned his fleet away for a while to avoid the torpedoes, and by the time he was able to turn it back in the right direction, the Germans had got away. They made it to port and they stayed there. For the rest of the war.

Who won the Battle of Jutland?

The arguments about who won at Jutland still go on. The Germans undoubtedly won the battlecruiser battle: they did far more damage to Beatty's squadron than he was able to do to them. The Germans certainly claimed they'd won and the British public was deeply disappointed that Jellicoe hadn't won a Trafalgar-style victory. But sea battles aren't really about sinking ships: they're about commanding the ocean. The Germans had recognised that they simply couldn't break Britain's command of the seas. Scheer realised that he'd been very lucky to get so many of his ships back in one piece, and he didn't intend to risk them like that a second time. As for Jellicoe, many people thought he'd let the Germans get away too easily at Jutland, and although he became First Sea Lord, he never held another command at sea.

How much did Jutland matter?

Whoever controlled the sea would win the war: the matter was as simple as that. The Allies needed to move troops across the English Channel and around the Mediterranean (and, eventually, across the Atlantic) and for that they had to control the seas. Both sides depended heavily on imports of munitions and of food: without these even the strongest military power can't carry on a war. German raiders and U-boats came close to starving Britain out, but the Allies worked out effective counter-measures in time to stop that happening. The Germans, on the other hand, never worked out a way of breaking the British blockade of their ports.

Jutland – the big showdown between the British and German navies – may not have been the crushing victory the British public hoped for, but it mattered because it left the British in command of the North Sea and the British blockade of Germany still in place. It was no coincidence that the winter that followed Jutland brought some of the hardest food shortages of the war. The war ended in 1918 (and Chapter 16 tells you exactly how) because Germany suddenly collapsed, and the British blockade – and Jutland – played an important part in making that happen.

Controlling the Skies

Humans have long dreamed of flying, but it was not until 1783 that the Montgolfier brothers were the first to leave the ground under their own power – in balloons. Since then, armies had used balloons in war for observation and, in 1871 Parisians used them to get messages out of the city during the Prussian siege. But balloons had major disadvantages: they were easily visible to an enemy, who just had to follow a balloon and capture its occupants when it came to earth, and balloons were almost completely at the mercy of the elements. One balloon carrying a message out of besieged Paris in 1871 carried its bewildered crew all the way to Norway! In the First World War, both sides used balloons for observation, and the crews were even given parachutes so they could jump to safety if the enemy started firing at them.

However, in wartime people were starting to see that having control of the skies was as critical to success as having control of the seas. To have control, you needed to be able to attack your enemy from the air, and to attack your enemy from the air you needed powered flight. Balloons just weren't enough.

Powered flight saw some of the most dramatic technological advances made during the war. The Wright brothers had made their famous pioneering flight at Kitty Hawk in 1903, and the first flight over the English Channel took place in 1909. Less than ten years later airships were conducting the first ever airborne bombing raids and fighter planes were staging dogfights in the skies above the trenches on the Western Front and carrying out long-range bombing missions against the British Isles. Aircraft hadn't yet reached the stage where they could decide the outcome of wars on their own, but the First World War took air power a long way down that road.

I lost my home to an airship trooper

Airships were developed in 1900 by Count von Zeppelin, after whom they became known, for carrying mail and passengers, but they were quickly taken up by the German army. Unlike a balloon, an airship has an engine to drive it to specific points, which meant that the army could use Zeppelins for reconnaissance at sea and to drop bombs to help with ground attacks in Belgium and in Poland, which they did from 1914. However, Zeppelins were vulnerable to the weather and many of them crashed.

Airborne attacks

After the Germans had conquered Belgium, they set up Zeppelin bases there from which they could conduct air raids against Britain. The Kaiser took some convincing before he authorised these raids, because he was fond of England, but in January 1915 he finally authorised the attacks. In return, the British launched raids on the Zeppelin bases at Cuxhaven and Friedrichshafen using aircraft launched from ships (these were the world's first naval air raids), but they couldn't prevent the Zeppelins from setting off (see Figure 10 in the insert section).

Zeppelins conducted several raids on the Allies:

✔ **19 January 1915:** First Zeppelin raid on Britain, at Yarmouth on the Norfolk coast.

✔ **21 March 1915:** First Zeppelin raid on Paris.

✔ **31 May 1915:** First Zeppelin raid on London.

✔ **8–9 September 1915:** Major Zeppelin raid on London.

Zeppelin raids caused considerable panic in London and angry crowds started attacking foreign-owned shops and homes, even when the owners weren't German. By comparison with the Second World War, Zeppelin raids were tiny: a serious raid on London killed 22 people, whereas the Blitz of 1940–1 killed nearly 20,000 people there and left a quarter of a million homeless. But at the time, in a world that had never known bombing from the air, the damage wrought by these huge monsters in the sky was terrifying. The big Zeppelin attack of 8–9 September alone destroyed half a million pounds' worth of property.

Zapping the Zeppelins

Zeppelins flew too high for British aircraft to reach them and ordinary machine gun bullets couldn't bring them down in any case. Gradually, however, the British developed effective anti-Zeppelin measures:

✔ **'Archie':** The British nickname for anti-aircraft gunnery. Archie didn't often hit a Zeppelin but could force it to change course.

✔ **Incendiary bullets:** These bullets set light to the hydrogen in a Zeppelin's gas bag. On 2 September 1916 a British fighter plane armed with incendiary bullets shot down a Zeppelin over north London.

✔ **Blackout:** Lights were dimmed or switched off to make it harder for Zeppelins to spot their targets.

✔ **Searchlights:** These lights would pinpoint Zeppelins to help anti-aircraft guns fire at them.

The incendiary bullet ended the Zeppelin raids: too many airships were being shot down and the Germans halted the campaign. Now they would concentrate on their aircraft.

Airplane!

Information is vital to military commanders, and at the start of the war the best use for aircraft seemed to be to get accurate information about enemy troop movements. Such information could sometimes prove crucial. For example, an air reconnaissance report caused the Germans to pull back from the Marne in 1914 and led to the decision on both sides to dig in. As the war went on, though, and technology progressed, aircraft began to be used for other purposes, too.

Spies in the sky

The earliest aircraft only had room for one pilot, who had to fly the plane, note what he saw on the ground and fly back to base to report it. Soon, however, factories started producing two-seater planes: one pilot could concentrate on flying while the other took photographs of the enemy position with a specially adapted camera designed for aerial photography (see Figure 11 in the insert section). Reports from aerial reconnaissance like this could have devastating effects on the ground: if a pilot reported a big build-up of troops behind the enemy lines, which usually meant a large attack was coming, the artillery could start shelling where the troops were gathering and cause enormous casualties. Seeing an enemy plane overhead was therefore very bad news for the men in the trenches. The only way to combat these aerial snoopers was to shoot them down, but how?

Flying bullets

In the early days of the war, enemy reconnaissance pilots would occasionally take shots at each other with pistols or rifles, or else they just waved and carried on with their business. But as the military value of aerial reconnaissance became clearer, so the military value of shooting down enemy planes became clearer too. Pilots would have to stop waving and get serious about killing each other.

The most obvious weapon to use in the air was a machine gun, but the problem was where to place it. If it went at the front, where the pilot could aim and fire it, it would shoot away the plane's propeller. It could go on the upper wing, but that meant a pilot would have to stand up in the cockpit to fire it, which wasn't a very safe thing to do. To start with, therefore, most planes carried a machine gun at the back, which was operated by the co-pilot. However, whereas a machine gun could be very useful for defending a plane against an attack from behind, it wasn't much good for attacking other aircraft. If military aircraft were to be any good at attacking enemy planes, they had to be able to fire their machine guns from the front.

Meet the Fokkers

Tackling the problem of how to fire machine guns from the front exercised brains on both sides of the war. The first man to come up with a solution was the French pilot Roland Garros, who fixed metal plates to his propeller to deflect the bullets. That idea certainly allowed Garros to fire at the enemy; unfortunately it also made it difficult to aim, because the propeller could deflect the bullets in any direction. Nevertheless, his was the only idea about how a plane could shoot forwards. However, in April 1915 Garros ran out of fuel and had to land behind enemy lines. The Germans inspected his plane and discovered the metal plates on the propellers. They were impressed but reckoned they could improve on the design.

A Dutch aircraft designer called Anthony Fokker, who was living and working in Germany and whose factory was run by the German government, worked out a mechanism that synchronised the propeller and the gun, so the bullets always passed between the propeller blades. With this advantage, the Germans turned the tables on the Allies and dominated the skies.

For most of 1915 the Germans in their Fokker aircraft completely dominated the skies above the Western Front. In contrast, Allied pilots could measure their life expectancy in mere weeks. They often arrived at the Front with minimal training, and for much of the war Allied pilots had to make do with planes that were decidedly inferior to the Germans'. The Allies simply had no response to what they called the 'Fokker scourge'.

Aircraft were now performing two quite distinct roles. Some were still carrying out vital reconnaissance work, spotting enemy troop movements and 'artillery spotting' and reporting on the effectiveness of artillery bombardment. Others were specifically designed to be fast and manoeuvrable, to seek out reconnaissance planes and shoot them down. These planes become known as *fighters*. If one side could dominate the skies above the front so that its reconnaissance planes could operate unhindered, it would give a huge advantage to its military commanders. From 1915, reconnaissance planes were equipped with radio sets (albeit rather cumbersome ones), so they could report their observations directly without having to wait till they landed. It was vital, therefore, for fighter pilots to shoot down as many enemy reconnaissance planes as possible. The pilots who proved best at doing this became national heroes (see the nearby 'Aces high' sidebar).

Aces high

Newspapers on both sides soon made heroes out of the *aces,* the young pilots who shot down the most enemy planes. Here are just a few of those aces, with the number of enemy planes they took out:

- René Fonck (France): 75
- Edward Mannock (Great Britain): 73
- William 'Billy' Bishop (Great Britain): 72
- Ernst Udet (Germany): 62
- Georges Gynemer (France): 54
- Albert Ball (Great Britain): 44
- Edward Rickenbacker (USA): 26
- Alexander Kazakov (Russia): 17

Some of these pilots were very young: Albert Ball, for example, was just 21 when he was killed.

The single most successful pilot on either side was Baron Manfred von Richthofen, who shot down 80 Allied planes. He led a squadron that became known as his 'flying circus', and he painted his planes red to add to his opponents' fear, earning him the nickname 'The Red Baron'. Richthofen became a national hero in Germany, and a hate figure in Britain and France. He was finally brought down, in April 1918, possibly by the Canadian pilot Roy Brown though more likely by Allied anti-aircraft fire.

Fighting the Fokkers

At the start of the war the air forces on both sides operated as part of their national army or navy. The British Royal Flying Corps (RFC), for example, was the army unit, concentrating on reconnaissance, and a separate Royal Naval Air Service (RNAS) supported the navy and provided home defence. While the RFC was desperately trying to survive the Fokker scourge, the RNAS was undertaking attack missions against German targets: it ran airship missions from bases in Britain to attack German U-boats and it commissioned the Handley-Page bomber, one of the most successful bombing aircraft of the war, to bomb the Zeppelin bases in German-occupied Belgium.

In 1915, General Hugh Trenchard took over the RFC. He wanted to take a much more aggressive policy towards the Germans: pilots weren't allowed parachutes, for example, in case knowing they had them made pilots give up too easily in a fight. During the period of the 'Fokker scourge', Trenchard repeatedly called for better aircraft to fight back against the Germans and in 1917 he finally got one: the Sopwith Camel.

The Sopwith Camel was the most successful Allied fighter plane of the war: it shot down nearly 1,300 German planes and could also shoot down Zeppelins. To Trenchard's delight it could also be used to attack enemy troops on the ground. The Sopwith Camel finally put an end to the Fokker's dominance and allowed the Allies to turn the tide of the war in the air.

Bombs away

The Sopwith Camel didn't completely turn the war the Allies' way. In 1917 the Germans started using long-range 'Gotha' bombing aircraft to attack targets in Britain. Like the Zeppelin raids, these attacks probably shocked the British more than they disrupted Britain's war industry, but the reaction was furious. The press said Britain had been humiliated, and the Prime Minister called for huge bombing raids on German towns in retaliation, even though the British didn't have the means to launch these – and he knew it.

Gothas could fly higher and farther than the British fighters, which made shooting them down difficult. In one bombing raid, in July 1917, one Gotha was shot down, but 57 people on the ground were killed. The fighters would keep trying to get at the bombers, but the only sure defence against the Gotha was either to capture its bases – or to win the war.

Air power at sea

One of the most significant – and dangerous – technical advances made during the war was the *aircraft carrier*. The British experimented with launching planes from battleships, but they really needed ships specially designed to carry planes, so they converted two vessels, HMS *Ark Royal* and HMS *Furious,* into flat-topped aircraft carriers. Other navies soon followed suit.

Aircraft carriers gave the British a big advantage: their sea-based planes could attack targets both far inland or out to sea. The war of technology was racing ahead.

Chapter 9

Turkish Delights

In This Chapter

▶ Decision making with the Ottomans and the Young Turks

▶ Encouraging holy war

▶ Dealing with disaster at Ctesiphon and Kut

▶ Courting catastrophe at Gallipoli

▶ Carving up the Middle East

The war with Turkey witnessed some of the hardest fighting and most serious suffering of the war. Despite this, many people in Britain and France saw the war against Turkey as a sideshow compared with the importance of the Western Front. Underestimating the Turks, however, proved a common – and disastrous – Allied mistake. The war in the Middle East was to have huge and complex consequences that still resonate loudly today. If you want to know the origins of the modern problems in the Middle East, of the Palestine–Israel conflict, of the difficult relations between Iran, Iraq and the west, this chapter is the place to start.

The Ottomans and Their Declining Empire: Choosing a Way Forward

If you travelled back in time to the 16th century, you'd find that the Ottoman Sultan was probably the most powerful ruler in the world. At its height, the Ottoman Empire, run from Constantinople (nowadays called Istanbul), covered North Africa, Syria, Palestine, Iraq, the Caucasus, the Crimea and deep into Europe, almost to Vienna, as well as its heartland, Turkey. By the 20th century, however, the Ottomans were a shadow of the power they'd been, and other European countries thought they were too weak and decadent to put up much of a fight. Nevertheless, the sheer geographical size of the Ottoman Empire could give an advantage to whichever side it joined, so the other European powers were very interested in what the Turks might decide to do: would they stay neutral or would they join one of the warring sides?

Old Turkey?

The Ottoman Empire had declined in power because it had been hit by two powerful new forces:

✔ **Nationalism:** This new idea from western Europe had inspired the Empire's Balkan provinces to rise up in revolt against Turkish rule (see Chapter 2). As a result, by 1914 Turkey had lost nearly all its lands on the European mainland, except for the ancient city of Constantinople, the Turkish capital. But other peoples in the Empire could turn to nationalism as well, including the Arabs – and even the Turks themselves.

✔ **Industrialisation:** While other European countries were developing into industrial powers, Turkey had kept to its traditional ways. This wasn't a good policy: by the 19th century any country wanting to be a Great Power had to industrialise.

The Turks knew that other Great Powers, such as Russia and Austria-Hungary, had ambitions in the region and would seize any chance they could get to carve their lands up. In 1908 a group of young Turkish army officers decided that they had to act to modernise and industrialise the country. They seized control of the government, and a year later they overthrew Sultan Abdulhamid II and put their own man, Mehmed V, on the throne. Officially, they were called the Committee of Union and Progress, but everyone called them the *Young Turks*. The Young Turks sacked old and incompetent officials and started to bring the Turkish government into some sort of 20th-century shape.

Hmm – ruling isn't as easy as it looks

The Young Turks soon found that reversing years of Ottoman decline wasn't going to happen overnight. They suffered several military defeats:

✔ **War with Italy (1911–2):** The Turks lose control of Tripoli (Libya) and the Dodecanese Islands in the Aegean Sea (see Chapter 3).

✔ **Balkan Wars (1912–3):** The Turks lose control of their lands in the Balkans (see Chapter 3).

To make life even more difficult, the Young Turks found themselves coming under pressure from two very different directions. Islamic revivalists within the Empire were unhappy with the Ottoman government, not because it wasn't modern enough, but because it wasn't Islamic enough. They thought the Sultan should either start acting as a proper Islamic *caliph* – the spiritual successor of the Prophet Mohammad and leader of Muslims all over the world – or else he should recognise someone else as successor (see 'The Arab Spring', later in the chapter). And then there were the Germans.

We'd very much like to be your friends: The Germans court the Turks

For many years the Turks had been allied to Britain against their deadliest enemy, Russia, but now the war had started Britain and Russia were allies. In the meantime, Kaiser Wilhelm II, seeing another opportunity to move against the British, had been trying to interest the Turks in an alliance with Germany. Germany could promise heavy investment in Turkish industry and even a railway link from Berlin to Baghdad that would run right through Ottoman territory and connect the Ottoman lands directly with northern Europe (see 'The train at Platform 3 is non-stop from Berlin to Baghdad'). The German General Liman von Sanders even arrived in Constantinople to advise the Turks on how to run their army. The trouble was, as the Turks soon discovered, the German version of 'advising you on how to run your army' turned out to be 'we will take over your army'.

Germany hadn't been a major player in the affairs of the Ottoman Empire before now. The Russians, Austrians, British and French had all been directly concerned with the area for their own political reasons, and the Italians were also interested in events in the Balkan region, which was just over the water from their own territory. Germany, though, was the one major power that didn't have a direct interest in the region. So when the Germans started to get active in Turkey, and especially when they started offering the Turks military and political support, the other powers were worried. A variety of potential wartime scenarios featuring a resurgent Turkey, supported by Germany, began to appear before the other powers' eyes:

- ✔ **The Turks and the Austrians between them could control the Balkans.** In this scenario, Serbia would be crushed and Russia cut off from any contact through the Mediterranean with its western allies.

- ✔ **The Turks could open another front against the Russians, in the Caucasus.** In this situation, Russia would have to divert troops from fighting the Germans and Austrians on the Eastern Front in order to fight the Turks. This was bound to weaken the Russians.

- ✔ **The Turks might move against the British in Egypt and seize the Suez Canal.** This move would cut Britain and France off from their possessions in Asia and could pose a serious threat to Allied shipping.

The Allies held on to the impression that the Ottoman Empire didn't look strong. After all, the Turks had lost every war they'd fought for the previous half century, including since the Young Turks had taken control (okay, they were on the winning side in the Second Balkan War of 1913, but they'd joined in an attack by every Balkan state against the Bulgarians, so it doesn't really count). What the

---

The train at Platform 3 is non-stop from Berlin to Baghdad

It might not seem like it when you're waiting for a delayed train to take you to work, but railways have long been prestigious political projects. The 19th century went for long railway lines of big symbolic importance, such as the first trans-continental railroad that united east and west in the United States, or the Trans-Siberian railway that connected European Russia with its lands in the Far East. The famous Orient Express already linked Paris with Constantinople; Kaiser Wilhelm wanted to go one better and build a railway that would run all the way from Berlin to Baghdad. He wasn't trying to fill a gap in the market. He wanted to declare to the world that Germany was a global power and that it regarded the Middle East as its own sphere of influence. The railway itself was some 300 miles short of its destination when the First World War broke out, and it didn't reach Baghdad until the start of the Second World War.

Allies overlooked was that the Turks had shown in every war that they could be very skilful and dogged defenders of their own territory against invaders, and they would show this again when the First World War started.

This means war! With one side. Or maybe the other

When the war broke out in 1914, the Turks had a dilemma: should they stay neutral, should they join the Allies or should they join Germany? If they stayed neutral, they'd still have to get ready to defend their neutrality: the other powers wouldn't hold back from attacking Turkey just because it was neutral. Britain and France had been very strong allies of the Turks, so it might make sense to fight on their side. On the other hand, joining the Allies would mean being on the same side as their old enemies the Russians, and few Turks liked that idea. In any case, it was fairly obvious that the French had their eyes on the Turkish province of Syria and the British were after the oil fields of Mesopotamia (Iraq). There again, joining the Germans would almost certainly mean the Germans taking more control of Turkey itself. The Turks didn't much like that idea either. They had a tough decision to make.

In the end what made the Turks' minds up for them was a saga of four warships.

Hey! Give us our ships back!

When war broke out between Britain and Germany in 1914, British shipyards had nearly finished work on two brand new battlecruisers of the latest design that had been ordered by the Turkish government. The Turks didn't really have a navy so these new British-built warships had attracted a lot of public attention. They were very expensive too, and the Turks had had to launch a huge public subscription campaign to pay for them, which meant that ordinary Turks looked on the ships (to be called *Sultan Osman* and *Reshadieh*) as their own special property. But then, as the crisis over Bosnia grew in July 1914, Winston Churchill, Britain's First Lord of the Admiralty, faced a tricky decision. Should he

- ✔ **Let the ships go to Turkey as agreed?** This course of action was the legally proper thing to do: the ships were Turkish property. But if Turkey were to declare war on the Allies, the ships would be able to do serious damage to Allied shipping in the Mediterranean.

- ✔ **Seize the ships for the Royal Navy?** Legally, such a move was allowed – in fact, it was common practice – when two countries were at war with each other, but Britain and Turkey weren't at war. Seizing the ships would be bound to infuriate the Turks and might even drive them to join the Germans. On the other hand, Britain needed every ship it could get to meet the German threat in the North Sea. It seemed crazy not to take hold of two modern battleships being built in British shipyards.

Churchill decided to seize the ships. They were taken into the Royal Navy as HMS *Agincourt* and HMS *Erin*. They certainly helped Britain's Grand Fleet fight the Germans; whether it was worth the risk of bringing Turkey into the war on the German side is a matter of opinion.

The elusive Admiral Souchon

To show the Turks that the British weren't the only ones with flashy warships, in 1912 the Germans had sent Admiral Souchon with two modern battlecruisers, the *Goeben* and the *Breslau*, to Constantinople, where the German crews soon made themselves very popular with the locals. The ships were still based there when war broke out in 1914. Souchon took his ships out into the Mediterranean to attack the French, but he ran into a British squadron and had to make a run for home. Souchon outran the British and made it back to Constantinople, where the Turks announced that these German ships now belonged to them (to replace the ones the British had stolen, they said) and Admiral Souchon was now Commander-in-Chief of the Ottoman navy. Which consisted, essentially, of the *Goeben* and the *Breslau*.

The Allies hadn't expected Souchon to get back to Constantinople (neither had the Turks) and they certainly didn't expect what he did next. Despite the fact that his ships were now flying the Turkish flag, Souchon took them out into the Black Sea and to the southern coast of Germany's enemy, Russia. Then he opened fire on a series of Russian ports, including Odessa, Sevastopol and Yalta. Because Turkey wasn't at war with Russia – or indeed with anyone – the Russians, understandably, were keen to know just what the 'Turkish' Admiral Souchon thought he was doing, as was the Turkish government!

The Turkish government still hadn't decided whether to stay neutral or join the war, and if so, on which side. The Young Turks' leader, Enver Pasha, wanted Turkey to join in on the German side. So he signed a secret alliance with the Germans and then didn't bother telling the Turkish Cabinet anything about it. They'd find out soon enough, he reckoned, when the Allies declared war. He was right. After Souchon's attack on their coast, the Russians declared war on Turkey and Churchill sent a British squadron to the Dardanelles, where it did serious damage to the forts guarding the Straits. Turkey was now well and truly in the war on Germany's side (see Figure 12 in the insert section). Enver Pasha was relieved, but many Turks weren't at all sure that going to war with Britain and France was a good idea. And they weren't entirely wrong.

Is a World War Not Enough? Have a Holy War Too!

The Turkish sultan wasn't just the secular ruler of the Ottoman Empire, he was also the caliph – in theory. In practice, the Ottoman sultans of the 19th century had been an unimpressive lot and few Muslims took much notice of them.

Meanwhile, Kaiser Wilhelm was busy trying to promote himself as the great protector of the Islamic world against the big, bad British and French. This was why he'd claimed to be protecting Morocco against France back in 1905 (see Chapter 3 for more on the Kaiser's machinations) and it was also how he sold the idea of a German alliance to the Turks. After war had broken out in 1914, the Germans persuaded the Young Turks to issue a call to *holy war* to all the world's Muslims, calling on them to rise up against their British, French or Russian masters. All three Great Powers had large Muslim populations: the British ruled over Muslims in India and Singapore, the French in North Africa, the Russians in Central Asia. A Muslim holy war, the Kaiser hoped, would bring these mighty empires crashing to the ground.

Unfortunately for the Kaiser his holy war idea didn't work. Some Muslims in British India talked excitedly about setting up a new Caliphate – the term they used was *khilafet* – with a Muslim sultan in Constantinople who'd lead the Islamic world in a great religious revival. But otherwise the call to holy war ended up in the waste paper baskets of the Muslim world. Here's why:

✔ Very few Muslims thought the Ottoman sultan had enough religious authority left to start telling them what their religious duty was.

✔ In any case, the Young Turks said they wanted to make Turkey less religious and more secular. The actual Young Turk minister who issued the call to Islamic holy war wasn't even a Muslim, he was a freemason!

> ✔ This call to Islamic holy war was being issued to help the Kaiser (who wasn't a Muslim) fight a war against the British (who weren't Muslim), French and Russians (and they weren't Muslim either). Muslims didn't see why they should get involved.

Apart from a few localised mutinies by Muslims in Britain's Indian army, the call to holy war fell flat. However, if the Allies thought that meant the war against the Turks was going to be easy, they were in for a shock.

A Mess in Mesopotamia

When war with Turkey broke out, Allied eyes were fixed on one vital aspect: oil. The British were concerned that the Turks might attack the oil fields in Persia (modern-day Iran), so they launched an invasion of the neighbouring Ottoman province of Iraq, then known by its ancient name, Mesopotamia. This attack wasn't run from London but by the government of British India, based in Delhi. At first it was supposed to be only a relatively small raid. The British and Indians took the port of Basra so the Turks couldn't launch attacks on Persia from there. But then the government in Delhi decided to extend the war farther into Mesopotamia. They sent a force up the Tigris Valley to take the capital, Baghdad.

This advance on Baghdad ran into problems right from the start. The government in Delhi hadn't checked with London before authorising it, and the government in London wasn't pleased when it heard about the offensive. Delhi didn't have anything like enough troops, transport or supplies to undertake such a campaign, but London wasn't prepared to release extra men or supplies from the Western Front or from Gallipoli (see the next section, 'Disaster at the Dardanelles', for details of this campaign) to reinforce them. So the British and Indians advanced on Baghdad, got beaten back at Ctesiphon, about 25 miles short of Baghdad, and had to take refuge in the town of Kut-al-Amara. There the Turks cut the British and Indians off and beat back all attempts to relieve them. Eventually, on 29 April 1916 the British and Indian army at Kut had to surrender to the Turks. The defeat was a massive blow to British prestige and a huge boost to the Turks.

The prisoners who surrendered to the Turks at Kut-al-Amara had a terrible fate in store. Of 10,000 who went into captivity, 4,000 died from starvation and ill-treatment. Mistreatment of prisoners was found on both sides in the war, but the Turks were particularly brutal.

Meanwhile, the Allies had suffered an even bigger disaster and the Turks an even bigger victory: Gallipoli.

Disaster at the Dardanelles

The Dardanelles, or Gallipoli, campaign of 1915 was by far the biggest of the Allied offensives against the Ottoman Empire, but it was a complete disaster and cast a very long shadow. Even years later, in the Second World War, Allied leaders – especially Winston Churchill – were very wary about launching amphibious landings such as the 1944 D-Day invasion because of how badly the landings at Gallipoli had gone wrong in 1915.

Uh-oh: Winston's had a bright idea

The Allied governments in 1915 faced a straightforward question: how to win the war? The obvious answer seemed to be to break the Germans on the Western Front, but by 1915 the Germans had given no sign of being broken and the Western Front showed no sign of being won either (see Chapter 5). The Allies could react to that situation in one of two ways:

- ✔ **Keep on trying to break through on the Western Front.** The 'westerners' said that the Western Front was the only front that mattered in winning the war; the trouble was that their policy was costing thousands of lives and not getting anywhere.

- ✔ **Find somewhere else and break through there instead.** This idea sounds clever, but everything depended on where the breakthrough would come. It also supposes that breaking through somewhere else would actually win the war, but this outcome was far from guaranteed.

The Allied situation was even bleaker on the Eastern Front, where the Russians were still reeling from their defeat at Tannenberg (see Chapter 4 for more on this Allied disaster). At the very beginning of 1915, they asked the British and French whether they could do something to relieve the pressure on the Eastern Front. It wasn't easy to see what the western Allies could do to help the Russians. If they sent too many troops to the Eastern Front, the Germans might break through in the west, and that wouldn't help anyone except the Germans themselves. Lord Kitchener, Britain's Secretary of State for war, told the Russians that any help Britain gave would have to take the form of a naval attack somewhere. But where? The question passed to the First Lord of the Admiralty, Winston Churchill.

Churchill's idea was to use the Royal Navy *on its own* to attack and take the Dardanelles. He thought this was a brilliant idea; the First Sea Lord, Sir John Fisher, the man who'd single-handedly modernised the Victorian navy, thought the plan was crazy, and here's why.

Winston Churchill

Forget the famous Winston Churchill of 1940 defying Hitler's Luftwaffe and seeing Britain through the Blitz: the Churchill of 1915 was a much younger, maverick politician. He was the son of a famous but erratic Victorian statesman and Winston seemed to have inherited something of his father's mixture of brilliance and unreliability. He hadn't shone either at school or at Sandhurst, Britain's famous military academy. He served as a cavalry officer and soon developed a reputation for writing articles and pamphlets telling senior officers how they ought to be running their campaigns. Even when he was no longer in the army he headed for war zones as a war correspondent. He was captured during the Anglo–Boer War (1899–1902) and became a national hero when he escaped with a price on his head.

Back in Britain, Churchill entered politics as a Conservative and then changed his mind and joined the Liberals in time for their huge electoral victory in 1906. As Home Secretary he gained a reputation, not entirely fairly, for being prepared to send troops in to solve almost any dispute that might arise. As First Lord of the Admiralty he got the fleet up to strength to face the German threat and saw the navy through the difficult first few months of the war (see Chapter 8 for more on the Royal Navy's war). Churchill was one of those people who could have several bright ideas at any one time, and one or two of them might be quite brilliant ones. The trouble was, he wasn't always good at spotting which ones. Gallipoli is a good example of where he got this wrong.

The Dardanelles is a very narrow sea passage that runs from the Mediterranean towards the Black Sea. It broadens out in the middle but at the two ends it's hardly wider than a canal. Churchill thought the navy could sail into the Dardanelles, open fire on the Turkish forts along the shoreline and destroy them. Then, he thought, the Turks would surrender, the Allies would take hold of Constantinople, and they'd be able to rush troops and supplies through the Black Sea to Russia. These reinforcements would so strengthen the Russians that they'd rise up like a mighty giant and crush the Germans beneath their mighty boots. That, at any rate, was the theory.

Historians don't agree on whether or not Churchill's plan had any chance of success: some think it did, others think it was too ambitious. What is clear is that Churchill's plan made a number of highly questionable assumptions:

✔ **Questionable Assumption No. 1: Ships can defeat forts on their own.** Fisher didn't believe this; neither, back in his day, did Nelson. Both men thought that ships should leave forts well alone and only attack them in conjunction with ground troops.

✔ **Questionable Assumption No. 2: When the forts have been destroyed, Constantinople will fall and Turkey will surrender.** It wasn't clear why the Turks should do this. Major cities don't usually surrender to fleets and Constantinople could defend itself quite adequately.

> ✔ **Questionable Assumption No. 3: Knocking Turkey out of the war would mean the defeat of Germany.** It might, but it might not. The Germans might simply move troops down to Turkey to carry on the fight.

The Dardanelles offensive was therefore a massive gamble, with no guarantee that it would achieve its aims, even if it went well.

Phase 1: The naval attack – or 'How not to win a quick victory'

On 19 February 1915 British and French ships moved into the Dardanelles and opened fire on the Turkish forts. The Turks were taken by surprise and the ships did serious damage to the Turkish defences, but the Turks soon started firing back and laying mines so the Allied ships had to pull back for their own protection. The British decided it would be crazy to risk losing a dreadnought battleship – they desperately needed these powerful ships to fight the Germans – so they withdrew the most powerful ship in the attack force, HMS *Queen Elizabeth,* and carried on the attack with battlecruisers. These ships had to get in close to do any real damage to the Turkish forts, but with the Turks lobbing shells at them from howitzers and with minefields in the narrow waters of the straits, the ships had to keep their distance.

Through the rest of February and into March the Allied ships continued battering the forts but they were getting nowhere. The French realised that they needed to commit ground troops. Duly, on 10 March they sent 18,000 colonial troops from French North Africa to the Dardanelles zone. The British too were coming to the conclusion that naval power on its own wouldn't win this battle, but before the army arrived in strength and took over, the naval commanders decided to have one last go to show what they could do without army support. On 18 March British and French ships moved in to attack the Turkish forts – and ran into a minefield. Two French ships, *Gaulois* and *Bouvet,* and one British ship, HMS *Ocean,* were sunk, and two British ships, HMS *Irresistible* and HMS *Inflexible,* were badly damaged. Soon, on 23 March, Churchill told the British Cabinet that the naval attack had failed and that they had no choice but to use troops on land.

Phase 2: The landings – or 'How not to take your enemy by surprise'

You may think that a major naval attack on the Dardanelles would give the game away that the Allies were planning an assault in the area. If so, you'd be right. The Turkish leader, Enver Pasha, was badly worried about the prospect of an Allied landing and was preparing to evacuate the Gallipoli peninsula on the northern shore of the Dardanelles. He didn't think the Turks would be able to resist such an attack if it came. But the German General Liman von Sanders thought Enver Pasha was too pessimistic. He took over command and started to prepare the Turkish defences for when the Allies came back. And sure enough, they did.

The Allies' best hope to beat the Turks was to land large numbers of troops on the Gallipoli peninsula as soon as possible, before the Turks had a chance to recover from their surprise at the Allied attack and put their defences in order. Instead, the Allies spent a whole month arguing about whether they should land, where they should land, which troops should land, who should be in charge of them and so on. Liman von Sanders could hardly believe his luck, and he used this month's delay to prepare defences for the whole Gallipoli peninsula.

Von Sanders didn't have enough troops to cover the whole coastline, so his plan was for the troops at the coast to delay the Allies for as long as possible, while his mobile reserve troops rushed to the danger spot and stopped the invaders advancing any farther. It was a plan that depended on the Allies making lots of mistakes and getting into serious muddles. Once again, von Sanders' luck was in – the Allies were about to do both of these things.

Next time, study the map more carefully

In some ways, the Allies' Dardanelles plan can seem quite clever if you look at a map showing the whole of Europe, but when you look more closely at the land involved it doesn't look anything like such a bright idea. The Gallipoli peninsula is very rocky, and most of its coastline is dominated by steep cliffs and hillsides, with lots of rocky gullies and hills inland: perfect terrain for an army to defend against an enemy landing; not such great terrain to encounter if you're on the attacking side (see Figure 9-1). The Allied commander, Sir Ian Hamilton, had the right maps showing all the details, but he still seemed surprised by the terrain he found.

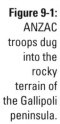

Figure 9-1:
ANZAC troops dug into the rocky terrain of the Gallipoli peninsula.

© *Imperial War Museums (Q 13400A)*

D-Day in the Dardanelles

The date for the landings in the Dardanelles was set for 25 April 1915. The plan was for three main Allied forces to head for the Gallipoli peninsula:

- ✔ A French force was going to land on the eastern side.

- ✔ A British force would land at the southern tip and on the western side.

- ✔ The Australian and New Zealand Army Corps (ANZAC) would be landing at the far north of the landing area.

The plan was for the three forces to travel to Gallipoli on ships and get into lifeboats and other rowing boats to get ashore – no landing craft existed in 1915. One ship's captain had what seemed a good idea for one of the British beaches: instead of making the troops climb into small boats, where they would be helpless targets for Turkish rifle fire, an old converted collier, the *River Clyde,* would sail inshore and beach itself, and then the troops could pour out of specially cut holes in the ship's sides, straight into action.

The best-laid plans sometimes go awry, however, and at Gallipoli they did:

- ✔ **French troops landed successfully on their landing beach.** They had effective covering fire from the British fleet.

- ✔ **British troops landed successfully on the western side of the peninsula.** They faced virtually no opposition.

- ✔ **The ANZAC troops landed in the wrong place and headed in the wrong direction.** Then they advanced inland too far, too fast and got thrown back again towards the beach.

- ✔ **The British landing from the *River Clyde* went disastrously wrong.** The Turks massacred the troops as they emerged from the ship. The British suffered 1,200 casualties out of 1,500 men.

ANZAC

One third of the Allied army in Gallipoli was made up of the Australian and New Zealand Army Corps, or *ANZAC.* Australia and New Zealand had sent troops to help Britain in the Boer War and now they were pleased to be fighting alongside the 'motherland' in her hour of need.

The ANZAC troops caused quite a stir. The British were taken aback at the way the Australians had no regard for rank or class and treated everyone as equal. Australian soldiers fought for their mates, not for any of that king and country stuff (see Figure 13 in the insert section). British Tommies were even more taken aback that Australian soldiers were paid five times more than they were. But not everyone was equal, even in ANZAC. Only white soldiers were to serve at Gallipoli: New Zealand's Maori troops, who were fearsome fighters, were packed off to garrison duty on Malta.

The Allied commanders had been prepared to accept heavy casualties, so despite the *River Clyde* disaster, their main concern was that the troops were now ashore.

The British are coming – to the rescue!

The Gallipoli front was in two main sectors (see Figure 9-2):

- **Cape Helles, at the southern end of the peninsula:** British and French troops had advanced inland and were sitting, facing the Turks, in a trench line that stretched across the peninsula. Neither side was able to break through. This was ironic, because the whole idea of the Gallipoli campaign was to get past the trench line on the Western Front that no one was able to break through!

- **ANZAC Cove, farther up the west coast of the peninsula:** This front, where the Australians and New Zealanders had landed, was bogged down in trench warfare too, though unlike at Cape Helles, the ANZACs were dug into the cliffs only just inland from the beach.

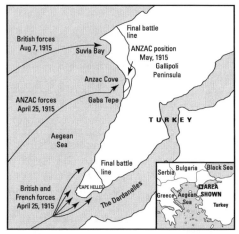

Figure 9-2:
The Gallipoli
front.

With the Gallipoli front now as badly bogged down as the Western Front, the only way to break the deadlock seemed to be to stage another landing to outflank the Turks. So the British landed troops at Suvla Bay, just north of ANZAC Cove. Just like the ANZAC landings, though, the British landed in the wrong place and weren't able to advance very far inland. The two Allied landings, at ANZAC and at Suvla, were able to join up, but they weren't able to break through the Turkish lines.

By the autumn of 1915 it was impossible to avoid the awful truth: the entire Dardanelles campaign had failed.

The Turkish officer who led the very successful defence against the ANZACs and the British at Suvla was Mustafa Kemal. Kemal was a tough commander and he led his men in fierce attacks against the Allied positions. His success at Gallipoli made him a national hero. He would go on to become the most successful Turkish general of the war and would eventually take power himself, with his name changed to Kemal Atatürk (you can read more about him in Chapters 17 and 19).

Should we stay or should we go?

After six months it was clear that the whole Dardanelles campaign – which had been intended as a way to break the deadlock of the Western Front, bring help to Russia and win the war – wasn't going to achieve any of its aims. However, deciding what to do about it didn't prove easy. The sequence of events went like this:

1. **The British government discusses withdrawal from the Dardanelles.**

2. **The British commander, Sir Ian Hamilton, recommends withdrawal.**

3. **Sir Ian Hamilton is sacked for being defeatist and replaced by General Monro.**

4. **General Monro recommends withdrawal.**

5. **Lord Kitchener says, 'No, the campaign must go on,' and he goes to Gallipoli to show Monro how to run it.**

6. **Lord Kitchener recommends withdrawal.**

Ironically, withdrawing the men before the Turks knew what was happening was about the only part of the campaign that can be called a success. The Allies were able to slip away so quietly that the Turks had no idea they'd gone. But this success couldn't disguise the fact that the campaign had been a complete and very costly disaster. It was a serious blow to the prestige of the Allies and it caused serious resentment among the Australians and New Zealanders, who felt their young men had been sacrificed for nothing. To add insult to injury, the Allied failure convinced the Bulgarians to join the war on the German side (see Chapter 5). As a result of the campaign's failure, Winston Churchill resigned from the government and rejoined the army, serving for a time as a colonel at the front in France.

And still the Ottoman war was far from over.

The Arab Spring

Nowhere did the First World War have a greater and longer-lasting impact than in the Middle East. In fact it was in this period that the term *Middle East* was first used to refer to the region: it meant the area between Europe and its colonial territories in Asia (also known as the *Far East* – that is, far from Europe). The British and French knew perfectly well that this area of desert and mountains was very rich in oil and they intended to get their hands on this precious resource if they could take the area away from the Turks. The Arabs who lived there, however, took a different view.

The Land of Araby rises up

Arabia wasn't very clearly defined at the time of the First World War: it was a region stretching over modern-day Saudi Arabia, Jordan, Palestine, Lebanon and Syria. The whole area fell within the Ottoman Empire, though the Turks didn't exercise much control over it. Outside the cities of Syria and Palestine, most of the area was inhabited by Arab tribes who were ruled by local chiefs and sheikhs, forever quarrelling among themselves and not particularly interested in what was going on elsewhere. One important exception was Sherif Hussein Ibn Ali, whose lands included the Muslim holy cities of Mecca and Medina. The title *Sherif* indicates a descendant of the daughter of the Prophet Mohammad; that title made Sherif Hussein the only serious rival to the religious authority of the Ottoman Sultan himself.

Sherif Hussein wanted to rule a large, independent Arab state as the new caliph, the successor to the prophet. However, he couldn't hope to take on the Turks without help, so in October 1916 he contacted the British high commissioner in Cairo, Sir Henry McMahon, to see whether the British were interested in an alliance. Not knowing quite what to make of Sherif Hussein's offer, but knowing that the Gallipoli campaign against the Turks was going down the drain fast, Sir Henry agreed and promised Sherif Hussein he could have a large Arab state after the war except for some areas, such as Palestine and Syria, which the British and French had earmarked for themselves. So in 1916 Sherif Hussein launched his revolt.

When Sykes met Picot

Just as the Arab Revolt was getting under way, a British official, Sir Mark Sykes, met his French opposite number, Georges Picot. They drew up an agreement about what should happen to the Middle East if the Allies were to defeat the Turks (this wasn't as remote a possibility as you might think). The Sykes–Picot Agreement, which was to be kept hush-hush until the war was over, stated that Russia should get land in the Caucasus and Kurdistan, France would get a large swathe of land across Syria, Lebanon and southern Turkey, and Britain would get a large area covering Palestine, Jordan (known then as Transjordan) and Mesopotamia. This secret agreement didn't say a word about giving any land to Sherif Hussein and his Arabs.

Hang on! I thought the Turks were winning everything?

The Turks had been very successful in the war so far, but now the Gallipoli campaign was over (see 'Disaster at the Dardanelles', earlier in the chapter) things began to change. They lost in a campaign against the Russians in the Caucasus and the British began to advance far more effectively in Mesopotamia, wiping out the memory of the fall of Kut-al-Amara (see the earlier 'A Mess in Mesopotamia' section).

The Arab revolt was underway too. It wasn't very well organised, but the British – whose new Prime Minister, David Lloyd George, was determined to drive the Turks out of the whole Middle Eastern region – managed to get enough help to the Arabs to keep it going and the Turks weren't able to stamp it out. Even so, the Arab Revolt might have remained a sideshow had it not been for the appearance on the scene of a rather unusual young Englishman: TE Lawrence, known as 'Lawrence of Arabia'. You may have heard of him.

TE Lawrence was a rather intense young man who'd developed a love of the Arabs and their lifestyle while travelling through Arabia to study Crusader castles for his dissertation at the University of Oxford. He was employed by the British Arab Bureau to liaise with Sherif Hussein's son, Prince Feisal, and the two men got on well. Lawrence became a sort of semi-official military adviser to Feisal and he hit on the crazy idea of leading a party across the desert to attack the Turkish-held port of Aqaba. The Turks didn't use Aqaba much, but the British could. Lawrence, who had a powerful personal charisma, gathered support for the attack. When the attack came, the Turks, who hadn't prepared for an attack out of the desert, were taken completely by surprise and beaten out of town. The British could now send supplies for the Arabs through the port. The Arab Revolt had suddenly become a much more serious problem for the Turks.

The twice-promised land: Arthur Balfour's Declaration

As well as the Arabs, the British, the French and the Turks, one other group had an interest in what would happen to the Middle East after the war: the Zionists. *Zionism* was the Jewish nationalist movement that worked to set up a national home for the Jewish people in Palestine. The British Prime Minister, David Lloyd George and the Foreign Secretary, Arthur Balfour, were sympathetic to Zionism. They wanted to win over Jewish opinion in the United States (American Jews were wary of supporting the Allies because Russia was violently anti-semitic).

KEY PEOPLE

Lawrence of Arabia

Stripping the legend from Lawrence of Arabia is a challenge because so much of it he deliberately created himself, though he had considerable help from an American journalist, Lowell Thomas, who turned Lawrence into an international sensation. Lawrence knew that Arabs expected their leaders to be dramatic, flamboyant hero figures and he played the part perfectly. This quiet, studious student became a guerrilla fighter of genius, continually harassing the Turks, attacking their vital railway line across the desert. At one point he was captured and sexually abused by the Turks, but they let him go without realising who he was.

Lawrence wanted to see an independent Arab kingdom set up after the war and he even accompanied Prince Feisal to the Paris Peace Conference at the end of the war as part of the Arab delegation to try to get it, but he failed. He retired to England and wrote his memoirs of the Arab Revolt, *The Seven Pillars of Wisdom,* but he left the manuscript in a train and had to write it again from memory. He joined the Royal Air Force and the army under assumed names, first 'Ross' and then 'Shaw', hoping to escape his fame, but in 1935 he was killed in a motorcycle accident in Dorset. David Lean's classic film *Lawrence of Arabia* takes some liberties with the historical detail but captures brilliantly the dangerous charm of a remarkable man.

So on 2 November 1917 Balfour wrote a letter to the British Jewish leader Lord Rothschild that became known as the *Balfour Declaration.* It stated that the British government viewed with favour the establishment of a Jewish state in Palestine, so long as nothing was done that might 'prejudice the civil and religious rights of existing non-Jewish communities in Palestine'. He didn't say *how* this could be done and no one has worked out a way of doing it since.

To Jerusalem and beyond!

Nineteen seventeen proved a very disappointing year for the Allies (Chapter 15 explains why), so British Prime Minister David Lloyd George was determined to provide some good news. He told General Edmund Allenby that he wanted Jerusalem to be in Allied hands by Christmas. And it was.

Closing in on Turkey

Allenby was advancing from Egypt against the Turkish defence line in Palestine, between Beersheba and Gaza. He was well equipped: he'd received reinforcements from the Salonika front, he had plenty of cavalry and armoured cars, he had a huge concentration of heavy artillery, and British fighter planes prevented German reconnaissance flights from seeing what he was up to.

At the end of October Allenby launched his attack. His men cut round the Turks' flanks, captured the essential wells before the Turks could poison them and drove the Turks back towards Jerusalem.

The defending Turks weren't alone. The Germans had set up a special army called *Yilderim* (or *Thunderbolt*) *Force* under General von Falkenhayn, who had been Chief of the German General Staff (you meet him in Chapters 4, 5 and 6). The Yilderim was originally supposed to fight the British in Mesopotamia, but the threat in Palestine was more urgent. Unfortunately for the Germans, the Yilderim was short of men and relied for supplies on a railway that kept having to stop because the track was different gauges. Allenby pressed on to Jerusalem and Falkenhayn wasn't able to stop the Allies taking Jerusalem in time for Christmas (see Figure 9-3).

Figure 9-3:
General Allenby hears the proclamation of the British occupation of Jerusalem.

© Imperial War Museums (Q 12617)

But Allenby wasn't finished yet. In 1918 he launched an attack over the Jordan river in conjunction with the Arab Revolt, against the Yilderim forces in Transjordan under General Liman von Sanders, who'd overseen the Turkish victory at Gallipoli. This time Liman had met his match: Allenby's attack worked and he took Transjordan's capital, Amman.

Endgame: The Armageddon

The end came in September 1918 when Allenby's troops converged on the Turks at Megiddo, also known as Armageddon – the place where, according to the Bible, the great battle will take place at the End of Time. As it turned out, the battle of September 1918 didn't bring about the end of the world, but it did end Turkey's hold over Palestine and Syria. (Chapter 16 has the details.) In October 1918 Allenby moved into Damascus, and by November, when the war finally ended, he'd advanced as far as Aleppo.

Allenby had achieved what he set out to achieve – and what he kept completely secret from his Arab allies: he'd captured all the land the British and French were proposing to take over under the terms of the Sykes–Picot Agreement. The British had made promises in both the McMahon–Sherif correspondence, which promised the Arabs a large, independent state, and the Balfour Declaration, which promised a Jewish homeland in Palestine after the war. But the Sykes–Picot Agreement was the only one that they intended to honour. And no one could convince them otherwise. (You can find out how the map of the Middle East was redrawn in Chapter 17.)

Chapter 10

The Imperial War

In This Chapter

▶ Following colonial troops to war

▶ Watching the rise of national identity

*T*he Great Powers of Europe had all amassed huge overseas empires in the years before 1914, and the quarrels between them in Europe inevitably meant that their overseas colonies were brought in as well when those disputes turned to war. Almost the whole of Africa and most of Asia, for example, was directly ruled from Europe, with the effect that when one of the European imperial states, such as France, Britain or Germany, went to war, it had an immediate impact on people living in Africa or Asia. Likewise, the self-governing dominions of Britain's empire rallied enthusiastically to the flag when war broke out. As the former Canadian Prime Minister, Sir Wilfrid Laurier, put it, 'When Great Britain is at war, we are at war'. The Australian Labour Party leader Andrew Fisher, who became Prime Minister shortly afterwards, declared that Australia should defend Britain 'to the last man and the last shilling'.

Colonial troops fought not just in the colonial theatres of war but also in Europe. Soldiers from French North Africa and from British India, as well as from British dominions such as Canada and Australia, all served in the trenches alongside soldiers from their colonial rulers.

These overseas territories meant that what started as a European quarrel quickly became a world war, a war that deeply affected and irreversibly changed those empires too. In this chapter, you find out how.

The Imperial World of Warcraft: Europe's Empires

By the time the First World War broke out, European states ruled empires that stretched right across the globe. (Chapter 2 fills you in on exactly who ruled what.) Having colonies made for tensions among the Europeans.

Not only did they often want to have more colonies than their neighbours, but they often feared that one of the other European powers was about to take over land they wanted for themselves, or move against one of their own colonies. Colonial tensions like these had been the reason for Britain's *entente* agreements with France and Russia and for the Kaiser's attempts to interfere in French Morocco (you can read about all this business in Chapter 3). When war broke out, therefore, it was natural that the troops stationed in the Europeans' colonies should start by launching expeditions against their enemies' colonies nearby.

Answering imperial calls to arms: The colonial soldiers

All the European colonial powers recruited troops from the peoples they'd colonised. Often these troops were highly trained and professional, and were widely used in the fighting in the colonies. Many troops were also deployed on the Western Front: both Britain and France, for example, sent troops from their African and Asian colonies to the Western Front.

The Europeans' overseas colonies were based on the idea of a hierarchy among peoples of different ethnic backgrounds: the white European colonisers were seen as better suited to lead than the non-white peoples of the colonies: that was why the Europeans were ruling these territories in the first place. So although all the European colonial powers recruited troops from among their colonised peoples, usually only white Europeans were allowed to be officers.

Here are some of the colonial troops who made big impressions during the war:

- ✔ **Askaris:** *Askari* was an African word for a soldier. Both the British and the Germans employed Africans as soldiers and bearers after fighting began. Askaris often had no particular uniform and they came from different African tribes and peoples, so the First World War in Africa often came down to one set of Africans tracking and fighting another.

- ✔ **Chinese and Indo-Chinese Labour Corps:** The British employed Chinese labourers to undertake all the support work for troops, and the French did the same with labourers from Indo-China. Support work was vital and often dangerous, and many men from these labour corps were killed on the Western Front.

- ✔ **Gurkhas:** The *Gurkhas* came from Nepal in northern India and were one of those Indian peoples the British thought of as manly and trustworthy. The Gurkhas had a fearsome reputation as fierce fighters, especially with their famous fighting knives or *kukris*.

- **King's African Rifles (KAR):** The KAR was formed in 1902 by merging various rifle units the British had formed mainly to fight against slave traders in West Africa. The KAR was a disciplined, uniformed unit and formed the main part of the forces Britain used to fight against the German colonies in Africa.

- **Sepoys:** *Sepoys* were soldiers of the Indian army, which had Indian troops but British officers and which came under the government of India, not the British government. They were recruited from among those Indian peoples the British thought of as 'martial' or 'military' races, such as the Rajputs and Sikhs of northern India.

- **Tonkinese Rifles:** The French had formed units of native riflemen to help them fight their enemies in Indochina. When war broke out in 1914, the French used these troops both on the Western Front and against German colonial possessions in China and the Pacific.

- **West India Regiment (WIR):** The British West India Regiment was a professional force with a history going back to the 18th century. The British used WIR soldiers in Africa and on the Western Front, though the commanders there didn't like the idea of black soldiers fighting alongside white Europeans, so the WIR in France was kept for support duties such as bringing up shells and running depots.

- **Zouaves:** *Zouaves* were soldiers from French Algeria who had a ferocious reputation. In 1915 the Zouaves on the Western Front had the dubious privilege of being among the first troops on the receiving end of a German gas attack.

An officer and a footballer (and a gentleman)

If you're thinking of the empire soldiers of the First World War just as men who were forced to fight and die for other people's quarrels then consider the story of Walter Tull, the first black officer in the British army – at a time when black people weren't allowed to be officers!

Tull came from a very poor family (his own mother put him in an orphanage) and he had a bleak future ahead of him until he was spotted by a football scout for Tottenham Hotspur (or 'Spurs'), one of the leading football teams in the English game. He became Britain's first ever black professional footballer and played for Spurs and Northampton Town, until war broke out. Tull joined the army and was quickly promoted, first as a sergeant and then he was recommended for training as an officer. He served on the Italian front as the first black officer ever to lead white British troops into battle. He was a very popular officer, known for taking care of his men and not exposing them to unnecessary risk.

Sadly, Tull was killed in action in 1918. His body was never recovered.

(Driving the Germans) out of Africa

As soon as the war started, British and French troops and settlers in Africa gathered forces to drive the Germans out of the continent. They thought the whole business would be over in a matter of weeks, and to start with it looked as if they were right.

The troops both sides used in the war in Africa were overwhelmingly African askaris that came from the tribes living within the Europeans' colonial borders. So the First World War set Africans against each other according to which Europeans happened to rule over them.

Taking Togo and capturing Cameroon

British and French forces invaded the German colony of Togo in West Africa and took it over within three weeks. The nearby German colony of Cameroon (or 'the Cameroons', as it was known then) proved a little trickier: the Germans fought back with a guerrilla campaign, using their African askari troops. However, the British and French had overwhelming numbers and they were able to stamp out the guerrillas. They also divided the country between them, with most of it going to the French, who governed much of West Africa.

A Boer war

While the British and French were having success in West Africa, South African troops were preparing to move into the neighbouring German colony of South-West Africa (today's Namibia). This invasion, however, didn't entirely go according to plan. The South African premier, General Louis Botha, led a (segregated) force of black and white South Africans into South-West Africa. But instead of a quick walkover, he found himself up against a much larger and well-prepared all-white German force of professionals, and he had to retreat, gather more troops and try again.

By no means all South Africans had supported Botha's decision to enter the war on Britain's side. Many had strong memories of the Anglo–Boer War (1899–1902), when they'd fought against the British, and they didn't see why they should fight for the British Empire hardly more than a decade later. When news arrived that the Germans had defeated Botha's invasion of South-West Africa, these anti-British South Africans saw their chance. Led by two old Boer War Generals, Christiaan de Wet and CF Beyers, they rose up in rebellion against Botha's government. Botha had to break off from his renewed invasion of German South-West Africa to deal with them. Doing that didn't prove easy.

Eventually, Botha forced de Wet to surrender and Beyers was drowned trying to escape from Botha's troops. But that didn't end South African opposition to the war: the anti-war Boers took to politics instead. A new anti-war Nationalist Party was founded under James Hertzog and it nearly won the 1915 elections. Botha had to give up his military campaigning to concentrate on defending his political position, and he handed over responsibility for war and foreign policy – and the task of destroying German power in Africa – to another old Boer War General, Jan Christian Smuts. Smuts reignited the campaign against South-West Africa with renewed energy, and the Germans finally capitulated in July 1915.

A cunning German fox

The defeat of the German forces in South-West Africa left only one German territory in Africa for the Allies to conquer: German East Africa (roughly modern-day Tanzania, Rwanda and Burundi). Unfortunately for the Allies, the local German commander was one of best generals of the war: General Paul Lettow-Vorbeck.

Lettow-Vorbeck knew that he had no chance of defeating an Allied invasion of German East Africa: he had only 160 European officers and 2,400 African askaris. The British, French and Belgians (and Portuguese, after Portugal declared war on Germany in 1916) all had troops in East Africa and could send many more, and with Britain controlling the seas, Lettow-Vorbeck couldn't hope for reinforcements to arrive from Germany. However, he knew that he could evade capture and launch raids on Allied forces so as to stop them from actually conquering the country. That way they'd have to pour troops into Africa instead of using them against his fellow Germans on other fronts. And as Lawrence of Arabia would show in the Middle East (see Chapter 9), a guerrilla war made for great publicity back at home.

How to win African friends and influence people

Unlike the South Africans, Lettow-Vorbeck had no problems putting white and black troops together in the same units. His African askaris were devoted to him and often continued the fight against the Allies even when Lettow-Vorbeck himself had been forced to pull back. Because he treated his African troops with respect, they fought all the better for him.

Tangling at Tanga

In 1914 a German warship, the *Königsberg*, which had escaped from the German defeat at the Falkland Islands (see Chapter 8), turned up near Dar-es-Salaam – the capital of German East Africa. The British quickly blockaded the port so the ship couldn't put to sea again, but Lettow-Vorbeck didn't worry about that. He was able to get hold of all its equipment and guns, so he was ready for when the Allied troops landed.

The Allied landing in German East Africa came in November 1914. A force of 8,000 British and Indian troops under General Aitken came ashore at the port of Tanga. The British assumed that because Indian troops were used to hot sun, they'd be well suited to fighting in Africa, so they hadn't bothered to give the Indians any proper training for fighting in African conditions. The British soon learned why doing that might have been a good idea: Aitken's men walked into a devastating German ambush and many of the Indian troops just turned and fled. To compound the situation, a swarm of angry bees then attacked the rest of Aitken's men. Lettow-Vorbeck launched a counter-attack and the British and Indians had no choice but to run back to their boats. Conquering German East Africa clearly wasn't going to be the doddle the British had assumed.

When news of Lettow-Vorbeck's success spread, more Germans and Africans joined him. By the end of 1915 his force was up to 3,000 Europeans and 11,000 Africans. Lettow-Vorbeck was proving a very difficult headache for the Allies.

In 1916, the Allies appointed the South African General Jan Christian Smuts to take charge of the hunt for Lettow-Vorbeck. They reckoned that an old Boer commando fighter such as Smuts should be able to deal with another guerrilla fighter like Lettow-Vorbeck. However, although Smuts certainly inflicted some heavy losses on Lettow-Vorbeck's force, the South Africans found the forests of East Africa very different from the grasslands they were used to at home. Smuts was never quite able to defeat or capture the wily German.

KEY PEOPLE

Jan Christian Smuts

Jan Smuts was a Cambridge-educated lawyer, but he fought as a very successful guerrilla commander on the Boer side in the Anglo–Boer War. After that war ended, he quickly decided that South Africa's best hope for the future lay within the British Empire and he had very little patience with those Boers who couldn't see this. He then went into politics and worked closely with the South African premier, Louis Botha.

Smuts' successes during the First World War in helping to put down the anti-war Boer uprising, leading the successful South African invasion of German South-West Africa and invading German East Africa made him something of a hero figure in South Africa and in Britain. By 1917 he had a seat as South Africa's representative on Lloyd George's Imperial War Cabinet. Then in 1919, after the war's end, he was part of the British delegation at the Paris Peace Conference, on whose behalf he undertook a tricky diplomatic mission to Hungary to check whether the recently set up communist government really did control the country. (Smuts reckoned it didn't – and he was right.) After the war, he twice served as Prime Minister of South Africa and he represented South Africa in London during the Second World War as well. Smuts was the only person to sign the peace agreements at the end of both the First *and* the Second World Wars.

Go away and fight your own wars!

Not all Africans were happy to fight and die in the Europeans' wars. The Europeans tried to enlist thousands of Africans into their forces as askaris, and this sometimes provoked serious trouble. In January 1915 an anti-British rising broke out in Nyasaland (modern-day Malawi) led by John Chilembwe. The French faced even more serious trouble: a revolt against French rule erupted in 1915 in Tunisia, and a whole local war lasting a year started the same year in French West Africa when French administrators tried to lock up local Muslim leaders to prevent an outbreak of Muslim holy war. These revolts were never likely to succeed, and they didn't, but they serve as an important reminder that Africans didn't always take the Europeans' domination of their continent lying down.

In 1917 the Allied forces in East Africa got another South African commander, General van Deventer. Deventer made more use of African askaris instead of Indian troops or white South Africans, who'd never really adapted to the terrain. Deventer's men gradually isolated and destroyed various parts of Lettow-Vorbeck's forces until finally, in October 1917, Deventer brought Lettow-Vorbeck himself to battle. The battle was hard-fought, and both sides lost so many men they each had to withdraw from the battlefield. Lettow-Vorbeck managed to escape to Portuguese territory, where he went on to evade the Portuguese too (Portugal had joined the war against Germany) just as successfully as he'd evaded Smuts and Deventer. He was still launching guerrilla raids against Allied troops when the war ended. Lettow-Vorbeck's was the only completely undefeated German force of the whole war.

We're gonna wash those Germans right outta our hair: The Pacific

Germany controlled various islands in the Pacific. After war broke out in 1914, Allied countries were determined to get them:

- ✔ Australia took over the island of New Britain in the Bismarck Archipelago, in modern-day Papua New Guinea, and the Solomon Islands.
- ✔ New Zealand took over western Samoa.

However, the Allied country with the biggest ambitions for taking over German colonies in Asia and the Pacific was Japan.

Strictly speaking, the alliance between Japan and Britain didn't state that the Japanese had to declare war on countries Britain was fighting in Europe, but the Japanese had their own plans for Germany's colonies, so they claimed that the alliance gave them no choice and they declared war on Germany on 23 August 1914.

The Japanese wanted bases in the Pacific, and above all, they wanted land in mainland China. Getting this wasn't going to be easy, because China was neutral. But Germany had land in China along the Kiaochow coastline and including the port of Tsingtao, so the Japanese knew they could always attack there.

The Japanese had no trouble taking the German island colonies in the Pacific – the Marianas, the Marshalls and the Carolines – but they hit difficulties when they tried to take Germany's territory in China. The Germans had a strong force in Tsingtao and had prepared its defences well. The Japanese had to bring a large force, with British and Indian reinforcements, and lay siege to the town. They dug trenches and then launched a huge attack, repeating the same tactic that had worked so well for them in the 1904–5 war with Russia. It worked well in 1914 too: the Germans surrendered, though at a heavy cost to the Japanese, who lost 1,400 men in the attack.

After the German colonies they'd attacked had fallen, the Japanese sent their navy farther afield to escort Allied convoys and carry Allied troops along the African coast and in the Mediterranean. However, they hadn't quite finished with China yet. In 1915 they sent the Chinese government an ultimatum of 21 demands, including allowing Japan to control the huge Chinese region of Manchuria and to take over the running of some of China's heavy industry. China had to agree: it was in no fit state to refuse. The Chinese resented this treatment, though (it's hard to blame them), and in 1917 they came into the war on the Allied side, partly to protect themselves from any further demands from the Japanese.

Empires on the Western Front

Colonial troops didn't fight just close to their homelands. From the start of the war, the British and French – unlike the Germans – decided to use colonial troops in the colonies *and* on the Western Front. Throughout the war, the French were joined by troops from North Africa; the British forces were joined in the trenches by large numbers of Canadians, Australians, Newfoundlanders and Indians. The colonial troops proved very good fighters. They played a particularly important part in some of the most celebrated battles of the war, such as the Somme (where the Newfoundlanders showed particular heroism), Vimy Ridge and Passchendaele. (I describe the Somme in more detail in Chapter 6 and Vimy and Passchendaele in Chapter 15.)

ANZAC in action

The Australian and New Zealand Army Corps (ANZAC) is best known for fighting at Gallipoli (see Chapter 9), but that was far from its only campaign. The ANZAC commander for much of the war was a British General, Sir John Birdwood. Birdwood was one of the few British commanders to emerge with some credit from the Gallipoli campaign and he went on to lead ANZAC on the Western Front until he was replaced in March 1918 by the Australian (and, frankly, much better) General Sir John Monash.

ANZAC forces had gained a tough reputation at Gallipoli, and they lived up to it in full on the Western Front. The Australian forces were involved in some of the thickest fighting of the Battle of the Somme in 1916 (see Chapter 6) and over the whole of the war they had a casualty rate of 65 per cent, one of the highest figures in the British Empire. And the New Zealanders captured the Belgian village of Messines in 1917 in one of the most successful Allied attacks of the war.

ANZAC cavalry was also attached to General Allenby's forces in Palestine and played a crucial role in routing the Turks at the Battle of Megiddo in 1918 (see Chapter 16 for more on this campaign).

Er, could we go somewhere nicer, please?

The Indian troops on the Western Front, who were divided into two divisions named Meerut and Lahore after places in Northern India the troops were familiar with, played an important part in the British victory at Neuve Chapelle, the only real Allied success on the Western Front in 1915 (see Chapter 5). However, the sepoys soon grew disillusioned by the horror of trench warfare and heavy bombardment. 'This is not warfare,' one sepoy wrote, 'it is Hell.' Indian troops began to try to deliberately get themselves wounded, usually in the hand (doing this was quite easy: you just raised your hand above the parapet and German machine gunners did the rest) so they could be sent home.

In 1915 the British decided that the Western Front was bad for the morale of their Indian troops and withdrew them from the European war. Instead Britain used Indian troops against the Turks in the Middle East and in Africa against the Germans.

Different places for different races

Britain and France both drew strict racial distinctions between different types of colonial troops on the Western Front. They had no problems about using white colonial troops. The 'problem' (as the commanders saw it) came with non-white troops. The French used their North African troops in the trenches; the British kept their black troops, even the men of the experienced West India Regiment, behind the lines, working in support roles. The British put Indian troops into the trenches but not Chinese, who were only allowed to carry out labour duties; the French felt the same about their troops from Indo-China.

Labour and support units were essential for keeping the Western Front together: they maintained the trenches, kept the artillery supplied with shells, and drove supplies and men to and from the front line. The work was highly dangerous and many men from support units were killed in action. No shame at all was attached to the work. Nevertheless, the Allied leaders saw this work as a service role, particularly suitable for some races of colonial troops. They thought that some people, such as North Indians and North Africans, were fierce warriors who'd fight well, but that others, such as the Chinese and other Africans, were less warlike and disciplined and would do more harm than good if they were given rifles and sent into action. Racial attitudes like these would be unacceptable today but they were very common at this period: after all, they help explain why the Europeans had these empires in the first place!

The military and civil authorities were particularly worried about what would happen if colonial troops got too friendly with the local womenfolk in France or England. White communities had a particular horror of what they called *miscegenation,* which meant people of different races having sex and producing 'half-caste' children. In fact, this happened quite commonly in the colonies themselves. A huge mixed-race 'Anglo-Indian' population existed in British India, for example, and similar communities existed in colonial Africa. Yet the British and French liked to pretend that inter-racial sex didn't happen, and they certainly didn't want it to start among the colonial troops in Europe.

Despite the best efforts of the generals to keep colonial troops away from local women, many soldiers seem to have managed to get close to French women: some of the men boasted in their letters home about it happening. Of course, quite possibly these men were all talk . . . .

The empire on the Somme

The British assault on the Somme on 1 July 1916 (see Chapter 6) may well have been a disaster, but colonial troops played an important part in the effort. The attack was to be almost entirely British-run, which meant that it involved troops from many different parts of Britain and the empire, particularly Ireland, Newfoundland and South Africa:

✔ **Ireland:** Ireland was part of the United Kingdom, but it had been granted *home rule* (that is, dominion status) before the war. This was to cause serious trouble in 1916 (I explain the Irish situation in 'The Easter Rising – Ireland's terrible beauty', later in this chapter). Irish troops were involved in some of the hardest fighting in the Battle of the Somme:

  • **The Royal Irish:** Three Irish regiments, the Royal Irish Fusiliers, the Royal Dublin Fusiliers and the Royal Inniskilling Fusiliers, went into action at Beaumont Hamel on 1 July. The Germans knew they were coming because a huge mine exploded under the German line just before the attack. As a result, the Germans brought up more troops quickly and the Irish regiments, along with the other British regiments attacking alongside them, suffered very heavy casualties and had to fall back.

- **The Tyneside Irish:** The Tyneside Irish were troops recruited from among the Irish community living and working on Tyneside, in the north-east of England. Three thousand of them attacked on 1 July and managed to penetrate far behind the German lines. However, no one was able to support them and they had to fall back. By the time they got back to their lines, only 50 men were left alive and unwounded.

- **Ulster:** The Ulster Division 'went over the top' on 1 July opposite the Schwaben Redoubt, a very strong German position near Thiepval. They took the position but then they found themselves stuck out on a limb: the attacks on either side of them had failed, so they had to fall back. Nine Victoria Crosses were awarded to British troops for their actions on 1 July 1916, and three of them went to the Ulsters.

  Every year a big march is held at Drumcree on 1 July in honour of the Ulstermen who died that day. In the difficult politics of Northern Ireland, this march often provokes trouble with the Catholic community, but it's worth remembering why the Somme is so important to people of Ulster to this day.

- ✔ **Newfoundland:** Newfoundlanders responded enthusiastically to the outbreak of war. They served in their own unit and 'went over the top' on 1 July 1916 opposite the village of Beaumont Hamel. More than 90 per cent became casualties, a devastating blow both for the troops and for the small community back home.

- ✔ **South Africa:** The South Africans attacked at Delville Wood, a deadly area that got nicknamed 'Devil's Wood'. The South Africans took the wood from the Germans and held on for three days until eventually they were relieved. Theirs was one of the most heroic actions of the day, and the area now holds the South African memorial to all those from South Africa who died on the Western Front.

Victory at Vimy, passion at Passchendaele

Canadian troops had a fearsome reputation as tenacious fighters on land and in the air. Billy Bishop, for example, was one of the deadliest fighter pilots of the war. The Canadian forces' moment of glory on the Western Front came in the battles of 1917 at Arras and Ypres (see Chapter 15).

Under the British General Sir Julian Byng (another one of those successful British generals of the First World War whom most people have never heard of) they captured the fortified German position on Vimy Ridge, a steep slope dominating the countryside all around, where the Germans had beaten off all previous attacks (see Figure 10-1). The Canadian assault was one of the most successful Allied attacks of the whole war. Today a huge memorial to the Canadians who died on the Western Front stands on the spot.

Figure 10-1: Canadian troops tend to a wounded German soldier on Vimy Ridge.

© Imperial War Museums (CO 1189)

In June 1917 Byng was replaced by the Canadian General Sir Arthur Currie (Byng's link with Canada continued: in 1921 he became Governor-General of Canada). British commander Field Marshal Sir Douglas Haig was preparing a major Allied offensive in Belgium, near Ypres, and the Canadians were an important part of his plans (see Chapter 15). Canadian tunnellers helped set up the huge mine that successfully destroyed Messines Ridge before the battle began, but Currie was very concerned about the plans for the main attack at the village of Passchendaele. He told Haig that the ground was impossibly bad and his men would suffer horrific casualties. Haig, however, insisted on the attack, so the Canadians had to valiantly fight their way through impossible mud and slime. Yet they still managed to take and hold the village. It was a sign of just what good soldiers the Canadians were. Unfortunately, Currie's prediction about horrific casualties proved all too true.

Forging National Identities

Many people in the British dominions were very proud of their British identity: Canadians, for example. Even the French Canadians of Quebec, who normally opposed English-speaking British rule, could support the war, because it was being fought to push the Germans out of France (though they mounted serious opposition to conscription when it was introduced in Canada in 1917). Conservatives and Liberals put their quarrels on hold for the duration of the war, and in 1917 they formed a coalition government of national unity under the Conservative leader Sir Robert Borden. All agreed that Britain's war was Canada's war.

Canadians tended to hold on to their British identity, not least because it helped differentiate them from the United States. The Canadian successes in the war, such as Vimy Ridge, gave Canadians a great sense of national pride. However, in Canada, as in other parts of Britain's empire, the heavy losses gave Canadians an equally strong sense of the high price they'd paid for their loyalty to Britain.

Across the Pacific, much the same was true of Australia and New Zealand, which had only recently been formed into unified nations. Like Canada, both were proud of their British identity, but in Australia and New Zealand the war had a huge impact on the way these two new nations developed.

Under southern skies: Australia and New Zealand

The First World War provided Australia and New Zealand with a great opportunity to start asserting themselves as independent nations. The war didn't break the two countries' relationship with Britain; in fact, in some ways the shared sacrifices they'd all made strengthened that relationship, but the war also gave each country a sense of equality with Britain. Although Australia and New Zealand retained their strong trading links with Britain after the war and throughout the 1920s and 1930s, when war with Germany broke out again in 1939 and once more they rallied to Britain's side, this time they each wanted to keep control of their own armed forces. Britain's dominions had grown up.

Australia

The British had founded different colonies in Australia and it was only in 1901 that they came together as a federation to form a single country. Australians were an independently minded lot, fond of speaking their minds but also very proud of being British. Australian faith in British leadership took a severe knock, however, after the Gallipoli campaign (you can find the details in Chapter 9). Australians thought their young men had been sacrificed in futile attacks ordered by the British commander Sir Ian Hamilton. (Hamilton became a genuine hate figure for many Australians during the war and for many years afterwards.) Within a year of the Gallipoli campaign, the anniversary of the landings at Anzac Cove was being celebrated in Australia as *Anzac Day,* to commemorate those who died at Gallipoli. That date – 25 April – is still one of Australians' most important days of the year.

Charles Bean's national narrative

Australian suffering at Gallipoli at the hands of their British commanders became a sort of cherished national narrative thanks to the writings of Charles Bean, an Australian schoolmaster who wrote the Australian *Official History* of the war. Bean was outraged by the sufferings of the ANZAC troops at Gallipoli and his version of events showed them as helpless victims of incompetent and uncaring British generals.

Bean's work was central to how Australians were beginning to identify themselves as a separate people from the British. You'd never guess from reading Bean's version of events that the great majority of the Allied troops at Gallipoli were actually British and French, but if his account isn't strictly accurate, it was very popular in Australia and has shaped the way Australians view the war to this day.

Billy Hughes is in charge

In 1915 the Labour leader Billy Hughes became Prime Minister of Australia. Like most Australians, Hughes was staunchly pro-British and remained so even after the news of the disaster at Gallipoli, when many politicians criticised him for his pro-British stand. Hughes reckoned that it was in Australia's best interests to stick close to the 'mother country': he even promised to introduce conscription into Australia, but he met such strong opposition to it in his own party that he had to put the issue to a referendum which he narrowly lost, though he soon recovered his political fortunes and won a big majority in the next elections.

Australia remained very pro-British throughout the war, and in the years that followed it continued to maintain strong trade links with Britain. However, the war had shown that some groups in Australia, especially the Irish community, the Catholic Church and the trade unions, wouldn't go along with absolutely anything the British might want, such as conscription. When the Second World War broke out, some of these groups would start looking to develop closer ties with the United States.

New Zealand

New Zealand had long been in Australia's shadow: its first white settlers had come from Australia, and Europeans often thought of New Zealand as a sort of Australian suburb. Like Australia, New Zealand hadn't been a single country for very long; only since 1907, in fact. And like Australians, New Zealanders were very proud of their British identity and heritage.

New Zealand had a much smaller population than Australia, so it was the junior partner within ANZAC. Nevertheless, per head of population New Zealand suffered higher casualty rates than almost any other country in the war. Perhaps because they saw themselves as different from Australians, New Zealanders remained loyal to Britain even after Gallipoli, and didn't join in the Australians' attacks on British military leadership. In 1916 New Zealand introduced conscription with very little controversy.

New Zealanders fought with great courage in all theatres of the war, including a major contribution to the Battle of Passchendaele. The war was New Zealand's opportunity to make its mark on the world stage and the New Zealanders intended to make the most of it. Historians agree that they did.

India's aspirations

India was by far the most important part of Britain's empire: it provided a huge amount of wealth and a substantial part of Britain's armed forces. Strictly speaking, India wasn't a colony but a sort of empire-within-an-empire: the British monarch had a separate title as Emperor of India.

The British had developed many of the institutions of a fully-functioning state, as a result of which India had excellent systems of railways, communications, education and government. However, the administration of the country was almost entirely in the hands of the British. Indians were only allowed a very small role in the government of their own country.

An Indian nationalist movement called the Indian National Congress (INC) tried to put pressure on the British government to grant more self-government to India, as it had already done to the dominions, such as Australia and Canada. When the war broke out, the INC supported it because they hoped that the British would grant India self-government in return for its help. So Indian troops served on all fronts – in Europe, in Mesopotamia, in Africa and in Palestine (see Figure 14 in the insert section).

In 1917 the Secretary of State for India made a statement in Parliament in which he said that India should indeed move towards 'responsible government' when the war was over. Indians thought he meant that they would get home rule at the end of the war, and that's what they expected to happen.

When the war ended, however, they soon released that the British had no intention of granting India home rule. Before long, protests were breaking out all over India against what they saw as a huge British broken promise. In the end, the First World War proved an important point in the story of how India won its independence.

I say more about the impact of the war in India in Chapter 17.

The Easter Rising: Ireland's terrible beauty

Ireland had been a part of the United Kingdom since 1801. However, Irish nationalists had campaigned vigorously for years for Ireland to be granted home rule, such as Australia or Canada.

Home rule? No, thanks!

The idea of home rule alarmed the Protestants of Ulster, in the north of Ireland, because they knew that a self-governing Ireland was bound to be dominated by Catholics. So the Protestants campaigned equally vigorously to maintain the union between Ireland and Britain. The British government introduced home rule for Ireland in 1912 and it finally passed into law two years later, but this move nearly provoked a civil war between the two camps. To avoid any more trouble, in 1914 the British government suspended Ireland's home rule until after the European war had ended.

Fight for Ireland by fighting for Britain

Suspending home rule presented the Irish with a puzzle: would the British keep their promise and re-enact home rule after the war (which is what the Catholics were hoping for), or would they change their mind and keep Ireland in the United Kingdom (which is what the Protestants wanted)? One way to influence the British decision, many Irishmen thought, was to join the British army and fight in the war.

Thousands of Catholic Irish joined the British army to show they were loyal to Britain and that Britain could safely re-enact home rule as soon as the war was over. Likewise, thousands of Protestants joined up to show *they* were loyal to Britain too and that Britain should repay their loyalty by keeping Ireland in the United Kingdom after the war. Not surprisingly, these two different Irish groupings tended to join different regiments.

Although most people in Ireland supported the war, a small group didn't. They weren't interested in home rule within the British Empire: they wanted an independent Irish Republic, and they wanted it now.

The Easter Rising

At Easter 1916, Irish nationalists, led by Patrick Pearse and James Connolly, seized Dublin's General Post Office and proclaimed an Irish Republic. British troops soon crushed the rising after heavy street fighting. The people of Dublin were furious with the rebels: they thought that staging an uprising while Irishmen were away fighting and dying in the trenches was an unforgivable act of betrayal. One nationalist, the consular official Sir Roger Casement, had even landed in Ireland from a German U-boat with arms for the rebels.

But then the British shot themselves in the foot by starting to execute the prisoners they'd taken, including Sir Roger Casement. Suddenly, the rebels became martyrs and support for an independent Irish republic skyrocketed. The Irish poet William Butler Yeats wrote that 'a terrible beauty' had been born – the blood-soaked beauty of an independent Ireland.

Although the British had put down the Easter Rising, they'd far from defeated support for an Irish Republic. As soon as the war was over, a much bigger uprising against British rule began. I look at this in Chapter 17.

An empire state?

In 1917 British Prime Minister David Lloyd George decided that the empire's contribution to the war was so important that it needed to be involved at the highest level. He invited the prime ministers of the self-governing colonies and dominions to form an Imperial War Cabinet, which he would chair, rather as if the empire was a single federal state.

The tragedy of Tom Kettle

Tom Kettle was an Irish nationalist lawyer and poet. He devoted his life to fighting for *home rule* for Ireland – that's a form of devolution that would leave Ireland within the United Kingdom but governing its own affairs. He joined the British army to show that Irish nationalists were loyal to Britain and would help in its hour of need. And then the Easter Rising broke out and people in Ireland forgot home rule and demanded an independent Irish republic. Suddenly, home rulers such as Tom Kettle looked naïve and out of date.

Tom Kettle was killed at Guinchy on the Somme in July 1916. After the war, when Ireland had won its independence, a memorial to him was erected in Dublin. His widow wanted it to have the words 'Killed in France', but the Irish government didn't like to be reminded of the Irish who fought in the British army. The most they would allow were the words 'Killed at Guinchy', which meant nothing to anyone who didn't know where Guinchy was or why Tom Kettle was there.

In fact, apart from a photo opportunity at the start, the Imperial War Cabinet never fully operated. It consisted of Lloyd George plus whichever colonial representative happened to be in London at any one time. But the fact Lloyd George had formed it was a sign that Britain's relationship with its colonies was changing quite rapidly: perhaps the time was coming when the colonies would find they didn't really need British leadership at all.

Chapter 11

America Goes to War

Up until the First World War, the United States had always taken a simple line on foreign policy: it stayed out of Europe's quarrels and it expected the Europeans to stay out of America's. Yet by the end of the war, the United States had not only come into the war and tilted the balance of power in favour of the Allies, but President Woodrow Wilson was even proposing plans to change the shape of the world.

In this chapter, I explain how a country that had for so long deliberately turned its back on foreign war, especially in Europe, came to enter into and play such an important part in the First World War.

Woodrow Wilson's World

The man who took the United States into the war was President Woodrow Wilson. Wilson had an academic background: he'd been president of Princeton University, where he lectured in modern history and politics. Wilson had a clear idea of the sort of higher-profile role he thought the United States ought to play on the world stage.

Not long after the war broke out in Europe, Wilson envisioned a special role for the United States as a peacemaker, mediating between the warring sides. The United States had played that role in ending the war between Russia and Japan back in 1905 and Wilson thought that peacemaking could be the country's special contribution to world affairs in the 20th century. However, although the United States stayed neutral, Wilson himself wasn't quite so even-handed. He came from the southern United States and, like many southerners at the time, his general outlook was pro-British. He thought that the Allies were fighting to defend Christian, civilised values against German militarism and aggression. If Wilson's attempts at mediation failed, however, and especially if it looked as if German militarism might prevail, then, he thought, America's place was alongside the Allies. However, by no means all Americans agreed with him.

The American melting pot

In the early 20th century America was changing rapidly, probably more so than any other country on the planet. Thousands of immigrants were arriving in New York every day, completely transforming the nature of American society. By 1914 the predominant British influence was being rivalled by the new cultures of the immigrants, and the country had to get used to a whole range of new national communities, such as Italian-Americans, Hungarian-Americans, Polish-Americans, German-Americans and Jewish-Americans.

These immigrants went to America to make a new life for themselves because their own countries offered them no future. Many went because they were poor and were likely to stay poor. Some, such as the Jews of Russia, went to escape persecution. Whatever the reason for their going to America, they had no wish to return home. America was their home now. This attitude lay at the root of what historians call American isolationism, and because these new Americans had the vote, the President had to take their views very carefully into account.

Don't go there! America's isolationists

Ever since the founding of the United States after the American Revolution, America had maintained a long tradition of *isolationism,* meaning that Americans liked to leave other countries, especially European countries, to sort out their own problems without Americans having to get involved. The United States certainly had a foreign policy but it didn't want to get tied down in any entangling alliances that might drag it into other people's wars.

Most American governments followed an isolationist policy, and with good reason:

- ✔ Americans believed their country was special – richer, happier and more morally upright than other countries. Why would anyone want to spoil that situation by getting dragged into other people's wars?

- ✔ Americans didn't have a very large army, so they felt tangling with the huge European armies on their home ground would be a bad idea. Americans were proud of their victories in the past over the British, but those had been fought on American soil. Travelling over to Europe to fight a war was a very different, and much riskier, proposition. It would also mean investing in a bigger navy, to protect both the troopships and American merchant ships, and that would mean yet more expense for the American taxpayer.

✔ Americans came from so many different European countries that taking sides in any European war was bound to divide Americans too. German-Americans, for example, would never agree to fight alongside the British. On the other hand, Italian-Americans and all those of British descent would want to fight on the Allied side and against the Germans. The best way to avoid trouble between these different groups of Americans would be for America to stay out of any war in Europe.

After the war broke out, news of the appalling losses being suffered by all sides simply added to the list of good reasons many Americans had for thinking their country was much better off keeping out of it. Prominent people and groups began demanding that America continue to stay neutral and out of the war:

✔ **Henry Ford:** The famous industrialist was a prominent opponent of getting involved. He thought the war was a European matter and that it would be an economic disaster for the United States to get dragged in.

✔ **Women's groups:** A large number of women's groups existed in America in the 1910s, campaigning for a wide range of issues, including closing down bars and securing votes for women. Women's groups were strongly opposed to the idea of America getting involved in a major European war – they didn't want to send their own sons off to get killed in someone else's war.

✔ **Churches:** The many churches and religious groups within America called on Wilson to negotiate a peace settlement between the two sides fighting in Europe, but not to get involved in the war itself. Wilson did offer to negotiate between the two sides but they turned him down.

✔ **Irish-Americans:** The Irish were a powerful political lobby, especially in New York. They'd never agree to fight alongside Britain, the country they blamed for dragging Ireland into poverty. They became even more hostile to Britain after the 1916 Easter Rising in Dublin (Chapter 10 has the details).

Beware U-boats!

When Germany's Admiral von Tirpitz decided to launch unrestricted *U-boat* (that is, submarine) warfare in 1915 (and Chapter 8 tells you why he reached this decision) he knew perfectly well that American merchants ships would be torpedoed. Americans were naturally outraged to learn that German U-boats could stop and sink unarmed merchant ships flying the American flag in international waters. But even though American shipping losses soon began to mount, President Wilson still couldn't bank on getting enough support at home to take America to war. Many Americans thought the U-boat sinkings merely showed what a nasty business the European war was and how wise the US was to stay out of it.

Then the U-boats went too far. On 7 May 1915 a German U-boat sank the British passenger liner *Lusitania,* with the loss of 128 American lives (see Chapter 8). Americans were aghast and angry, and it began to look as if the sinking would bring America into the war. But the Germans had given warnings in the American press that they considered it a legitimate target and advising American passengers that they travelled at their own risk. Horrifying though the sinking was, it wasn't enough on its own to win over those Americans who were determined to stay out of the war.

To appease American isolationists Wilson announced that the United States was too proud to fight, no matter what outrages the Germans might commit. This approach didn't go down well in the Allied countries: some people in Britain thought that Wilson should have said the United States was too *scared* to fight. However, Wilson knew that the German U-boat campaign was making war much more likely, so he ordered a fleet of new battleships for the navy, though they wouldn't be ready until 1919. The United States wasn't in the war yet, but it was certainly getting its boots on.

He kept you out of war! The 1916 election

Nineteen sixteen was a presidential election year and Wilson was standing for a second term. With so much feeling against getting involved in the war, winning the election wouldn't be easy if he allowed his personal sympathy for the Allies to become an election issue.

By 1900 American politics had settled into the two-party system you see today, with Republicans and Democrats. By the time of the 1916 presidential election, these two parties had been joined by two other political groups, both of whom were putting pressure on Wilson:

- **The Preparedness Movement** thought that America was far too weak compared with the Europeans. Preparedness Movement members, which included many Republicans, wanted to build up America's position in the world and to see conscription introduced in order to get America's armed forces up to a suitable level for a Great Power. They thought that Wilson should be doing much more to protect American shipping from German attack and that America needed something much bigger and more efficient to defend it than the existing National Guard.

- **The Progressive Party** thought that America needed a big dose of social reform, in order to iron out inequalities between rich and poor and make government more efficient and answerable to people's needs. They wanted to see women get the vote, limits imposed on alcohol consumption, working conditions in factories improve and an end to child labour. They believed that Wilson was already spending too much on new battleships and that the only people who'd benefit from them would be the rich arms manufacturers and profiteers.

By and large, President Wilson sympathised with the Preparedness Movement. He too thought America needed a larger army and a much larger navy in order to make its presence felt in the world. However, the Progressives disagreed. They thought that building up the army and navy was just an excuse for government not tackling the question of poverty among America's immigrants and farmers. Both the Progressives and the Republicans opposed Wilson's spending plans (the Progressives did this because they didn't approve of spending on armaments; the Republicans did it because Wilson was a Democrat), so he couldn't increase America's fighting forces by quite as much as he'd hoped.

Wilson knew that many Americans feared getting dragged into the war, so he kept his campaign slogan very simple: 'He kept you out of war!' This slogan suggested, of course (though it didn't actually say – Wilson was a politician, remember), that Wilson would carry on keeping America out of the war if he was re-elected.

The election result was close: Wilson got 52.2 per cent of the electoral vote, whereas his Republican rival got 47.8 per cent. However, Wilson had clearly won and he got his second term of office.

Five months later he took America into the war.

KEY PEOPLE

Woodrow Wilson

Woodrow Wilson's reputation has gone up and down like a rollercoaster ever since his death in 1924. At the end of the war many people thought he had the key to world peace and that, thanks to him, war would be a thing of the past. When it became clear that that wasn't going to happen, people turned against him and blamed him for being so naïve and making the world situation after the war even more dangerous and unstable than it had been before 1914.

Wilson suffered from very poor health, and he was seriously ill at the time of the peace conference in 1919, which might explain why he didn't do more to force the Europeans to accept his ideas. But Wilson could also be very narrow minded and intolerant himself. He was a southerner and he shared the common prejudice at the time against black people: one of his favourite films was DW Griffith's controversial epic *Birth of a Nation,* which has the Ku Klux Klan as its heroes. He tended to think that if people didn't accept his ideas, something was wrong with them, so it was pointless to try to win them over. This attitude won him many political enemies, who undermined his cherished project for America to take a leading role in a new League of Nations he wanted to set up.

Wilson had many good political ideas, but in the end he didn't have the political skills he needed to make them happen.

You Know How President Wilson Kept America Out of the War? Well, He's Changed His Mind

In 1915, and again in 1916, Wilson sent his close friend and adviser Colonel Edward House to Europe to try to negotiate a peace settlement. House didn't get very far, but his talks with the British did convince the Germans that, whatever Wilson might say in public, he did, in fact, support the Allies.

The Allies had one major advantage in their dealings with the United States: the transatlantic telegraph cable, which was under British control. The British cut the German cable, so that all messages between Germany and the United States – even German ones – had to be transmitted via Britain. This gave Britain control over exactly what messages the United States did or didn't get from Europe.

By 1917 the Germans regarded the United States as, in effect, an enemy country, so they put plans in place to attack the United States both at sea and closer to home:

✔ **Unrestricted U-boat warfare:** In 1917, Germany announced that it was resuming unrestricted U-boat warfare after a period during which international outcry had led to its temporarily cancelling the policy. U-boats would now sink any ship, anywhere at sea, if the Germans thought doing so was necessary in order to win the war. American ships carrying food or supplies to England were regarded as entirely legitimate targets, and the Germans promptly sank three of them. (Chapter 8 tells you more about the German U-boat campaign.)

Americans couldn't simply accept that the Germans would sink American ships whenever they felt like it.

✔ **German plans for Mexico:** In 1917 the British intercepted a telegram from the German Foreign Minister, Arthur Zimmermann, to the German Minister in Mexico City. The telegram gave instructions to the Minister to negotiate a deal with the government of Mexico whereby Mexico would invade the USA and, with German help, recover all the land it had lost over the years to the USA: Texas, New Mexico and Arizona. The British reckoned the telegram would make interesting reading in Washington, and they were right.

This evidence of a German plot to help an invasion of the United States caused a wave of angry indignation in America. Even staunch isolationists reckoned the Germans had gone too far this time. In fact, the telegram suggested it might be more dangerous for America to stay out of the war and be invaded than it would be to join in.

Sabotage!

On 30 July 1916 New Jersey and everywhere for miles around was shaken by a huge explosion when a large ammunition dump on Black Tom Island, near Jersey City, blew up. The force of the blast was felt through the centre of New York: it blew out the stained-glass windows of St Patrick's Cathedral and even badly damaged the Statue of Liberty. The explosion caused $20 million of damage – that's not exactly small change nowadays, but it was a huge sum of money then. It was the worst terrorist attack New York would see until 9/11.

Everyone assumed the explosion was caused by German sabotage, because the firm that owned the ammunition dump was exporting munitions to Britain. And the assumption proved to be true, though it took the Germans some time to accept responsibility – not until 1953, in fact!

Another explosion at an arms factory at Lyndhurst, New Jersey, also seemed to be the result of German sabotage. These examples of German attacks on American soil made Wilson's task of persuading Congress that German aggression could only be halted by military action all the easier.

The Zimmermann telegram finally won Americans over to the idea of joining the war. Wilson made a speech to Congress outlining why repeated acts of aggression by the imperial German government against American shipping and now against the territory of the United States itself (see the nearby 'Sabotage!' sidebar) gave them no choice: they had to declare war. He reassured them that it wasn't going to be a war for conquest; he called it a war to safeguard democracy and to end all wars. Congress agreed, and on 6 April 1917 the United States declared war on Germany.

Even though America was now in the war, Wilson wanted to make it clear that the US wasn't lowering itself to the level of the European powers. America had been forced into the war by German aggression. It would send troops over to France and do whatever was necessary to bring the war to an end and then it would ship its boys home again. For this reason, the United States joined the Allies but didn't join their alliance. The United States would be an *Associated Power,* supporting the Allies, fighting alongside the Allies, but not one of the Allies and definitely not under the Allies. Think of it as the political equivalent of an 'I'm with these idiots' T-shirt.

What were the Germans thinking?

Trying to understand what the Germans thought they were doing can be difficult. They knew perfectly well that at some point unrestricted U-boat warfare would bring America into the war – that was precisely why German

Chancellor Bethmann-Hollweg had opposed it. And anyone knows that if you start plotting to take some of a country's own national territory, that country will defend itself. So what on earth were the Germans thinking?

With hindsight, you can see that bringing America into the war meant that Germany and its allies had no hope of winning. However, that wasn't quite how the situation seemed to the Germans at the time. Their thinking was as follows:

✔ **The United States has only a small army.** America had no conscription and its armed forces were very small by European standards – good for fighting against native American tribes or the Spanish in 1898, but hardly up to European standards. To put it bluntly (American readers, keep calm here!) the Germans thought the United States was so feeble that they didn't particularly care even if America did come into the war.

✔ **The U-boats will sink the Americans anyway.** The Germans reckoned their U-boats would be able to sink so many American troopships that America would hardly be able to get any men to the Western Front.

✔ **The Mexicans will make mincemeat of the Americans.** The Mexico plot wasn't as odd as it might seem. An attack on the American homeland, the Germans thought, might cause the United States to keep more troops at home rather than sending them to Europe. Mexico was a good country to approach because it was going through a period of radical revolution and civil war, and the United States had tried – not very successfully – to intervene. In 1914 the United States had occupied the port of Veracruz, and two years later Wilson sent General Pershing into Mexico with a large force of troops to seize hold of the Mexican revolutionary leader Pancho Villa, who'd launched a brief raid into the American state of New Mexico in search of supplies for his men. The Mexicans ran rings round them. The Germans reckoned the Mexicans might very well be interested in launching their own invasion of their overbearing northern neighbour.

✔ **The Russians are out of the war and nothing can stop Germany from winning.** The Russian Revolution broke out in February 1917 (see Chapter 15 for more about this) and the Eastern Front virtually collapsed. The Germans reckoned they'd soon be able to transfer thousands of troops from the Eastern Front to the Western Front, break through the Allied lines, take Paris and win the war – all before the United States knew which day it was.

All this shows that provoking the United States wasn't quite as mad an idea as you might think, although it's hard to see that *deliberately* getting a country the size of the United States to declare war on you is ever a sensible idea. Even so, the Germans had badly miscalculated. Each one of their assumptions proved to be wrong:

✔ The American army could quickly get a lot bigger, and it did. (The Germans had made exactly the same miscalculation about the British army at the start of the war. Some people never learn.)

- The British were developing effective weapons to destroy U-boats. The Germans wouldn't be able to stop American troopships getting through after all.

- Mexico very sensibly decided not to have anything to do with the German plans to invade the United States.

- Although the Eastern Front did indeed collapse and the Germans did move their troops west, they just weren't strong enough to win the war quickly – Chapter 16 shows why.

When we win: Wilson's Fourteen Points

Declaring war presented the United States with a big problem: what would it want to gain if – as seemed entirely possible – it emerged on the winning side? Wilson consolidated his thoughts about this question into a set of Fourteen Points that he announced in January 1918. His points made clear what he thought had caused the war in the first place and what the Allies could do to make sure these things never caused any trouble again.

Wilson's Fourteen Points fitted into three main categories:

- **General points:**

  - Future international agreements should be open for everyone to know about, with no more of the secret diplomacy that had caused the war.

  - Everyone should have complete freedom of the seas, with no danger of merchant ships being sunk by submarines or warships.

  - International trade should be completely free.

  - All countries should disarm.

  - The future of colonial territories should be decided impartially, taking into account the colonised people's wishes as well as those of their rulers.

- **Points about specific countries:**

  - Russia should be left to sort out its own future.

  - The Germans should get out of Belgium.

  - The Germans should get out of France and give Alsace-Lorraine back.

  - Austria-Hungary should give its Italian-speaking lands to Italy.

  - Austria-Hungary should also allow all its different peoples to set up their own states.

- The Balkan states should be restored and their frontiers and territorial integrity guaranteed, giving Serbia access to the sea.

- The Ottoman Empire should allow its non-Turkish peoples to set up their own states and keep the Dardanelles open for everyone to use.

- Poland should be liberated, with internationally agreed borders.

✔ **A League of Nations:** A special international association should be created to solve international disputes in the future.

To the Great Powers in Europe, Wilson's Fourteen Points seemed rather ambitious and not very realistic. At home, however, they did reassure Americans that the country wasn't going to war to get hold of anyone else's territory, and that after the war was over the world was indeed going to be a much safer and more peaceful place.

All the Americans had to do now was win the war.

Gearing Up for Action: A Nation at War

The last time the United States had geared itself up for a major war had been when the Civil War broke out back in 1861, so by 1917 the Americans were a bit out of practice in how to set about it. They had a whole army to recruit (see Figure 15 in the insert section) and train, methods of trench warfare to learn from scratch, weapons and equipment to get hold of, and the whole question of how to transport their troops over to Europe and what they'd be doing when they got there to work out. As if that wasn't enough, they also had to raise money, keep their factories and farms going while their young men were away and generally get the whole country involved in the war effort. Doing all this was never going to be easy, and for the first few months the United States' war effort was pretty chaotic. No one knew exactly what they needed to do or who should be doing what.

Apart from a small U-boat raid in Massachusetts, the Germans pretty much left the Americans alone after the declaration of war. They thought the Americans were doing a splendid job of hampering their own war effort and didn't need any German help!

There's no place like the home front

The Europeans had needed to gear their peoples up for war right from the start (Chapter 12 has the details), and Americans also soon realised that the war would be won or lost on the home front. To fight the war a country needed money and labour, and it was up to people at home to provide both. (Food was just as vital to the war effort at home; Chapter 12 looks at how America fared here.)

Money

Wars are phenomenally expensive and governments always have trouble paying for them. They usually borrow heavily and raise people's taxes, but the American government also sold *Liberty Bonds,* which were a form of government borrowing in order to pay for war materials, but borrowing from ordinary people instead of from international finance. People would buy bonds from the government and the government would pay them back interest at a fixed percentage each year until the end of the war – when, in theory, they'd get the original price back. The more bonds you bought, the more interest you'd get and the more money you'd make from supporting the war. (The government made even more money from bonds by charging tax on people's income from the interest – in effect making them pay for having loaned their own money in the first place. Clever, eh?)

The first sale of Liberty Bonds wasn't a great success, so the government upped the rate of interest and began promoting them more vigorously. A special Committee on Public Information put out propaganda posters urging people to do their bit for the war by buying Liberty Bonds, especially if they weren't able to do much in any other way. Film stars led Liberty Bond drives in front of crowds and cameras to proclaim that it was every citizen's patriotic duty to buy as many bonds as he could. Even boy and girl scouts sold Liberty Bonds: the government reckoned no one could walk by these earnest young people and refuse to buy from them, and by and large it was right.

Liberty Bonds had one problem that the government didn't advertise: the government wasn't only using the bonds to pay for the American war, but also to finance American loans to the Allies. After the war, the Europeans weren't able to repay their debts and so many Liberty Bond holders never got their money back.

Labour

Like the food supply, control of the workforce was essential to winning the war. That meant the government would have to deal with the two main labour unions:

- **American Federation of Labour (AFL):** The moderate AFL was led by the veteran unionist Sam Gompers. Gompers assured the government that the AFL supported the war and would support the government in whatever measures it needed to take in order to win it, especially letting women take over the jobs the men had left behind them. This was just what the government wanted to hear, and Sam Gompers was taken onto the Council of National Defense that was overseeing the war effort at home.

✔ **The International Workers of the World (IWW):** Very different to the moderate AFL, the IWW (nicknamed 'the Wobblies') was a radical socialist organisation committed to world revolution. Like other socialist movements around the world, the IWW denounced the war as a quarrel among international capitalists that would only benefit the rich, and it said working people should have nothing to do with it.

Many Americans thought the IWW's opposition to the war was profoundly unpatriotic, especially after the Russian Revolution broke out in February 1917. Various groups, including many employers and even a branch of the Ku Klux Klan, arranged violent attacks on IWW meetings and some IWW members were killed. In 1917 the US Department of Justice organised a series of raids on IWW meetings by federal agents and many members were arrested and given long prison sentences.

The great majority of America's working people supported the war. However some, including American socialists and communists, remained strongly opposed to it. At the end of the war, many of these radical opponents of the war were arrested in a big swoop operation organised by the Attorney General, Mitchell Palmer.

With so many men going off to fight, America's women had to come forward to fill the gaps in the factories and in the fields. The war provided a huge opportunity for women in the United States and the other countries to explore types of work they'd never have got a chance to try in peacetime. (You can look at how the war affected the lives of women in Chapter 13.)

Why we fight

The American government reckoned that, given how strong isolationist feeling had been before the war (see the earlier section 'Don't go there! America's isolationists'), Americans needed to have a good idea of why they were in the war and what they were fighting against. After all, the problems of Belgium or Bosnia-Herzegovina seemed a very long way from Wisconsin or Kansas.

To this end, the government put out posters showing the Germans and their allies as vicious, inhuman brutes who would dominate the world unless they were stopped. The government also deliberately suggested that German militarism might even endanger the United States itself. It organised big public meetings with flags and military bands to explain why the United States had gone to war and what ordinary Americans could do to help.

Of course, the most important thing men could do was join the army.

Lock 'em up!

All countries in the First World War faced the problem of what to do with enemy aliens, but none faced it on quite the scale of the United States. The United States was virtually made up of immigrants, and they came from countries on both sides of the war in Europe. The government decided that recent immigrants should be put on a fast track to becoming fully Americanised, with intensive language lessons and special courses on American history, culture and values. This fitted in with the government's message that the war wasn't just between the United States and Germany, but between American democracy and German militarism. Some German-Americans were happy to go through the process, but others didn't want to take any part in the war against their homeland, and 2,000 of them were interned in special camps.

The Yanks Are Coming!

The famous American marching song 'Over There!' sums up the American approach to the First World War: 'The Yanks are coming,' it proclaims, 'And we won't come back till it's over Over There!' In other words, Americans were going to war to sort out the mess the Europeans had got themselves into, they'd stay till the job was done *and then they'd come home.*

You're in the army now

From the moment that the United States entered the war, it was clear that the government would have to introduce conscription, known as the *Draft,* to bring the army up to fighting strength.

Rich or poor, you're in!

Years before, during the Civil War, those who had enough money had been able to buy their way out of the army by paying for a substitute to take their place. This time the Draft was to be run on more democratic lines and it wouldn't be possible for young men from well-to-do families to dodge it.

Under the Selective Service Act, young men of military age were registered with local registration boards, who then started selecting at random from among the young, unmarried men on their lists. The very first name was drawn by a blindfolded secretary of war. The first draft brought in 2.8 million men; later drafts brought in married men. With the existing army, Marines and National Guard, by the end of 1918 the United States was looking at a total fighting force of something like 4 million men: that was more than enough to strengthen the exhausted British and French.

Fight for liberty and equality! Sorry – whites only

Even though black soldiers had fought very well back in the Civil War, most American generals didn't want them fighting alongside white soldiers in the First World War. They could only serve in support roles.

The movement calling for civil rights for black Americans was getting going around the time of the First World War, and its leader, WEB Du Bois, called on President Wilson to let black Americans fight for their country. However, too many American generals thought black people were simply unable to fight as well as white people.

Two divisions of black soldiers were put together, though only one – the 92nd – fought together as a division: the other, the 93rd, was split up into different units. The French, who thought highly of black troops (they had their very good Senegalese troops fighting with them) specifically asked for the 92nd to fight alongside them. Unfortunately, it didn't do very well in battle. The reason was a wonderfully circular argument: American generals had no confidence in black soldiers, so they didn't bother training them properly, so they did badly in battle, so American generals had no confidence in them.

The American army was still segregated along racial lines in the Second World War. It wasn't really until the Vietnam War that white Americans finally got rid of the idea that people's ethnic identity determined whether or not they could fight.

Lafayette – we are here!

The American entry into the war was almost the only good news the Allies had in 1917 (find out why in Chapter 15), so it was important to make the most of it. Maximum publicity and razzmatazz was generated by the news, so as to cheer up people in the Allied countries and dismay people in Germany and its allies. American 'doughboys' (the origins of the term are unknown) in their distinctive 'Canadian Mountie' hats staged spectacular parades through Paris, fast marching (which showed they were fresh and strong) or cleverly making out patterns of the Statue of Liberty or the Stars and Stripes.

It was particularly important that American troops were landing in France because a young French nobleman, the Marquis de Lafayette, had crossed the Atlantic with a band of volunteers and had fought alongside George Washington during the War of Independence. Now it was time for the United States to return the favour. 'Lafayette,' as one banner the American troops carried proclaimed, 'we are here!'

The Lafayette Escadrille

Some Americans didn't want to hang around waiting for their government to declare war so they set off for France and joined one of the Allied armies. The *Lafayette Escadrille* (*escadrille* is French for *squadron*) was a team of American fighter pilots who formed a squadron within the French air service. They learned the tricks of aerial fighting and became a very effective unit. When the United States finally came into the war, the men of the Lafayette Escadrille were invaluable in training and preparing the pilots of the American army: they were the most experienced fighter pilots America had.

Learning the hard way

By 1918 American troops were arriving in France at the rate of 10,000 a day. The Allied leaders were thinking of sending American units in wherever the British or French were under-strength, but the American commander, General Pershing, was determined to keep the American Expeditionary Force (AEF) together as a single unit under his command.

Pershing couldn't ignore his allies, though. Despite their numbers, the Americans were still much less experienced than their British and French allies, had almost no military equipment and depended on supplies from Britain and France for their tanks, machine guns, artillery and so on. For example, American troops went into action wearing distinctive British 'soup plate' helmets and American pilots had to learn to fly French planes. Moreover, Pershing insisted on sending his men into battle in huge frontal assaults on the enemy lines. The British and French had long stopped launching those, because of the heavy casualties. The Americans soon found the same thing happened when they attacked.

In the spring of 1918 the Germans launched their big offensive in the west and broke through the Allied line (Chapter 16 has all the details). In the emergency and Allied counter-attack that followed, Pershing realised he'd have to allow American troops to be sent into action where they were needed, even if doing so meant breaking up the AEF and even though it often meant American troops were serving under non-American command. The Americans were very quickly learning the harsh realities of the First World War.

Into battle

The Americans' first real taste of fighting on the Western Front came in the German spring offensive in 1918, when in June they fought with the French in a major counter-offensive at Chateau Thierry in the Second Battle of the Marne (see Chapter 16 for more on what was happening in 1918) and when, in July, four units of the AEF fought alongside the Australians under Sir John Monash.

The first battle in which the Americans went into action in their own right, rather than supporting one of the other armies, came at St-Mihiel, which was part of an Allied offensive on the rivers Meuse and Argonne. The attack was a success (see Figure 11-1), though many of the Germans managed to fall back safely. However, the Americans found the follow-up attack two weeks later much harder than they'd expected. (Chapter 16 looks at what else was happening in 1918, after the Americans joined the war.)

The Americans had arrived, but the war was very far from over.

Figure 11-1:
Americans in St-Mihiel change 'Hindenburgstrasse' to 'Wilson USA' to celebrate their success against the Germans.

© Imperial War Museums (HU 56409)

Part IV
Home Fronts

For a bonus article that looks at whether changes brought in by the war, at home and away, signalled the end of an era, go online and take a look at www.dummies.com/extras/firstworldwar.

In this part...

✔ Tour the factories and fields to see how the First World War was fought on the home front as well as in the trenches.

✔ Take note of how the war affected the lives, the role and the status of the women who kept industry and transport systems running while the men were away fighting.

✔ Keep your finger on the political pulse of the time as you see the power struggles, changes of government and, in some cases, violent revolution produced by the war.

1. Volunteers outside the Whitehall recruitment office in London (1914). Thousands of men rushed to volunteer as soon as war was declared. (Chapter 4)

2. An officer reads out the Kaiser's German mobilisation order to a Berlin crowd (1914). (Chapter 4)

YOUR KING & COUNTRY NEED YOU

A WEE "SCRAP O' PAPER" IS BRITAIN'S BOND.

TO MAINTAIN THE HONOUR AND GLORY OF THE BRITISH EMPIRE

3. This recruitment poster shows a Scottish soldier on duty in Belgium. The 'scrap o' paper' is the Kaiser's dismissive description of the 1839 Treaty of London that guaranteed the independence of Belgium. (Chapter 4)

4. Russian troops marching in the Balkans (1916) – only months away from revolution. (Chapter 6)

5. A ward in a Royal Flying Corps hospital of the First World War. Hospitals placed great emphasis on light and fresh air to aid recovery. (Chapter 7)

6. The 'Lusitania medal'. It was produced as a cynical comment on the shipping line risking the lives of its passengers, but it was used in Allied propaganda as an example of heartless German rejoicing in the deaths of innocent civilians. (Chapter 8)

7. The reverse of the 'Lusitania medal'.
(Chapter 8)

8. *The Second Division at Jutland* by WL Wyllie, showing British ships at the Battle of Jutland (1916). (Chapter 8)

9. Shell damage to HMS *Kent* at the Battle of Jutland (1916). (Chapter 8)

10. A Zeppelin emerging from its hangar. Zeppelin raids did serious damage until the Allies worked out the most effective way to shoot them down. (Chapter 8)

11. A Royal Air Force officer showing a reconnaissance pilot the area to photograph. The aerial camera is attached to the plane, underneath the map. (Chapter 8)

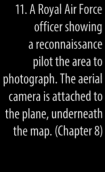

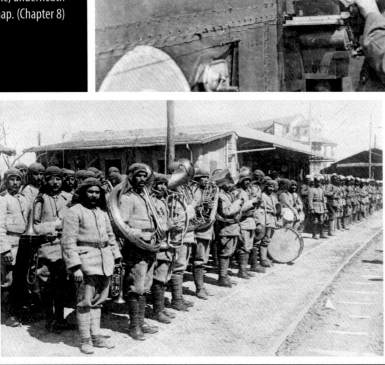

12. Turkish troops, including their band, waiting to 'entrain' in the Palestine campaign. (Chapter 9)

13. An Australian soldier carrying a fellow soldier to a medical aid post at Gallipoli (1915). The Australian army was based on the strong bond of friendship between 'mates'. (Chapter 9)

14. Indian troops at bayonet drill. Indian troops were fearsome fighters. (Chapter 10)

15. A United States Navy recruiting poster from 1917. American and British propaganda often used female images to shame men into joining up. (Chapter 11)

GEE !!
I WISH I WERE
A MAN

I'd JOIN
The NAVY,

NAVAL RESERVE
OR COAST GUARD

16. An Australian propaganda poster, showing a map where the country's name is scored out and replaced with 'New Germany'. Several major cities are also given new German names. (Chapter 10)

17. Women took on skilled, as well as unskilled, work from men, here shaping an aeroplane propeller. (Chapter 13)

18. The Women's Land Army uniform. With U-boats trying to starve Britain out, women's work in agriculture was essential. (Chapter 13)

19. A British nurse of the First World War, by AO Spare. (Chapter 13)

20. A car of a Voluntary Aid Detachment convoy in Italy, skidding on the mountainside snow. (Chapter 13)

21. The British Prime Minister, David Lloyd George (centre, left) at Fricourt – the scene of some of the heaviest fighting on the Somme just two weeks before (1916). He was critical of the heavy losses on the Somme and reluctant to provide troops for similar offensives. (Chapter 14)

22. The deadly mud of the battlefield at Passchendaele (1917). (Chapter 15)

COMMISSARIATO DI PROPAGANDA
ED ASSISTENZA CIVILE
Pro Befana dei Bimbi delle Terre redente

VITA, MORTE E MIRACOLI.....
DI UN IMPERO

Giovedì 2 Gennaio alle ore 16,30, nella SALA PICHETTI (Via del Bufalo) si aprirà una Mostra di 100 caricature di AMOS SCORZON con un commento di GINO CUCCHETTI.
La Mostra resterà aperta nei giorni 2, 3, 4, 5.

23. An Italian propaganda poster showing a double-headed Austro-Hungarian eagle being decapitated. The sword, held by an unseen man, is inscribed with the motto of Italy's ruling House of Savoy. (Chapter 16)

24. The Cenotaph, in London's Whitehall, was unveiled on Armistice Day, 1920. The Unknown Soldier was buried on the same day. (Chapter 18)

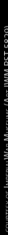

Chapter 12

The Civilian War

When past wars had broken out, they'd been fought by armies; ordinary civilians were only involved if they got caught up in the actual fighting. The First World War was different. For the first time in history, everyone in the combatant countries was involved in the war effort. No one could just stand by and watch.

From the start, it was clear that the First World War was going to be a much bigger conflict than any previous war. The armies were huge and they made use of all the very latest technology, but no one was prepared for the scale of the fighting. For example, each country went to war in 1914 thinking it had enough shells to last until the end of the war, which they all thought would be in a few months' time. But the war didn't end in 1914, and by the spring of 1915 all the major countries were beginning to run out of shells. This meant that industry at home had to be reorganised to completely support the war effort, at the expense of domestic needs. Other changes were needed too. Because each country was doing all it could to starve its enemies out, grocers' shops and kitchens suddenly became vital to winning the war.

No part of ordinary life, from workplaces to the shops and right into the home itself, could escape the reach of the First World War. This was to be the world's first experience of *total war,* and the different countries took to this new experience in varied ways, some with more success than others. This chapter shows you how they fared.

Blurring the Lines between Soldiers and Civilians

In past wars the difference between soldiers and civilians had been quite obvious, but in the First World War the distinctions began to get very blurred. In many countries, some people who were civilians when the war broke out found that they weren't civilians after all, because they were part-time reservists and they were being called back into the army. In Britain, which didn't have conscription in 1914, civilians were queuing up to join the army. This wasn't necessarily the good idea that it seems, because some of the men who worked in vital industries (such as coal mining, engineering and shipbuilding) but joined the army or were called up as reservists could contribute far more to the war effort by staying at work than by sitting in a trench. The Austrians made the mistake of drafting so many of their key industrial workers into the army that their war production fell disastrously, and they had to un-enlist them and send them back to work.

As the war went on, the question of who was a soldier and who wasn't became more deadly. When the Germans started bombing civilian areas in England (see Figure 12-1), they justified their action by saying that people working in munitions factories were just as much their enemy as the soldiers who were firing the shells produced by the factories. And if it was acceptable for the British to blockade German ports to stop food supplies getting in, surely it was acceptable for the Germans to sink merchant ships carrying food to Britain? That was how the Germans justified their U-boat campaigns (see Chapter 8).

Figure 12-1: German shell damage to a family home in Scarborough.

© Imperial War Museums (Q 53484)

The First World War was the first conflict in which people started to talk about a *home front*. That phrase meant that people living and working at home were just as important to the war effort as the men fighting at the actual front.

Taking on Special Powers

When the war started, the governments of the combatant countries started to take on special powers to take over the resources they'd need and to deal with any trouble or opposition they might encounter. Some governments, such as those of Russia and Germany, already possessed very extensive powers, and extending them further to meet the demands of the war wasn't too difficult. The German government, for example, took over Germany's mines and heavy industry and just shut down any industry it deemed non-essential. In Russia, the tsar gave the army complete control over the civil authorities in the war zone in the western part of the country, while the government took over all essential industries. And in Austria-Hungary, any factory workers who went on strike were drafted into the army and sent off to the front.

The switch to wartime powers was much harder for countries with a strong tradition of civil liberty, such as Britain and France.

Meeting DORA

Only four days after declaring war on Germany, the British Parliament passed the *Defence of the Realm Act,* known as *DORA.* DORA overturned the normal workings of the British parliamentary system and enabled the government to rule by decree, without having to pass laws through Parliament at all. The government promptly used DORA to bring in a series of rules that took away people's normal freedoms:

- No talking about military matters in public or spreading rumours.

- No trespassing on bridges or railway lines.

- No purchasing binoculars (because you might be a spy), using invisible ink to write abroad (ditto – though how would they know?), feeding bread to animals (it was a waste of food that humans could eat), flying kites or lighting bonfires (they might be used to guide Zeppelins to their targets).

- No buying rounds of drinks in pubs (factory workers needed to stay sober at all times) and no afternoon drinking. (The government used DORA to force pubs to close in the afternoon, to make sure workers were back at work after lunch sober and in good time. Mind you, DORA made the breweries water the beer down in any case.)

In 1916, the government even changed time itself. Following a move by the Germans, it introduced what's still known as British Summer Time, moving the clocks forward an hour in the spring and back an hour in the autumn, in order to get maximum use of daylight in the different seasons.

Although people could be prosecuted for breaching the rules, these changes were irritating rather than a major change to their civil liberties. However, DORA also enabled the government to take on much more extensive powers. From now on, the government would

- Take over any factory or industrial plant deemed essential for the war effort, and changing its production processes and patterns to meet the demands of the military

- Take over any land needed for the war effort, whether for military training or for growing food

- Censor the press and other publications, especially to stop secret information leaking out or to suppress criticism of the war

- Prosecute offenders against any of these rules

These changes represented major extensions to the government's power and they seemed to overturn every liberty the British had always claimed they stood for. The Victorians had believed passionately in free trade and free enterprise, but now the government was nationalising large parts of industry, turning them over to war production and introducing its own rules, quotas and working practices. In some areas, such as the coalfields of South Wales, industry was even taken over by the military. Huge areas of unused agricultural land were taken over for food production. Even more startling was the clampdown on free speech. In theory, Britain still allowed people to express their views freely, just as long as doing so didn't undermine public morale or harm the war effort. However, because in practice the courts would be deciding what did or didn't constitute harming the war effort, DORA had in fact suspended Britain's long tradition of free speech.

Across the Channel in France, the French government brought in similar controls and restrictions on its citizens' freedoms. The government censored the press, banning anyone from criticising the war or the way it was being run. The censorship was so heavy that one newspaper changed its name from *The Free Man* to *The Man in Chains*. The French government took control of food prices and rents and even forbade people to own radio receivers so they couldn't get information from anyone except the government.

Taking forced labour

Right at the start of the war, many governments – not just the British – started taking over the running of essential industries. But in some areas this process of government control of industry had a more sinister meaning: *forced labour*. In areas the Germans had taken over, such as Belgium and Poland, working people were taken by force, or were tricked with false promises of good wages, and sent to Germany to work as forced labour. On one occasion in Poland, the Germans announced free entertainment at the local theatre and then grabbed all the men who turned up to see it.

A tragedy

One part of German industry produced a very sad tragedy. Fritz Haber was a brilliant German chemist who won the Nobel Prize in 1918 for his work on fertilisers to increase food production. During the war, however, he worked on the development of poison gas for use on the battlefield. Haber had no worries about the ethics of using poison gas: he didn't think killing troops by gas was any worse than shooting them or blowing them up. His wife, however, disagreed. Her name was Clara Immerwahr and she too had a doctorate in chemistry. She was appalled by her husband's work and they often argued about it. On 2 May 1915 she took her husband's revolver, went out into the garden and shot herself through the heart.

Clara Immerwahr was a victim of turning industrial production over to the demands of war.

Forced labourers had no rights and had to live on the tiny pay that farmers or factory workers gave them. If they caused trouble, the German military authorities could punish them by taking away blankets or lights, or cutting their already meagre rations.

Although Germany was desperate for people to work in its factories and farms, forced labour turned out not to be the most sensible way to get it. The people they took were often badly suited to the work and they certainly didn't work willingly.

Dealing with strikes and soldiers

Each country tried to ensure that industry produced the necessary goods with as little trouble as possible from the workers. In Austria-Hungary strikes were banned, and when workers came out on strike anyway in 1917 the army simply took over the factories and forced the workers to go back to work. In Germany, the army took over the running of the country's industry and brought in compulsory labour service for all men aged 16 to 60. Doing this didn't work: by 1918 Germany was paralysed by workers striking for food and better wages.

The Allied countries managed a little better, though they too had problems. In France, the government created a special government department to run French industry, under the socialist minister Albert Thomas. By and large he did a good job, but even so in 1917 French industry was hit by a wave of strikes. In Britain, the government agreed to a truce with the trade unions at the start of the war, even though the unions were very suspicious of plans to 'dilute' their work by bringing women into the factories (you can read more about women's role in the war in Chapter 13). The British minister of munitions was the dynamic David Lloyd George, who completely reorganised the armaments industry to increase shell production massively. Even so, in 1917 the miners of South Wales came out on strike.

The South Wales strike was different from other strikes. The men weren't protesting against shortages or low wages: they were angry that some of the rich were making a profit from the war and not making the sort of sacrifices that others were having to make. 'Profiteering' was one of the main working-class complaints in Britain about the way the government was running the war.

Conscription Comes to Britain

All the major European powers conscripted men into their militaries – other than Britain. The answer to why Britain was different lies deep in British history and in the national characteristics the British thought they were fighting to protect.

Britain's constitution was (and still is) a balance between the monarchy and Parliament that had been established back at the time of the English Civil War in the 17th century. Back then, the main charge against King Charles I was that he was trying to rule through military force instead of through Parliament and he paid for this fault in full: Parliament put him on trial and cut off his head. But after the civil war, Oliver Cromwell ruled England directly through the army – the whole country was governed by a group of major generals. The British had never allowed themselves to forget how Cromwell had closed theatres, banned dancing and even abolished Christmas – and how it was his military power that enabled him to do it.

Ever since Cromwell's day, the British had kept to a set of strict rules about their military:

✔ **Political power stays in civilian, not military hands.** Generals and admirals took their orders from the government of the day, and never vice-versa.

✔ **Britain should have no, repeat no, standing (that is, peacetime) army.** Obviously, Britain did have an army, but Parliament had to pass a law every year to legalise it for the following 12 months, otherwise the army was an illegal organisation. Moreover, all soldiers, even the highest ranking, remained subject to the ordinary laws of the land.

✔ **The army should consist of volunteers only – no one should be forced to join.** The navy used to use press gangs to force men into service, but that had been in wartime only and had long been outlawed. The redcoats who'd fought Britain's wars in the 19th century had all been volunteers.

This suspicion of standing armies was shared by the British colonists in America and survived in the United States after they won their independence. This fact explains why the United States was the only other major power that didn't have a peacetime conscription system before the First World War. (Chapter 11 looks at how the United States handled the challenge of getting their army up to strength to fight in the war.)

Britain's overseas dominions shared its suspicions of conscription. Like Britain, Canada, South Africa, Australia and New Zealand all relied entirely on volunteers for their armed forces.

Let's try volunteers first

When the war broke out in 1914, Lord Kitchener, the British Secretary of State for war, warned that it would be very long and costly and that Britain would need a much larger army. However, instead of moving for conscription, the British government opted for a mass appeal for volunteers: this was the recruiting drive that produced the famous poster with Lord Kitchener's picture on it. Even in wartime, the British remained committed to their principles about avoiding compulsory military service.

The volunteering appeal was phenomenally successful, and it brought in some 2.5 million men in the first two years of the war. Like the other combatant countries, Britain was swamped by a wave of patriotic fervor. (Chapter 4 tells you a bit more about the reasons why young British men rushed to join the army in 1914.) So many men volunteered that the army couldn't cope: it didn't have anything like enough equipment, arms or uniforms for these new recruits. Yet still they came, in their thousands. All through the autumn and winter of 1914 and right through 1915 they kept coming forward to volunteer to fight for king and country. They were so numerous that these volunteers became known as Kitchener's *New Army.*

All right, conscription it is, then

Despite the surge in numbers that the recruitment drive had brought about, it still wasn't enough. The big offensives of 1915 failed and it became clear that the war was going to stretch into 1916. The commanders had learned that attacks would only succeed if the attackers had huge numbers of men. Then the Battle of the Somme in 1916 taught them that even overwhelming numbers couldn't guarantee success if you didn't properly prepare the attack (you can pick up the same lesson in Chapter 6). So by 1916 the British government had to face up to the need for some form of conscription.

Plenty of people, both in the government and outside, were profoundly unhappy about this idea. The Labour Party and the trade unions opposed conscription, and Sir John Simon, the Home Secretary, resigned in protest against it. Their opposition was in vain: the demand for men at the front was too great and conscription was coming in whether they liked the idea or not.

Britain introduced conscription in several phases:

- ✔ **Derby Scheme (July 1915):** A voluntary registration scheme suggested by Lord Derby. Men could place themselves on the register and wait to be called up. Single men would usually be called up first. Results: disappointing.

- ✔ **Military Service Act No.1 (February 1916):** All single men aged 18 to 41 were made liable for military service.

- ✔ **Military Service Act No.2 (May 1916):** All single men aged 18 to 41 were called up for military service, as were married men and widowers. Full conscription had arrived.

After the heavy battlefield losses of 1916, the governments of Australia, New Zealand and Canada all did the same as Britain and introduced conscription measures into their parliaments. The parliaments of New Zealand and Canada both passed conscription (though French Canadians protested), but in Australia, where the Irish settlers and trade unions opposed it, the government had to put the issue to a referendum, which narrowly rejected the proposal (see Chapter 10).

Introducing conscription was a massive change in British society. For the first time, the whole of the population was engaged in one massive enterprise: either men were away at the front, or men and women were working at home in industry to produce the materials to supply them with. To win the war, the British were accepting huge limitations on everyone's individual freedom to work, speak and act as they chose. Only two groups of people were allowed to opt out of conscription. The first group was the Irish. The British had a very good reason for not enforcing conscription in Ireland. It was only a month since the 1916 Easter Rising in Dublin (Chapter 10 has the lowdown) and anti-British feelings in Ireland were running very high. Forcing Irishmen to join the British army would be asking for a lot of trouble, so the government simply avoided doing so. Dealing with the second group – conscientious objectors – was much trickier.

Conscientious objectors

Some people continued to oppose conscription on grounds of conscience: they were known as *conscientious objectors* (COs). COs had varied reasons for their opposition: some had a political objection to the state taking on so much power over individuals; some had a moral objection to fighting and killing; and some were morally opposed to war itself and would do nothing whatsoever to contribute to it.

Few people had much respect for COs. They were often nicknamed 'conchies' and insulted or abused in the street.

People who registered their objection to military service had to explain their objection to a local military tribunal. The tribunal had to decide:

✔ **Did the CO only object to fighting and killing, but not to war itself?** If so, it was usually possible for him to serve in a non-combatant role such as stretcher-bearer or ambulance driver.

✔ **Did the CO have a moral objection to all war or only to this war?** *Pacifism* was an acceptable reason for not fighting, if it was genuine, but political opposition to the war wasn't – it was regarded as almost as bad as treason.

✔ **Was the CO's pacifism genuine?** If the tribunal thought the CO wasn't genuinely opposed to all forms of violence then it could judge that his objection wasn't real and enlist him into the army by force.

Tribunals usually regarded the cases brought before them with utter contempt: they simply saw COs as cowards. Tribunals tried asking all sorts of questions to trick COs into admitting that in some circumstances they would fight, such as 'What would you do if a German assaulted your sister?' or 'What would you do if the Germans invaded England?'. If they weren't convinced that a man's objection was serious, they could order him to be enlisted into the army. After a man accepted a shilling's pay or put on a uniform, he was deemed to have enlisted and he was then subject to military discipline, which meant that a man who refused to obey orders could be shot.

Some COs who hadn't managed to convince the tribunal of their sincerity had their clothes taken from them and had only a military uniform to put on; some were even taken by force to the front and then court-martialled for disobeying military orders.

Even if a CO was accepted as genuine, he wasn't free to go home. Conscientious objection was still regarded as a breach of the law, so most COs were sent to prison with hard labour, which usually consisted of breaking rocks. The British had come a very long way from the time when the army itself was an illegal organisation: now it was opposition to the army that was illegal.

Did conscription work?

Ironically, conscription actually brought in *fewer* men than volunteering did!

These are the numbers of men who joined the British army during the years of the First World War:

- ✓ **1914:** 1,180,000
- ✓ **1915:** 1,280,000
- ✓ **1916 (conscription introduced here!):** 1,190,000
- ✓ **1917:** 820,000
- ✓ **1918:** 493,000

Nevertheless, conscription did help to keep the size of the British army up and ensured that by 1918 it was larger than it had ever been.

Round 'Em Up and Drive 'Em Out!

It was probably inevitable in the circumstances, but the war provoked a very ugly wave of anti-German feeling in Britain, especially after the Germans started their bombing raids on British cities. Britain was unused to war damage, so attacks like these fuelled anti-German sentiment. Angry crowds attacked any shop or business with a German-sounding name, even when it turned out the owners were in fact Russians or Poles. Under the *Aliens Restriction Act,* enemy aliens were rounded up and put into internment camps on the Isle of Man, in the middle of the Irish Sea.

Even dogs suffered from this anti-German hysteria. Reports suggested that people had started kicking dachshunds (also known as 'German sausage dogs') in the street, and in Britain the German Shepherd dog was quickly rechristened the Alsatian, which means 'from Alsace', one of the areas the Germans had taken from the French. So overnight a suspiciously German mutt became a patriot!

Not surprisingly, this lashing-out at foreigners wasn't confined to Britain. Canada experienced a similar wave of anti-German feeling: a Canadian town called Berlin was even renamed Kitchener after the British military hero! Similar outbreaks of anti-German violence happened in France, as the Germans advanced through the country. In Moscow in 1915, violent mobs attacked foreign-owned houses and shops; many Russians blamed the Jews for their country's problems and 1915 saw some violent attacks on Russia's large Jewish population.

Propagating racial hatred and rumour

All countries involved in fighting wars use propaganda to stir up public support for a war by portraying the enemy in the worst possible light, and the First World War was no exception. Each side accused the other of committing terrible atrocities. Sometimes the stories were based on truth, but sometimes they were made up (see Figure 16 in the insert section).

Allied propaganda posters showed the Germans as a heartless and cruel race of people who weren't to be trusted. 'Once a German, always a German,' said one poster, showing a German soldier burning cities and bayoneting babies, and then turning up in civilian clothes after the war to sell German goods (see Figure 12-2). Another showed a German nurse heartlessly pouring water on the ground in front of a wounded British prisoner, desperate with thirst. Fearing your enemies in wartime is quite normal, but First World War propaganda was something new: it was fostering genuine racial hatred.

Figure 12-2: British anti-German propaganda portraying Germans as inhumane and suggesting that they'll remain the same after the war.

© Imperial War Museums (Q 80141)

Some of the fiercest racial stereotyping was to be found in recruiting posters, because it helped persuade recruits of what they'd be fighting against. After Britain introduced conscription in 1916, fewer of these posters were needed, but Australia narrowly rejected conscription in its referendum on the subject. As a result, Australian recruiting posters used increasingly extreme racial caricatures in an increased effort to persuade men to join up to fight the Germans and their allies, even despite the heavy Australian losses that were being reported from the Western Front.

Rumours also played an important role in determining how the people on both sides of the war thought about their enemies. These are a few of the best-known examples of rumours and propaganda stories from the First World War:

✔ **Germans cutting off Belgian girls' hands and bayoneting babies:** When the Germans invaded Belgium, stories of atrocities committed against the civilian population quickly began to circulate and these were two of the most common. In 1915 a British government committee looked into the stories and concluded they were true.

Phantom Russians and mysterious clouds

Many rumours circulated during the First World War of ghosts and apparitions, and of strange events and weird phenomena that no one could explain but that everyone *knew* about. Here are three of the strangest First World War stories:

✔ **The phantom Russians:** At the start of the war in 1914 it was widely reported and believed in Britain that a huge Russian army had travelled all the way from Scotland through England and on to the Western Front. Everyone knew someone else who'd seen the soldiers – 'still with snow on their boots', as people recounted at the time.

Verdict: No Russian army passed through Britain or fought on the Western Front. The story is completely untrue.

✔ **The mysterious cloud:** Many stories circulated during the war of mysterious clouds or mists descending onto the battlefields and swallowing up whole military units, which were never seen again. One such story was told about a company of soldiers from the royal estate at Sandringham in Norfolk who went missing in action at Gallipoli, but similar stories can be found about other units on other fronts.

Verdict: Completely untrue, but a comfort for the families of men missing in action whose bodies were never found.

✔ **The wild men of no-man's-land:** Soldiers on both sides of the war told stories of encountering groups of wild-looking men, supposedly deserters from all armies, who roamed the battlefields at night and fed on human flesh.

Verdict: No evidence exists of such gangs operating on the battlefields. Deserters on the Eastern Front often operated in groups, but that was because whole units often deserted *en masse*: no evidence has emerged of such groups operating on the Western Front.

Verdict: The stories were completely untrue. The Germans did shoot civilians, but no evidence has ever emerged that they bayoneted babies or cut off people's hands. The British government report had simply accepted hearsay with no evidence whatsoever to support it.

✔ **Melting corpses down for glycerine:** It was widely reported in Britain that the Germans ran 'corpse factories' that melted down human corpses and turned them into glycerine. The story was run in the international press and debated in Parliament and the German government had to issue stringent denials.

Verdict: The British may have mistranslated the German for dead horses (which were commonly melted down in all countries), but it's much more likely that the story was a deliberate British fabrication.

✔ **The crucified Canadian:** The Germans were supposed to have nailed (or maybe tied) a captured Canadian sergeant (though some said he was a Highlander) to a cross (or maybe a gate, or a fence, or a tree, or a door, depending on which version of the story you heard) and then thrust bayonets into him. No one could ever give the man's name or come up with any eye-witnesses, but that didn't stop the story being widely repeated (though the Canadians themselves were sceptical and the Germans angrily denied it).

Verdict: The story was almost certainly invented to build on international outrage after the *Lusitania* was sunk by a German U-boat (see Chapter 8). The Canadians investigated after the war and found one Canadian soldier had indeed been tied up and killed – by some Belgian farmers.

The House of ~~Saxe-Coburg-Gotha~~ Windsor

The anti-German hysteria that swept Britain during the First World War even touched the royal family. The British royals were of German descent. They were descended from the 18th-century House of Hanover, and Queen Victoria's marriage to her German cousin, Prince Albert, made their links with Germany even stronger – after all, Kaiser Wilhelm himself was King George V's cousin.

Even the royal family's surname was about as German as it was possible to be: they were the House of Saxe-Coburg-Gotha. As if that wasn't bad enough, 'Gotha' was also the name of the German planes that started bombing Britain in 1917. So in July 1917, very reluctantly, the King agreed to an announcement that the British royal family would be dropping all its German titles and honours and taking a new name: the House of Windsor, after the castle in Berkshire where they lived for much of the year. Their cousins, the Battenbergs, also changed their name to the more English-sounding Mountbatten.

Spies R (all around) Us

All countries in the First World War were fearful of enemy spies and sometimes this fear tipped over into genuine hysteria. Anything that went wrong was blamed on spies. In Britain, 'German spies' were blamed for a stampede by 300 cavalry horses at a depot in Essex (it was probably started deliberately but not by German spies) and for a spate of reported attacks on policemen by armed men on motorbikes – though not one case turned out to be genuine.

People in Britain could be arrested for all sorts of activities that suggested they were spies, such as the following:

- ✔ Handing out sweets (everyone *knew* the Germans poisoned sweets to kill British children)

- ✔ Wearing a flamboyant or wide-brimmed hat ('If he's not a spy, why does he wear a hat like that?' asked one local schoolmistress after denouncing an innocent visitor to the police)

- ✔ Having an American accent (this got the American poet Robert Frost into trouble)

- ✔ Having a German chauffeur (a Cabinet minister was accused of this – and it's true: he had one)

- ✔ Having (or, worse, building) a concrete-bottomed tennis court or ornamental lake (which was clearly intended as a secret gun platform for the Germans, of course)

The tragic tale of Mata Hari

Mata Hari ('sunrise' in the language of Java) was the stage name of a Dutch exotic dancer called Gertrud Magarete Zelle who very foolishly allowed herself to get involved in the glamorous but dangerous world of wartime espionage. She'd grown up in the Dutch East Indies before ending up as a nearly-nude dancer in Paris with a long line of lovers on the side.

Her reputation as a femme fatale led the Germans to offer to pay her for any useful information she might glean from her French officer lovers and, very unwisely, she agreed. Perhaps not realising the risk she was taking, she also offered to spy for the French and she did pass them some not-very-important information. However, the French got wind of the fact that she'd agreed to work for the Germans and arrested her. No evidence has ever come to light that she passed anything to the Germans, but this didn't save her. The French government was keen to have a high-profile spy to shoot, to reassure the public that the German threat was under control, so in October 1917 the famous Mata Hari stepped in front of a firing squad and was executed.

Fighting the War for Food

One of the most important weapons in any war is food. Armies, cities and even nations can't continue a war without enough food. Not only do the soldiers at the front need to keep their strength up to fight, but so do all those people working on the home front. Children's nourishment too needs to be maintained. Moreover, food shortages often lead to protests, riots and mutiny.

With food being such an important weapon, armies often seek to starve their opponents out by destroying crops or cutting off food supplies. All things considered, in all countries, the outcome of the First World War would depend upon who was able to retain control of the food supply. That meant

- Taking action against food hoarders, to ensure that what food was available got spread around to those who needed it

- Growing as much food as possible at home and finding ways to replace food that used to be imported, so that stocks could be maintained

- Introducing rationing, so that governments could control the supply and demand of the available food

To make the food situation even more difficult to manage, many factors, even the weather, sometimes got in the way of governments' attempts to keep their people fed. The food situation became so serious that it unquestionably determined the final outcome of the war.

Britain: Relying on the merchant navy

As an island, Britain was reliant on merchant vessels bringing in food. In 1917 German U-boats were sinking so many British merchant ships that at one point Britain had only enough food to sustain the country for six weeks (see Chapter 8). If it hadn't been for the new convoy system hampering U-boat efforts to find the merchant ships, Britain simply couldn't have continued in the war. Nevertheless, the British did run an efficient system of rationing and they made good use of all available land for growing food. The government was even able to offer meals to schoolchildren in the school holidays.

France: Coping with less

France wasn't as dependent on food imports as Britain was, but a fifth of its national food supplies were lost when the Germans occupied the northern part of the country. The French had long-established practices for governing the food supply in wartime, which they'd been implementing ever since the French Revolution: they laid down rigid controls on mills and bakeries and fixed the price of bread by law. Anyone charging too much could be arrested. Doing that put bakers out of business, but it usually went down well with the voters.

Germany: Focusing on the military

Germany's supply of food was hampered by the British blockade of the country's ports, which meant that no imports could arrive by sea, and its internal system for distributing and selling food was chronically inefficient. The German government was spending so much on war production that it never managed to devise a proper system of rationing and food distribution. It rationed bread and then had to steadily reduce the ration until 1917, when it was halved. The winter of 1916–17, when the potato crop failed, was a terrible time, known as the 'Turnip Winter', because that was about all that people could find to eat, and thousands died from the effects of malnutrition. In response, the Germans put their chemicals industry to work developing substitutes (*ersatz*) for essentials such as coffee and butter.

By 1918 the Germans were suffering badly from hunger and were staging protests demanding food in the shops and an end to the war.

Russia: Heading for a fall

The Russian government was so incompetent that by 1916 almost no food was on sale in the shops. This severe food crisis led almost directly to the Russian Revolution.

Russia's system of food distribution was even worse run than Austria-Hungary's (and that's saying something). By 1916 Russia was suffering from serious food shortages and riots were breaking out in the streets. Then strict food rationing brought in at the start of 1917 sparked off panic buying and further rioting, followed by strikes, which turned into a revolution that overthrew the whole tsarist regime.

You can find out more on how the war sparked off the Russian Revolution in Chapter 15.

Austria-Hungary: (Not) helping your neighbours

The food situation in Austria-Hungary was desperate. Austria-Hungary lost a third of its arable land when the Russians invaded in 1914, and the Hungarians, faced with their own food shortages, refused to export grain to Austria, even though they were both meant to be part of the same empire.

Such was the situation in Austria-Hungary that horses were killed for their meat (which hit the war effort, because the military needed horses) and bread had to be filled out with barley or potato – it was called *war bread,* and it was strictly rationed. Coffee, milk, sugar and fats were all rationed too, and Austrians had to go without meat for two days a week. To make matters worse, the 1916 harvest was a disaster and those people who had any bread started hoarding it. Result: rations had to be cut even further.

By 1917 Austria-Hungary was gripped by food riots and the government was desperate to get out of the war – at almost any price. They even risked war with their German allies when they seized a grain shipment from Romania to Germany as it passed through Austria. It's fair to say that Austria-Hungary was defeated as much by the food crisis as it was by the Allies.

United States: Helping your allies

Because the United States was so big, the Germans couldn't use their U-boats to starve the country out, as they were trying to do to Britain (see Chapter 8), but after the United States joined the war it needed to export food to its allies, including Russia, so food production was vital.

With so many young men leaving home for the war, farming was bound to suffer. That meant women would have to help out on the farms; it also meant the United States had to organise its food supply efficiently. The man put in charge of this was Herbert Hoover. He supervised food exports and encouraged Americans to do their bit for victory by cultivating special gardens, known as victory gardens, where they could grow their own vegetables. Hoover's work helped to give all Americans a sense that they were making an important contribution to the outcome of the war.

I'm just going down the allotment

As industrial cities grew in the 19th century, more people who lived in them craved a garden where they could grow their own produce. In Russia they were known as *dachas* and in German they were named *Schrebergarten,* after the man who pioneered them. In Britain the land for these gardens was allotted to people by the local council, so they were known as *allotments*.

When the war broke out, these gardens became more important because they could be a way of alleviating the food shortages that European powers suffered. Britain made particularly good use of allotments: in 1917 allotment renting surged as people grew their own food to supplement their rations. Americans started digging 'victory gardens' when they came into the war. What had started as a hobby for townspeople became an important way of winning the war.

Chapter 13

Women at War

The First World War had a major impact on the life and role of women. With the combatant countries in a state of total war, every aspect of life had to be reorganised to help the war effort, and this meant involving women. Women played their part from the start by fulfilling their traditional roles in nursing and in supervising hospitals. But as more men went off to fight, women were needed in greater numbers to keep industry going, to maintain agricultural production and to run transport networks.

For the first time in history, women became fully integrated into the public and economic life of the industrial countries. The big question was whether the changes for women ushered in by the war would carry on after the war was over. This chapter looks at how those changes came about, and how the future looked for women when the war ended.

Welcome to the Women's Sphere

In the 19th century, it was common to hear people talk of the worlds of men and women as being two 'separate spheres' – one that included politics and public life and belonged to men, and the other covering life in the kitchen, the nursery and the boudoir that belonged to women. Gentleman's clubs or working men's clubs were 'male' spaces into which women sometimes weren't even allowed, whereas the home was a 'female' space where the wife and the (female) housekeeper were in charge. However, in all countries, the war challenged this perception of separate spheres. With so many men needed at the front (and so many getting killed) all countries involved in the war needed women to step out of their sphere and take on jobs and roles that had previously belonged exclusively to men.

This is a man's world . . .

The world that went to war in 1914 was very much a man's world. Women didn't have the vote in any of the European Great Powers, and in the whole of the western world they could vote only in Finland, New Zealand and some parts of Australia and the United States. Around the world, men controlled governments and industry and it was generally accepted that this was how the world had been made and was meant to be.

War too was a man's occupation: all the politicians, diplomats and generals involved in the war were men. Women took no part in running wars or deciding policy, though they'd long accompanied armies, providing the soldiers with drink and other comforts, and since the pioneering work of Florence Nightingale in the Crimean War of 1854–6 women had worked in a proper nursing profession. However, most military commanders regarded a female presence on the battlefield or at headquarters as a wretched nuisance.

. . . but sisters are doing it for themselves

The idea of women having their own separate sphere of life was beginning to change by 1914. In many parts of the western world, feminist movements were campaigning to remove some of the restrictions that 19th-century society placed upon them. They campaigned for the vote, for better social and medical conditions, for improvements in education, and for changes in the law about prostitution and sexually transmitted diseases.

Not all countries loosened up the rules at the same rate as others, but by and large, by 1914 women in Europe and North America had won the right to train as doctors and nurses, to enter schools and universities, to work in the sciences and the arts, to control their own property and to run their own businesses. And despite the fact that few women had the right to vote, women were very active in politics, writing pamphlets, whipping up support for different parties and making speeches.

Suffering Suffragettes

Probably the best known pre-war feminist movement was that of the British *Suffragettes,* who ran a high-profile, militant campaign for the vote, with posters, marches and protests. They disrupted meetings, smashed windows and even planted bombs in post boxes and empty buildings. The authorities treated the Suffragettes with appalling brutality, locking them up and subjecting them to force-feeding (a form of torture), but the Suffragettes continued their campaign.

Their organisational skills and militancy suggested that the Suffragettes could be very useful to the war effort. (It also indicated that women deserved the vote – see 'Winning the Vote' a bit later on.) Sure enough, when the war started, the Suffragettes called off their campaign and threw themselves into the war effort. They turned their campaign newspaper, *Votes for Women,* into a patriotic and very anti-German newspaper called the *Britannia.* They also helped organise a campaign to hand white feathers (a sign of cowardice at the time) to young men seen out of uniform.

Work for (young) women

By the time that war broke out in 1914, young women in major cities had massively improved job prospects thanks to two inventions – the telephone and the typewriter. These two inventions led to positions for thousands of young women in telephone exchanges and offices. Young women were also finding work in the big department stores that were opening in major cities across the world by the 1910s. As countries expanded their education systems, women found they could often get work as teachers in elementary schools or in girls' secondary schools. However, women were usually expected to give these jobs up if they got married: it was generally thought that a married woman's duty was to her husband and that nothing as petty as a job should get in the way of that.

Some of the skills these young women learned would prove very useful in wartime. Armies and governments need thousands of typists, telephonists and secretaries. However, women would soon show that these skills were far from being the limit of what they could do.

With such an active women's movement in so many parts of the world, women were bound to break out of their own sphere and get heavily involved in the war – and they did.

Women of Britain say 'Go!' (and so do women of America)

At the start of the war women played an important part in the big recruitment campaign in Britain to persuade young men to join the army. Posters and songs all suggested that women looked on soldiering as a manly pursuit and they expected any young man to do his duty and enlist. A famous poster of the time showed a group of women watching as their menfolk marched off to war: the women look as if it's

a wrench to let them go, but the poster still proclaims, 'Women of Britain say "Go!"' One poster even showed a mother telling her own son it was his duty to go.

American posters also used images of women to encourage men to enlist, or else to buy Liberty Bonds (see Chapter 11 for the lowdown on what these were).

Freeing Men for the Front: Women at Work

The First World War was the first real chance that women of all classes had to show that they could do work that everyone had always assumed could only be done by men. Much of the factory work, for example, was highly skilled precision work, and women soon showed they could do it just as efficiently as men (see Figure 17 in the insert section). Many women learned to drive and could be seen driving ambulances or buses. Women even undertook heavy physical work such as hauling heavy coal sacks to keep the power stations running.

Many of the assumptions people (okay, mostly men) had made about women were based on the idea of 'separate spheres' (see 'Welcome to the Women's Sphere', earlier in the chapter) – the notion that men and women simply *belonged* in different areas of life and work. The work women did in the First World War showed that that idea simply wasn't true: women could do pretty much anything men could do, and sometimes they could do it better.

Clocking in: Women in the factories

One of the most important things that women could do to help the war effort was to 'free a man for the front' by taking on the work that he'd usually do, in an office or a factory. However, at first governments didn't always see this. One woman who turned up at the British War Office to volunteer her services was told to 'go home and sit tight'. The British Suffragette leader, Emmeline Pankhurst, was so frustrated with the British government for not involving women in the war effort that in 1915 she led a march of 30,000 women demanding to be given some sort of war work. This time the government listened and agreed to start employing women for war work. All countries employed women, but Britain involved women in more aspects of the war than any other nation (see Figure 13-1).

France too recruited women into the factories in huge numbers: near the start of the war, in August 1914, 80,000 women were working in the French manufacturing industry; by the end of the war, that number had risen to 1.24 million. In Austria-Hungary, somewhere close to a million women volunteered for war work (though employers often gave them only small jobs to do, which meant they could pay the women lower wages). By way of a contrast, although the government in Germany tried to attract women into war work, especially in offices, it never made this sort of work compulsory and far fewer German women volunteered for it. In reality, German women had more than enough to do at home just getting their families through the hardships of food shortages and high prices.

Making munitions

Probably the most important war work women undertook was in the factories. Particularly vital was their work in munitions factories, because without a constant production of bullets and shells no army could continue to fight.

(This situation nearly occurred when, in 1915, both sides on the Western Front suffered a serious shell shortage and the war nearly ground to a halt. Chapter 5 gives you the lowdown.) To this end, over 700,000 young British women (nicknamed *munitionettes*) and 430,000 French women worked in munitions factories. The French munitions industry was so productive, in fact, that France was able to export arms to other Allied countries and supply the American army when it arrived in 1918.

Figure 13-1: Glasgow women carrying out precision factory work to aid the war effort.

© *Imperial War Museums (Q 109912)*

The dangers of working in a munitions factory

Many munitions factories experienced accidents and explosions, some of them very serious:

- **1916, Faversham, Kent, England:** Two hundred tons of TNT exploded, killing 115 people. (The accident happened on a Sunday, when no women were working, so the victims were men and boys.)

- **1917, Silvertown, Essex, England:** An explosion at a munitions factory killed 73 people and left 400 wounded – mainly women.

- **1917, Quickborn-Heide, Germany:** An explosion at a munitions factory set off a chain of explosions that killed some 200 people, most were young women workers.

- **1917, Pilsen (now Plzeň), Austria-Hungary:** Over 200 workers were killed and nearly 700 injured when a series of explosions destroyed the Škoda factory.

- **1918, Chilwell, Nottinghamshire, England:** In an explosion at the National Shell-filling Factory 134 people were killed and 230 wounded. All but 30 of the dead were so badly disfigured that they couldn't be positively identified.

- **1918, Syracuse, New York, United States:** An explosion in a munitions factory followed by a fire destroyed the plant and killed some 50 workers.

Working in a munitions factory was no easy option. Girls (they often came straight from school) had to learn to make shells, bullets and grenades accurately and safely – a big responsibility. As well as needing the supply of munitions to be constant, armies needed those munitions to be reliable: a small mistake made by a factory girl could mean a shell landing on the battlefield without exploding or, worse, it might explode in the gun before it was fired and injure the soldier using it.

One of the worst parts of munitions work was the job of filling shells physically with high explosive. The girls had no protection against the chemical effects of working with substances such as TNT, and it often turned their skin a yellow colour that no amount of washing could get rid of. The poor girls got nicknamed 'canaries'.

As well as being unpleasant and unhealthy, munitions work was extremely dangerous (see the nearby sidebar, 'The dangers of working in a munitions factory'). And because the risks were serious, the rules in munitions factories were very strict. Carrying matches, for example, was a serious offence (this was a time when smoking was very popular, so people often carried matches around with them). Anyone found with a match on her could be prosecuted for attempted sabotage.

It's only for while the war's on, mind

In Britain, the government had to negotiate with the trade unions to let women work in factories and other workplaces. The Trade Union Congress (or TUC), the body that represents all British trade unions, didn't like the idea of women moving into its members' places of work: they called this process *dilution,* as if the work was like a beer that the women were watering down. The TUC agreed to allow this 'dilution' as long as it lasted only for the length of the war. As soon as the war was over, the women were to go and the jobs they'd been doing were to be filled by men again.

Shoot at the goal! No, not that kind of shooting!

One unexpected by-product of having so many British women working in munitions factories was a big uptake for women's football. Munitions girls were allowed to play football in their lunch breaks, as good, healthy exercise that kept morale up. Soon factories put their own teams together and started challenging other factories, and whole competitions with cups and prizes were formed for munitionette teams. Sometimes the teams played matches to raise money for charity and some professional clubs allowed them to play on their grounds. Professional football had almost entirely stopped because so many players were at the front, so it was good to get some football going again.

Munitionette football was popular while the war lasted, but most people only saw it as a wartime novelty. At the end of the war the teams were disbanded, the professional teams took their grounds back, and the women players hung up their boots and headed back to the kitchen.

Sylvia Pankhurst, the Suffragette (and daughter of Emmeline Pankhurst; see the nearby sidebar for more about her) insisted that women should get the same pay as men had received for doing the same work. The government assured her that they would, and the TUC reluctantly agreed. In fact, few women got the same pay as men, though they were generally much better paid than they'd been before the war, so not many of them complained.

The situation was similar in France. French trade unions were wary of women workers, especially as they weren't usually union members and were paid less than men. Employers preferred to employ these cheaper women and it took some tough negotiations between employers, unions and women's groups to reduce the gap between men's and women's wages for the same work. Women were still paid less than men at the end of the war and the unions still expected women workers to stand down and let men take their jobs back when the war ended.

Mucking out: Women on the land

One area of work where Britain also went further than other countries in employing women was on the land. In 1916 a special women's unit was formed to recruit girls to work on the farms; the following year it became the Women's Land Army (WLA).

KEY PEOPLE

Sylvia Pankhurst

Sylvia Pankhurst was a daughter of the British Suffragette leader, Emmeline Pankhurst. Unlike her mother and her sisters, however, Sylvia was a socialist and one of the leading opponents of the war. She fell out with her mother during the Suffragette campaign, because Sylvia wanted to give the vote to all women, including working-class women, whereas her mother only wanted to give it to well-off ladies who could be trusted to vote Conservative. Even though she was her own daughter, Emmeline Pankhurst threw Sylvia out of the Suffragette movement.

During the war Sylvia was disgusted with the way the Suffragettes supported the war and tried to pressurise young men into joining the army. She led a campaign demanding that the government negotiate peace with the Germans (that campaign didn't get anywhere) and she was also active in the No-Conscription Fellowship that campaigned against the introduction of conscription (neither did that one). She was delighted when the Russian Revolution broke out and she even went over to Russia to meet Lenin, but when she got back the government locked her up. She went on to become one of the founders of the British Communist Party.

Women in the WLA were trained in how to plough, milk cows, shear sheep and every other job that kept the nation's agriculture going (see Figure 18 in the insert section). They were given a uniform with rough breeches instead of a skirt. It was very practical for farm work, but many people were worried that it made the girls appear too masculine. Volunteers for the WLA were warned to remember that, although they wore a 'male' uniform, they were women and they should maintain womanly standards of behaviour: no getting drunk, no getting slapdash and, above all, no getting pregnant.

One of the reasons Britain survived the war without collapsing was because it proved very efficient at growing and distributing its own food, and the WLA was crucial to that success. By the end of the war, well over a quarter of a million women were working in the WLA.

Across the Atlantic in the United States, the Women's Land Army of America (WLAA) operated in much the same way as the British WLA. The WLAA played a key role not only in ensuring that wartime America was well fed, but also in growing a surplus of food that the United States could export to its allies. In France, village communities took on the role of allocating work to make sure the harvest came in. Women and children worked long hours in the fields, ploughing and reaping, tasks which beforehand had always been the preserve of men.

The women and children of Lille

Women in areas occupied by the enemy were in a very vulnerable position. One particularly troubling example of their vulnerability comes from Easter 1916, when the Germans forcibly deported some 20,000 people, most of them women and children, from the French city of Lille. The Germans forced the inhabitants out of their homes and subjected the women and girls to invasive internal examination. Then they sent them to different areas, apparently at random, and made them do manual work, such as digging trenches or burying corpses. Historians still don't really know why the Germans did it, but the events may be connected with the fact that the Battle of Verdun was going badly at the time and strikes and protests had broken out in Germany: German labour was scarce, so the extra labour was needed, or the Germans may have wanted to get revenge for their losses at Verdun.

This episode is a reminder that in all wars armies often take out their frustrations by assaulting or abusing any women they can lay their hands on.

Nurses, you're needed!

All the countries at war needed women to work as nurses, both at the front and in the hospitals at home where wounded men were sent (see Figure 19 in the insert section). Nursing administration had been revolutionised in the 19th century by the work of Florence Nightingale, so it was much better organised than it had been in past wars. By the time of the First World War, most countries had a professional military nursing service. The Queen Alexandra Imperial Military Nursing Service (QAIMNS), for example, was founded in 1902 and recruited nurses from the different countries of the British Empire, but Australia, New Zealand and Canada all had their own nursing units as well.

Bedpan, scissors, moral fibre . . .

Any woman applying to work as a military nurse was going to be working with soldiers, and nurses were expected to maintain proper standards of morality at all time. The very first question on the reference form for people applying to the QAIMNS was: 'Is the applicant of sound health, both of body and mind, of good moral character and high principled?' Nurses were supposed to stay focused at all times, obey orders without question and certainly not form romantic attachments to their patients. Many of their patients (and some nurses, of course) had other ideas.

Nursing with a twist

The war produced some remarkable individual nursing stories:

✔ **Flora Sandes:** Even before Britain entered the war in 1914 this British nurse volunteered to serve with the Serbian army. When the Austro-Hungarians overran Serbia and the Serbs had to retreat, she enlisted in their army as a soldier and was soon promoted to Sergeant Major. She was wounded and went back to nursing, running a Serbian military hospital, but still found the time to write a book about her wartime experiences to raise money for the Serbs. Sandes stayed with the Serbian army after the war, becoming a captain.

✔ **Elsa Brandstrom:** This Swedish nurse worked in Russia with the Swedish Red Cross looking after wounded German and Austrian prisoners of war who called her 'The Angel of Siberia'. After the Bolshevik Revolution of 1917, the Russians revoked her work permit but she carried on her work until finally she was arrested as a spy. Eventually the Russians let her go and she continued her work for the welfare of prisoners of war.

✔ **Mairi Chisholm and Elsie Knocker:** These British nurses were also keen motorcyclists. They were snapped up to serve in Belgium with the new Flying Ambulance Corps when the doctor setting it up spotted Mairi Chisholm taking hairpin bends. The women were employed as motorbike riders, ferrying wounded men across the battlefield to the casualty clearing centres behind the lines. They soon decided they wanted to be more directly involved in nursing and left the corps to set up their own first aid post with their own money. The pair became celebrities and were awarded medals by both Britain and Belgium.

The dangers of nursing

The QAIMNS sent nurses to accompany the very first troops who went to the front in 1914, and the service operated on every front where Empire troops were involved: the Western Front, Gallipoli, Palestine, Mesopotamia, Salonika, Italy and so on. The work was hard and exhausting, and it could be very upsetting for women who weren't used to such things to see the soldier's appalling wounds.

Nursing was also dangerous work. Nurses often worked close to the front line and many were killed in enemy bombardments. In June 1918, 234 nurses and patients were drowned when a German U-boat sank the Canadian hospital ship the *Llandovery Castle*. Quite rightly, war memorials in different countries include a tribute to the courage of the military nurses.

VADs . . .

VAD stood for *Voluntary Aid Detachment,* a volunteer unit set up by the Red Cross before the war to back up the work of the QAIMNS. Volunteers (who were usually known simply as VADs) tended to come from rich middle-class families, where the women wanted to do something practical to help the war. Some very famous women became VADs during the war, including the American aviator Amelia Earhart and the British writers Vera Brittain and Agatha Christie.

QAIMNS nurses often resented VADs: they saw VADs as amateurs getting in the way of the professionals. To start with, VADs weren't able to do much more than clean and cook but, as the war went on, they developed better nursing skills and played a crucial role in keeping the war going (see Figure 20 in the insert section).

. . . and FANYs

Although nurses served in often dangerous locations behind the front lines, the battlefield itself was still regarded as an exclusively male space. That idea was challenged by *FANY*– the *First Aid Nursing Yeomanry,* a British female unit set up in 1907 by Captain EW Baker to provide immediate first aid to men on the battlefield itself. FANYs were trained to ride horses as well as give first aid because it was thought that riding horses would be the best way to get out to wounded men in battle (that's why they were called *yeomanry,* which is a type of volunteer cavalry corps). However, when the war came FANYs usually drove lorries and ambulances.

The British army command didn't like the FANY one bit: they thought it was an amateurish unit that would only get in everyone's way on the battlefield. Moreover, because FANYs weren't actually in the army, they didn't feel they had to salute army officers every time they saw them, and this made the army even more determined not to have anything to do with them! So instead the FANY worked with the Belgian and French armies, who were delighted to have its help. As well as driving ambulances and providing immediate first aid (a bit like combat medics nowadays), FANYs also ran soup kitchens and canteens, mobile bathhouses and even a cinema.

Two courageous nurses

Edith Cavell was a British matron working at a Brussels teaching hospital in 1914 when the war broke out and Brussels fell to the Germans. From her hospital, she operated an escape line that allowed some 200 Allied prisoners of war to escape. Eventually, the Germans realised what she was doing and she was arrested and shot. This was a bad mistake on the Germans' part because the act was widely condemned around the world and just added to the propaganda picture of the Germans as murderous bullies.

Less well known is Claire Trestrail, an Australian nurse who was also working in Belgium when the war broke out. She and a couple of other Australian nurses managed to evacuate 130 French and Belgian patients from their hospital in Antwerp while the Germans were shelling the place, and they flagged down or commandeered any transport they could find to get all the patients out of harm's way. Eventually, the nurses themselves managed to get a lift on a British bus that took them to safety behind British lines. This remarkable escape story was a sensation at the time, though it's largely forgotten now. That's how history works!

The French and Belgians thought very highly of FANY, and FANYs soon collected medals for bravery from Britain, France and Belgium, including 17 British Military Medals, 27 *Croix de Guerre* (the highest French military award) and a *Légion d'honneur* (a special award by the French state).

They also serve who only stand and wait

Not all women could work in factories or on the land. Many had no choice but to stay at home with their children and were often in the unenviable position of waiting for news of their sons or husbands away at the war.

Staying at home, getting on with ordinary life and waiting for news may not sound very glamorous compared with the other opportunities the war was opening up for women, but it wasn't an easy option. Women were the ones who had to queue for food and work out how to feed the family on the rations, which got tighter as the war went on (no wonder women were at the head of the food riots that broke out in Austria and Germany in 1916). You won't find so many photos of the women who stayed at home in the history books, but their contribution to the war was every bit as important as that of the ones who went off to work in the factories and on the land.

The children's war

Life during the war was very difficult for mothers with young children, despite the presence in some countries of clinics where mothers could get medical help and advice. For children, too, it could be very difficult to grow up without a father they could see and relate to. Children would write to their dads at the front and they'd get letters back, but it wasn't the same as having their fathers at home.

Men usually got home leave about once a year, and often just for three or four days, so it was important to make the most of it. Years later, people who were children during the war remembered the excitement they'd felt when their fathers came home on leave and they finally had a chance to see them. Asking dad about the trenches, though, wasn't a good idea. Soldiers found it impossible to tell people at home about life at the front; they usually kept quiet about it and talked about absolutely anything else.

The dreaded telegram

Before the war, receiving a telegram had been a special event: *telegrams* were the very latest in telecommunications technology. A telegram was sent over the wire to a post office, where the message was listened to by a telegraph operator and written out on a form. The form would be handed to a telegram boy who'd hop on his bike and pedal off to deliver it. During the war, however, women came to dread hearing the telegram boy ring his bicycle bell, because news that a soldier had been killed was often delivered by telegram.

Women Serving in Military Uniform

One major change that the war brought in for women was that for the first time they had the opportunity to serve in uniform. In 1917 Britain set up the Women's Army Auxiliary Corps (WAAC), which recruited 40,000 members. The thinking behind the WAAC was much was the same as with sending women into the factories: to free a man for the front. So WAACs didn't usually go into the trenches. Instead they took on much of the supply and support roles behind the lines that armies depend on, such as driving lorries, mechanical work, secretarial work and (of course!) cooking.

In 1917 the Women's Royal Naval Service (WRNS, known as the 'Wrens') was formed to provide a similar sort of support for the land-based role of the Royal Navy: driving, clerical work and help with naval intelligence. Finally, in 1918 a Women's Royal Air Force was created to provide the new Royal Air Force with mechanical and secretarial support. It was overwhelmed with volunteers (see Figure 13-2).

© Imperial War Museums (Q 12291)

Figure 13-2:
A motor-
cyclist
with the
Women's
Royal Air
Force.

Apart from a notable exception in Russia (see the later 'The Women's Battalion of Death' section), other countries' armies only used women as nurses and medical personnel, though some individuals did manage to disguise themselves as men and serve at the front. Most were sent home when they were discovered (often when they were wounded), though Milunka Savić, a feisty lady who slipped into the Serbian army, managed to stay at the front even after her identity was known. She proved a formidable soldier and went on to be highly decorated by the French, Russian and British governments, as well as her own.

Changing perceptions

Female uniformed units played an important role in changing people's perceptions of what women could and couldn't do. Before the war, factories and the armed services had seemed two areas of life that belonged to men. Now, women were demanding and getting the right to go into the factories in order to do their bit to win the war. Putting women into military uniform seemed to be challenging almost the last taboo: the idea that war was just for men. The *fighting* was still supposed to be just for men – women's units were supposed to keep to a support role. But when women are driving army lorries and ambulances or flying new aircraft, it's not hard to conceive of women beginning to take up arms and fight. One women's unit did just that.

The Women's Battalion of Death

In February 1917 strikes and food riots broke out in Russia and the crisis forced Tsar Nicholas II to abdicate. It was the start of the Russian Revolution (you can get more details in Chapter 15). The new Provisional Government (so called because it was only governing until the Russians could hold proper elections) decided to carry on the war, expecting that the Russian army, which was falling apart by 1917, would be so inspired by the Revolution that it would finally get its act together and crush the Germans. Not many Russian solders responded in the way the new government hoped, but one person who did was a peasant woman called Maria Bochkareva. She'd been in the army at the front and seen soldiers deserting in huge numbers or turning against their officers. She wasn't impressed.

When the new Russian government decided to authorise a women's army unit Maria Bochkareva was put in charge of it. Called the *Women's Battalion of Death*, the name was meant to strike terror into the hearts of the enemy. The women shaved their hair and wore exactly the same uniform as the men: it was only close up that you could tell they were women at all.

The Women's Battalion of Death went into battle against the Germans in 1918 and immediately put their male comrades to shame. The men weren't keen to attack, but the women took the enemy position and drove the Germans back. Unfortunately (this sort of thing often happened in the First World War), the units on either side of them didn't do well, so the women were left out on their own without support and they had to fall back. This experience confirmed Bochkareva's view that women were better fighters than men.

In October 1917 the *Bolsheviks* – a group of socialist revolutionaries under Vladimir Lenin's leadership – staged their own revolution, to overthrow the Provisional Government. Most of the government's troops had given up by that stage of the Revolution, but not the Women's Battalion of Death. When the Bolsheviks stormed the palace, they defended it fiercely. They couldn't fight off the attack or save the Provisional Government, however: they were taken prisoner by the Bolsheviks and rumours soon spread that they'd been assaulted in prison (and some of them indeed had been). The British ambassador to Russia got the women released and Maria Bochkareva eventually ended up in the United States.

Winning the Vote

Before the war, one of the biggest issues for women in many countries was whether or not they should have the vote. Finland, Australia and New Zealand had given women the right to vote, but other countries held back, and vocal women's suffrage movements existed in Britain and the United States calling for votes for women. Their opponents claimed that women weren't able to reason or work as well as men, but women in the combatant countries were disproving that idea with every day of work they put in. By the war's end, the case for granting women the vote looked overwhelming.

Hard bargaining in Britain

In Britain, the last general election had been held in 1911, so from 1916 a general election was overdue. However, by no means all British men had the right to vote and most people thought it would be a scandal if men who were fighting and dying for their country in the trenches were denied the chance to vote, so the government drew up plans to extend the vote to all adult men.

Hang on! What about us?

The woman who stepped forward to insist that if the British government was going to start extending the franchise it had better include women wasn't a Suffragette (see 'Suffering Suffragettes', earlier in the chapter), but the leader of the non-militant *Suffragists,* Millicent Fawcett. The government hadn't been intending to include women in the proposal at all, and when it discussed the matter with Fawcett, it proposed only giving the vote to women property-owners aged 35 or over. She argued that this was far too restrictive. After some hard negotiating, they agreed on a compromise: women property-owners aged 30 and above would get the vote. The new rules were passed into law in June 1918, in good time for the general election in December.

Why not just give the vote to everyone?

Nowadays people think of the vote as a right, but that's not how people saw voting at the time of the First World War. The vote was something you *earned* through hard work or by owning property and showing yourself to be a responsible citizen. By 1918 most people agreed that the working men of Britain had earned the vote through their sacrifice in the trenches, and women had earned the right to join the 'Voters' Club' too. But those in power argued that women still had to show they could use the vote responsibly. That's why the two sides argued so much about exactly which women would get the vote, instead of just giving it to all of them. In any case, the Prime Minister, David Lloyd George, was worried that young women might vote for the Labour Party and he didn't see why he should hand his opponents such an advantage!

Lloyd George was worrying about nothing. Young women were no more committed to one political party than any other age group was, and ten years later British women got the vote on the same terms as men.

Voting all over the world

The example of Britain giving women the vote in recognition of their war work made it easier for the United States to do the same for American women in 1920. Some American states had granted women the right to vote before the war, but most states held out. American suffragists had used similar tactics to the British suffragettes (see 'Suffering Suffragettes', earlier in the chapter): some went on hunger strike while others picketed the White House.

President Wilson himself supported votes for women, and in 1919 Congress agreed to the Nineteenth Amendment to the Constitution, allowing women to vote. As a result, American women voted for the first time in the presidential election of 1920. As in Britain, the war work women had undertaken helped to convince opponents of the case for female suffrage.

Many European countries also granted women the right to vote at the end of the war when they removed their monarchs and became republics. As new democratic states, they tried to get rid of inequalities, and doing that meant giving votes to women. The Provisional Government in Russia (see the earlier 'The Women's Battalion of Death' section) granted women the right to vote in 1917, the new republican governments of Germany and Hungary did the same the following year, and the Republic of Austria did so in 1919.

France had been a republic much longer than these countries, but French conservative groups were still opposed to votes for women: they thought women belonged in the home and should keep out of politics. They defeated an attempt to introduce female suffrage at the end of the war and it wasn't until after France's liberation from German rule in 1944, at the end of the Second World War, that French women finally got the vote.

What did women win?

One of the most important questions historians ask about the women of the First World War is the extent to which women's experiences changed their role in society as a whole. Did the war help women to achieve equal status with men?

While the war was going on, and especially in Britain (which used women more extensively than any other country), it looked as if the answer might well be 'yes'. The British writer HG Wells was certain that what he called the 'superiority of our women' had won the war, and many people agreed with him. In all combatant countries, though, women had played a key role in the war effort, even when it seemed to be falling apart at the front. Women had shown that they could do almost everything that men could do. At least in the industrialised world the 'separate spheres' idea was dead.

Or was it? At the end of the war, men came back home and reclaimed their old jobs. In many countries the war was followed by years of high unemployment and hardship, which made men even more anxious to get their jobs back. Women had to give up their wartime work and go back home to carry out their traditional tasks of washing, cooking, cleaning and looking after the children. In many countries, job prospects for women in the 1920s weren't much better than they'd been before 1914. Even so, no one could forget what women had proved in the First World War, and when the Second World War broke out 20 years later, women played an even greater role all over the world. The modern emancipation of women owes a huge amount to the women of the First World War.

Chapter 14

Struggles for Power

. . . .

In This Chapter

▶ Watching the showdowns in the German high command

▶ Controlling the generals in France and Italy

▶ Following the clash between Lloyd George and Haig

▶ Witnessing Austria-Hungary implode

. . . .

The combatant countries of the First World War weren't engaged only in fighting each other: conflict also arose between the political leaders of those countries and the generals in charge of their armed forces. As the war dragged on and demanded ever greater sacrifices from the peoples of the combatant countries, political leaders grew increasingly alarmed. They worried about how long people would put up with heavy casualties and food shortages and why the generals didn't seem able to hurry up and win the war so that life could get back to normal. But the generals thought that the reason they weren't able to break through the enemy lines was because the politicians back home weren't providing them with the men and materials they needed. Some military leaders even began to wonder whether things might run more smoothly if they took over the government from the politicians.

As the First World War unfolded, political leaders across Europe had to face the increasingly urgent question: who was more dangerous – the enemy, or their own military leaders?

Battling for the Soul of Germany

Germany was the most powerful of the Central Powers. But the country was gripped throughout the war by a deadly internal struggle for power between the civilian government and Germany's apparently all-powerful military leaders. The stakes could hardly have been higher: the whole future of Germany would depend on which of these two deadly rivals came out on top. This was a struggle for the soul of Germany itself.

Ooh, I do like a man in uniform

Two strange cases dating from before the war demonstrate how the German army viewed itself. In 1906, an unemployed Berlin drifter called Wilhelm Voigt decided to have a bit of fun. He gathered bits and bobs of an army captain's uniform, put them on, went out into the street and started barking out orders to people. Everyone he met obeyed his every word, simply because he was in a uniform. He even managed to put the local mayor behind bars before someone finally got on the phone to the local barracks! And in 1913, a more serious incident happened at Zabern (that's Saverne to the French), a town in German-occupied Alsace. A (genuine) army officer started arresting civilians and nearly provoked a revolt in the whole province by his high-handed behaviour.

These two stories are often taken as evidence of how all-powerful the army had become in Germany by 1914. The army saw itself as a law unto itself, beyond the control of mere civilians. When the country went to war in 1914, the army's sense of its own importance was bound to grow still further. It did.

Divisions running deep

The German constitution was specifically designed to let the army and navy have as much of an independent say in government as possible. The German armed forces even had their own Cabinet, separate from the German government. This situation made the likelihood of a division between the military and civilian members of the German government much greater and sure enough, the war provoked such a split. However, the German military leaders were also split, between those who thought Germany should concentrate its efforts in the east and those who thought Germany should concentrate on the west. These divisions would hamper the German war effort right to the end of the war.

Westerners v. easterners

In 1914 the civilians in the government and the military agreed to put their existing differences aside in order to unite behind the Schlieffen Plan (see Chapter 4). After the plan failed to deliver the quick victory it had promised in the opening campaigns (Chapter 4 tells you why), however, the old division re-emerged, but with a new twist. This time the military was divided too:

✔ **Westerners** believed that Germany's most dangerous enemy was Britain, and that Germany should put all its resources onto the Western Front. Some westerners, such as General Falkenhayn, the Chief of the General Staff, thought Germany had much in common with Russia and should make peace, maybe even an alliance, with the Russians as soon as possible.

> Major westerners: General Falkenhayn, Chief of the General Staff and therefore in ultimate control of the army; (up to a point) the Kaiser.
>
> ✔ **Easterners** thought the Eastern Front was the only one that counted and that Germany should just contain the Western Front and go for an all-out attack on Russia in the east.
>
> Leading easterners: General Hindenburg and General Ludendorff, winners of Germany's victory over the Russians at Tannenberg in 1914.

Hindenburg and Ludendorff were key figures within Germany because they'd become national heroes after their victory over the Russians at Tannenberg (Chapter 4 has the details). After Tannenberg they became steadily more important in politics and they used their influence to try to undermine their great rivals, the Chief of the General Staff, General Falkenhayn, and the chancellor, Bethmann-Hollweg.

Remind me – what are we fighting for, exactly?

As well as disagreeing over which front Germany should concentrate on, the German high command was also divided on what Germany should be fighting *for.*

In September 1914, a month or so into the war, Bethmann-Hollweg announced Germany's *September Programme,* a long list of territory in France, Belgium and Poland that Germany should seek to take over directly, as well as an even larger sweep of territory far into Russia that should be a sort of German empire. Many in the German high command supported this idea enthusiastically, but Falkenhayn wasn't convinced. As a westerner, Falkenhayn's hopes were to contain the war in the east, defeating the Russians without taking too much territory off them, but to break through in the west and to impose tough terms on the British and French.

Falkenhayn fails

Falkenhayn's biggest plan for breaking through in the west was the huge German attack on Verdun in 1916. Falkenhayn was hoping that success there would show that he'd been right to concentrate on the Western Front. Unfortunately, Verdun turned into a nightmare for the Germans, just as much as it was for the French (see Chapter 6). Even Bethmann-Hollweg, who normally supported Falkenhayn against Hindenburg and Ludendorff, was appalled at the casualties Germany suffered at Verdun. The last straw for Bethmann-Hollweg came when Romania declared war on Germany and its allies in August 1916, and Germany was faced with yet another front to fight on. Bethmann-Hollweg decided that these disasters were Falkenhayn's fault, sacked him and replaced him with his rivals, Hindenburg and Ludendorff.

As a nice little irony, Falkenhayn was sent to take charge on the Romanian front, on a sort of 'You got us into this mess; you can get us out of it' basis. (He did very well and had the Romanians beaten by the end of the year, though it probably didn't make up for being sacked.)

Look, who's actually running this war?

Bethmann-Hollweg took the view that, as chancellor of Germany, he was in charge of the country's war strategy. Hindenburg and Ludendorff saw matters differently, as did Admiral Tirpitz, who commanded the German navy. These military commanders had no intention of obeying a civilian just because he happened to be chancellor of Germany. In particular, they were determined to stop Bethmann-Hollweg negotiating any sort of peace settlement.

These were some of the issues on which these men clashed:

- **Unrestricted U-boat warfare:**

    - **For:** Admiral Tirpitz, who thought the policy would starve Britain into surrender. Also Hindenburg and Ludendorff.

    - **Against:** Bethmann-Hollweg and Falkenhayn, who thought the 1915 U-boat campaign had been a public relations disaster for Germany and that another such campaign would be bound to bring the Americans into the war.

    - **Result:** Falkenhayn changed his mind and Tirpitz got his way. Unrestricted U-boat warfare resumed in 1917 and, sure enough, America declared war.

- **A separate peace with Russia:**

    - **For:** Bethmann-Hollweg, who wanted to bring the war to an end and thought Germany could do a deal with the new Russian government that took office in February 1917 after the Revolution.

    - **Against:** Hindenburg and Ludendorff, who wanted to make the Russians eat dirt and thought the Revolution gave them their best chance to do it.

    - **Result:** Hindenburg demanded that any peace treaty should include an independent Polish state or he'd resign, so there. The Russians said no to an independent Poland and the peace plan was over. Which had been Hindenburg's aim all along.

- **A separate peace with Britain and France:**

    - **For:** Bethmann-Hollweg, who wanted to negotiate a deal before the Americans started arriving in large numbers.

    - **Against:** Hindenburg and Ludendorff, who thought they could still break through in the west and win.

    - **Result:** Hindenburg and Ludendorff refused to give up any land in Belgium and so Britain and France said no to Bethmann-Hollweg's peace plan. As Hindenburg and Ludendorff had known they would.

The problematic Hindenburg Programme

In 1916, with the Battle of Verdun bleeding Germany's army dry, the German military high command took a fatal step into the world of civilian policy. General Ludendorff announced that Germany needed to double its production of munitions and that the German economy would have to be turned upside down in order to do it. The new military-run economy was named the *Hindenburg Programme,* in honour of the famous general and national hero. A special Supreme War Office, run by the army, took over the German economy, closed down all non-essential industries and drafted 300,000 men to work in war production: this figure quickly rose much higher. Unfortunately, doing this meant taking men away from the land and from the army. Taking men from the front line meant that Germany wasn't able to build on the Allied disappointments of 1916 (see Chapter 6) but taking so many men away from food production was even worse: soon Germany was hit by serious food shortages and the price of what little food there was rocketed. The trade unions were strongly opposed to the Hindenburg Programme and the divisions and weaknesses in German society it caused were a major reason for Germany's collapse in 1918.

Hindenburg and Ludendorff systematically scuppered both Falkenhayn's military strategy and Bethmann-Hollweg's peace proposals in order to wage war their way. In July 1917 the two men persuaded the Kaiser to sack Bethmann-Hollweg, while Tirpitz helped to create a new Fatherland Party, a political party dedicated to supporting German expansion. They all got their chance to put their ideas into action when Russia finally signed a peace settlement in March 1918 and Germany demanded (and got) a huge area of Russian territory (see Chapter 15).

By 1918 Hindenburg and Ludendorff could feel pleased with themselves for having beaten off their domestic rivals. However, their success meant that the Allies would consider Germany a military state. They'd bear that in mind when they finally drew up their own peace terms (see Chapter 17).

Losing Heart in France: Do We Actually Want to Win?

The war had gone so badly for France by 1917 and cost so many lives that some people were beginning to lose heart. They didn't want to lose, but given the cost in money and lives, they weren't sure they wanted to carry on either.

France divided

France had been deeply divided, politically and socially, between left and right before the war. On the left, socialists tended to distrust the army because it was so conservative, and on the right, Conservatives and the Church thought that socialists wanted to plunge the country into bloody revolution. In 1914 the government declared that everyone should now put aside their differences so as to form a grand *Union Sacrée,* a 'sacred union' of the whole country. This new mood of national unity didn't last long: by the autumn of 1914 people were demanding to know who was to blame for the failure to drive the Germans off French territory.

To compound matters, in 1915 huge arguments broke out over the crisis in shell supplies: French factories weren't producing shells fast enough and the army simply didn't have enough to fire at the Germans. That crisis brought down the French government and started a long-running dispute between the government and the French generals over who was actually in charge of running the war. The new Prime Minister, Aristide Briand, rather thought he was, but the French commander General Joffre had his own ideas:

✔ In 1915 Briand and the National Assembly (the French parliament) demanded more of a say over military strategy. General Joffre told them he knew rather more about these matters than they did and they should leave everything to him, thank you very much.

✔ In 1916, after France's appalling losses in the epic Battle of Verdun, Briand decided that it was time for the government to take back control of the war. Joffre was removed from command. (They made him marshal of France to save hurting his feelings. It was a great honour and, even better, didn't involve his doing anything.) Never again would France appoint one soldier to command all the fronts of the war.

✔ In 1916 control of the war passed to the civilian minister of war, with General Pétain working *under* him as Chief of Staff (that is, head of the army). This way, the government could keep a close watch on what Pétain was planning. The new commander on the Western Front was General Nivelle.

✔ In 1917 General Nivelle announced that he'd launch the mother of all offensives on the Western Front and that the government had better start planning a massive victory parade. In fact, Nivelle's offensive was a disaster and the French army mutinied rather than go through that again. So the government sacked Nivelle and replaced him as commander on the Western Front with Pétain. Now France needed a new Chief of Staff.

Losing the will to fight

The French really wanted the Germans to get out of France and to hand back Alsace and Lorraine, but not everyone wanted to go through disasters like Verdun and General Nivelle's offensive (you find the full details in Chapter 15) in order to get these lands back. More and more French people thought that they'd already done enough fighting and that they should concentrate just on making sure the Germans advanced no farther into France. If the British or Americans wanted to launch huge offensives to drive the Germans back to Berlin, well, let them get on with it.

The French were disappointed because they wanted their generals to be like Napoleon: a great leader on the battlefield and a great political leader too. However, that little daydream had two very practical snags:

- ✔ France's politicians would never allow a general to set himself up as ruler, however good he was.
- ✔ France's generals weren't as good as Napoleon had been (though some of them thought they were).

What France needed in order to carry on the fight was a successful general who wouldn't try to take over the government and a tough Prime Minister who could stop the general if he tried. Luckily, in 1917, France got both.

Enter Clemenceau and Foch – the French dream team

In 1917 the French government collapsed because of a treason scandal based around a left-wing pacifist newspaper called *Le Bonnet Rouge*. The newspaper had links with figures in the government, including the interior minister, and in 1917 it turned out that the newspaper also had links with the German government, which was, in effect, bankrolling it. The interior minister was accused of turning a blind eye to the newspaper's activities (the implication was that he must have known the paper was in the pay of the Germans) and also to other pacifists in the French parliament who, it turned out, were also being paid secretly by the Germans. Not surprisingly, in November 1917 Aristide Briand's government resigned.

The President of France, Raymond Poincaré, now had to choose a new Prime Minister. The top two candidates were

- ✔ **Joseph Caillaux:** A former Prime Minister who didn't worry about people disliking him if he was doing the right thing. In this case, he reckoned, the right thing was negotiating a peace deal with Germany.

✔ **Georges Clemenceau:** A tough old radical, nicknamed 'the Tiger', anti-conservative and anti-socialist. He was anti-German, too: he wanted to carry on the war until the Germans had been cleared off every last scrap of French territory – including Alsace-Lorraine. On a personal note, he didn't like Poincaré and Poincaré didn't like him.

Poincaré chose Clemenceau. That decision meant Poincaré was accepting the need to fight the war right through to the end and not try to make a separate peace. This also meant that the French must find just the right general to fight on without trying to undermine the government. Luckily, they found one. The new army Chief of Staff was Ferdinand Foch, a tough general who could run successful military campaigns but had no desire to take over the government.

Clemenceau soon showed his determination to win the war whatever the cost. The French economy was falling apart, so he got parliament to let him deal with the crisis by ruling by decree. When the socialists objected, he just ignored them. This was the sort of Prime Minister Foch could work with, and the two men supported each other to the hilt. As a result of this unity, France went into the final stages of the war more united than it had been since 1914.

PLEASE Can We Sack General Cadorna? Italy and Its Men in Charge

Italy's war against Austria-Hungary in the Alps isn't as well known as the fighting on the Western Front, but it was every bit as traumatic for the Italians as Verdun and the Somme were for the French and British. The Italian commander General Cadorna launched a series of huge offensives against the Austro-Hungarian positions there, but all were defeated with huge casualties.

In his handling of Italy's war, Cadorna enjoyed the confidence of King Victor Emmanuel III, but not of anyone else. He had the knack of blaming everyone else for his own failures. Cadorna sacked generals and even had Italian soldiers executed for cowardice when really it was his own strategy that was to blame for Italy's lack of success at war.

The Italian government became increasingly alarmed at Cadorna's handling of the war, and in 1916 the Italian parliament set up a Committee of Inquiry to look into the matter. Cadorna simply ignored it. As long as he had the support of the King, he reckoned he could get away with defying Italy's elected politicians. Cadorna even refused to have any dealing with the Prime Minister: he'd deal with the Minister of War and with the King but no one else.

The last straw: Catastrophe at Caporetto

Meanwhile, ever-bigger protests were being staged in Italy against the war. In April 1917 Italian communists staged a rising in Turin and troops opened fire on the crowds. It was beginning to look as if Italy might fall into civil war. Then, in October 1917, the situation finally came to a head. The Austro-Hungarians launched a devastating attack on the Italian positions at Caporetto and broke through the Italian lines (you can find the details in Chapter 15). The Italians were thrown back in confusion. The Austro-Hungarians were even closing in on Venice. It looked as if the whole Italian front was about to collapse and Italy would be knocked out of the war entirely.

General Cadorna, as usual, blamed everyone else for the disaster. In particular, he said his army had been 'stabbed in the back' by all the riots and protests taking place in Italy, which had demoralised the men. This time, though, no one was listening to him. The defeat at Caporetto had brought down the Italian government and the new man in charge, Orlando, had no patience with the disastrous General. Even the King had finally realised that Cadorna had to go. Orlando sacked Cadorna and his replacement, General Diaz, set about completely reorganising the Italian army, ensuring it was better equipped and abandoning the huge offensives that Cadorna had insisted on launching. By 1918 the Italian army was significantly better equipped, better led and in a good position to strike back at the Austrians and get revenge for Caporetto.

Following Cadorna's example

The danger to Italy from ambitious generals hadn't gone away, however. Cadorna had tried to ignore the elected government and he might have got away with it had he been more successful in battle. Other Italians, such as the radical writer Gabriele d'Annunzio, also thought that military leaders should be free to do as they liked and that democratic politicians were just an irritating waste of space.

To make his point, d'Annunzio went on to take military action himself right at the end of the war, seizing the port of Fiume with an armed band of followers, in complete defiance of the law. Ultimately, Cadorna's and d'Annunzio's contempt for democratic politicians would find a great admirer in the Italian fascist leader, Benito Mussolini.

Bringing Out the British Bulldogs

Britain's long tradition of keeping soldiers out of politics (you can find this tradition explained in Chapter 12) acquired an important exception in 1914 when Lord Kitchener was made Secretary of State for war – the first serving soldier to sit in a British government since the 17th century. Kitchener looked at the war from an entirely military point of view and he resented the way civilian politicians 'interfered' with military decisions. Like his French and German counterparts, Kitchener thought that soldiers should be left to get on with fighting the war and that the politicians' job was simply to make sure the military had all the men and materials it needed.

Right from the start, Kitchener made an impact in Cabinet when he told them, in August 1914, that the war would last much longer than the Cabinet ministers thought and that it would require huge numbers of men. This message wasn't a welcome one for a Cabinet that had only reluctantly gone to war in the first place and which was hoping to get back to the normal business of government as soon as it could. Kitchener didn't like confiding in his Cabinet colleagues, even when he needed to change plans, because he reckoned they wouldn't understand military strategy: as a result, they thought of him as erratic and unpredictable. Ironically, although the Cabinet thought of Kitchener as a military man, the generals at the front thought of him as a civilian and resented being told by him what they should be doing.

However, if tensions developed between Kitchener and his civilian Cabinet colleagues, these were dwarfed by the bitter clash that developed later in the war between the Prime Minister and the British commander on the Western Front. Unlike in Germany or France, it was never very likely that British military leaders would try to seize power, but the divisions that developed between the government and the military high command were to have a serious impact upon the whole development of the war.

Sorting out the shells crisis

By the spring of 1915 Sir John French, commander of the British Expeditionary Force on the Western Front, was in trouble and he knew it. He hadn't delivered a knock-out blow to the enemy and his attack on Aubers Ridge had failed. After the battle he gave an interview to the *Times* newspaper in which he said the lack of success on the Western Front was down to the army not having enough shells. The *Times* ran the story. Kitchener assured the Prime Minister, Herbert Asquith, that the army had all the shells it needed, so that was what Asquith told the press. French, however, hit back: he fed documents to the *Times* correspondent to support his claim and he also sent them to senior politicians on both sides. MPs and newspapers began demanding answers about the 'shells crisis'.

At the same time as the shells crisis, the news from Gallipoli (see Chapter 9) was becoming increasingly bad, so Asquith agreed to form a coalition government that included both Conservatives and members of the new Labour Party. The key new role of minister of munitions went to the combative Welsh Liberal, David Lloyd George. It would be down to him to make sure the army got the shells it needed.

A very British coup

Kitchener had offered to resign over the shell shortage, which had ultimately been his responsibility. Asquith didn't accept his resignation, mindful of the bad headlines it would attract. But then Kitchener fell out of the picture when he drowned in June 1916 after his ship hit a mine off the Orkney Islands.

The man appointed to replace Kitchener as War Secretary was Lloyd George, who'd made a great success of his time as minister of munitions. Lloyd George now showed that politicians could be just as ruthless in their way as generals. He decided that to run the war properly he needed a small executive committee of only three ministers. He would chair the committee, and it would include the Conservative leader Andrew Bonar Law but not the Prime Minister. At first Asquith agreed to this arrangement, but then he realised that Lloyd George had taken the running of the war right out of the Prime Minister's hands. So he changed his mind and insisted on being part of this inner War Cabinet. Lloyd George didn't want him and resigned from the Cabinet. Bonar Law supported Lloyd George's position, but Asquith thought he had more support so he decided to show who was boss: he resigned.

Asquith's thinking was that everyone would be so horrified by his resignation that they'd beg him to come back. Bad mistake. To Asquith's horror, the King (who still had the power to appoint Prime Ministers) instead sent for Lloyd George. The Welsh Wizard, as he was known, had completely wrong-footed Asquith and taken his place as Prime Minister (see Figure 14-1 and Figure 21 in the insert section).

© Imperial War Museums (Q 70208)

Figure 14-1:
The dynamic British Prime Minister David Lloyd George – the 'Welsh Wizard'.

David Lloyd George

David Lloyd George was an old-fashioned radical from Wales. He'd made his name as a young firebrand chancellor of the exchequer, denouncing the rich, taxing their income heavily and airily describing the House of Lords as a bunch of people randomly selected from the ranks of the unemployed. Lloyd George was one of those dynamic politicians you either admired or you couldn't stand. Winston Churchill was a fan. The Prime Minister, Asquith, was not.

Lloyd George enjoyed cutting through red tape. When, as Prime Minister, he found that 10 Downing Street wasn't large enough to house all the secretaries he thought he'd need, he simply had a set of garden sheds erected in the grounds with tables and typewriters inside. He wasn't a man to be scared by important or high-ranking people: he'd beaten the powerful House of Lords in an epic political battle in 1911, forcing them to accept major limits on their own powers and he was quite prepared to force his will upon the British generals if he had to. Lloyd George relished political in-fighting, particularly if it meant taking on people he thought of as blinkered or conservative: such as Field Marshal Haig, for example.

Both Asquith and Lloyd George belonged to the Liberal Party. Many Liberals were horrified at what they saw as a gross act of betrayal by Lloyd George, and remained loyal to Asquith, to the extent that in the general election at the end of the war, the Liberals divided into two camps: pro-Asquith Liberals and pro-Lloyd George Liberals.

It's easy to feel a bit sorry for Asquith, but the fact is that he hadn't been a very good war leader. The year he was outmanoeuvred as Prime Minister, 1916, had also been the year of the Battle of the Somme and of the disappointing Battle of Jutland, which both followed on from the Dardanelles and the other failures of 1915 (see Chapter 6 for more about the Somme, Chapter 8 for more about Jutland and Chapter 9 for the Dardanelles). Asquith had to go and Lloyd George had found the perfect way to force him out.

No, Prime Minister! Lloyd George ruffles a few feathers

Lloyd George had a totally different leadership style to Asquith. For one thing, he brought into the Cabinet people from outside the main parties, such as the South African General Jan Christian Smuts and the historian HAL Fisher, but did most of his work with a small inner Cabinet that included the leaders of the Conservative and Labour Parties. And he certainly wasn't one to let the military boss him around.

After taking over the top spot, Lloyd George soon showed his tough side:

- ✔ Sir William Robertson, Chief of the Imperial General Staff, deeply disliked Lloyd George's War Cabinet and thought the army should be left to run the war as it saw fit. Lloyd George replaced him with the more pliant Sir Henry Wilson.

- ✔ In 1917 British socialists wanted to travel to neutral Sweden to attend an international peace conference. Lloyd George didn't want the world's socialists all banding together, so he refused to let them go. This act led many Labour Party supporters to turn against Lloyd George's coalition government. Lloyd George didn't let their decision worry him.

- ✔ Admiral Jellicoe, in charge of Britain's Grand Fleet, resisted the idea of making merchant vessels sail in convoy, to make it harder for the U-boats to find them. Lloyd George simply overruled him and ordered all merchant ships to sail in convoy from then on.

As a Liberal, Lloyd George believed passionately that Parliament and the government were sovereign, and that the army must obey the elected government. Opposing his opinion was Field Marshal Sir Douglas Haig. Haig resented Lloyd George and, like Kitchener before him, thought that civilian politicians had no place trying to tell him how to run his own war. Lloyd George, in turn, thought that Haig was far too wasteful in battle with the lives of his men, and he wasn't going to let Haig have endless reinforcements just because he demanded them. The appalling losses at Passchendaele in 1917 (see Chapter 15) confirmed Lloyd George's opinion that Haig was simply throwing lives away in pointless offensives.

Lloyd George would happily have sacked Haig, but doing so would've been politically risky: Haig was still very popular with the British public and identifying an obvious replacement for him wasn't easy. Lloyd George settled on the alternative of outranking Haig. He was very keen on the idea of an Allied supreme commander with direct authority over all the Allied armies – as long as that commander wasn't Haig. In the end this post went to the French Chief of Staff, General Foch. Haig wasn't very happy with the appointment, but he went along with it (see Figure 14-2). Lloyd George supported it enthusiastically. In his eyes, anything that put some sort of control over Haig had to be a good thing.

Figure 14-2:
Two architects of victory: Field Marshal Sir Douglas Haig and Marshal Ferdinand Foch.

© Imperial War Museums (Q 7179)

Clash of the Titanic egos: Lloyd George v. Haig

In March 1918 the Germans launched a huge attack on the Western Front (which you can read about in Chapter 16). They attacked the British lines on the old Somme battlefield and broke through. For the first time since 1914 the Germans were heading towards Paris. For the Allies this was the biggest and most serious crisis of the entire war. Immediately, the questions began. How had the Germans managed to break through the British lines with such apparent ease? Who was to blame?

Field Marshal Haig had no doubt about who was to blame for the crisis: Lloyd George. He already hated Lloyd George so much that he could barely bring himself to be in the same room as the Prime Minister. Now Haig told the press that the reason the Germans had broken through was because the Prime Minister had deliberately kept the British army short of men. Lloyd George angrily replied that Haig's allegations were entirely wrong. The army was actually stronger in the spring of 1918 than it had been a year earlier, he claimed, and here were the figures to prove it.

One of us is lying

Lloyd George's answer might have been the end of the matter, except that another General, Frederick Maurice, wrote a letter to the *Times* saying that Lloyd George's figures were wrong and giving what he said were the true figures. According to Maurice, the British army on the Western Front was much weaker in 1918 than it had been in 1917. Lloyd George's enemies demanded a debate in Parliament and got one. In the debate, Lloyd George announced that he'd got his figures from General Maurice's own department! Lloyd George won the debate and General Maurice was forced to retire from the army in disgrace for his insubordination.

Historians now know that more was at stake in this clash than at first appeared. Lloyd George *had* given misleading figures – the British army in France *was* smaller than in 1917, not larger, and he knew it. Maurice may have hoped his letter would force Lloyd George to resign, but Lloyd George had been cannier and much more unscrupulous.

Lloyd George later claimed that Maurice had been part of a plot by the generals to overthrow him. That such a plot existed, beyond the occasional general daydreaming of what he'd like to do to the Prime Minister anyway, is unlikely. Haig didn't think soldiers should interfere in politics any more than he liked politicians intervening in military matters. In any case, as the Maurice debate showed, the 'Welsh Wizard' was perfectly capable of running rings round his opponents. Lloyd George survived the debate and went on to represent Britain at the Paris peace conference at the end of the war.

Meeting the Last of the Habsburgs: Austria-Hungary

The power struggle in Austria-Hungary was different from the struggles going on in other countries. Instead of a stand-off between generals and civilians, in Austria-Hungary the tension was between the different nationalities that made up the empire. As the war dragged on, these groups began to demand the right to rule themselves. Moreover, by 1917 the food shortages and hardship the war was causing were creating so much suffering and tension in the country that the Austro-Hungarian government was desperate for peace.

Be careful what you wish for, Austria

The empire of Austria-Hungary was made up of two separate halves, Austria and Hungary, and their interests didn't always coincide. The trouble with Serbia that led to the outbreak of war in the first place, for example, was almost entirely an Austrian, not a Hungarian, problem (see Chapter 3). By 1914, many ordinary Austrians, as well as their leaders, had had enough of the Serbs and thought it was time they were dealt with once and for all. However, as the war dragged on and cost more and more lives, many Austrians changed their minds. What exactly, they asked, were they fighting *for?* But asking the government about its aims was difficult, because it didn't bother calling the Austrian parliament (Austria and Hungary each had their own parliaments). Austrian socialists demanded that parliament be called to discuss the war, and when they didn't get their way, one of them took out his frustration by assassinating the Austrian Prime Minister.

Austria-Hungary's wheels start falling off

Since 1867 Austria and Hungary had had a sort of power-sharing arrangement whereby Austria ruled one part of the empire and Hungary ruled the other. That suited the Hungarians, but it didn't suit the other nationalities, who didn't like being ruled by the Hungarians any more than they'd liked being ruled by Austria. Then, in 1916, Emperor Franz Josef died. He'd reigned for nearly 70 years and provided a symbol under which the empire could unite.

His successor, Karl I, didn't have the same hold over the different peoples of the empire, and they all started to fetch their coats and thank the Habsburgs for a lovely time but say they really must go home. The Czechs, for example, didn't see why they should risk life and limb fighting for Austria-Hungary, so whenever they could, they'd surrender to the Russians and then volunteer to fight on their side. Before long, the Russians had so many Czech soldiers that they formed a special Czech Legion, which went into battle against the Austrians quite convinced that they were fighting for their independence.

The Hungarians, too, saw the war as their chance to put the screws on the Austrians. Austria was dependent on imports of grain from Hungary. The Hungarians knew this, so they cut off Austria's grain supply and kept the grain for themselves. The time had come, they decided, to turn the tables on the Austrians and assert their independence. And when the Hungarians started talking about independence, the other nationalities within the Austro-Hungarian Empire began to do the same. The clock was ticking for Emperor Karl and his empire.

Oh no you don't, Emperor Karl!

Emperor Karl knew that his empire was desperate for peace, but he also knew that Austria-Hungary was dependent on Germany for military and economic support. The Germans were determined to fight on, convinced they could win the war. So, Karl opened secret negotiations with the French about a possible peace deal. Clemenceau, the French Prime Minister, however, was a wily old bird. He realised that the Allies would benefit even more if the Germans and Austrians fell out with each other: their alliance would collapse, the different nationalities would all declare independence and Austria-Hungary would simply cease to exist. So he published the news of the negotiations in the press. Sure enough, the Germans were furious. They already reckoned that being allied to Austria-Hungary was like being 'shackled to a corpse'. Now the Germans didn't trust their allies an inch.

As the war moved into 1918, the Germans would be drawing up their war plans without consulting their allies. If Austria-Hungary got into trouble, it could expect no help from Germany.

Part V
Armistice and Aftermath, 1917–1918 and Beyond

© Imperial War Museums (E(AUS) 1220)

For a great free article that asks whether the *First* World War caused the *Second* World War, go online and take a look at www.dummies.com/extras/firstworldwar.

In this part...

- ✔ Empathise with how desperate all the Great Powers were for the war to end by 1917 – and with how equally desperate they all still were to win.

- ✔ Prepare for a rough ride and some surprises as you watch the great plans for 1917 turn into some of the worst nightmares of the war (including Russia's collapse into revolution) and the sudden burst of movement in 1918 that came after years of sitting in trenches.

- ✔ Pull up a seat and join the peacemakers of Paris as they dictate a peace that hit the Germans hard.

- ✔ Take time to pay your respects with the poets, writers, historians and ordinary people who helped to foster the culture of remembrance that still exists today.

Chapter 15

1917: The Year of Big Changes

*1*916 had been a year of very hard lessons for both sides. The huge offensives of that year – the German attack at Verdun and the Allied attack on the Somme (which I describe in Chapter 6) – had led to disaster with unimaginable losses, and military leaders on both sides knew they had to seriously rethink their tactics. They planned to apply the lessons they'd learned in new offensives to be launched in 1917. However, these plans were to go just as badly wrong as those of the previous year: 1917 was the year of the Battle of Passchendaele, for example, when British and Empire troops slogged it out with the Germans in Flanders in possibly the worst conditions of any battlefield of the war.

1917 also turned out to be the year in which the war expanded in some unexpected directions. A major revolt against the Turks broke out in Arabia (you can read about it in Chapter 9); the Austro-Hungarian army broke through on the Italian front (see 'Italy's Darkest Day – Caporetto', later in this chapter); and, most importantly, this was the year when the United States finally broke its tradition of isolationism (Chapter 11 has the details) and entered the war on the Allied side.

Above all, however, in 1917 events in Russia took centre-stage. This was the year of the Russian Revolution. The Russians overturned the Tsar's government and installed a new Provisional Government. This new government decided to stay in the war but it proved no better at waging war than the Tsar had been, and in October 1917 it was overthrown in a second revolution, this time led by the *Bolsheviks,* Russia's most important communist group. The changes that took place within Russia had a dramatic impact not just on the way the war was heading but on the whole shape of the 20th century.

1917 was an epic year that changed the war – and the world. This is its story.

Revolution in Russia

The Russian Revolution was the event that would define 1917 in world history, and it also completely changed the balance of power and the shape of events in the war. So what exactly happened?

The Russia of the Romanovs

Compared with the rest of Europe, Russia in the early 20th century was bewilderingly backward. Apart from two major industrial centres in Moscow and Petrograd (that's how St Petersburg was renamed during the war), Russia was still overwhelmingly a country of small peasant villages. Russian industrial workers lived and worked in appalling conditions of poverty, overcrowding, dirt and disease. On top of that, Russia had serious internal weaknesses which the war only made worse.

Problems, problems . . .

Although Russia is rich in raw materials it had very few mines, so its industry was almost entirely dependent on foreign imports of essential materials, especially coal. However, the Germans and Turks were able to blockade Russia's western ports, and the country's geography dictated that imports now had to come via the distant port of Vladivostok in the Russian far east. Unfortunately, the Russian railway system wasn't robust enough to cope with carrying so many imports of raw materials such a long distance, and the whole supply system broke down. Without enough coal to feed it, the Russian electricity supply also began to collapse, and before long the railway system was collapsing, too: it didn't have anything like enough rolling stock and, with no imports of metal reaching Russia's factories, no replacements could be built.

To make Russia's misery even worse, the war ruined the country's agriculture, too. So many men were called up to serve in the army that villagers didn't have enough hands to get the harvest in: often whatever food they could produce was requisitioned for the army anyway. By 1915, food was running short, and by the end of 1916 hardly any food was available in the shops; what little food you could find was very expensive. Workers in the cities went on strike and staged protest marches, but the government didn't listen: instead, it banned trade unions and sent anyone whom it considered to be a troublemaker into exile. When any politicians and journalists tried to ask questions about the way the war was being run the government just accused them of being dangerous revolutionaries who wanted to pull down the whole tsarist system.

Unfortunately for the Tsar's government, it didn't even appear to most Russians that the country's war effort was gaining anything from the immense suffering that the people were having to go through. Although Russian commanders did well against the Austro-Hungarians in the south, the Russians had been crushed by the Germans in Poland and the Baltic, taking thousands of prisoners and areas of rich farmland (see Chapter 4). Every German advance made Russia's food crisis worse. The railway system and the army administration were in such chaos that thousands of Russian soldiers were expected to fight at the front line with no food, ammunition, boots or proper uniforms. No wonder they started to desert in their thousands.

Just popped out to war. Rasputin's in charge till I get back

Tsar Nicholas II of the Romanov dynasty was Russia's *autocrat,* meaning that – in theory – he was in charge of everything. However, the Russian Commander-in-Chief, Prince Nikolai Nikolayevich (who also happened to be Nicholas' uncle), was a popular figure with the army, despite Russia's huge military problems, and Nicholas feared that his uncle might be tempted to stage a military coup and take control of Russia himself. To stop him having such dangerous thoughts, Nicholas had decided in 1915 to take personal command of Russia's armies at the front. This was a strange decision, given that Nicholas had no military experience, but he thought it was essential.

However, if Nicholas thought that taking charge would solve Russia's problems at a stroke (and it's possible that he did) he was in for a shock. Holding so much power in how own hands meant that the responsibility for Russia's backwardness and its social problems, and for Russia's performance in the war, all fell squarely on his shoulders. A strong individual would've been up to the task, but Nicholas was too weak a character to impose his will and he was far too open to the influence of other people, notably:

- ✔ **His wife, Tsarina Alexandra,** who wanted him to be tougher on his critics. Alexandra, however, was German, and Russians were asking questions about just where her loyalties lay.

- ✔ **Rasputin,** a (not very) holy man with immense personal magnetism. He attracted a devoted following of aristocratic groupies, and he had the power – no one really knows how – to stop the internal bleeding that plagued the young Tsarevich (Prince) Alexis, the heir to the throne. Because of this, the Tsar and Tsarina grew ever closer to Rasputin and referred to him simply as 'our friend'. When Nicholas, at Rasputin's suggestion, left Petrograd for the front to take personal charge of the ailing Russian army, he left the government of the country in the hands of the Tsarina. Which meant, in effect, that he was leaving it to Rasputin. In turn, Rasputin appointed his drinking and séance friends to top ministerial posts, where they proved every bit as incompetent as you'd expect.

By 1916 it seemed as if Russia was rapidly imploding: the shops were empty, soldiers at the front were deserting, workers were on strike and the government didn't have a clue what to do about it all. A group of young noblemen were concerned enough about the way things were going to murder Rasputin, but doing that didn't solve anything. By February 1917 Petrograd was in the hands of rioters and strikers. The Tsar gave orders to his troops to restore order. But then the unthinkable happened: they said no.

Revolution!

When troops join in with a riot, it's no longer a riot: it's a *revolution*. With rebel and loyal troops firing at each other on the streets, Nicholas's ministers and generals persuaded him that he had no choice: he'd have to abdicate. With a heavy heart, Nicholas agreed. The long reign of Russia's Romanov dynasty was over.

Although I speak of 'the Russian Revolution' of 1917, in fact the country experienced *two* revolutions that year. The first one, which overthrew the Tsar and set up a Provisional Government, is known as the *February Revolution* after the month of the Russian calendar when it took place. In the *October Revolution,* later the same year, Lenin and the Bolsheviks overthrew the Provisional Government and took power themselves.

Give peace a chance. Or maybe not

Leading Russia now that the Tsar had abdicated was a Provisional Government led by Prince Lvov, a well-known reformer. The Provisional Government intended to turn Russia into a modern democratic republic with a proper constitution. Drawing up the constitution would be the job of a special assembly that the Russian people would elect in the autumn. In the meantime, the Provisional Government would work to get Russia back on its feet again.

The first decision that the Provisional Government had to take – the big one – was whether or not to stay in the war. This decision wasn't straightforward:

- **Reasons to pull out:** Russia desperately needed a complete overhaul of its economy and for that it needed peace. People needed reasonably priced food in the shops, workers needed decent housing and wages, and the country needed to get its head round a democratic voting system. Oh, and the soldiers at front were deserting in droves and were desperate to go home.

- **Reasons to stay in:** Russia was committed to its allies, and new governments aren't generally keen to get a reputation for breaking promises. If the Russians tried to make peace, the Germans would almost certainly demand huge areas of Russian territory and they'd possibly impose some sort of fine as well. But with its new revolutionary enthusiasm the new Russia could thrash the Germans and start Russia's new era with a famous victory.

It didn't take Lvov and the Provisional Government long to decide: Russia would stay in the war.

What time is the next sealed train? Lenin arrives

Many Russian revolutionaries had either been sent into exile or had escaped abroad from the Russian secret police. One group living in exile in Zurich, in neutral Switzerland, was known as the *Bolsheviks* and they were led by Vladimir Ilyich Lenin.

The Bolsheviks followed the teachings of the German political philosopher Karl Marx, who'd taught that industrial societies would all experience a workers' revolution which would establish a society without classes where industry and land and everything else would belong to the people.

Marx had suggested that countries needed to go through a fairly long period of middle-class rule before they were ready for revolution, which in Russia's case meant that the country wouldn't be ready for revolution for another 100 years or so. However, Lenin and the Bolsheviks wanted to stage a revolution in Russia rather earlier than that – immediately, in fact. They were desperate to get back to Russia and get to work, but their problem was how to get there. If they travelled through France or Italy, they'd be arrested as dangerous revolutionaries; if they went through Germany or Austria, they'd be interned as enemy aliens. Their problem was solved when a most interesting and unexpected offer of help arrived from, of all sources, the German government.

The Germans thought that Lenin and the Bolsheviks going to Russia and causing trouble could only work to their advantage. But they didn't want any revolutionary ideas causing trouble in Germany, and so they offered Lenin a deal. They'd provide him with a train to take him through Germany to the Baltic coast, where he could cross to Sweden and arrive in Petrograd via Finland, but it was to be a sealed train: it would have just one carriage, and no one would be allowed on or off it until it reached its destination. Lenin agreed. And so he arrived back in Russia in April 1917 and immediately called for a new revolution to overthrow the Provisional Government. The members of the German government rubbed their hands and sat down to watch the fun.

At first it looked as if the Germans were going to be disappointed. Lenin made a big splash when he first arrived back, but most Russians ignored his call to overthrow the Provisional Government. They were prepared to give Prince Lvov and his ministers a chance to govern the country. When the Bolsheviks tried to seize power in July 1917, the Provisional Government was able to deal with them swiftly and Lenin and the others had to flee to Finland in disguise. They'd be back.

The Russians get steamrollered

The dominant figure in Lvov's Provisional Government was a radical lawyer, Alexander Kerensky. Kerensky was confident that he could organise the army and lead it to victory over the Germans. Never mind that he was a lawyer with absolutely no military experience: gifted amateurs do exist and Kerensky believed that he was one. (He wasn't.)

Kerensky appointed Russia's best commander, General Brusilov, and told him to prepare a large-scale offensive to drive the Germans and Austrians out of Russian territory. Brusilov was a good general and the attack did work well against the Austrians (who were almost as fed up with the war as the Russians were). But it was much less successful against the Germans, who launched a major counter-attack and drove the Russians back.

The failure of the Kerensky offensive finally broke the will of the Russian army. One thing Kerensky was good at was giving rousing speeches, and he'd managed to reverse the mood among Russia's front-line troops and persuade them that they could win and, even more importantly, that thanks to the Revolution they now had something worth fighting for. So when the offensive petered out for all the usual reasons – the Russians' inability to keep their armies supplied with essentials such as food, clothing and ammunition – morale collapsed completely. Whole regiments mutinied and headed for home. Often they just murdered any officers who tried to stop them.

KEY PEOPLE

Alexander Kerensky

Alexander Kerensky was a radical lawyer and politician, one of the few socialists in tsarist Russia's *duma* (parliament). When the war broke out he opposed it, but he gradually changed his mind as he came to see it as a war against right-wing German militarism. The Provisional Government made Kerensky its Justice Minister, because doing so seemed a good way to keep the workers and socialists on side. They weren't wrong: Kerensky was by far the most popular figure in the Provisional Government. He quickly rose to the position of War Minister, and in July 1917 he became Prime Minister.

Kerensky fancied himself as a war leader, often having himself photographed in military uniform. But after his big offensive failed, he was overthrown by the Bolsheviks. He escaped from Russia and lived in exile, first in England and then in the United States. Kerensky had become one of those people who end up as a sidebar in a history book. Like this one.

The final nail in the coffin of Russia's war effort came at Riga in the Baltic, where the Germans launched a new-style 'lightning' attack. It began with a short but intensive bombardment with lots of smoke and gas to confuse and disorientate the Russian defenders. Then the Germans sent in hundreds of lightly armed, elite *stormtroopers,* who were specially trained in trench fighting. They captured the Russian front line and sent the Russians back, reeling. Kerensky's Russia was no more able to defeat the Germans than tsarist Russia had been.

And Kerensky's Russia was about to collapse too. In response to riots against the war that broke out in Petrograd, Kerensky sent in troops to restore order, losing credibility with Russians almost by the day as a result. By the autumn of 1917 he'd squandered all the support he'd enjoyed earlier in the year, and it was easy for Lenin and the Bolsheviks to decide to overthrow him. In October, they made their move.

Oh, well done, General Kornilov, you've let the Reds in

The October Revolution was an example of the Law of Unintended Consequences. Kerensky had sacked the commander of the Russian army, General Kornilov, who in September decided to get his own back. He marched on Petrograd at the head of his army, intending to overthrow the Provisional Government and take power himself. For a while, it looked as if he might succeed: very few soldiers were prepared to risk their lives defending the Provisional Government, so General Kornilov thought he'd be able to march unopposed into Petrograd.

His dreams of staging a coup, though, were shattered by the Bolsheviks, who didn't want a military take-over ruining their own plans for revolution. The Bolsheviks sent their own soldiers, known as the Red Guards, to stop Kornilov. The Red Guards didn't just block his way: they also convinced his men to desert and come over to join the Bolsheviks. General Kornilov's army melted away before his eyes and he himself had to escape. The citizens of Petrograd could breathe a sigh of relief: the Red Guards had saved the Provisional Government. Now the Bolsheviks prepared to overthrow it themselves. This wasn't at all what General Kornilov had had in mind when he planned his coup.

Lenin, working with a new recruit to the Bolsheviks, Leon Trotsky, planned an uprising to seize the Winter Palace in Petrograd, which was the Provisional Government's headquarters. By October 1917 the Bolsheviks had nearly all the army and navy on their side; the Provisional Government had only a small force, including the Women's Battalion of Death (see Chapter 13 for more on this remarkable unit). On the night of 24 October the Russian cruiser *Aurora* fired a blank round towards the Winter Palace and the attack began. The defenders put up a fierce fight, but they were too few. The Bolsheviks overran the palace and arrested the ministers, except for Kerensky, who managed to escape. Lenin and the Bolsheviks were now in charge.

Just sign here – the Treaty of Brest-Litovsk

Lenin had no intention of repeating the Provisional Government's mistake of staying in the war. He'd promised the Russian people peace and he intended to deliver.

In December 1917 Lenin suspended fighting along the Eastern Front and sent a delegation led by Trotsky to the German headquarters to discuss peace. The Germans, though, were in no mood to make concessions. They demanded that Russia give up a vast area, including the whole of Ukraine, or the war was on again. Even the Bolsheviks, who weren't too bothered about national borders, were taken aback by the extent of the German demands.

Trotsky deliberately dragged the negotiations out: the Bolsheviks reckoned that if they kept talking long enough, revolution would break out in Germany too. However, the Germans got impatient with the Russians' delaying tactics and ordered their troops to resume the war. That shook the Russians. Lenin sent orders to Trotsky to sign whatever terms the Germans were offering. Trotsky did, and Russia was out of the war.

The Treaty of Brest-Litovsk was a triumph for the Germans and its terms showed just how land-hungry German nationalists were (see Figure 15-1):

- ✔ Russia was to lose a huge area, including Ukraine, the Crimea, Lithuania, Estonia and Finland.

- ✔ Germany and its allies were to decide what happened to the areas Russia gave up, and Russia was to have no say in that decision. For example, Ukraine was to be independent and Russia had to recognise it as an independent state.

- ✔ Russia was to evacuate all the land it had taken off Austria-Hungary.

- ✔ Russia was to demobilise its army and keep its fleet in port.

- ✔ Russia wasn't to engage in anti-German propaganda.

- ✔ Each side was to return their prisoners of war.

Figure 15-1:
The Treaty
of Brest-
Litovsk.

The treaty had come just in time for Germany because the Western Front would soon be changing radically. Russia might have pulled out of the war in the east, but the United States was in the process of joining in the west. With all its prisoners returned from Russia, Germany would be able to transfer thousands of troops to the Western Front, ready to take anything the Allies might be planning to throw at them.

All Busy on the Western Front

Both sides began 1917 with plans that, they hoped, would bring the war to a speedy conclusion. The Allied plan was that the Russians and Italians would both attack on their fronts, and the British and French would launch a major offensive on the Somme. However, events soon forced the Allies to change their plans: first, the February Revolution in Russia delayed the Russian offensive from the spring to the summer; second, the French appointed a new commander, General Nivelle, who didn't like the idea of launching a second Battle of the Somme. Instead, he wanted two Allied offensives, a French one to the south of the Somme and a British one to the north. Before he could put his new plan into effect, however, the Germans caught the Allies out with some manoeuvres of their own.

Germany's list of priorities in 1917 looked like this:

- ✔ Deal with Russia in the east – bring the country to its knees.

- ✔ Hold on in the west – don't let the Allies break through.

- ✔ Launch a massive attack in the west – crush the French and British in good time before the Americans start arriving in large numbers.

The Germans achieved the first part of their plan with the Treaty of Brest-Litovsk (see the earlier section 'Just sign here – the Treaty of Brest-Litovsk'). The attack in the west to crush the French and British was planned for early 1918 – the latest point by which Germany had to try to win the war, because the Americans were on their way. America had declared war in April 1917 (see Chapter 11) but took time to then recruit, train and equip the additional troops it needed. (American troops wouldn't arrive in Europe in force until the spring of 1918, massively boosting the number of Allied troops facing the Germans.) Though the Germans underestimated American strength, they still planned to attack before American troops began to arrive in significant numbers.

In preparation for their big attack planned for 1918, the Germans had to hold on in the west and implement a plan they'd come up with to make life very difficult for the French.

Germany's deadly withdrawal

In February 1917 the Allies were very puzzled: the Germans in the opposite trenches appeared to be withdrawing. Indeed they were, but they weren't giving up. Far from it. *Operation Alberich* was underway.

The Germans knew the Allies were preparing a major offensive in the west. They also knew that their own line had weak spots where the Allies might break through. Instead of spending ages trying to strengthen these points, the Germans built a new, much stronger defensive line farther back, code-named the *Hindenburg Line.* Operation Alberich (Alberich was a tricky customer from German mythology) was the codename for the German withdrawal to this new, impregnable defence line.

As the Germans withdrew to the Hindenburg Line, they systematically laid waste to the countryside: they burned all food, crops, bridges, houses – anything that might help the Allies when they advanced through the area. To add to their enemies' difficulties, they also set plenty of booby traps. The French who lived in the area watched in dismay. Many of them had got on well with individual German soldiers, who'd often been billeted in their homes, but now those same soldiers were deliberately destroying their homes and their livelihoods.

The (not so) talented General Nivelle has a plan

In December 1916 the French government finally got rid of General Joffre (Chapter 14 has the details), who was a genial enough cove but not the man to deliver the killer blow to the Germans that was required on the Western Front. The new French commander was the dashing, confident and clever General Robert Nivelle. Nivelle reckoned that he, and he alone, could win the war and save France. He had political ambitions too, but first Nivelle had to break through the German line on the Western Front.

Nivelle's plan looked sound on paper. The German line bulged just at the point where the British and French forces joined, so he planned to attack there: they'd squeeze the Germans between a French attack from the south, a British-led attack from the north and then a French attack in the middle that would break through the German line – and the war would be as good as won. What could possibly go wrong? Well, the plan had two major flaws right from the start:

✔ The Germans had pulled back to the Hindenburg Line, so the bulge Nivelle wanted to attack had disappeared and the whole plan had to be reconfigured.

✔ The Germans knew about Nivelle's plan in detail because he'd distributed so many copies of it and the plan was virtually public knowledge (in any case, it was difficult to miss a million French troops gathering opposite the Germans' front line).

KEY PEOPLE

General Robert Nivelle

Looking back, it's hard to see why the French placed so much confidence in Nivelle. He'd done well at Verdun but had never commanded anything as large as his 1917 offensive. He rose to power mainly because he was so full of self-confidence and ideas that he gave the *impression* that he could win: he was like a French equivalent of Gilbert and Sullivan's Model of a Modern Major-General. Nivelle knew how to use the press to promote and publicise himself. He used his political contacts to get command of the Western Front when the French government wanted to drop Joffre.

Nivelle was half-English, through his mother, and he spoke the language fluently, so he was also able to take advantage of the bad relationship between the British commander Haig and Prime Minister Lloyd George: he charmed Lloyd George so much that the Prime Minister even placed the British Expeditionary Force under Nivelle's command, much to Haig's disgust.

After the failure of his offensive Nivelle was sacked and disappeared from the scene. He spent the rest of his army career in North Africa while the French army tried to recover from his disastrous time as its commander.

The moral of the story is: don't be fooled by confident generals who tell you they can win the war in a weekend.

When it became clear that the Germans knew about the planned attack, Haig – the British commander on the Western Front – argued that the plan needed a complete rethink. However, the Prime Minister, David Lloyd George, overruled Haig and even placed him under Nivelle's command. Haig fumed about this, but Nivelle was adamant: the attack would go ahead.

Nivelle's offensive has various names. Some people call it the Second Battle of the Aisne (the Aisne was the river where the Germans first dug in after the First Battle of the Aisne back in 1914); others call it the Battle of the Chemin des Dames, after the area where the main French attack came. The British, ANZAC (that is, the Australian and New Zealand Army Corps) and Canadian parts of the offensive are named after the particular places where they attacked: Arras, Vimy Ridge and, farther north in Belgium, Messines.

Phase 1: The Battle of Arras

The first phase of Nivelle's offensive was a British, Canadian and ANZAC attack against the German lines near Arras. Although the huge preliminary bombardment rather gave the game away that an attack was coming, the Arras phase of the offensive actually worked very well. The British had dug tunnels under the battlefield and were able to emerge much closer to the German lines than the defenders were expecting. They used gas and took advantage of a very helpful snowstorm, both of which made it much harder for the Germans to see them coming. The British had also learned how to make much better use of their artillery than before, especially how to fire a *creeping barrage* – a line of shell bursts just ahead of the advancing infantry, which moved forward at the same pace as the men.

The creeping barrage was a very effective way of protecting attacking infantry from enemy gunfire, but it did require nerves of steel in the advancing soldiers. Not only did they have to keep as close as they dared to the exploding shells, but they had to walk towards the enemy at a steady pace: if they ran (which would be most people's instinct in a battle), they'd lose the protection of the barrage and may very well be blown up by it.

The most important victory of the Battle of Arras came when the Canadians, under Sir Julian Byng, attacked the German position high up on Vimy Ridge and took it. Vimy Ridge was a difficult position to attack. It was up a steep slope that the French and British had attacked before and been beaten off each time. One hundred thousand Canadians launched themselves against the German position at Vimy, and both sides suffered very heavy casualties before the Canadians finally took it. Vimy Ridge was a major Canadian victory: they took the ridge, 4,000 prisoners and plenty of guns and mortars. The news from Vimy Ridge was a major morale-booster in Canada and Britain, at a time when the war seemed to be going Germany's way.

The Battle of Arras didn't all go the Allies' way, however. When the British and their allies reached the Hindenburg Line, they found it impossible to break through. The Australians in particular suffered very heavy casualties while attacking the impregnable German position.

Phase 2: The Battle of the Chemin des Dames

Following the British, Canadian and ANZAC attack at Arras, the French were due to attack farther south, north of Reims along the Chemin des Dames (*Chemin des Dames* means 'the Ladies' Way' – it was where ladies at Louis XIV's court liked to take their walks back in the 17th century). The Germans knew the attack was coming, though, and they were ready for it.

The Battle of the Chemin des Dames was a disaster for the French. The Germans had left behind plenty of carefully positioned machine gun posts when they withdrew, and these were able to decimate the French before they could get anywhere near the German lines. The French were in despair. One unit even went into battle baa-ing like lambs going to the slaughterhouse. The great Nivelle offensive took a bit of land off the Germans, but it didn't achieve anything like the great breakthrough Nivelle had been promising.

The Chemin des Dames offensive for the French was similar to the 1916 Somme offensive for the British: they'd built up huge expectations and everyone thought it would be a walkover, so it was all the more devastating when the attack failed so disastrously.

Hang on, this wasn't part of the plan: Mutiny!

The French people were stunned by the failure of Nivelle's offensive, which had promised so much, and the French soldiers were angry. In May 1917 they mutinied. They'd defend their own trenches against German attacks, but they refused to take part in any more pointless offensives. In one place the mutineers even set up a sort of rival French government, committed to ending the war. The real French government acted quickly. It had the ringleaders of the mutinies arrested and shot, and it sacked General Nivelle and replaced him with General Pétain, the man who'd saved the day at Verdun the year before (see Chapter 6). Pétain calmed the situation down, listened to the men and promised not to waste their lives in any more badly planned attacks. But even he couldn't get the men to commit to undertake any more offensives.

Remarkably, the French managed to hide the news of the mutinies from the Germans. If they'd known about the low morale in the French army, they might have been able to defeat the French as they were in the process of doing to the equally war-weary Russians. Even though the French had managed to limit their damage, the mutinies had one big result: the main burden of carrying on the offensive against the Germans now fell to the British.

Field Marshal Haig has a better plan!

If the British were to take over the main task of attacking the Germans (see previous section) then Haig wanted to shift the attack much farther north, towards their lines in Flanders and the British army's very vulnerable position at Ypres. Haig wanted to beat the Germans right back and fight through to the Belgian ports of Zeebrugge and Ostend, from where U-boats were still sailing out and devastating Allied shipping (see Chapter 8).

Haig planned the British-led attack to take place in two phases:

- ✔ An attack on the German position on the Messines Ridge, just south of Ypres
- ✔ An attack out of the *salient* (a bulge in the Allied line) at Ypres

Phase 1: The mines of Messines

The man with the job of taking Messines from the Germans was General Sir Herbert Plumer. Plumer might have looked like a caricature of a stuffy, old-fashioned officer – he was a bit tubby and he had a big, bushy white moustache – but don't be fooled: he was a very able tactician, one of the best commanders of the war.

Plumer prepared the attack very carefully. The Germans were in a salient and the British and ANZACs would be attacking all the different parts of the bulge simultaneously. They'd be using the usual preliminary bombardment, which would pound the German positions but also give them a good idea that an attack was coming. However, Plumer had a secret weapon: mines.

British engineers had been tunnelling under the Messines battlefield and had planted 20 huge mines, containing almost 600 tons of explosive, under the German trenches. The Germans knew something of what was happening and they dug their own tunnels to try to intercept the British, but they found only one mine: the British were able to plant explosives in *all* the others.

Irish from north and south

The Belgian village of Wytschaete was the scene of a remarkable piece of military co-operation during the Battle of Messines Ridge. The soldiers who attacked and took the village were Irish and Ulster troops, veterans of the Battle of the Somme. Back home, the Catholics of the south and the Protestants of Ulster were at daggers drawn over the future of Ireland, but on the Western Front their soldiers were able to put their differences to one side and work together. This sort of co-operation would become increasingly rare in the years ahead.

On 7 June 1917 the British exploded their mines on the Messines Ridge. The combined explosion was enormous: it could be clearly heard as far away as London. The Germans didn't stand a chance. Ten thousand of them were killed in an instant and the rest were either too badly wounded or too shocked to put up much resistance. Plumer's men took Messines and advanced farther. They took all their objectives, and although the Germans counter-attacked continuously, they weren't able to drive Plumer's men out.

Messines was a major British victory. It was also a sign that the advantage on the battlefield was beginning to swing back from the defender to the attacker.

The Monocled 'Mutineer'

Unlike the French, Russian and German armies, the British army in the First World War never experienced a full-scale mutiny. The closest it came to one was an outbreak of trouble in September 1917 at the large training camp at Etaples in northern France, where the officers and *NCOs* (non-commissioned officers, such as corporals and sergeants) seem to have enjoyed making the men's lives as miserable as possible. When a New Zealand soldier was arrested as a deserter (he'd actually just slipped out of the camp) his mates gathered to protest, and a military policeman fired and killed one of them. Trouble broke out and more troops had to be brought in to restore order. Afterwards, one man was shot and three others got heavy prison sentences. The authorities learned their lesson and improved the regime at the camp.

In the 1980s a fictional story about the mutiny, *The Monocled Mutineer,* was filmed by the BBC. It was about Percy Toplis, a soldier who liked to dress up as an officer, complete with monocle. In the film Toplis leads the Etaples mutiny. He didn't. In fact, he may not even have been on the Western Front at the time. But hey, why let the facts get in the way of a good story?

Phase 2: The pain of Passchendaele

The second part of Haig's plan was a breakout from the salient around the town of Ypres. The plan was actually quite good: a huge Allied attack, using British, Belgian, French, Canadian and ANZAC troops, would drive the Germans back from Ypres and head for Bruges, which was the headquarters for the German U-boats based at Zeebrugge and Ostend. Officially, this was to be the *Third Battle of Ypres;* however, the world soon came to know it by a different name: *Passchendaele,* a little village that Haig made one of his objectives.

Haig's tactics at Passchendaele sound very like the ones he employed at the Battle of the Somme in 1916 (see Chapter 6): a huge artillery bombardment followed by a massive infantry assault. But Haig thought that the attack planned for 1917 would have some significant advantages over the Somme attack the year before:

✔ The British and Canadians had just had two major victories, at Vimy and at Messines, so their morale was higher than the Germans'.

✔ The German defeat at Messines had shown (Haig reckoned) that the Germans were exhausted and in no fit state to withstand a British attack.

✔ The attack was on a much more limited front than the Somme attack had been.

✔ The advancing infantry would be protected by a creeping barrage.

In many ways Haig's analysis was right. The British and Canadians were more experienced and professional than the volunteers who'd been slaughtered on the Somme and they'd learned to use more effective tactics for their attacks. It was probably wishful thinking for Haig to expect the Germans to be too exhausted to put up a fight after the Battle of Messines, but it's true that they were in a much worse shape than they'd been in 1916. What Haig couldn't have anticipated were two pieces of bad luck:

✔ The British government decided to transfer men and equipment from France and Belgium to the Italian front (see 'Italy's Darkest Day – Caporetto' later in this chapter for the details).

✔ It rained. Heavily.

Of the two, the most serious blow was the rain. Water is never far below the surface in this part of Belgium anyway, and the British preliminary bombardment had completely destroyed the local drainage system. The result was that the battlefield was churned up into thick, liquid mud (see Figure 22 in the insert section). I don't mean the sort of mud you may encounter out on a country walk. This was like fighting in thick, liquid and very deadly caramel.

Men couldn't advance through it – they couldn't even walk in it: they had to use wooden 'duckboards' to walk on, and if they fell off the duckboards into the mud, they drowned (see Figure 15-2). The conditions were impossible to fight in: horses were useless and so were tanks.

Figure 15-2: Australian troops walk on duckboards through the remains of Chateau Wood, Ypres, in 1917.

© Imperial War Museums (E(AUS) 1220)

Even so, Haig chose to fight on. He's been fiercely criticised for this decision since. His thinking was that if the Allies could follow up their successes at Vimy and Messines with an even greater victory in Belgium, German morale in the army and at home would simply collapse. But if the Allies were to pull out, it would give the Germans new heart and might even jeopardise the safety of the British base at Ypres. So Haig pressed on with the attack long after it was clear that it was permanently stuck in the mud.

The battle became known as the *Battle of Passchendaele* because this village was where the attack finally petered out. The village itself fell to Canadian troops in the autumn (the Canadians were really proving their worth in 1917). However, it was clear that the mud wouldn't allow the Allies to press forward any farther. Passchendaele was as far as the advance reached and it gave its name to the whole battle.

It was here, at Passchendaele, that the Germans used possibly the most deadly weapon of the war: mustard gas. *Mustard gas* was by far the most lethal of the various gases used in the First World War. It could burn its way through clothing and was much more likely than other gases to kill its victims. Mustard gas inflicted a horrible lingering death: victims could die four or five days after being gassed. It also remained in the ground for days, which wasn't ideal if the army that had used the gas later wanted to advance across the same piece of land.

Cambrai – the day of the tank

Haig was deeply frustrated that his plans for breaking out from Ypres had been ruined by the Battle of Passchendaele and he wanted to counterbalance that failure with a success somewhere else. So in November he launched one more offensive, at Cambrai, near the Arras battlefield where the British had done so well in the spring.

This time they attacked with large numbers of *tanks* – the metal-plated armed and armoured vehicles (see Figure 15-3) that had so shocked the Germans when they first saw them on the Somme in 1916. On that occasion, the Germans had decided that tanks weren't actually as scary as they looked: they always seemed to break down and they were very vulnerable to artillery. But then the British had only had a handful of tanks and they were indeed prone to breaking down. For the attack at Cambrai, however, the British had amassed 381 tanks that finally showed what this new technology could do. They rolled right over the German front line and enabled the British to take a substantial area of the Germans' territory.

Figure 15-3: British tanks awaiting action in September 1917.

© Imperial War Museums (Q 11651)

Unfortunately for the British, the Germans had been using their defence in depth tactic. In practice, *defence in depth* meant keeping your front line relatively lightly defended but having some very strong lines of defence farther back. That way, when the enemy attacked your front line, you didn't lose too many troops. The enemy might well be able to take your front line, but you could then launch your reserves to take it back again. So the Germans were able to launch a major counter-attack, which not only pushed the British back again but also took a few extra bits of Allied-held territory. So the Germans still weren't that impressed with tanks.

Although the Battle of Cambrai was a failure for the Allies, it did show what tanks were capable of if they were used *en masse*. The Germans, however, had seen too many tanks running out of fuel or breaking down to take them too seriously and they didn't bother making too many for themselves. So the tank remained an almost exclusively Allied vehicle for fighting.

Italy's Darkest Day – Caporetto

The fighting on the Italian front was every bit as difficult and deadly as the fighting on the Western Front. The big difference was that it took place up in the mountains instead of in trenches (see Figure 15-4). The Italian General Cadorna had been launching ever more costly offensives against the Austro-Hungarians there and getting nowhere (see Chapter 14). The whole front just seemed like a great drain that was sucking the Italian army into it for no gain whatsoever.

Figure 15-4: Italian troops manning an anti-aircraft gun above Caporetto.

© *Imperial War Museums (Q 65158)*

The Austro-Hungarians had been fighting on two fronts, in the Alps against the Italians and in the east against the Russians. After the Russian Revolution and the defeat of Kerensky's summer offensive (see 'The Russians get steam-rollered', earlier in the chapter), the Austro-Hungarians were able to transfer many more men to the Italian front. They'd also appointed a new commander, Ars von Straussenberg. He proposed a joint Austrian–German attack on the Italians, and the Germans, who reckoned the only way the Austrians would break through the Italians lines was with German help, agreed. In October the Germans and Austro-Hungarians fell on the Italians at Caporetto.

The Italians hardly knew what had hit them: they hadn't faced a full-scale German offensive before. They might have done better if they'd been able to fall back and regroup. Unfortunately, General Cadorna wouldn't allow his commanders to order retreats: they had to stand and fight, which meant that thousands of Italians were taken prisoner. The Germans and Austro-Hungarians broke through the Italian lines and headed towards Venice. It began to look as if the Battle of Caporetto might knock Italy out of the war completely.

The Italians, however, just about survived Caporetto. They fell back to the river Piave, north of Venice, and managed to hold the line. To support the Italians, the British and French rushed troops from the Western Front to the Italian front, and they managed to hold the Germans and Austro-Hungarians back from Venice. By the end of the year, both sides were exhausted and the Italians had lost 300,000 men, mostly taken prisoner. Italians desperately wanted a victory to wipe out the memory of Caporetto, but for that they'd have to wait until 1918.

Any news from Salonika?

A large Allied army had been stuck in appallingly unhealthy conditions at Salonika in northern Greece since 1915 (Chapter 5 has the details), during which time they'd launched one attack after another without getting anywhere. To try to break out of their deadlock, the Allied commander in Salonika, the French General Sarrail, launched another useless offensive in 1917 that got nowhere: the best result from the Allied point of view was that General Sarrail was finally sacked.

Greece came into the war on the Allied side, when the pro-Allied Prime Minister Venizelos forced the pro-German King Constantine to abdicate, and in due course the Greeks would be able to help the Allies break out of Salonika. But, for the moment, the Salonika front was, in effect, as the Germans joked, a very useful way for the Germans and Austrians to keep a large Allied army cooped up where it could do them no harm at all.

Chapter 16

1918: Victory and Defeat

*T*he previous year – 1917 – had been a very costly one for both sides, but as I reveal in Chapter 15 it brought in some massive changes: the Russians were out of the war and the Americans were in. With these developments in mind, both sides drew up plans for the new year:

✔ **The Allies** set up a Supreme War Council to oversee the fighting on all fronts – especially the Italian one, where the Central Powers had made a major breakthrough the previous year.

✔ **The Germans** held a military staff conference at Mons in Belgium on 11 November (remember this date) 1917 where the German commander General Ludendorff proposed an all-out offensive in the west for the spring. The conference agreed.

As you may expect, 1918 turned out to be very different from the other years of the war. Although it started with troops sitting in trenches on the Western Front, it soon witnessed the end of trench warfare and the war returned to the sort of movements and manoeuvres that commanders hadn't been able to use since 1914. The Germans launched their great offensive to punch through the Allied line and win the war; the Allies rallied and pushed the Germans back. This was going to be a very interesting year.

Springtime for Germany

Nineteen seventeen had been a mixed year for Germany. The German people had come close to starvation thanks to the British naval blockade of their ports (along with the Germans' surprisingly inefficient methods of food distribution – Chapter 12 has the details of the desperate hardships the German people were suffering). On the plus side, they'd survived two major Allied offensives. Even better: revolution had broken out in Russia and the new Russian government was negotiating peace terms (you can find the details in Chapter 15). As a result, Germany gained a new empire in the east and could move its troops from the Eastern Front to the west, ready for a big offensive in the spring.

General Ludendorff's gamble

The German government and high command were only too aware that the war's great unknown X factor – the United States – was about to be thrown into the equation against them. The German government hadn't initially seemed too worried whether the Americans came into the war or not, but now that they were in the war it was clear that they were busy training an absolutely enormous army. Yes, they'd mostly be new to battle when they first arrived, but even new troops learn quickly when they've been on the

KEY PEOPLE

General Erich Ludendorff

General Erich Ludendorff often gets mentioned in the same breath as Field Marshal Paul von Hindenburg, but they were very different figures, and by the end of the war it was Ludendorff who'd amassed more power in his own hands. In fact, much of what Germany did in 1918 came down to decisions that Ludendorff took.

Ludendorff had made his name as a very effective commander during the invasion of Belgium in 1914. He and Hindenburg were then sent to the Eastern Front to put things right after the Russians had invaded German territory. After their great victories over the Russians in 1914 Hindenburg and Ludendorff became national heroes (they didn't actually deserve all the credit, but Ludendorff was always good at

manipulating his media image to make sure he got any credit going). By 1917 Ludendorff was virtually in charge of the German government. He pressed for the harsh terms of the Treaty of Brest-Litovsk with Russia and he planned the great German spring offensive in the west.

Ludendorff's weakness was his tendency to crack up under pressure: when things began to go badly wrong in the summer of 1918 he broke down in tears and tantrums, blaming everyone else for disaster except himself (not unlike Hitler: the two men worked together later). If any one person is responsible for the disaster that engulfed Germany in 1918, that man is probably General Erich Ludendorff.

battlefield a few weeks. Nineteen eighteen would bring a great flood of fresh American troops to the Western Front, and so time was no longer on the Germans' side. If they wanted to win the war, it was now or never.

General Ludendorff needed to do what had eluded every commander, German, British and French, since the war broke out in 1914: he needed to break through the enemy line of trenches and into the open country beyond. The problem was *how* to do in a matter of months what so many other generals had failed to achieve over the previous three and half years. The answer to Ludendorff's problem was obvious: look at the precedents.

Learning from successful attacks of the past

People tend to think of First World War offensives as costly failures, but in fact by 1918 the war had seen some very impressive, successful attacks:

- **Carpathians, 1916:** The Russians under General Brusilov defeated the Austro-Hungarians. No preliminary bombardment; attacked on a very wide front; used gas. (See Chapter 6.)

- **Caporetto, 1917:** The Germans and Austrians broke through the Italian lines. No preliminary bombardment; attacked in huge numbers on a short front. (See Chapter 15.)

- **Riga, 1917:** The Germans defeated the Russians in the Baltic. No preliminary bombardment; used lots of gas and fast-moving *stormtroopers* – special shock assault troops trained in trench fighting. (See Chapter 15.)

Ludendorff planned to use the tactics that had worked so well in these assaults. He'd avoid using a preliminary bombardment (this tactic only churned up the ground you wanted your men to advance over and alerted the enemy to the fact that you were about to attack), but would, however, release a lot of gas and send in stormtroopers.

Picking the right spot

Having decided *how* to attack, the big question remaining for Ludendorff was *where* to attack the Allies. He had three possibilities:

- **Belgium:** The Germans could plan to attack and break through the British lines at Ypres. However, the British had defended the Ypres salient very effectively since 1914 and it was unlikely the Germans would be able to break through now. Even if they did, the Allies could easily fall back and stop the advance a little farther on. Verdict: no.

- **The French front:** It was hard to see why this possibility was any better than the Belgian one. The French were well dug in and the last attempt to drive them out, at Verdun in 1916, had been a disaster. Ludendorff needed a weak spot where he could punch his way through, and the French line didn't appear to provide one. Verdict: no.

✔ **The right-hand end of the British line:** This position lay along the old Somme battlefield. What made it perfect for Ludendorff's plan was that this was where the British line ended and the French line began. When troops have to fall back, they usually head towards their base, where they can get fresh ammunition and supplies and where they can report for new orders. If you attack at the point where two different armies join, they each fall back to their separate bases, which almost certainly means that they retreat in different directions. This opens up a gap between the two armies and – hey presto! – you've split them apart and can deal with each of them in turn at your leisure. This was how Napoleon used to operate and Ludendorff had every intention of doing the same. Verdict: yes.

Ludendorff had chosen his spot very well: he couldn't know this, but that particular section of the British line was a lot weaker than it would normally be. The Prime Minister, David Lloyd George, thought Field Marshal Haig had been far too wasteful with his men's lives, especially at the disastrous Battle of Passchendaele the year before (see Chapter 15), and was refusing to let him have all the reinforcements he was demanding. Haig's priority was reinforcing the lines in Belgium, which meant leaving somewhere else lightly defended. That somewhere was the sector manned by Sir Hubert Gough's British 5th Army, stationed exactly where Ludendorff was planning to attack.

Fighting Foch

In the spring of 1918, the Allies moved to appoint a new commander in chief: the French General Ferdinand Foch. Foch was handed command of all the Allied fronts, and all other generals, French, Italian, British and American, would come under him. Giving a general this much power wasn't something the French were usually happy to do, but in Foch's case the French Prime Minister, Clemenceau, reckoned that Foch wouldn't try to take advantage of his position for his own ends, and he was right.

Foch had been a successful general, but his real skill was in being able to get on well with and, where necessary, command the other Allied generals, even Haig, who didn't usually like French generals. The American General Pershing wasn't too happy at first to take orders from another general, and he didn't like the way the first American units to arrive were just thrown into the battle line to bolster the British, Belgians or French wherever they were most needed. He wanted to keep the American Expeditionary Force together. However, even he came to accept Foch's leadership after he'd seen that Foch did know what he was doing. In any case, the Americans depended entirely on their allies for their arms, ammunition, equipment and training, so Pershing decided he didn't have a lot of choice in the matter!

Foch ultimately provided the leadership and co-ordination that would be essential to the Allies if they were to meet Ludendorff's offensives.

On my command, unleash hell! The Kaiser Battle

Ludendorff's German spring offensive was codenamed the *Kaiser Battle,* which was appropriate because the men leading it were commanded by the Kaiser's eldest son, the Crown Prince. The first attack came on 21 March.

Breakthrough! A surprise attack

The attack was carefully planned and it caught the British completely unprepared. The Germans started with a short bombardment of the British trenches, and then the stormtroopers moved in. The morning was misty, which made it difficult for the British to see them coming, as did all the gas the Germans released. German stormtroopers came out of the gas cloud and leapt into the undermanned British trenches. The Germans outnumbered the British in the assault area about three to one, and the British didn't have any reserve positions to fall back to. They'd have to surrender or run. So, after the Germans had taken the British front line, they were into open country.

Talking (German) tactics

How did the Germans manage to do the one thing that had defeated both Allied and German commanders ever since the two sides dug in on the Western Front back in 1914, and break through? The Germans had put a lot of thought into their attack and had learned both from their own mistakes and those of their enemies to work out these successful techniques:

✔ **Using two different types of gas: tear gas and mustard gas.** *Tear gas* irritated the eyes and throats of any Allied soldiers who breathed it in before they could get their gas masks on. That made them tear off their gas masks, so they had no protection against the deadly mustard gas.

✔ **Directing highly accurate artillery fire to hit the British guns and command posts far to the rear.** The biggest danger for

attackers was being shelled by the defenders' artillery, so targeting that artillery from the start made good sense. The Germans also managed to hit some petrol and ammunition dumps far behind the Allied lines.

✔ **Sending in fast-moving stormtroopers behind a creeping barrage.** The *creeping barrage* was a technique the Germans had learnt from the British where the artillery fired a sort of curtain of shells in front of the advancing infantry. The stormtroopers themselves were under orders to advance *quickly:* if they ran into a position that was well defended, they were to ignore it and press on. The idea was to penetrate as far behind the British front line as fast as possible.

The unthinkable had happened: after over three years of stalemate, the Germans had broken through the Western Front.

The Germans pushed the Allies back 40 miles, which was astounding – most First World War attacks were lucky if they managed 40 *yards* – and took 90,000 prisoners. And sure enough, just as Ludendorff had expected, the British retreated north, towards their base, and the French retreated south, towards Paris. The Germans came charging through the middle.

The German advance looked impressive on a map, but on the ground it was very bad news for the German soldiers. They'd advanced so far, so fast that they were soon exhausted. In open country, with little shelter or cover, they were soon suffering heavy casualties and their supply columns couldn't keep up. Without regular supplies of food and ammunition any attack would peter out, and the Kaiser Battle was no exception. The Germans had created a huge bulge in the Allied line, but they had to stop. So they halted, got some rest, allowed reinforcements to catch up with them, got their big guns into position and then attacked again.

British backs to the wall

Ludendorff was still aiming his attacks on the British lines. After his March offensive had run out of steam, he launched a second one in April, this time along the River Lys in Flanders, against the British positions around Ypres. This was probably the greatest crisis for the British of the entire war. The British knew that if the Germans broke through here, they'd be able to attack towards Dunkirk and Calais and cut Britain off from the whole of the Western Front. The Germans might even win the war.

With the situation more critical than ever before, Haig issued what for him was an unusually eloquent order of the day to his men. 'With our backs to the wall,' he said, 'and believing in the justice of our cause, each one of us must fight on to the end.' His words struck a chord. The Germans did push the British back and took much of the land the British had been holding to the south of Ypres, but the British held onto the town itself and once again the German attack fizzled out.

Although it may look as if the Germans were winning, with each new offensive they launched, the Germans lost more men – a quarter of a million in March and April alone – and the survivors were ever more exhausted and hungry. Meanwhile, not only were the British getting ever more reinforcements thanks to the conscription they'd introduced in 1916, but the Americans had finally started arriving in significant numbers. It might seem like a paradox, but the Germans' success actually made them weaker; the Allies were quickly getting stronger.

The Americans have landed!

Sending American troops over to Europe was a major step for the American people, many of whom had turned their backs on Europe when they emigrated (see Chapter 11). But it was also a big moment for the Europeans.

For many people in Europe, 'America' wasn't so much a country but more a sort of fabled land where people went to make new lives for themselves and then sent letters or money to their families back at home. So the American soldiers landing in France seemed like beings from another world, especially because they looked so fresh and smart compared with Britain's and France's own exhausted troops.

General Pershing made full use of the propaganda value of his men's arrival in France: he had a million American troops under his command and he wanted the world to know it. So the Americans staged elaborate parades with lots of flags and brash music to send a message both to the Allied countries and to the Germans that a young, vigorous and above all enormously powerful new international power had arrived on the Western Front. He was serving notice to the Germans that America intended to bring this war to an end as soon as possible.

Ludendorff's luck runs out

In May 1918 Ludendorff launched the third of his big offensives, which came to be called the *Second Battle of the Marne*. This time he was pitting his forces against the French and heading for Paris itself. The last time the Germans had been anywhere near Paris was back at the very start of the war in 1914, when they'd been beaten back at the First Battle of the Marne (Chapter 4 gives you the lowdown). Now, four years later, they were heading for those same battlefields along the rivers Aisne and Marne.

Once again, the Germans drew perilously close to Paris and thousands of Parisians fled the city. But, like the other 1918 offensives, this attack petered out: the Germans never did take Paris (well, not until the Second World War at any rate). The attack wasn't just a failure for the Germans: it marked the beginning of the end for them. Foch was able to pile troops, including Pershing's Americans, into the Marne-Aisne region to halt the German advance. In fact, the whole German advance collapsed, and now it was the Allies' turn to start advancing and pushing their enemy back (see Figure 16-1). From then on the Germans won no more victories, and through the rest of 1918 they were forced to retreat all the way back to their own frontiers.

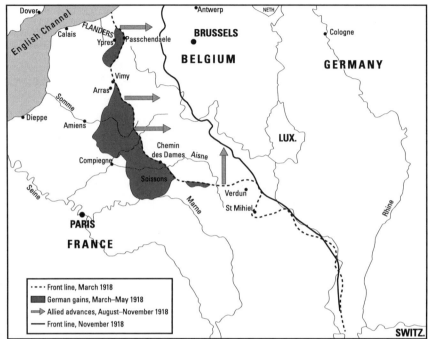

Figure 16-1:
The German break-through and the Allied counter-attack of 1918.

Legend:
- - - - Front line, March 1918
■ German gains, March–May 1918
⇨ Allied advances, August–November 1918
── Front line, November 1918

Understanding why the German advance collapsed

On a map, the German spring offensive in 1918 looks very impressive. The Germans overran a huge area and pushed their enemy back for miles – something that no army had managed to do since 1914. But then put the map away and think about what that advance was like for the men on the ground:

✔ **The German troops were short of food right from the start of the offensive because the German food supply system at home had virtually collapsed.** You try advancing 40 miles or so on foot, carrying a heavy pack of equipment on your back, without enough food to keep you going, and see how far you get.

✔ **Many of the Germans were showing symptoms of the terrible flu epidemic that struck Europe in 1918.** American troops arriving in Europe were suffering from flu too, but the American army was large enough to absorb these losses. The Germans couldn't afford to lose a single man to flu. (You can find more on the flu epidemic in Chapter 17.)

The Zeebrugge Raid

While things were moving so rapidly and dramatically on land, the war at sea was still going on. German *U-boats* (submarines) were still attacking Allied shipping from their bases in the Belgian ports of Ostend and Zeebrugge. To try to ensnare the U-boats the British laid a huge barrage of mines across the North Sea, including the very latest magnetic mines, but the U-boats got through. With the American troopships now crossing the Atlantic so vital to the Allied effort, the British decided they needed to deal with the U-boats once and for all, so they launched raids on Ostend and Zeebrugge to stop the U-boats getting out to sea in the first place. At Zeebrugge, they tried to block the harbour by positioning some old naval ships across the entrance and then sinking them. Unfortunately, they weren't able to get in close enough. One of the sunken ships *nearly* blocked the harbour but not quite. The U-boats still managed to squeeze through.

✔ **The farther the Germans advanced, the fiercer the defence they encountered became, because they were running into British and American reinforcements.** The British were piling so many reinforcements into Belgium and France that in 1918 the British army became the largest Allied army on the Western Front. This was a major change from the situation in 1914 when the British Expeditionary Force had been so tiny. The Americans weren't as experienced as their allies, and they made mistakes that cost them heavy casualties, but they learned quickly and they had plenty of reinforcements.

By the summer of 1918 the Allies had recovered their nerve and their strength, and were outnumbering and out-gunning the Germans on every front. Put all these factors together and you can see why the German offensive petered out.

Then, in August, Foch launched his counter-attack.

Downfall – the Allied Hundred Days' Counter-Offensive

In the summer of 1918 the mighty German army died. It wasn't stabbed in the back or let down by anyone or any of the stories that got told in Germany after the war (see Chapter 17). It completely collapsed. The campaigns of summer and autumn 1918 saw Germany defeated in some of the most remarkable Allied victories of the war.

Many people have a vague notion that the fighting ended in 1918 because everyone was so exhausted they all just stopped. It's certainly true that the troops on all sides were worn out, but it's not true that the war ended because of it. The fighting stopped because it was crystal clear that the Allies had won and Germany had completely lost, and the German high command knew it.

By the end of June the balance of advantage between the Germans and the Allies had completely changed from the way it was when the Germans launched their offensive in the spring. The Germans were exhausted and couldn't advance any farther. The Allies, meanwhile, were gathering huge forces for a massive counter-attack.

French and American troops had already halted the German advance on Paris in the *Second Battle of the Marne* on 2 July (see 'Ludendorff's luck runs out', earlier in the chapter). The Germans had to pull back in disorder as the Allies advanced to drive them right back from the French capital. And then, on 8 August, the British were ready to launch their own counter-attack, in which British, Australian and Canadian troops crippled the German army in the Battle of Amiens. This huge British-led counter-attack became known as the *Hundred Days*.

The Battle of Amiens

Very few people nowadays have heard of the Battle of Amiens, but it ought to be up there with Agincourt and Waterloo as one of the very greatest victories in British history.

Foch had agreed that the British should lead a major attack on the Germans, who'd started to retreat after the failure of the spring offensive. Haig had a huge force of British, Australians and Canadians with which to attack, as well as support from the French. And for the first time in the war, this attack was to make full use of tanks and aircraft, working in conjunction with each other: the British deployed over 400 tanks and nearly 2,000 aircraft. Ironically, it was more like the sort of *blitzkrieg* attacks the Germans themselves would be launching in the Second World War.

The Germans crumbled in the face of the Allied attack. The Allies took 16,000 German prisoners, and Australian cavalry even managed to capture a German military train complete with its artillery. Ludendorff was aghast: the mighty German army, which had made Germany the most powerful nation on the continent, was collapsing before his eyes. He called 8 August 1918, the day of the Allied attack at Amiens, 'the Black Day of the German army'. Two days later, he offered the Kaiser his resignation and told him to end the war before Germany itself fell apart. The Kaiser wouldn't accept his resignation, but

Ludendorff made it clear that from now on the Germans would only be fighting on the defensive: they wouldn't be launching any more offensives. The famous German army, once the finest military machine in Europe, was completely spent.

The Battle of Amiens was a huge success for the British and their allies. Even victories have their downsides, though. Many tanks still broke down, and in the August sun the heat inside a tank could drive a man mad – and often did. Just as in the days of trench warfare, it was difficult for headquarters to keep in communication with the infantry as they advanced. So the Allied advance slowed and the Germans were able to withdraw to a better defensive position. The Germans might have been reduced to fighting a defensive war, but they weren't planning to give in without a fight.

Endgame on the Western Front

As summer 1918 moved into autumn, the British, Canadians and Australians were continuing the Allied attacks on the German army by leading an assault in northern France, near Amiens and Albert, the region that included the old battlefield of the Somme. Foch decided to follow up these attacks with a big offensive in the French and American sector in north-eastern France along the river Meuse and into the Argonne forest, near Verdun. This time, he reckoned, the Allies would finish off the German army. He was right.

By the autumn, the Allies were pushing the Germans back on all fronts:

- ✔ **The Canadians broke through on the Somme and captured Peronne.** Ironically, this town had been the Allied objective on the first day of the Battle of the Somme back in 1916.

- ✔ **The Americans won a victory at St Mihiel.** Pershing had insisted on having his own battle, to show what the Americans could do when they fought as a unit of their own, and not in support of one of their other allies (though they had support from French planes and artillery). Strictly speaking, the St Mihiel attack wasn't needed as part of Foch's offensive, but it was a success and it showed just how good the comparatively inexperienced Americans really were.

- ✔ **The British, Americans and Australians took the St Quentin Canal.** The canal was part of the Hindenburg Line, Germany's apparently impregnable line of fortifications keeping the Allies back from the German frontier. The canal had almost sheer slopes on either side of it and it was heavily fortified. The Americans and Australians were beaten back with very heavy losses, but a British unit managed to slip across and the Allies took the canal.

A defensive line like the Hindenburg Line only works if it remains intact. If breached, it becomes useless: the enemy can attack it from both sides, and the back of the line is never as strongly protected as the front. By October 1918 the Canadians had also broken through the Hindenburg Line and taken Cambrai, the scene of the first major tank attack the year before. (Ironically, the Germans did do some damage to the British and Canadians forces at Cambrai with some tanks they'd captured from the British in 1917.)

After the Hindenburg Line was breached, nothing stood between the Allies and Germany itself. Ludendorff, in tears of rage and despair, knew the German situation was now hopeless: the German army, once the most formidable fighting machine in Europe, had completely collapsed: all discipline had gone and the men were deserting and heading for home. On 27 October 1918 Ludendorff resigned as German commander– and this time the Kaiser accepted. Now the Germans would have to ask for peace terms.

The Germans did have one big ray of hope, however. US President Wilson had declared the Fourteen Points on which the United States was prepared to discuss peace terms (you can find more about these points in Chapter 11). A peace treaty based on these points would be harsh but bearable for the Germans. And so, on 8 November, delegates from the German high command arrived at Foch's headquarters in his personal railway carriage in a clearing in Compiegne forest to discuss the possible terms for an armistice (see 'The Fighting Ends', later in the chapter).

Make no mistake about it: an *armistice* is a surrender. Strictly speaking, an armistice is an agreement by both sides to cease fire; it doesn't have to last and many such agreements don't. But if one side asks for an armistice, it's because it knows it can't continue. It's the best way to end the fighting before losing everything. This was what the Germans were thinking when they asked for an armistice (see 'The Fighting Ends') and it's what was in the minds of Germany's allies when they too asked for an armistice.

Endgame on All Fronts

Germany's allies were already desperate to get out of the war by the time 1918 got underway. In Austria-Hungary, the economy had collapsed, food was scarce and what could be obtained was astronomically expensive, and the different parts of the empire were preparing to pull away and set up their own states. The Turks were being beaten in Palestine and a struggle for power was beginning in Constantinople. Bulgaria, too, was in trouble now that Greece had come into the war and attacked it, with help from the Allied forces in Salonika. If Germany, their most powerful ally, collapsed, then their chances of winning, or even surviving, the war looked very slim. What happened on the different fronts in 1918 seemed to confirm all their worst fears.

Sending the Turks packing from Palestine – the Battle of Armageddon

Armageddon is the place where, according to the Biblical Book of Revelation, a great battle will one day be fought at the end of the world. Armegeddon is a real place in Palestine, though it's better known to locals as Megiddo, and in September 1918 it was the scene of a great battle that ended the Ottoman world.

The British commander in Palestine, General Allenby, had put together a huge Allied army of some 70,000 men, equipped with over 500 guns, plus aircraft. He also had TE Lawrence and the Arab Revolt (see Chapter 9 if you're wondering how these people came into the story) on his side. In contrast, the Turks' numbers were reduced, because they'd sent large numbers of their troops up to the Caucasus to try to take some land off the Russians. Moreover, their German commander, Liman von Sanders, seemed to have lost his touch. Not only was he unable to stop the British attack at Megiddo, but he himself was nearly captured at his headquarters in Nazareth when a troop of British cavalry trotted into town early one morning and Liman had to run for it – still dressed in his pyjamas! In the battle itself, Allied cavalry (see Figure 16-2) played havoc with the German and Turkish positions, and they fled or surrendered.

Figure 16-2: Australian troops saddle up for the Battle of Megiddo.

© Imperial War Museums (HU 75737)

The Battle of Megiddo was such a devastating defeat for the Turks that it virtually destroyed the Ottoman Empire's power in the Middle East. Already, since the start of the century the Turks had seen their hold over the Balkans, north Africa and the Middle East gradually whittled away by different enemies. After Megiddo, the Allies would be able to march into Turkey itself and divide the country up between them if they wanted to (and the Allies had plans to do just that). The Turks could do nothing now except seek peace and bring the war to an end.

Portugal? Brazil? Who else was in this war?

By the end of the First World War, many more countries had come into the conflict than you might realise. Portugal, for example, had declared war on Germany back in March 1916: the Portuguese were angry about German U-boat attacks on neutral shipping and the two countries were rival colonial powers in Africa. Portugal sent 50,000 troops to the Western Front, where they performed well against the German attack in Belgium in April 1918 (you can see them in this photograph).

Several Central and South American nations also joined the war, including Brazil, Panama,

Nicaragua, Cuba, Haiti, Honduras and Costa Rica, many of them following the example of the United States. The Brazilians had close links with the Portuguese and they too were angry about German U-boat attacks. These Central and South American nations mostly contributed to the war by supporting the Allied naval campaign against German U-boats.

By the end of the war, the number of neutral countries, such as Switzerland, Sweden and Spain, was much shorter than the list of countries that had joined in.

© Imperial War Museums (Q60295)

Italy's revenge – the Battle of Vittorio Veneto

The Italians had spent the early months of 1918 trying to recover from their disastrous defeat at Caporetto the year before (Chapter 15 fills you in). By October 1918 they had a new government and a major retraining programme for their army in place, and were ready to launch a big attack to drive the Austro-Hungarians right out of Italy.

It's not easy being neutral

Some European countries – Spain, Sweden, Denmark, Norway, the Netherlands and Switzerland – wondered at the start of the war whether they were about to suffer the same fate as neutral Belgium (which the Germans had invaded and occupied), but managed to remain neutral throughout the war. Staying neutral wasn't an easy option: all the neutral countries depended heavily on foreign trade and under international law they were allowed to trade with whomsoever they liked. In reality, they came under heavy pressure from the combatant countries. For example, the British threatened to stop trading with Norway unless the Norwegians stopped selling food to Germany. The Norwegians agreed, whereupon German U-boats started sinking Norwegian ships.

Neutral countries were very useful for negotiating between the combatants: King Alfonso XIII of Spain, for example, negotiated with the Germans to get better treatment for French prisoners of war (PoWs), and much work for PoWs was done by the International Red Cross. By the end of the war, many neutral countries were suffering almost as badly as the combatant countries: food shortages in Switzerland, for example, were so severe that the Swiss had to introduce rationing.

The Austro-Hungarian army was close to collapse by then and the Austro-Hungarian government was desperate to make peace and pull out of the war, so the Italians could perhaps have just dug in, sat tight and waited for the Austrians to collapse. But the public mood in Italy was in favour of making an attack, with good reason:

- ✔ **The Italians wanted to show the world that they could beat the Austro-Hungarians.** That defeat at Caporetto in 1917 had been so humiliating the Italians felt it was a slur on their national honour. They didn't just want revenge for Caporetto: they wanted to wipe out the very memory of it. The only way to do that, they reckoned, was to win a massive victory.

- ✔ **The Italian government had its eye on the peace settlement.** By the autumn of 1918 it was pretty clear that the Allies had won the war and would soon be imposing some sort of peace settlement on the defeated powers. The best way that Italy could make sure of getting some land in the peace settlement was to conquer it before the war was over. And the best way to do that was – you've guessed it – to win a massive victory.

The Italians gathered an army that included large numbers of British and French troops, and equipped it with plenty of heavy artillery. The combined Allied forces, which heavily outnumbered the Austro-Hungarians and Germans, launched their attack near the town of Vittorio Veneto. Right from the start, the Austro-Hungarians and Germans crumbled: they were weary, short of supplies and keen to get home and end the war (see Figure 23 in the insert section). The Italians and their allies pushed them right back to the Austrian frontier.

All change at Salonika

If you've read this book chapter by chapter, you may vaguely recall seeing mention of a front at Salonika, in northern Greece, at various points. Salonika was where the Allies opened a front after the Austro-Hungarians overran Serbia in 1915. The Greeks were divided over whether or not they liked the idea of a battle front on their territory, and it took them until 1917 to decide to come into the war on the Allied side. Meanwhile, a sizeable Allied army of French, British and Serbian troops under the not-very-gifted French General Sarrail had been pinned down at Salonika, not able to do much. The Austro-Hungarians, Germans and Bulgarians defeated every attempt they made to break out.

By 1918 the situation had changed. General Sarrail had gone and in his place came a much better French commander, General Franchet d'Esperey (known rather endearingly to the British troops as 'Desperate Frankie'). Franchet d'Esperey planned to take advantage of the way the war had changed by launching a massive breakout offensive, and this time the plan worked. The Allied troops burst through the enemy lines and started making real progress:

- ✔ **The Bulgarians surrendered, the Bulgarian Tsar abdicated and communist revolution broke out across Bulgaria.** So much for Bulgaria.

- ✔ **The Serbs retook their capital, Belgrade.** The war had originally started with this conflict between the Austro-Hungarians and the Serbs. Now the Serbs could rightly claim that they'd won this war.

- ✔ **Allied troops reached the river Danube.** The Danube is the river that ran through the heart of the Austro-Hungarian Empire. After the Allies had reached the Danube, the game was up for Austria-Hungary and the Austrians knew it.

Where's Austria-Hungary gone? It was there a minute ago

On 3 November 1918, in a desperate situation and in retreat on the Italian front, and facing a comprehensive defeat in Salonika, the Austro-Hungarians finally asked for an armistice. In doing so, they didn't just surrender: they imploded. All the different national groups that had made up the Austro-Hungarian Empire – the Poles, the Czechs, the Croats, the Slovenes and all the others – set up national committees and declared themselves independent. These peoples wanted separate representation at the peace conference that would be held at the end of the war, and they wanted control of their own territory, just as soon as their borders had been agreed by the Allied powers (and with everyone making their own land grabs, this wouldn't be an easy question to resolve, believe you me).

Even the Austrian people wanted to get rid of the regime that had dragged them into this disastrous war. They thought the ruling Habsburg dynasty had been far too cosy with the Germans. In 1918 Emperor Karl even had to agree to his empire being effectively taken over by Germany, with German generals taking command of the Austro-Hungarian army. By November Karl knew the game was up, and on 11 November he abdicated. No new emperor would be taking over: with the different peoples declaring independence, nothing was left to be emperor *of*. Austria itself was declared a republic, as was Hungary. The famous empire of the Habsburgs, one of the oldest dynasties in Europe, had simply ceased to exist.

Sunset at sea

Even as events were drawing to a close on the Western Front, the Italian front and in Salonika, one last front of the war was still fighting – in theory: the naval war.

The German High Seas Fleet had been sitting in harbour ever since the Battle of Jutland in 1916 (see Chapter 8), the job of keeping the sea war going having passed to Germany's fleet of U-boats. But the German Admiral Scheer hated this situation: he wanted to have one last climactic battle against his British enemies. The sailors who'd have to fight his battle for him, however, had other ideas.

During all the time that the German fleet had been in harbour, the sailors had been stuck in German ports. That meant that they knew at first hand how bad the situation was at home – how little food shops had to sell and what prolonging the war meant for German civilians. It also meant that German sailors came into contact with anti-war messages from socialist groups far more directly than most German soldiers did. For most of the war, anti-war Germans, such as the socialist leaders Rosa Luxemburg and Karl Liebknecht, had been imprisoned and ignored, but by 1918 the situation within Germany was so desperate that many more Germans were listening to socialists and communists who urged them to do something to end the killing. The sailors of Germany's High Seas Fleet were in a position to do a bit more to end the war than just read pamphlets and listen to speeches.

In April 1918, Admiral Scheer took the fleet out to sea for his big battle, but the German and British fleets missed each other and he had to head back to port. But then in the autumn, with the German army collapsing in France, Scheer decided it was time for the Last Great Battle. He gave orders for the fleet to prepare for action, and the unthinkable happened: the sailors said no. The whole German fleet mutinied. The war was over and Germany had lost, so what, they demanded, was the point of setting sail to fight a battle just for the sake of it? So Admiral Scheer never did get his big battle. But he did have one last card up his sleeve (see 'The Germans' last act', later in this chapter).

We'd Better Get a New Government: Germany Implodes

The previous year, the Russians had learned that when your armed forces refuse to obey orders, you have a revolution on your hands. Now it was Germany's turn to learn that lesson.

By November 1918 Germany was imploding: the army had collapsed and the fleet was in mutiny. Protesters on the streets were demanding that the Kaiser go and German communists were openly parading with weapons, planning to seize power. On the other hand, more right-wing Germans (and Germany had no shortage of these people) were defying the protestors and said the Kaiser should stay. Germany was falling into chaos.

With his throne in grave danger, Kaiser Wilhelm tried one last move to save it. He appointed a new Chancellor, Prince Max von Baden, who was to have full authority over the German army – or what was left of it. But no one in Germany thought that appointing a new Chancellor was enough to solve the crisis the country was in. Prince Max knew what had to be done and, when he could be forced to face it, so did the Kaiser. Field Marshal Hindenburg and Admiral Scheer finally convinced the Kaiser that the war was lost and he'd have to abdicate. On 10 November 1918 Kaiser Wilhelm left Germany and fled to Holland. (The Dutch gave him a rather nice house to live in and his first words when he got in were, 'Now for a nice cup of English tea'!) The next day Prince Max announced that the Kaiser had abdicated and Germany was now a republic. And he himself resigned.

The first president of the new German Republic was a socialist, Friedrich Ebert. Ebert would have some very difficult problems to solve. Many people in Germany were unhappy about the way the republic had been set up. Right-wingers wanted the Kaiser back; communists wanted to set up a Russian-style Bolshevik state. The fighting between the two groups in Berlin was so intense that it wasn't safe for the government to meet there and so it was set up at the pretty little provincial town of Weimar (which is why people who didn't like the republic used to sneeringly call it the *Weimar Republic* – it was like calling it the chicken or scaredy-cat republic).

As well as trying to keep order within Germany, Ebert was going to have to negotiate peace terms with the victorious allies. (Chapter 17 shows how difficult a task that was going to be.)

The Fighting Ends

Having finally accepted the hopelessness of their position on the battlefield and the severity of their situation at home, a German delegation arrived to discuss the Armistice with Marshal Foch on 8 November (see the earlier section 'Endgame on the Western Front'). If the Germans had any hope of being able to negotiate terms, they were in for an unpleasant surprise. Foch was a tough bargainer, and he informed the Germans that they'd have to surrender unconditionally or the Allies would resume their advance. All fighting was to end along the whole Western Front at 11 a.m. on 11 November, and the German fleet was to sail to Scapa Flow (the main British naval base during wartime) in the Orkney Islands where it would be interned by the British. The Germans had no choice, and they knew it. They signed.

Soldiering on until the eleventh hour

One of the hardest things to understand about the war is what happened in some areas of the trenches after the Armistice was signed, but before it came into effect. In many areas both sides stopped fighting: no one could see any point in carrying on. But in some sectors, soldiers kept the fighting going – killing 'enemy' solders right up to 11 a.m. on 11 November.

Understanding why anyone should have carried on fighting until the last minute can be difficult. In some cases, men were firing off all their ammunition so the Allies couldn't get hold of it after the war was over. Other soldiers thought it was a question of honour and duty to keep the war going as fiercely as possible right up to the minute it ended. Some may have wanted revenge for their friends who'd been killed. One British soldier later recalled how a German machine gun kept firing right up to the last minute. Then, exactly at 11 a.m., it stopped firing and the officer stood up in full view of the British and bowed politely to them. No one shot at him.

The Germans' last act

The war had one last dramatic act to play. Crowds went wild with excitement in the Allied countries when it was announced that the war was over: people sang and danced in the street. Soon after, the German fleet began steaming across the North Sea to the main British naval base at Scapa Flow, where it was to be interned by its old British rivals. Crowds came out to watch the huge battleships arriving in the harbour. The ships stayed interned at Scapa Flow whilst politicians decided what should happen to them. And then, on 21 June 1919, the

Germans took matters into their own hands. As people looked on from the shore, the great ships slowly began to sink into the water. The Germans had scuttled their own fleet rather than hand it over to the enemy.

The Germans may have been beaten, exhausted and demoralised, but they hadn't lost any of their national pride.

Chapter 17

Aftermath: The World After the War

*W*hen the news arrived that the war was over, people in the Allied countries rejoiced wildly in the streets. In the new countries, such as Poland and Czechoslovakia, people celebrated their independence. But in Germany, the mood was much more sombre: the people were shocked by their defeat and apprehensive about their future.

Although the fighting was over, however, the world still had to face the problems the war had produced – and there were a lot of them. President Wilson of the USA in particular had a lot of new ideas about how to make the world a better place, but there was no guarantee that he'd be able to put them into operation.

After living through more than four long years of fighting, destruction and suffering, the world's people in 1918 were desperately hoping that better times lay ahead. They were going to be terribly disappointed.

Hitting the World When It's Down: The Great Influenza

As if the war hadn't been enough for the people of the world to cope with, 1918 had an even deadlier fate in store.

Even before the fighting had ended cases of violent sickness began to appear in the Middle East and the infection soon spread. It was a particularly deadly form of influenza that struck very quickly and could kill its victim within a day. Sufferers often started by coughing up blood, and then their body fluids drained out and their temperature soared. It was a horrible way to die.

The infection, known as *Spanish flu* (simply because the Spanish press were the first to report it in detail), spread quickly and soon seemed unstoppable. It swept through the western world at a frightening rate. Around the world, it killed many more people than the war had done, possibly as many as 30 million. Half a million Americans died from it, for example, often in crowded troopships crossing over to Europe to join in the fighting. The influenza was highly contagious and it flourished in overcrowded towns and cities, as well as in trenches, barracks, troopships and even hospitals – anywhere, in fact, where people were crammed together. At its peak, the influenza was killing 7,000 people in Britain *a week,* and one prominent victim was Sir Mark Sykes, who'd negotiated the Sykes–Picot Agreement (you can find out what this was all about in Chapter 9).

For many years historians said that the influenza was so deadly because people were so weakened by the war that they had no natural resistance, but this explanation doesn't account for the huge death rate in other areas such as the United States, where people were generally well fed and healthy. Nowadays historians reckon the influenza was a pandemic that would've happened anyway. It just happened to coincide with the end of the war, just when the world was on its knees and needed it least.

Peacemaking in Paris

A hundred years earlier, in 1814, at the end of the wars against Napoleon, the leaders of Europe had gathered in Vienna to draw up a peace settlement and redraw the map of Europe. The system for keeping Europe at peace that those statesmen established at the Congress of Vienna lasted exactly a century, until the outbreak of the First World War in 1914. Yet the leaders who gathered in Paris to make peace after the First World War reckoned the Congress of Vienna was a good example of how not to draw up a peace treaty, and that it had been a major cause of the war they'd all just come through. They would show the world how peacemaking was done properly. Their 1919 peace settlement, however, was to last barely 20 years.

Working out who won and who lost

Identifying which countries were on the winning side wasn't too difficult. The Allied powers – France, Britain, Italy and Japan – along with their allies – such as Belgium, Serbia, Portugal and Greece, and their associate, the

United States – had clearly won the war. It was harder to see which countries had lost because some countries that had gone to war in 1914 either didn't exist any more or had completely changed:

- ✔ **Austria:** *Went into the war as:* one half of the dual monarchy of Austria-Hungary under Emperor Franz Josef. *Came out of the war as:* a small German-speaking state with no empire and a new republican government.

- ✔ **Czechs and Slovaks:** *Went into the war as:* a constituent part of the dual monarchy of Austria-Hungary. *Came out of the war as:* a new, independent state, Czechoslovakia, that insisted it had nothing to do with the Austrians or the Hungarians and shouldn't be treated as a defeated country at all.

- ✔ **Germany:** *Went into the war as:* an imperial monarchy under the Kaiser. *Came out of the war as:* a democratic republic with a socialist president, Friedrich Ebert. The Allies would have to consider whether or not it was right to punish the republic for the faults of the old regime.

- ✔ **Hungary:** *Went into the war as:* half of the dual monarchy of Austria-Hungary. *Came out of the war as:* a small central European state with a communist government and no means to defend itself.

- ✔ **Poland:** *Went into the war as:* mainly part of Russia, but also part of Austria-Hungary and Germany, so Poles had fought on both sides in the war. *Came out of the war as:* a new, independent state that didn't want to be tied to the Germans, Austrians or Russians and certainly shouldn't be considered as one of the defeated countries.

- ✔ **Turkey:** *Went into the war as:* the Ottoman Empire, covering Turkey, Armenia and the Middle East. *Came out of the war as:* Turkey, still with an Ottoman sultan but with no Ottoman Empire for him to be sultan of.

In the end, the Allies decided to identify five countries as the defeated powers: Germany, Austria, Hungary, Bulgaria and Turkey.

Sitting down to talk: The peace conference

In 1919, having identified exactly which countries they considered as defeated, the Allies sat down at a peace conference in Paris to discuss all the areas of the globe they needed to discuss, with the aim of drawing up a separate peace treaty for each of the defeated countries and getting them to sign. A *peace treaty* is the formal way of ending a state of war between two or more countries. Normally, each side makes a few compromises, and when both sides have signed, the state of war between them is over, but this was no normal peace conference.

We didn't lose! We were stabbed in the back

The German defeat in 1918 happened so quickly that many Germans found it difficult to believe it had happened at all. In the spring the German army had broken through the Allied line and had been closing in on Paris, so how could they possibly have been beaten so badly by the autumn? The Germans had such faith in their army and its commanders that they found the idea that they could be beaten by other generals simply impossible to believe. Instead, they thought their glorious soldiers must have been betrayed by cowards and traitors at home. One of the great heroes of German mythology, the warrior Siegfried, meets his end when he's stabbed in the back by a villainous character called Hagen von Tronje. To Germans in 1918 it seemed that their army had suffered the same fate: it had been stabbed in the back. And who did most

Germans believe had 'stabbed Germany in the back'? The socialists and Jews who'd staged the revolution that got rid of the Kaiser and set up a republic, that's who.

But was this theory true? Was Germany stabbed in the back? No. The evidence is very clear: the Allies comprehensively defeated the Germans in 1918, and if the Germans hadn't asked for an armistice, the German army would almost certainly have collapsed. The 'stab in the back' idea was a complete myth but, nevertheless, it did a lot of damage. It made the Germans very bitter about the way the new republic accepted defeat and made peace with the Allies. It was also an important reason why, a few years later, Germans started turning to the Nazis.

How (not) to run a peace conference

Should you ever be given the task of running an international peace conference after a major war, here are some tips on how to do it:

- ✔ **Hold the peace conference in a neutral country.** Emotions are bound to run high after a war, especially one as long and destructive as the First World War, so to keep everyone's feelings under control and allow everyone to focus calmly on the task in hand, finding a neutral country to host and chair the peace conference is a good idea.

  What the Allies did: They held the conference in Paris, where the French had every intention of using the conference to get revenge for what the Germans had done to their country.

- ✔ **Negotiate frankly and openly with your opponents.** If both sides agree the terms, even if they don't particularly like them, you have a good chance that your peace settlement will last.

  What the Allies did: They didn't even invite the Germans to take part in the peace conference and they certainly didn't negotiate with them. The Germans were only invited to turn up right at the end to sign the treaty. They had no say whatsoever over its terms.

✔ **Don't humiliate your opponents.** No one likes being humiliated and people who are tend not to forget it.

What the Allies did: They stage-managed the signing ceremony so as to humiliate the German delegates in every way possible when they arrived to sign the treaty. They also drew up the most humiliating treaty terms they could've imagined and even made the Germans agree that they were to blame for causing the war in the first place.

What the Allies did when dealing with the other defeated countries – the Austrians, Hungarians, Bulgarians and Turks – was much the same. Like the Germans, these countries were simply presented with a document and told to sign. Also like the Germans, they resented the treatment dished out to them by the Allies, and they didn't forget it either.

Although the Allies set out to forge a lasting peace settlement that, as they saw it, would be more effective than the Congress of Vienna had been a century before, they got these key considerations wrong. In doing so, they stored up a lot of trouble for the years to come.

Meeting the statesmen

Leaders of all the countries that had taken part in the war gathered in Paris to discuss the shape of the peace settlement, but the most important were the leaders of France, Britain and the United States:

✔ **Georges Clemenceau:** The French Prime Minister, was an old radical and a tough cookie. He had no respect for rules and regulations if they got in the way of what needed to be done. Clemenceau could remember when the Germans had invaded France and humiliated the French back in 1871, and he was determined to crush the Germans so thoroughly that they could never do it again.

✔ **David Lloyd George:** The British Prime Minister was a dynamic Welsh radical politician, a plain speaker who enjoyed a good battle. Lloyd George was in touch with public opinion in Britain and he knew that, for the moment at least, the British people wanted revenge for what they'd gone through. Only a very tough peace treaty that would stop Germany ever threatening the peace of Europe would satisfy British public opinion. Accordingly, Lloyd George promised to squeeze Germany, as one of his ministers put it, 'till the pips squeak'.

Although the British Prime Minister represented the British Empire, Australia, New Zealand, Canada and South Africa all sent their own representatives to the peace conference. Insisting on separate diplomatic representation at such an important international gathering was a sign that these countries were beginning to assert their identity as nations in their own right.

✔ **Woodrow Wilson:** The American President was a former college professor, and he thought of himself as an expert on the ins-and-outs of modern European history. Wilson had enormous belief in himself and his ability to resolve issues that the Europeans couldn't solve on their own. Unfortunately, this meant that he took little notice of his political rivals. He didn't invite a single member of the Republican Party to accompany him to Europe, and as a result almost any settlement he might negotiate was bound to appear one-sided and biased to political opinion back home. In the end, this oversight was to prove fatal to Wilson's hopes, but he didn't realise this until it was too late.

People all over Europe had enormous hopes for Woodrow Wilson in particular. He was the first American President ever to leave the country while serving in office, and the fact that he was coming in person to the peace conference seemed like a guarantee that it would come up with the right decisions. For many Europeans, America was the land of hope, the place to which they could emigrate if things went badly wrong at home. The idea that the President of this fabled land of liberty was actually coming to Europe to solve the problems of the world was almost too much to take in. As Wilson's train sped through the French countryside on its way to Paris, people in the fields stopped what they were doing and said a prayer, almost as if Wilson's arrival was like the second coming of Jesus.

The reasons people put such faith in Wilson are easy to see. His ideas looked fresh, new and exciting. It also helped that they came from an American, and not from yet another representative of the old European Great Powers. When people have such high expectations, however, even the most able statesmen usually can't match them all. Wilson was no exception.

Woodrow Wilson's new ideas

Wilson arrived in Paris bearing his 'Fourteen Points' plan for peace (see Chapter 11 for a full run-through). Of his Fourteen Points, he was brimming with excitement about two in particular – major new ideas that, he thought, would ensure that this settlement would guarantee 'a just and lasting peace':

✔ **National self-determination:** This idea, Wilson believed, was crucial. It meant that all the people of a particular national group should have their own independent nation state. When they had this, all disputes over territory would simply disappear, because everyone would have all the land they wanted. All Poles would live in Poland, all Hungarians in Hungary, all Greeks in Greece and so on.

✔ **A League of Nations:** This idea was Wilson's most radical and exciting one: an international government that would have the power and authority to stop the nations of the world going to war with each other, like a sort of global teacher breaking up fights in the playground. Although international meetings and even organisations weren't new, no one had ever tried to set up a global government before.

In many ways, Wilson's ideas were indeed very good. The trouble was that putting them into practice fairly and equally would be very difficult. Here are a few of the problems Wilson found:

- ✓ **All nations deserve national self-determination. But some nations deserve it more than others.** National self-determination was a good idea when it meant giving the Poles or the Estonians their own state, but sometimes national groups were too small to form viable nation states on their own and they needed to join up with their neighbours, such as the Czechs and the Slovaks (Czechoslovakia), or the Serbs, Croats and Slovenes (Yugoslavia). Also, the British and French made it quite clear that they wouldn't allow national self-determination to apply to any of the lands they ruled, such as their colonies in Africa and Asia, or to Ireland. Above all, the Germans and Austrians weren't allowed to join together as one state even though they were all ethnically German.

  Wilson's idea of national self-determination soon turned into one rule for some and another rule for others. That situation never goes down well.

- ✓ **Everyone should join the League of Nations. Except you. And you.** The theory was that the League of Nations should include everybody on equal terms, but Wilson soon realised that the British and French wouldn't allow their colonial possessions to sit in it. Moreover, the Allies agreed that Germany shouldn't be allowed to sit in it, as a punishment for starting the war, and they didn't want communist Russia to sit in it either.

  So, right from the start Wilson's great vision wasn't really a League of Nations at all. It was more of a League of Some Nations That We Allies Think Are Reliable.

These lands are up for grabs – I mean, for discussion: Making a pitch

Usually, peace treaties are negotiated across a table, with the two sides sitting opposite each other and bargaining. The Paris peace conference worked rather differently. The *Big Three* – Wilson, Clemenceau and Lloyd George (they were joined at first by the Italian Prime Minister, Orlando, but they gradually started to work as an exclusive group of three) – operated like a sort of interview panel. Representatives of different nations and national groups came and made a sales pitch, saying what territory they thought their country was entitled to and why they should have it.

Some representatives came from countries that were arguing for a bit of their neighbours' lands. Belgium wanted some land from Germany, for example, and Italy wanted some land from Austria-Hungary. But in many cases, delegates represented a new nation that hadn't existed in 1914 and they were arguing for the whole territory they thought their country should have. For example, Poland had disappeared from the map back in the 18th century when its neighbours, the Russians, Germans and Austrians, partitioned it and took over it. The Polish delegation looked at their old historical atlases and argued that the new Polish state should have *all* the land that had ever been part of Poland, which would have included all of Ukraine and all of Lithuania as well.

The Big Three listened politely to all these claims, but delegates were under no illusions: the British, French and Americans would make the final decisions and they'd make them to suit their own ends. They had an impressive list of parts of the world whose future they needed to settle. These were some of the most important hotspots:

- **Africa:** Germany had owned large parts of Africa, including Cameroon, Togo, South-West Africa and Tanganyika. The Big Three had to decide what should happen to these areas now that they'd defeated Germany.

- **Central Europe:** At the end of the war, the old state of Austria-Hungary had suddenly collapsed. All the different national groups that had been part of it had declared their independence and were now queuing up in Paris to make their case to the Big Three for the land they thought was rightfully theirs. Many of them had territorial disputes among themselves, especially with Hungary, which had been joint partner in the old monarchy, alongside the Austrians. Deciding where the borders should go in this ethnically varied part of Europe was going to need very careful thought indeed.

- **China and Japan:** Both countries had been on the Allied side. The problem was that the Japanese were much stronger than the Chinese and had made an important contribution to the war effort, and now they expected their reward. They hoped for land in the Pacific and in China. They were also talking about inserting a clause about racial equality into the final peace treaties, which the European powers, which all ran large overseas empires, were not prepared to grant under any circumstances.

- **France and Belgium:** Both countries had suffered enormously from the war and wanted compensation for the huge damage done to their territory. They also had land claims on Germany: France wanted Alsace and Lorraine back and Belgium wanted the return of some of its territory – Eupen and Malmedy.

- **Germany:** Germany was the most important country that the Big Three had to deal with. It had been the most powerful military power in Europe in 1914 and it still had enormous military potential. The challenge for the Allies was how to make sure that Germany would never again rise to threaten the peace of the world.

- **Hungary:** At the end of the war, a communist coup had taken place in the Hungarian capital, Budapest, and a provisional government had been set up by a revolutionary called Bela Kun. The Allied leaders sent a small team to Budapest to meet Bela Kun and see whether he really was in charge of the country. They reported back that he wasn't, so the Allies wouldn't accept a Hungarian delegation in Paris and Hungary's neighbours just helped themselves to Hungarian land.

- **The Middle East:** Sharif Hussein of Mecca understood that the British had promised that he would rule over a huge, independent Arab state stretching from Arabia to Palestine and Syria. However, the British and French had privately agreed to divide the area up between them.

They also had to consider the little issue of the Balfour Declaration, Britain's undertaking to create some sort of homeland in Palestine for the Jewish people (see Chapter 9). Deciding how to settle the boundaries in the Middle East would be a particularly thorny problem.

✔ **Russia:** Russia had made its own peace with Germany at Brest-Litovsk in March 1918 (see Chapter 15), but the Allies had declared that treaty null and void. Russia was now a communist state, committed to starting off a world-wide communist revolution to bring down the governments of all capitalist countries. Not surprisingly, those governments weren't too keen to talk to the new Russian government, and the Russians weren't invited to the Paris conference. Its decisions would still affect Russia, though.

✔ **Turkey and the Balkans:** The war had started with quarrels in the Balkans and much fighting had taken place there. Bulgaria had fought on the German side and its neighbours would almost certainly want to take some of its land. The Allies had plans to carve Turkey up, too.

Who's going to pay for all this?

The First World War had been more destructive than any war in history. It was difficult to understand just how appalling the destruction had been if you hadn't seen it with your own eyes, and so the French made sure that the delegates coming to Paris did see it. All the trains bringing delegates to Paris were diverted so that they ran at walking pace through the areas where the trenches had been. It must have been a very sobering sight: the trenches still have the power to move visitors today, but in 1919 they were fresh and the full extent of the destruction was obvious. This had been prime farming land before the war; it also included some of France's most important industrial areas. Not surprisingly, when they arrived at the peace conference the French and Belgians asked very pointedly, 'Who's going to pay for all this damage?'

Peace treaties often include a heavy fine, sometimes known as an *indemnity*, that the defeated country has to pay. Usually, paying the indemnity means dipping fairly deeply into the national savings bank, but after the defeated country pays up then the debt is ruled out and the defeated country can make up the money again by putting up taxes. But the destruction of the First World War was so great that the Allies thought that a fine simply wasn't enough. Instead of a fine, *reparations* should be paid, they argued, to cover the costs of the actual repairs the French and Belgians were going to have to undertake.

Paying reparations would mean paying for physically rebuilding French and Belgian factories and railways, but other costs would need to be factored in as well. The war had produced thousands of widows who were now entitled to claim a war widow's pension, and thousands of men who'd been severely wounded in the war now needed permanent medical care. Someone had to pay all these costs. Who? The country the Allies blamed for starting the war in the first place: Germany.

Who's to blame? The war guilt clause

Making the defeated enemy pay for all the damage the war had created was a new idea, and its legal position wasn't entirely clear. If Germany should pay for French war widows' pensions, for example, then what about similar payments that countries would have to make after other wars? Did this new idea mean that *every* defeated nation should bear these costs?

To cover themselves against any legal problems, the Allies took a very important decision: they'd include in each peace treaty a clause to say that the defeated countries, Germany, Austria, Hungary, Bulgaria and Turkey, accepted responsibility for starting the war and therefore accepted that they should pay reparations. Most of the defeated countries just gritted their teeth and agreed to sign, but the Germans, who faced by far the heaviest reparations bill, were outraged. They refused to accept that the war had been their fault and that they ought to pay reparations to anyone.

The *war guilt clause,* as it became known, has always caused a lot of argument. Historians don't agree about who actually caused the outbreak of war in 1914, and although many historians agree that Germany bears much of the blame, it's important to remember that the war started with a showdown between Austria-Hungary and Serbia (see Chapter 3). The Germans certainly remembered this, and they felt it was desperately unfair to put all the blame on them for the outbreak of war, especially because doing so meant they'd have to pay the lion's share of reparations payments.

Making Germany safe

One of the reasons the Allies blamed Germany for causing the war and making it so destructive was that they thought imperial Germany had been such an aggressively militaristic state. They decided that just altering the map of Europe or setting up a League of Nations wasn't enough: they needed to change Germany itself and make the Germans a less militaristic people. The way to do this, the Allies thought, was to destroy Germany's means of waging war, to forbid it from having a large army or navy, and to deny it an air force and any submarines. The idea behind the Allies' plans was that without an air force, a fleet of submarines and a sizeable army, the Germans would soon forget about playing at soldiers and become a peaceful people.

Sign This! The Peace Treaties

When the talking of the peace conference was over, the time came to invite the defeated countries to sign their treaties. The signing ceremonies for the five treaties would take place in the rather posh suburbs to the south and west of Paris: Versailles for the Germans, St Germain for the Austrians, Trianon for the Hungarians, Neuilly for the Bulgarians and Sèvres for the Turks.

Dazed and confused – the Germans

The Germans had got the armistice they sought in November 1918 (see Chapter 16); the peace treaty, they hoped, would make the ceasefire permanent without inflicting too much pain. They were in for a shock.

At Versailles, the French stage-managed everything carefully. The members of the German delegation were put up in a small house and kept under armed guard, as if they were prisoners. The delegates were given a copy of the treaty and told they had no choice: if they didn't sign, the Allies would start the war again. The Germans couldn't believe what they read. No victor in history had imposed such a harsh peace settlement (though some said the Germans had imposed just such a harsh settlement on the Russians only the year before). Above all, the Germans resented the way the Allies were imposing the treaty on them, without any possibility to discuss any of it.

The German Foreign Minister was aghast at the treaty's terms and refused to sign, so the Transport Minister had to rush out from Berlin to take his place. The German delegates walked up the staircase between lines of magnificently uniformed French guards, again as if they were prisoners, and then they had to walk the whole length of Louis XIV's magnificent Hall of Mirrors, where the Allied leaders were waiting for them. (Holding the ceremonial signing in the Hall of Mirrors was no accident. That room was where the Germans had proclaimed their unified empire after they'd defeated France back in 1871. By choosing this particular room as the setting where the defeated Germans' would sign a humiliating peace treaty, the French were deliberately rubbing their old enemy's nose in the dirt.) The treaty was laid out on a table. The German delegates asked if they could raise a query but Clemenceau told them no: they had to sign. They did. Then they turned and walked out of the room with as much dignity as they could muster.

Here's what the German delegates had signed:

- **Germany accepted responsibility for starting the war.** This was the 'war guilt' clause that provided the legal basis for the Allies' demand for reparations.

- **Germany agreed to pay reparations in cash and in kind to the Allied countries, especially France and Belgium.** Total sum: unlimited. Payment period: no end-date set.

- **Germany agreed to give up lands on its borders.** Alsace-Lorraine was to be returned to France, Eupen and Malmedy to Belgium, Northern Schleswig to Denmark and a large area of West Prussia, including the port of Danzig, to the new state of Poland. Danzig was to be a Free City administered by the League of Nations.

- ✔ **Germany agreed that it wasn't allowed to join up with Austria.** The Allies feared that a combined German–Austrian state could soon become very powerful.

- ✔ **Germany agreed to hand over all its overseas colonies to the Allies, principally to Britain, but also to Australia, New Zealand and South Africa.** In fact, these territories were handed over to the League of Nations, which *mandated* (that is, handed them over) them to the British and their allies.

- ✔ **Germany was only allowed to have an army of 100,000 men.** That's about the size of a decent police force.

- ✔ **Germany wasn't allowed to have any tanks, submarines, large battleships or any military air force whatsoever.** The Allies would be sending in teams of weapons inspectors to check that Germany observed this ban.

- ✔ **Germany wasn't allowed to station any troops in the Rhineland, the area along the French frontier.** The Germans were lucky here: the French had originally wanted to take the Rhineland for themselves.

- ✔ **The Saarland, along the French frontier, was to be governed by France for 15 years.** This was another League of Nations mandate. After 15 years the people would vote to join either Germany or France.

- ✔ **Germany wasn't allowed to join the League of Nations.** This was a blanket ban: no terms were laid down under which it could be reversed.

The Germans called the Treaty of Versailles a *diktat* – a dictated peace. They were right: it was.

Crimes of war

The war had been so horrible that the victorious Allies decided to try to punish those who, they thought, had broken the rules of civilised behaviour. In effect, that meant putting German commanders on trial for things such as using poison gas or sinking unarmed ships. It proved very difficult, however, to come up with a proper legal definition of a war crime, and they weren't able to get the man they really wanted, the Kaiser, because he'd fled to Holland and the Dutch refused to hand him over. Some officers stood trial before a German court in Leipzig in 1921, charged with mistreating prisoners of war or attacking a hospital ship. Some got short prison sentences; most were acquitted.

It wasn't until after the horrors of the Second World War that the idea of putting people on trial in an international court for war crimes and crimes against humanity was finally put into effect with the establishment of an International Military Tribunal at Nuremberg, Germany, which put the Nazi war leaders on trial.

Spreading the humiliation – the Germans' allies

Germany's allies were just as outraged by their own treaties, which imposed similar terms to those imposed on the Germans in the Treaty of Versailles. In the Treaty of Neuilly, Bulgaria agreed to give up land to the Greeks, Romanians and Yugoslavs. In the Treaty of St Germain, the Austrians had to accept the loss of all their empire. The Treaty of Trianon obliged Hungary to give up huge areas of its territory to Romania, to Yugoslavia and to Czechoslovakia, as well as smaller areas to Poland and Austria. For years, Hungarians hung samples of soil from their lost territories in the streets, as a permanent reminder of the injustice they felt the Allies had dished out at Trianon in 1919.

The Treaty of Versailles would have enormous consequences because it was such an important factor in starting the Second World War, but the other treaties caused just as much bitterness and resentment. That the Austrians, Hungarians and Bulgarians were all on the German side in the Second World War was no coincidence.

Turkey: Don't get mad, get even

One country did manage to do something about its peace settlement. The Treaty of Sèvres with Turkey took time to prepare and was only signed in 1920. By the terms of the treaty, the British were to take over Palestine and Iraq while the French took Syria and Lebanon. The Turks would also have to give land to Greece, accept an independent Armenia and give up control of the Dardanelles, as well as paying reparations and handing over 'war criminals' for trial.

The Turkish government thought it had no choice but to sign, but the Turkish war hero Mustafa Kemal led a military coup and set up an alternative Turkish government. Kemal refused to accept the Treaty of Sèvres and in order to get a better deal he went to war with the Greeks, the French and the Armenians, and he nearly went to war with the British. He got the better deal. In 1922 the Allies agreed to the Treaty of Lausanne, which recognised Turkey as an independent republic and prevented the Allies carving the country up between them. Kemal became a national hero, known as Kemal Atatürk – Father of the Turks.

New kids on the European block

The map of Europe looked very different by 1919 (see Figure 17-1). The old empires had gone, replaced with a number of much smaller republics, such as Austria, Poland and Czechoslovakia. Serbia finally got its dream of a big Slav state: at first it was called the Kingdom of Serbs, Croats and Slovenes, but that proved a bit of a mouthful and it was changed to Yugoslavia: the Land of the Southern Slavs. These new states seemed rather small and vulnerable, but this was nothing to worry about: as everyone knew, war was now impossible because the League of Nations would deal firmly with any aggressor. That, at any rate, was the theory.

Figure 17-1:
The new-look Europe after the First World War.

Did the peace treaties cause the Second World War?

Many people have linked the 1919 peace settlement with the outbreak of the Second World War 20 years later, and it's easy to see why. Even at the time, some people thought the treaties would only cause more trouble. The British economist John Maynard Keynes thought the reparations policy was crazy and some people thought the settlement had merely sown the seed for war a generation later. Certainly, Germans supported Hitler because he promised to tear up the Treaty of Versailles. The treaty denied the Germans any aircraft, submarines and tanks, which inevitably meant that the Germans became determined to get their hands on aircraft, submarines and tanks. And the war guilt clause in particular was one of the major reasons that Germans in the 1920s and 1930s hated the Treaty of Versailles so much and would support anyone who promised to tear it up. However, this doesn't mean that the peace treaties *directly* caused the Second World War. That was down to decisions taken by statesmen in the 1930s.

The League of Nations and Its Fatal Flaw

The most important result of the Paris peace settlement was meant to be President Wilson's visionary idea of a world government committed to keeping the peace. Unfortunately for the world, the League of Nations was doomed from the start by a series of flaws and – most of all – by a fateful decision made by the President's own country, the United States.

Roll up! Roll up! Come and join the League of Nations!

Before the United States could accept the Treaty of Versailles and the League of Nations, the United States Senate had to agree to it. Wilson might have been able to get the League of Nations idea through the Senate if he'd tried to bring his political opponents, the Republicans, on board, but the Republicans (who had a majority in the Senate) just saw it as Wilson's pet project. Wilson thought he could outflank his enemies by appealing to the American people. He went on a whistlestop speaking tour of the United States, trying to explain the League of Nations and why America should be part of it. To many people, though, the League sounded like a scheme to get America tied up in more foreign quarrels and get their sons killed in more foreign wars. Many Americans wanted to go back into *isolationist* mode and have nothing more to do with the Europeans and their quarrels. And that meant saying no to President Wilson's League of Nations.

Wilson's battle to get the Treaty of Versailles through the Senate brought on a series of strokes. But he wouldn't give in or negotiate, so the Republicans wouldn't help him. The Senate rejected the treaty, which meant the United States wouldn't sit in the League of Nations. Wilson was distraught at his failure, and his health virtually collapsed. In 1921 he finally retired as President. He had good reason to be upset: the Senate's vote was a death-blow for the League of Nations – and Wilson knew it.

Okay, the League of Some Nations, then

The League of Nations had two main components: an *Assembly,* in which every member state was represented equally, and a *Council,* on which the Great Powers sat. The League could impose economic sanctions on any troublesome countries and could take military action if necessary, but members had to agree to this unanimously, and no country was obliged to provide troops for the League in any case.

Responsibility for enforcing the League's authority lay with the Council, and that meant, in effect, France, Britain and Italy. However, all three countries had been too badly weakened by the First World War to act as a sort of 'world police'. And without Russia, Germany or the United States, the League of Nations was fatally flawed from the start. It would prove unable to stand up to aggressive dictators such as Mussolini and Hitler when they started making their territorial demands in the years that lay ahead.

What's the difference between a mandate and a colony?

The League of Nations *was* heavily involved in handling *mandates* – the territories and colonies taken off Germany and Turkey by the Allies and given to the League. The League *mandated* – or commissioned – one of its members, usually Britain or France, to govern the mandated territory on behalf of the League until the territory was ready to govern itself. Mandated powers had to observe certain rules (they couldn't usually put military bases in mandates, for example) and the League could always take the territory back if things went badly wrong. Nevertheless, in reality the British and French regarded their mandates as colonies, coloured them in the appropriate colour on the map and governed them accordingly.

Mandates came in three groups:

- ✔ **Class A (nearly ready for independence):** Palestine and Transjordan (to be governed by Britain); Syria and Lebanon (to be governed by France); Mesopotamia (Iraq) (to be governed by Britain).

- ✔ **Class B (not ready for independence):** Tanganyika (to be governed by Britain); Cameroon and Togo (each to be divided between Britain and France); Rwanda (to be taken into the Belgian Congo and governed by Belgium).

- ✔ **Class C (never likely to be independent):** New Guinea (to be governed by Britain and Australia); Nauru (to be governed by Britain, Australia and New Zealand); Samoa (to be governed by Britain and New Zealand); South-West Africa (to be governed by Britain and South Africa).

The mandating of Palestine, Transjordan, Syria and Lebanon came as an unwelcome surprise to Sharif Hussein, who'd been expecting to rule the Middle East (see Chapter 9), so the British and French gave him and his sons consolation prizes. Sharif Hussein himself kept the Hejaz (that is, Arabia); his son Abdullah became King of Transjordan (a British mandate, so he wasn't independent); and another son, Feisal, became King of Iraq.

At the time, it seemed that the British and French had got the best parts of the Middle East (see Figure 17-2). When western companies started to find oil in Arabia and Iraq, however, those 'consolation prizes' began to look rather more attractive. The First World War had marked the start of world interest in the Middle East region, and its territories and its assets, which was to dominate the rest of the 20th century.

Figure 17-2: The peace settlement in the Middle East.

From World War to Civil Wars – and Civil Unrest

When peace came in 1918, Russia was in the middle of a violent revolution and in 1920 it fell into civil war between the communist Red Army and its opponents, known as the *Whites*. The Allies didn't want to see a communist government in Russia. They didn't invite them to the peace conference in Paris, and they even went so far as to send troops to support the Whites in the civil war. It didn't affect the outcome: the Red Army won. However, the Russians never forgot or forgave the Allied intervention in their internal troubles. From then on, the new Soviet Union (that was the name the communist government gave to the country) regarded the western powers as its enemies.

Ireland also erupted into civil war. In the British general election of 1918, the Irish republicans, *Sinn Fein,* won a huge majority of the parliamentary seats in Ireland but, instead of taking their seats in London, the Sinn Fein representatives declared a provisional government for an independent Ireland. The British refused to accept this rival Irish government, and a violent guerrilla campaign against British rule flared up until eventually the British agreed to withdraw from Ireland. They did, however, allow the Protestants of Ulster to opt out of the newly independent Ireland – a situation that was written into the 1922 Anglo–Irish Treaty.

Many Irish republicans were outraged by this partition of the country and the new state immediately fell into an even more violent civil war, between those republicans who accepted the treaty and those who rejected it. The pro-treaty group emerged victorious, but Irish anger over the partition didn't go away and was a major reason for the terrible violence that plagued Northern Ireland in the last decades of the 20th century.

Major trouble was brewing for the British in India as well. Indians' hopes that their huge contribution to the Allied victory in the First World War would be rewarded with some sort of self-rule within the British Empire were soon dashed. All the British did was to allow a few more Indians to sit on some of the administrative councils that ran India. When Indians started to protest, the British brought in strict police powers of arrest. And when people in the Punjab area of northern India *still* protested, the British commander on the spot in the Sikh holy city of Amritsar, General Rex Dyer, took drastic action. He took a body of troops to where a peaceful meeting was taking place and he gave the order to open fire. Over 1,000 Indians were casualties, including many women and children.

The Amritsar Massacre shocked opinion around the world, especially when many British people expressed their support for what General Dyer had done. For many Indian nationalists, however, the massacre was the defining moment when they recognised that British rule wasn't benevolent and that it would have to end. The next decades saw a growing protest movement against British rule in India that led eventually to Britain's withdrawal in 1947. In many ways, India's experiences in the First World War started the process by which British and other European imperialist powers would eventually have to bring the age of European empires to an end.

A Whole New World?

The First World War had been so destructive that, by the time it ended, many people were thinking that it would *have* to lead to the creation of a much better world. Less clear was what this better world would look like, and who'd build it.

Homes fit for heroes

Back when the war had broken out in 1914, many people in Europe's cities had been living in appalling squalor. As Europe had industrialised during the 19th century, unscrupulous builders had thrown up cheap tenements and terraced housing, often with no sanitation, into which factory bosses could cram their workers. Surely, many people thought, the men who survived the trenches deserved to come home to something better than that. Lloyd George, the British Prime Minister, announced that the government would provide 'homes fit for heroes'. Keeping that promise proved to be a lot harder than making it in the first place had been.

In the years after the war, the governments of all the combatant countries constructed housing for the poor. Often they built estates of flats for workers and their families – one famous example was the Karl-Marx-Hof estate in Vienna – but they weren't able to build as many homes as were needed. London's slums, for example, weren't finally swept away until the bombing raids of the Second World War.

All people are equal – aren't they?

In many ways, for most countries the war had been surprisingly democratic: officers shared the same conditions and dangers in the trenches as their men, and food rationing applied to *everyone,* no matter how wealthy or high-up they might be. Historians even think the war finally broke the power of Europe's landed aristocracy: the new republics that were set up in Europe after 1919 were *republics* which had no place for a powerful landed nobility. These new states also gave votes to women, which Britain and the United States also did at the end of the war. Some people wanted all this equality to go a lot further. In 1919, the Russian Bolsheviks called on working people around the world to stage their own communist revolutions and sweep away the rulers and the middle classes who'd plunged them into such a disastrous war.

However, the war didn't bring as much social change as some people hoped for. The old aristocrats were replaced by wealthy industrialists, and the years after the war saw high levels of unemployment, inflation and poverty. Even the First World War couldn't quite sweep away the old differences of rich and poor.

An American century

The world that had gone to war in 1914 was a world dominated by Europe. Europeans controlled most of the surface of the globe and it was a series of European problems that had sparked off the war. However, after 1918 Europe's hold on the world was severely dented. Britain and France still had worldwide empires, and Germany would soon be flexing its muscles again, but the most powerful country to emerge from the war was undoubtedly the United States. Only the United States had the wealth to help the Europeans recover from the war, and by the 1920s the Europeans were heavily dependent on American investments and trade.

Many Americans might have wished that they could remain isolationist and cut themselves off from the rest of the world, but there was no escaping the fact that the 20th century was going to be the American century: the First World War had seen to that.

Chapter 18

Remembering the War

The world was stunned after the First World War. Nothing like it had ever happened in the history of humankind. Never before had devastation been caused on such a monumental scale, never had so many lives been lost and so many communities been destroyed, and never had such acute wartime sufferings been endured by so many civilian populations. No war had ever led to such radical political and social changes, either. People across the world were left in a state of shock.

In all countries people were only too aware of all that they'd lost in the war, and they sensed that they needed to do something special to commemorate the suffering they'd gone through. In this way, the war produced a whole new culture of commemoration and remembrance, a culture that's as powerful and moving now as it was when it was created.

How Many Died?

The scale of the killing in the First World War was monumental, but being precise about the casualty figures of the war is very difficult, simply because so many bodies were never found and countries didn't always manage to keep accurate records.

These figures from the main countries involved in the war are rough estimates of the dead *only;* they don't include the even higher figures for the horribly wounded, who'd have to live with their injuries for the rest of their lives:

- **Austria-Hungary:** 1.1 million
- **British Empire:** 920,000 (including approximately 720,000 British)
- **Bulgaria:** 87,000
- **France:** 1.4 million
- **Germany:** 2 million
- **Italy:** 578,000
- **Russia:** 1.8 million (military)
- **Turkey:** 770,000
- **United States:** 114,000

Don't fall into the trap of looking at these figures as a way of scoring points about who lost the most men. For *all* countries, these numbers were horrific. The United States figure was a terrible blow for a country that had only been actively engaged in the war for a year: in addition to the dead, the Americans suffered nearly a quarter of a million badly wounded or missing. The Italian figure looks a bit small until you remember that the Italians spent nearly the whole war fighting on a narrow front in the Alps against the Austrians: this figure shows just how deadly that front was. And the German figure doesn't include over 5.5 million missing and wounded – that's almost as many as would die years later in the *Holocaust,* the genocide of millions of Jews during the Second World War. Never before in Europe's history had so many died with such violence in such a short space of time.

Commemorating the Dead

It seemed a long time ago in 1919, but the war had started five years earlier as a quarrel between the European Great Powers about territory and prestige. Everyone had been expecting that it would be a short war – that it would be 'over by Christmas' – and that the Germans would quickly be thrown out of Belgium or the Austrians would soon be marching through Serbia's capital, Belgrade.

When it became clear that the war was going to be a long one and that thousands, even millions, of people were going to be killed, people began to talk about the war rather differently, as 'the war to end all wars', a war so vast and so terrible that it *had* to be the very last war in human history.

US President Wilson even called it a 'war to make the world safe for democracy'. Labelling the war in this way meant that people who'd lost loved ones in the fighting could comfort themselves with the thought that they'd died for something that was genuinely worth fighting for.

Sadly, these phrases, 'the war to end all wars' and 'the war to make the world safe for democracy', proved to be just that – nice phrases. Democracy looked decidedly sickly in the years that followed the war as more and more countries turned to dictatorship to solve their problems. And as for ending all wars – well, that idea turned out to be wishful thinking.

Burying the dead

Battlefields in the 19th century were grim places. Burying the dead wasn't always someone's particular responsibility, especially if an army had to move on quickly. Bodies sometimes lay unburied for weeks or months after a battle. Even when they'd been buried the dead weren't always safe: after the Battle of Waterloo in 1815 British dentists used to travel to the battlefield and dig up corpses to use their teeth to make dentures! No one wanted a repetition of such grisly scenes after the First World War.

The usual practice was for armies to bury slain soldiers on the field of battle. No means existed to transport bodies over long distances without their rotting, and the number of bodies in the First World War was far too large in any case for such an idea to be workable. Often soldiers were buried in mass graves behind the lines. However, the Americans had created some proper war cemeteries during the American Civil War and the British had put up many memorials to the dead of the Boer War. It seemed only right that similar memorials and cemeteries should commemorate the dead of the First World War.

Sir Fabian's lists

In the British army, no one at first had the job of keeping a record of who'd died where. It was one Red Cross officer, Sir Fabian Ware, who had the idea and started to keep an unofficial list of where the British dead lay. Eventually, the military authorities recognised the value of what he was doing and gave him the job of running a special unit to register British graves on the western front. Soon this unit became the Imperial War Graves Commission or IWGC (the IWGC is now the Commonwealth War Graves Commission). The IWGC had the task of keeping a record of every British and Empire grave in every theatre of war. When the war was over, it would have the task of buying land on the battlefields to create cemeteries where they could rebury the dead under suitably designed headstones.

The IWGC made some important decisions right from the start:

- ✔ **Graves and monuments were to make no distinction between officers and men.** This hadn't always been the case with memorials in the past, which often kept the two groups separate and sometimes didn't even bother listing the ordinary soldiers by name at all.

- ✔ **The dead of the war deserved the very best quality of memorial the country could produce.** Some very eminent figures, including the architect Sir Edwin Lutyens and the poet Rudyard Kipling, were recruited to work for the IWGC. Lutyens came up with the simple and elegant design of the cemeteries. Kipling coined the wording for the graves of soldiers who were too badly mutilated to be identified: 'A Soldier of the Great War Known Unto God'; and for the stone altars in many of the cemeteries: 'Their Name Liveth for Evermore'.

The IWGC's work inspired other countries to set up their own organisations to oversee the burial of their war dead. In 1923, the United States set up the American Battle Monuments Commission, for example. And the French government took its role in recording the names of the dead very seriously: it was considered a great honour for a soldier to have the words *Mort Pour la France* (which means 'died for France') inscribed on his tomb.

War cemeteries and battlefield memorials

The IWGC set up hundreds of war cemeteries on battlefields in all the theatres of the First World War. Each soldier was given an individually carved headstone bearing his name, unit, age, date of death, the badge of his regiment or unit, and sometimes a suitable quotation, usually chosen by the man's family. The graves were laid out neatly in rows and the cemeteries were beautifully maintained (they still are). Some cemeteries were very small; others were huge. Tyne Cot cemetery, near Ypres, for example, has some 12,000 British and Empire graves; in contrast, the small cemetery at Mametz on the Somme holds the bodies of just 153 men of the Devonshire Regiment on the site of the trench from which they advanced on the first day of the Battle of Somme.

So that anyone who wanted to travel to France or Belgium to visit the grave of a loved one could do so, the IWGC kept detailed records of exactly who was buried where, and it could direct people to the correct cemetery and even the exact burial plot.

In French war cemeteries, graves were marked with simple crosses, and the French government erected a number of imposing monuments to commemorate the sacrifice of their soldiers at Verdun. American graves were also marked with simple white stone crosses carrying each individual's name, unit, home state and date of death. The Germans usually buried their dead in groups of four, each group designated by a dark stone cross with two names on each side.

My boy Jack . . .

The writer Rudyard Kipling, author of *The Jungle Book,* was very badly affected by the war. He'd used all his influence before the war to get his son John ('Jack') enrolled in the Irish Guards, even though John Kipling, like his father, was appallingly short-sighted and depended utterly on his very strong spectacles. John Kipling was killed during the horribly bungled British attack at Loos in 1915: a shell ripped his face apart, but his body was never found.

Kipling, who adored his son, was driven frantic by the news. He and his wife sent appeals out everywhere they could think of and interviewed every soldier of their son's regiment they could find, to try to find out exactly what had happened to him. They clung to the hope that he might somehow have survived, but eventually they had to accept that he'd been killed. Kipling penned a moving poem about his loss, taking pride that his son had died as a true Englishman: *'Have you news of my boy Jack?' Not this tide. 'When d'you think that he'll come back?' Not with this wind blowing, and this tide. . . . 'Oh, dear what comfort can I find?' None this tide, Nor any tide, Except he did not shame his kind.*

War memorials along the western front took many different forms. At Menin, in Ypres, Belgium, the names of the dead were inscribed on a large stone gate at the entrance to the town where, to this day, the 'Last Post' is sounded each night to honour the dead. The monument to the men of Ulster who died on the Somme is a replica of Helen's Tower, a familiar sight on the Northern Irish coast near Belfast. The Canadians who died at Vimy Ridge are commemorated in a huge monument dominated by two rough twin pillars representing Canada and France. One of the most striking monuments on the western front is the huge arch designed by Sir Edwin Lutyens at Thiepval on the Somme and dedicated to the memory of *the missing,* those whose bodies were never found. It has over 72,000 names inscribed on it.

An empty tomb and an unknown soldier

To coincide with the first anniversary of the end of the war, the British architect Sir Edwin Lutyens was asked, with only a couple of weeks' notice, to design a large wooden monument to stand in London's Whitehall symbolising an empty tomb, or *cenotaph.* The soldiers would march past it in tribute to their comrades who weren't coming back. The design worked so well that the government decided to commission Lutyens to design a permanent cenotaph in stone. Unveiled by King George V on 11 November 1920, the permanent cenotaph is a very plain and dignified monument that carries the words 'The Glorious Dead', as well as the Union Jack and the flags of the armed services (see Figure 24 in the insert section).

Other cenotaphs were set up all around the British Empire, modelled on Lutyens's design. Cenotaphs are found in all the major Canadian cities, including one by Niagara Falls; you can also see them in Sydney, Hobart, Auckland, Hong Kong, Singapore, Colombo and Belfast. A cenotaph stands even at Victoria Falls in Zambia.

The London cenotaph quickly became the focus of British commemoration of the dead of the war. Men used to take off their hats as they passed it, as a sign of respect for those who'd died. Each year, on 11 November, the anniversary of the Armistice, the king would lead the nation in a service of remembrance at the cenotaph, with representatives of the Empire and Commonwealth and a march-past by old soldiers. When *Big Ben,* the bell of the famous clock in the Palace of Westminster, sounded the hour, the crowd would observe two minutes' silence. This ceremony still takes place each November, though now it commemorates the dead of both world wars and other recent conflicts. Similar ceremonies are held each year at cenotaphs and war memorials all around the world.

In addition to Remembrance Sunday and national memorials to the dead of the war, a British army chaplain called David Railton came up with an idea of how to commemorate the millions of soldiers who had no known grave. He suggested burying one of these soldiers with full ceremony in Westminster Abbey, where the British have always buried their most famous figures. From a group of coffins containing the bodies of British soldiers who'd been so badly mutilated that they couldn't be identified a blindfolded officer chose one at random. No one knew who the soldier inside the coffin was, what regiment he served in or what rank he held: all they knew was that he was a Briton who had served in the war. The body was transferred to Britain and buried with full military honours in the presence of the king inside the West Door of Westminster Abbey. He was known as the *unknown soldier.*

Railton's idea of burying an unknown soldier as a way of remembering all those soldiers with no known grave caught the public imagination, and other countries buried their own unknown soldiers. France's unknown soldier lies under the Arc de Triomphe in Paris; the American Tomb of the Unknowns is in Arlington Military Cemetery; Italy's unknown soldier is in the huge Victor Emmanuel memorial in Rome.

Local memorials of war

Although national monuments served as the focus for national commemorations of the war, ordinary people in towns and villages across the world wanted to honour the sacrifice of their young men by putting up their own war memorials. The forms of these memorials varied a lot, which says much about how people at the time reacted to the war.

Many places erected a simple cross, but some raised the money for a memorial with a statue. Some of these memorials show classical figures of victory, holding laurel wreaths aloft (you can often see these in French villages). In Britain war memorials more commonly have a statue of an ordinary soldier, sometimes in an attitude of mourning, leaning on a reversed rifle (you can see a good example in Enniskillen in Northern Ireland). Often these statues are very detailed and give a realistic idea of what the troops wore. The war memorial at Paddington Station in London shows a British soldier in his rain cape and helmet, with a thick scarf wrapped around him.

Usually, the tone of the memorials is very sombre, but occasionally it's more hopeful. The war memorial in Cambridge, for example, is called 'The Homecoming' and has a statue by a Canadian sculptor showing a young man coming back from the war with a definite spring in his step. The German war memorial in Munich is another surprising one, though for a different reason. It shows a German soldier in full kit lying sleeping on a stone slab. The inscription makes it clear that the soldier represents Germany itself: it might be sleeping for the moment, but one day it would rise again.

These war memorials were an important sign that many people wanted to pay tribute to all those who'd fought and died in the war, and not just to officers.

Dr Spooner's plaque

You may have heard of the famous Dr William Spooner, Dean of New College, Oxford, who gained a reputation for getting his words muddled. 'You've wasted two whole terms', for example, is supposed to have come out as 'You've tasted two whole worms', and 'You've missed all my history lectures' as 'You've hissed all my mystery lectures'. In fact, these examples, like many others that are told about him, are almost certainly not true (though he could be very absent-minded). But no doubt exists about one thing Dr Spooner did. After the First World War he made sure that a plaque went up in the beautiful college cloister in memory of those *German* members of the college who'd died fighting for their country. The plaque reads: 'In memory of the men of this college who, coming from a foreign land, entered into the inheritance of this place & returning fought and died for their country in the war 1914–1919.' Other colleges in Oxford and Cambridge did the same: they honoured all their students, from whichever country they came and for whichever country they died. And that's as it should be.

Visiting the battlefields

Almost as soon as the war had ended, the governments of France and Belgium decided to preserve parts of the Western Front as a permanent memorial to the men who'd died there. The Turkish government took a similar view about the battlefields near Gallipoli. (On the Eastern Front, the terrible memory of what happened in Poland and Russia in the Second World War tended to blot out memories of the First World War.) Very soon, people began to travel to the battlefields, to visit the monuments and cemeteries and to pay homage to their relatives and friends who'd been killed and were buried there. The beach in Turkey where the Australians and New Zealanders had landed became known forever as Anzac Cove and the Turkish President, Kemal Atatürk, announced that the land now belonged to all the men who'd fought on it, whatever their nationality.

Over the years, more and more people have visited the battlefields of the First World War. Schools often organise trips for their pupils and some tour companies specialise in taking groups of tourists to visit the battlefields and the memorials. For many years men who'd fought in the war would visit the battlefields, but as they began to die out, their place was taken by their children or by people from their local communities. Towns that had sent Pals' Battalions (see Chapter 4) to the front often felt a particularly strong bond with the cemetery or monument that marked where they'd all fallen. Even after the carnage of the Second World War, people still travelled to visit the battlefields from the First World War, and Armistice Day, 11 November, remains the day to remember the dead of the First World War and of all the wars that followed it.

In Flanders fields the poppies grow

A Canadian officer, John McCrae, wrote a poem entitled 'In Flanders Fields' about the red poppies that grew on the battlefields around Ypres. They were the only form of wildlife that survived the destruction and their red colour seemed a very appropriate touch on the battlefield. McCrae's poem proved very popular and the red poppy quickly became a symbol, at least for the British and their empire, of the dead of the First World War. The wreaths laid at war memorials each November are made of artificial poppies, and people still buy a poppy to wear on Remembrance Sunday each year.

The poppies that people wear each November in Britain are made in a factory on Richmond Hill in south-west London, and the money raised from their sale supports the work of the Royal British Legion, which looks after old servicemen. Just a little farther up the hill from the poppy factory is a very elegant red-brick building called the Star and Garter Home – a hostel for badly wounded ex-service personnel, where some badly injured veterans of the First World War were living as recently as the 1980s. Some servicemen from the home work in the poppy factory, but others are too badly injured to be able to help.

The man in charge of the annual poppy appeal in its early days was Field Marshal Earl Haig, who had commanded the British armies on the Western Front. Haig devoted himself to the welfare of former soldiers, in whom he took enormous pride. However, not everyone agreed with the red poppy and the Remembrance Day parades. Some people thought that the war memorials and commemorations were too militaristic, especially because Haig was so closely associated with them. They produced a white poppy as an alternative way of honouring the dead without appearing to support a war of which they disapproved.

The Cry of Men in Face of Their Destiny: The Cultural Impact of the War

Rather surprisingly, the First World War produced some of the most important cultural and artistic work of the 20th century. The experience of the war was so intense, and the suffering and destruction so shocking, that it had a profound effect upon writers, artists and musicians. Some of the war's cultural impact can be traced in the memorials people put up to the dead or in the museums that sought to keep the memory of the war alive. Some of it went into the poetry and artwork the war inspired. For many people today, it's the artistic response to the war that brings the experience of the men of the First World War most vividly to life.

Meeting the war painters and poets

The First World War produced some very striking artwork. Some of it was produced by artists who served at the front; others by artists who visited the front and recorded what they saw. The artwork of the First World War is very varied, but it all gives a powerful idea of the impact the war had on those who lived through it.

Here are just some of the artists who were inspired by the war:

- **John and Paul Nash** were two British artist brothers who both served in the Artists' Rifles, a special military unit for painters and artists. They produced paintings of life in the trenches presented in a very simple, naïve style, rather like folk art, that made the Western Front seem an almost dreamlike, surreal place – which in many ways it was.

- **John Singer Sargent** was an American artist who lived and worked in London, where he was known for his very elegant portraits of people in high society. In 1918 he visited the Western Front and saw a group of men who'd been blinded by gas. This encounter inspired him to paint *Gassed,* a large painting showing a line of men, each blinded and with bandages over his eyes, holding on to the man in front as they're led along in a long line. Sargent's painting brought home the horrors of the war to people at the time, especially coming from someone so well known for a very different type of painting, and it's still a very powerful image today.

- **Otto Dix** fought in the German army on both the Western and the Eastern Fronts. He was appalled by the conditions he found and his paintings show the trenches as a sort of hell, in the style of the nightmare visions of the Renaissance painter Hieronymus Bosch.

- **George Grosz** was a lifelong pacifist and he used his paintings to attack the hypocrisy of the German ruling classes who'd taken the country into the war in the first place. He showed German generals and politicians as fat, selfish caricatures, happy to send others to their deaths while they lived lives of comfort.

One of the most unusual cultural products of the war was the sheer volume and quality of the English-language poetry it produced. Many of these writers came from a British public school background, and they fitted their writing around their work as serving officers. The poet Siegfried Sassoon even won the Military Cross for gallantry, though he threw it away when he turned against the war.

First World War poets such as Sassoon, John McCrae, Wilfred Owen, Edmund Blunden and many others (see Chapter 21) give a very vivid picture of what the fighting was like on the ground and they also reflect their growing disillusionment and bitterness about the men in charge. In one of Sassoon's poems a couple of Tommies remark that their General seems a cheery old sort, 'But he did for them both with his plan of attack'. Other diverse writers, diarists and playwrights such as Robert Graves and RC Sherriff (also see Chapter 21) also produced memorable accounts of the war. All these accounts stressed how the war had betrayed the hopes and ideals of the young men who'd joined up so enthusiastically to fight for king and country.

In 1975 an American literary professor, Paul Fussell, wrote a study – *The Great War and Modern Memory* – of how these literary writings shaped views of the First World War. Fussell thought that the war profoundly impacted how the British regarded the world and themselves, and that it was the experience of the trenches, as described by the poets and writers, that got the British so fond of irony and satire. He said that after the war the British never again viewed authority figures with the sort of respect they'd always received before 1914.

The war poets in particular pose a problem for historians looking at the war. No one can deny the power of the poets' imagery and the sense of immediacy they convey, but many people see the poets as the most vivid and accurate witnesses of the life in the trenches. They assume that all the soldiers shared the poets' feelings of disillusion and anger. The trouble is that by no means all the war was as described in the poems. Men weren't being shelled and gassed *all the time.* And just because Siegfried Sassoon didn't think the war was being fought for anything valuable doesn't mean later generations have to agree with him – and, increasingly, modern historians don't.

Historians often point out that the poets were a small group of highly articulate officers from well-educated backgrounds and that their views were by no means shared by all the men. Ordinary soldiers tended to produce far more earthy songs and jingles, and they didn't always share the outlook of their literary officers. After all, the British army never mutinied and Haig was highly respected by his men both during and after the war. However, the poetry is so vivid that it still dominates most people's understanding of what the war was like.

An Imperial War Museum

The idea of having a national museum dedicated to the events of the war was a British one, and it came from the Liberal MP Sir Alfred Mond, who, perhaps fittingly, was the son of German immigrants into Britain. Sir Alfred put the idea forward in 1917, while the war was still going on, for a museum that would showcase people's memories and experiences, as a permanent memorial of the war. Other parts of the British Empire got wind of the scheme and were keen to have their contributions acknowledged too, so the proposed museum became known as the Imperial War Museum, the name it still bears today. The Museum, based in London, England, houses a huge collection of photographs and documents relating to the war, as well as vehicles and artefacts from all the fronts on which Empire troops served, and is regarded as one of the finest military history institutions anywhere in the world.

Nowadays people are used to such museums, so it's easy to overlook what a radical idea Sir Alfred had. Museums in those days usually showed artefacts from distant history. To have a museum that told a story that had only just finished and didn't really feel like history at all was a new and very exciting idea. It added to people's sense that they were engaged in a war that would change history and the very future of humankind itself.

KEY PEOPLE

What happened to them all?

You may already know that Winston Churchill, First Lord of the Admiralty and the man behind the disastrous Dardanelles campaign in 1915, went on to lead Britain in the Second World War. Here's what happened to some of the other colourful figures of the First World War:

✔ **Gavrilo Princip:** The young man whose pistol shot started the First World War died in prison of tuberculosis in April 1918. To the end of his short life he remained unrepentant about his assassination of the Austrian Archduke Franz Ferdinand. If he hadn't done it, he said, the Germans would have found some other excuse to launch a war.

✔ **Kaiser Wilhelm II:** After abdicating in 1918, the German Kaiser headed into exile in Holland. The Allies wanted to put him on trial for war crimes, but the Dutch refused to extradite him. The Kaiser was still in Holland when the Germans invaded in 1940: He disliked the Nazis but he felt his duty was to support Germany, and he declined a British offer to help him escape to England. He died in Holland in 1941.

✔ **Sir Douglas Haig:** After the war, Field Marshal Haig was made an earl and he served as Commander-in-Chief of British Home Forces before he retired. He helped set up the Royal British Legion for veterans and he oversaw the annual sale of poppies to raise money for wounded ex-servicemen. Haig died ten years after the end of the war, in 1928.

✔ **Sir John Jellicoe:** Admiral of the British Fleet Jellicoe's reputation never recovered from the disappointment of the Battle of Jutland: he was sacked in 1917 by David Lloyd George. After the war he served as Governor of New Zealand. He died in 1935, the year Britain agreed to allow the Germans to start building up their navy again.

✔ **Paul von Hindenburg and Erich Ludendorff:** Germany's most famous generals remained in the public eye. Ludendorff hated the democratic republic that came to power at the end of the war and in 1923 he joined with Adolf Hitler's Nazi Party in its failed attempt to seize power in the Beer Hall putsch. He became more difficult to deal with, and turned against Hindenburg and Hitler. He died in 1937. Hindenburg also went into politics, with more success. He was popular with the German people, who elected him President in 1925. It was Hindenburg who appointed Hitler Chancellor in January 1933. He died in 1934.

✔ **Philippe Pétain:** The hero of Verdun was made a marshal of France after the war. He served as French ambassador to Spain after the Spanish Civil War. When the Germans defeated France in 1940, Pétain led the nominally independent French state based at Vichy. Petain was accused of collaborating too closely with the Germans, and after the Second World War he was found guilty of treason and sentenced to death, though the sentence was changed to life imprisonment. He died in 1951, in prison.

✔ **Alexei Brusilov:** Russia's best general of the First World War was sacked by the Russian Provisional Government in August 1917 and was out of work for the next three years while the Russian Revolution raged. In 1920, as Russia slid into civil war, the Bolsheviks offered Brusilov the chance to serve in the Red Army. He accepted. He died in 1926.

✓ **Woodrow Wilson:** The US President was ill during the Paris peace conference, though he hid it well. He wore himself out campaigning through the States to get the League of Nations through Congress and he suffered a series of strokes. He remained in office, even though he was too ill to function, until finally he retired in 1921. He died three years later.

✓ **David Lloyd George:** The British Prime Minister remained active in politics for the rest of his life. In 1922 his Conservative coalition partners turned against him and he had to resign as Prime Minister. He was impressed

with the way Hitler transformed Germany, though he opposed the policy of appeasement. He died in March 1945.

✓ **Georges Clemenceau:** The formidable French Prime Minister resigned in 1920 and devoted himself to working for good relations between France and the British and Americans as well as to writing history and philosophy. He was very critical of French foreign policy in the 1920s. He died in 1929.

✓ **Mustafa Kemal:** The Turkish hero of Gallipoli went on to end the Ottoman Empire and become President of Turkey. He transformed the country into a tough, secular modern state. He brought in the Latin alphabet, gave women equal rights and put an end to Islam's hold on the country. He took the name Kemal Atatürk – Father of the Turks.

The First World War: From a Distance

After the First World War ended (though they called it 'the Great War' at the time), people all over the world hoped that it had ended war for ever. That hope didn't last long; in 1939 a second world war broke out. To some people, it seemed as if the Germans had some sort of addiction to inflicting destructive wars on their neighbours.

As the world approached the 50th anniversary of the outbreak of the First World War, in 1964, that view changed, especially among younger people. Many of them thought that the war had been a tragedy caused by the rulers of all the Great Powers, and that no one country was more to blame than any other.

The satirists' war

A satirical theatre show called *Oh! What a Lovely War,* by radical British theatre producer Joan Littlewood, told the story of the war as a sort of variety show gone horribly wrong. The show stressed how many young men had been slaughtered by their incompetent and callous generals, who didn't care about the losses or about the misery they caused. The show had a huge impact. It was very popular with amateur theatre groups, so it became the main way that many people learned about the war. It contributed to the growing worldwide opinion that the First World War was a pointless exercise, in which men were slaughtered for no good reason. (You can read about the film version of *Oh! What a Lovely War* in Chapter 20.)

In the 1980s the BBC produced a satirical comedy show called *Blackadder Goes Forth* that was set in the First World War and made exactly the same sort of point about the war for a generation who didn't remember *Oh! What a Lovely War.* In the last episode of the series all the characters go over the top and are killed by German machine guns. The show ends with a scene of poppies in a field. Teachers still use *Blackadder Goes Forth* when they teach about the First World War today.

The lions and the donkeys

One of the most bitter arguments over the war is about the quality of the generals, especially Haig and the British commanders. The German General Falkenhayn is supposed to have said that ordinary British soldiers were like lions, but they were led by donkeys. 'Lions led by donkeys' became a familiar phrase for describing the British soldiers of the First World War, and some historians began to produce books with titles such as *Butchers and Bunglers of the First World War* or *The Donkeys* to argue the case that British generals were incompetent and uncaring.

More recently, historians have been much less ready to condemn the generals of the First World War quite so easily. No one denies that some disasters occurred: the first day of the Battle of the Somme, 1 July 1916, when the British suffered 60,000 casualties within one day, was a total shambles, and the Battle of Passchendaele in 1917 saw some appalling slaughter in the worst conditions anyone could possibly imagine. But historians point out that the generals were having to adapt very quickly to very new technology, and although they had some huge failures, they had some huge successes too. Both sides achieved huge victories in 1918, for example. Above all, some historians say that the people who criticise the generals don't offer any practical suggestions of what alternatives the generals had. The topic often arouses strong passions and the arguments still rage to this day.

The last Tommy

By the 2000s nearly all the men who'd fought in the First World War had died. Some historians and TV companies made one last attempt to interview the few survivors and get their memories before they too died. In 2009 Harry Patch, the last British Tommy to have fought in the First World War, died at the age of 111. Other last survivors included Frank Buckles, who was an ambulance driver in the American army and who died in 2011 aged 110, and a Canadian, John Babcock, who died in 2010 aged 109.

Towards the end of his life, Harry Patch became a sort of TV star. Everyone wanted to hear from this last surviving link with the men who'd served in the trenches. He warned that the war had been a hellish thing to go through and people should do everything they could to avoid going to war ever again.

Was it worth it?

Everyone will have their own view of whether or not the Great War was worth all the suffering and destruction it caused. Many people say that nothing could justify the war, and that the great majority of those who were killed died for no good reason. Others say that the causes of the war were just as valid as the causes of other, equally horrible wars: it was just as bad for the Germans to invade Belgium in 1914 as it was for them to invade Poland in 1939.

In the end you have to make your own mind up about this question. Some people think all war is wrong; others think war can sometimes be justified. What we can say is that many people at the time thought that the war would at any rate mean the end of all wars: in that, they were very badly mistaken.

Part VI

The Part of Tens

For some thoughts about what lessons the First World War can teach, head to www.dummies.com/extras/firstworldwar for a bonus Part of Tens chapter.

In this part...

- Spark your curiosity and head out on the path of finding out more about the First World War. Take a read through my thoughts – and they are only my thoughts – on the best generals, which writers and poets give the best accounts of the war and the best First World War films to watch.

- Discover a lot more about the war in the best possible way: by going to visit some of the places associated with it. In this part, you find my suggestions for where you might like to go.

Chapter 19

Ten Key Generals of the First World War

*T*he generals of the First World War haven't had a good press, and it's certainly true that they made some catastrophic mistakes that cost thousands of lives. But it's not true that they were all uncaring or incompetent. Some generals were extremely able and successful. They paid attention to detail, analysed the battlefield closely, took pains to avoid unnecessary casualties to their own men and made full use of the latest technology.

In this chapter, I steer clear of the really famous generals, such as the British Field Marshal Sir Douglas Haig or the German Field Marshal Paul von Hindenburg. You can read about them elsewhere in the book. Instead, here I present some generals who deserve to be better known, including some who deserve a place among the very best.

Max Hoffman (1869–1927)

Let me put this simply: Max Hoffman won the war against Russia. People usually think Hindenburg and Ludendorff did it, but a strong school of thought holds that Hoffman really deserves the credit. He planned the German victory at Tannenburg in 1914 (see Chapter 4): Hindenburg and Ludendorff simply inherited Hoffman's plan and followed it. As Chief of Staff to the rather neurotic Ludendorff, Hoffman also planned the crushing victories against the Russians in Poland (which you can also read about in Chapter 4). He even arranged for Lenin and the Bolsheviks to get to Russia and stage the revolution, knowing they'd pull Russia out of the war, and then he negotiated the crushing Treaty of Brest Litovsk with them to get maximum advantage for Germany (see Chapter 15).

Hindenburg and Ludendorff couldn't have done what they did without Max Hoffman.

Sir Henry Rawlinson (1864–1925)

Yes, Rawlinson was in charge of the disastrous British attack on the Somme on 1 July 1916 (you can read about it in Chapter 6). But he was actually a very able commander, who paid the sort of painstaking attention to detail that victory in the First World War demanded. The British plan for the Somme offensive was a mixture of Haig's and Rawlinson's ideas: it might have gone better had Rawlinson had more freedom to do things his way. Later, he went on to win a stunning victory at Amiens in 1918, when the British broke the German offensive and drove the German line right back: Ludendorff called it the black day of the German army (see Chapter 16).

So Rawlinson was responsible for the worst disasters of the war for both the British *and* the Germans. An interesting and often underrated man.

August von Mackensen (1849–1944)

Like Max Hoffman, Mackensen did much more for German success in the east than people usually remember. A striking figure in his cavalry uniform, Mackensen worked out the best way to break through the enemy lines: by attacking only a small stretch of the line but with overwhelming force. He applied his tactics with great success against the Russians in Poland (you can read how in Chapter 4), where he did so well he was promoted to Field Marshal. In 1915 he took command of the forces that crushed Serbia, and the following year he repeated the trick by organising the different armies that crushed Romania too (see Chapters 5 and 6).

He's been rather overshadowed by Hindenburg and Ludendorff, but Mackensen was definitely not a man you wanted to find facing you across a battlefield.

Sir Herbert Plumer (1857–1932)

The problem with Plumer is that, with his bald head and thick white moustache, he looked exactly like everyone's idea of a blimpish, old-fashioned general with his mind stuck in the past (he even went to Eton!). In fact, Plumer was one of the most successful British commanders of the war. He took command at Ypres in 1915 and retrieved the situation after the Germans' heavy offensive had come close to taking the town (see Chapter 5). His mastery of meticulous planning lay behind his biggest victory, at Messines in 1917, where his attack plan involved a huge concentration of artillery and gas and a series of enormous mines that exploded underneath the German lines. Messines was a devastating British victory where, for once, the defenders lost far more men than the attackers (see Chapter 15).

If you hear people saying the British generals were all incompetent fools, tell them about Plumer: they probably won't have heard of him but you might change their ideas.

Mustafa Kemal (Kemal Atatürk) (1881–1938)

Mustafa Kemal was the most successful commander to emerge from Turkey's very mixed war record. He'd fought in Libya and the Balkans before the war, but he became a national hero at Gallipoli, where he played a major role in defeating the Allied landings at Suvla Bay, launching one fierce attack after another on the Allied lines (see Chapter 9). After Gallipoli, Kemal found himself trying to pick up the pieces after other Turkish commanders' disasters, in the Caucasus against the Russians and in the Middle East against the British. Turkish politics had been getting ever more dangerous since the Young Turks revolution in 1908 and Kemal had enemies in high places, including the Turkish leader, Enver Pasha. When the Young Turks government collapsed at the end of the war, Kemal managed to prevent the Allies from carving the country up and he seized power.

Kemal did more than anyone to keep Turkish heads held high during the war and to turn Turkey into a modern, secular state. He became known as Atatürk – 'Father of the Turks'.

Sir John Monash (1865–1931)

Ask who was the most successful general on either side on the Western Front and many experts on the war would name an Australian, Sir John Monash. Yet outside Australia very few people nowadays have even heard of him. Monash pioneered a new way of attacking, known as *peaceful penetration* (also known as 'winkling' or 'nibbling'). Instead of sending huge numbers of men against well-defended enemy lines, Monash used small raiding parties to seize isolated German positions during quiet periods, or else he'd send in large numbers of machine guns, aircraft and tanks to attack a small part of the enemy lines, and only then did he send the infantry in to occupy the whole sector; meanwhile the mechanised units moved on to attack the next section.

Monash developed his successful peaceful penetration tactic in the spring of 1918 when the Allies halted the great German offensive and started to drive the Germans out of France (see Chapter 16). He provided the Allies with the key to defeating the Germans, and in that way you could say that he won the war in the west.

Sir Arthur Currie (1875–1933)

The Canadians consistently proved some of the toughest troops fighting on the Allied side and Sir Arthur Currie was their suitably tough-minded commander. He showed his worth at Ypres in 1915, when his Canadians were the only troops not to run when the Germans used gas for the first time in the war (see Chapter 5). Currie was also responsible for the Canadians' greatest success, the attack on Vimy Ridge in 1917 (see Chapter 15). The British and French had lost thousands of men trying to take Vimy ever since the Germans first dug themselves into the chalk there in 1914, and the Germans were determined to hold on to their position. Currie had tunnels built so his men could approach unseen and he pushed the attack forward through a snowstorm. The Canadians suffered heavy casualties, but their capture of Vimy Ridge was the greatest Allied success on the Western Front until the great battles of 1918.

Canadians are rightly proud of their fighting record in the First World War, and Currie deserves the credit for leading them against the Germans with such devastating effect.

Alexei Brusilov (1853–1926)

Brusilov was by far the most consistently successful of the Russian generals in the First World War; in fact during the German offensives in Galicia (Poland) in 1915 he was just about the *only* successful Russian general (see Chapter 5). Brusilov made his name with his famous offensive in 1916 that finally achieved the elusive breakthrough that commanders in all armies had been groping for (you can read about his achievement in Chapter 6). Brusilov dispensed with the preliminary bombardment, which was basically a very noisy way of announcing to your enemy when you were about to attack and telling him where. Instead he amassed huge numbers of men and attacked over a very wide area, not just concentrating on a small one as most generals did. Brusilov's plan worked: the Austrians didn't know where the main Russian thrust was, so they didn't know where to send their reinforcements.

Brusilov also served under the Russian Provisional Government in 1917, but they replaced him with a much less successful general who promptly lost and had to be sacked. But then that was the Russian Provisional Government all over. (You can find out about it in Chapter 15.)

John J Pershing (1860–1948)

Pershing was already an experienced commander when he arrived at the head of the American Expeditionary Force in France in 1917. He'd started out in the wars against the American Indian tribes, fought in the Spanish–American War and, in 1917, led the US invasion of Mexico. When he arrived in France later the same year, Pershing was very critical of Allied tactics, which he thought wasted lives for minimal gains, and he reckoned that Americans could do better. They certainly had a convincing victory at St Mihiel in 1918 (see Chapter 16), but Pershing made mistakes trying to follow it up, mainly because he didn't want to follow advice from other Allied commanders.

Pershing kept the American Expeditionary Force as a separate army: he was the first American commander ever to operate in a war on the European mainland and he wasn't going to start taking orders from anyone else. His presence on the Western Front was an important sign of the United States' commitment to gaining victory over Germany and achieving a lasting peace settlement.

Ferdinand Foch (1851–1929)

Foch was a 'fighting general': he believed armies were for attacking the enemy, not wasting time sitting around in trenches. He once said: 'My centre is giving way, my right is in retreat: Situation excellent – we attack!'

Foch first made his name as a pugnacious commander in the French invasion of Alsace-Lorraine at the start of the war (see Chapter 4), but it was towards the end of the war that he really came into his own. He'd performed well co-ordinating the different Allied forces in Italy in 1917 (see Chapter 15) and was appointed to command all the Allied forces on the Western Front after the German spring offensive had broken through the Allied lines. He proved surprisingly good in this role. He got on particularly well with Haig, who shared his preference for attacking.

When the Germans asked for an armistice, Foch met them in his personal railway carriage and imposed heavy terms, so as to make sure the Germans couldn't suddenly start fighting again. In that way, it was Foch who actually brought the war to an end.

Chapter 20

Ten Great First World War Films

In This Chapter

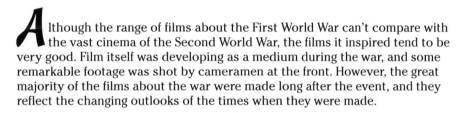

▶ Viewing feature films from the time of the war

▶ Watching films made since the war

▶ Appreciating the changing perspective of directors

Although the range of films about the First World War can't compare with the vast cinema of the Second World War, the films it inspired tend to be very good. Film itself was developing as a medium during the war, and some remarkable footage was shot by cameramen at the front. However, the great majority of the films about the war were made long after the event, and they reflect the changing outlooks of the times when they were made.

This chapter gives you a quick whistlestop tour of what I think are some of the very best films made about the war.

The Battle of the Somme (Geoffrey Malins and John McDowell, 1916)

This silent film of the battle (see Chapter 6) still has the power to grip audiences. It was filmed during the battle itself (these aren't actors – they're the real soldiers) and it was shown in cinemas in Britain and at the front when the battle was still in its final stages. Film historians have pointed out that some passages showing men going over the top were staged for the camera, though the men who actually fought in the battle found the film entirely realistic. One soldier wrote to the press saying that the only thing missing from the film was the sound of the guns. But as he was watching it in a tent just behind the front line, that was provided for real, free of charge.

To get beyond the still images and get a better sense of how a major Western Front offensive really felt to the men who took part in it, you really can't do better than looking out *The Battle of the Somme.*

Shoulder Arms (Charlie Chaplin, 1918)

Shoulder Arms is a bit of typical Chaplin slapstick, but instead of his trademark bowler hat and cane he's in doughboy uniform and carries a rifle. American *doughboys* (that was the popular nickname for American soldiers in the First World War, a bit like *GIs* in the Second World War) enjoyed the scenes sending up all the marching and drill sergeants they had to endure, and some of the comedy still works very well – see how Charlie deals with three German soldiers while disguised not very convincingly as a tree!

The First World War might not seem an obvious subject for comedy, but laughter is essential just as much in wartime as at other times. This film delivers just that.

All Quiet on the Western Front (Lewis Milestone, 1930)

All Quiet on the Western Front, based on Erich Maria Remarque's novel of the same name, is perhaps the most important film made about the First World War. It tells of an idealistic young German going straight from school into the army and on to the trenches, where the reality of war shatters his illusions one by one until the tragic final scene.

The film was remade very successfully in 1979, but the original has more of a feel of the period. It's a classic anti-war film, and you won't be surprised to hear it was banned by the Nazis. All the more reason to see it.

La Grande Illusion (Jean Renoir, 1937)

On the face of it, *La Grande Illusion* ('The Great Illusion') is an escape adventure film. It's about a French officer pilot shot down and captured by the Germans and his attempts to escape, and you may at first be hard pressed to see why it's always described as an anti-war film. The film's anti-war message is subtle, but it is clear. The Frenchman comes from the same aristocratic background as the German commandant, who stands for the old ways and believes men of the same class should stand together, whatever their nationalities. That belief is the *Grande Illusion* of the title: the war is killing off the old ways and bringing in a harsher, less honour-bound reality.

Paths of Glory (Stanley Kubrick, 1957)

Stanley Kubrick's great indictment of criminal folly starts with French generals exchanging merry banter in a comfortable chateau – a world away from the trenches they command. There they dream up an impracticable attack that duly proves disastrous, so they cover up their own incompetence by blaming the failure on three innocent French soldiers and having them shot for cowardice.

Paths of Glory is a shocking indictment of the cynicism and folly that undoubtedly operated in various headquarters, and also on what happens when the men in charge lose direct contact with the men they command.

Oh! What a Lovely War (Richard Attenborough, 1969)

Oh! What a Lovely War (the title comes from a popular music hall song) was a ground-breaking stage show put on in 1964 by London's radical Theatre Workshop and its famous director, Joan Littlewood. The show mixed songs, jokes, photographs and extracts from the diaries of the British commander, Sir Douglas Haig, in a devastatingly satirical attack on the folly of the First World War. Turning it into a film wasn't going to be easy, but Richard Attenborough rose to the challenge, presenting the war as a sort of seaside holiday gone disastrously wrong, with the high command playing leapfrog and riding round-abouts and helter-skelters while the men fight in the mud of the trenches.

Oh! What a Lovely War is a brilliant piece of satire – very unfair on Haig, of course, but then, it is satire.

Lawrence of Arabia (David Lean, 1962)

Laurence of Arabia is often regarded as David Lean's best film and it's easy to see why. You really need to see this famous epic on the wide screen to get an idea of the majestic scale of the desert, with Omar Sharif making his famous appearance out of a mirage and Anthony Quinn doing his 'Zorba the Bedouin' act.

Allowing for some simplification, *Lawrence of Arabia* shows how the British cynically exploited the Arab Revolt (see Chapter 9) for their own purposes and then took the region over for themselves. Above all, though, this film is a portrait of Lawrence, the complex, irresistible and frankly rather unnerving character behind the hero image conveniently created for him by the press.

Gallipoli (Peter Weir, 1981)

Bring a box of tissues for this story of how Australia lost its innocence. *Gallipoli* tells of two Australians, both keen amateur athletes, who become good mates and join up together to fight. They're young, they're Australian, they don't take anything too seriously – and then they land at Gallipoli and find themselves in another world (see Chapter 9). The climax of the film comes when one has to run with a message that will stop the suicidal attack his friend is going to take part in. Even though you know just what's going to happen, it's a heart-stopper of a film.

The history is simplistic, but that hardly matters. *Gallipoli* is where Australia comes of age.

Regeneration (Gillies McKinnon, 1997)

This film is based on the *Regeneration* book trilogy by Pat Barker, which tells of a number of officers, including the poets Wilfred Owen (see Chapter 21) and Siegfried Sassoon, who were treated for shellshock at the famous Craiglockhart hospital in Scotland. The central character is the doctor in charge of the hospital, Dr Rivers, who has to address the question of where the real madness lies: in his patients or in his job, of getting them fit and well enough to send them back into the trenches?

Regeneration is a thought-provoking film that raises much deeper questions about the war than just telling the story of the poets. And when you've seen the film, make sure you read the books.

Flyboys (Tony Bill, 2006)

The fighting in the air is about the only aspect of the First World War that has kept something of its glamour, and various film and television directors have made films about it. *Flyboys* tells the story of the American Lafayette squadron that flew with the French air force before the USA came into the war. The film has all the action sequences you'd expect but it's also a moving and intelligent reflection on the nature of the war and on what these American volunteers were going through. This isn't a romantic adventure: these boys are engaged in a vicious and deadly combat, and the strain tells.

Flyboys is an honest and very necessary piece of myth busting.

Chapter 21

Ten Famous Wartime Writers and Poets

*T*he writing of the First World War is so famous that it can sometimes seem as if the war was entirely fought by men with one hand on a gun and the other on a pen. Many people *only* know about the war from the writings of some of the famous authors it produced, such as Wilfred Owen and Robert Graves. The poetry of the First World War is very moving, describing the life the men led in the trenches and the feelings they went through, often in harrowing detail, and the lyric beauty of the work of the war poets can't be denied. But their poems don't give the whole story of the war; they don't even tell the whole story of those who wrote about the war. Here, however, is my selection of some writers well worth following up.

John Buchan (1875–1940)

Buchan was the Scottish journalist and politician who in 1915 produced one of the most famous spy stories ever written, *The Thirty-Nine Steps.* Buchan was a staunch believer in the British Empire and his central character, Richard Hannay, is clearly meant to be Buchan himself. The book tells of a dastardly German plot to invade pre-war Britain and it involves a famous chase across the Scottish Highlands. Less well known, though just as historically important, are the two follow-up books in the trilogy. *Greenmantle* tells of an equally dastardly German plot to undermine Britain's position in India and the Middle East. *Mr Standfast* has a dastardly German plot back in England, but this time helped by a group of tweedy, woolly-minded, weak-spined English liberals and pacifists for whom Hannay (and thus Buchan) has withering contempt.

The three books together give a very good idea of what patriotic Britons were convinced they were fighting for – and against.

RC Sherriff (1896–1975)

Sherriff served in the trenches as an officer before turning his hand to playwriting after the war. His most famous work, *Journey's End*, was based on the letters he wrote home from the front. It shows the tensions that arise among a group of officers in their dugout on the eve of the great German spring offensive in 1918 (see Chapter 16). It's a particularly poignant portrayal of the innocent idealism that many of those who'd been through public school still had when they arrived at the front. You won't be surprised to hear that the idealism doesn't last very long.

Journey's End made Sherriff's name and it's still regarded as one of the best dramatic presentations of the war. In 1976 it was made into a film, *Aces High*, this time set among the pilots of the Royal Flying Corps – which was appropriate because Sherriff had gone on to write the screenplay for the Second World War film *The Dambusters*.

Wilfred Owen (1893–1918)

Owen had only five poems published in his lifetime. His complete works were published in the 1960s and only then did he become the best known of that remarkable generation of British war poets. He spent time at the famous Craiglockhart hospital recovering from shellshock before returning to the front, where he was killed during the final Allied advances, only one week before the Armistice (see Chapter 16). The bitterness of his *'Dulce et Decorum Est'*, which tells of how one young soldier is caught without his gas mask in a gas attack, still has the power to move and shock. 'Strange Meeting' tells of how the spirit of a British soldier meets the spirit of the German he killed; it was used in 1961 by Benjamin Britten in his *War Requiem*.

Owen was a rather shy, modest man, but with a pen in his hand he tells the story of what the war meant to the men who fought it with a lyricism that few can match.

Jaroslav Hasek (1883–1923)

Soldiering isn't all about heroics or trench fighting: it's also about keeping your head down and looking after number one. That's the message of Hasek's brilliant comic novel, *The Good Soldier Schweik*. Schweik is a Czech solider in the Austro-Hungarian army, but he's not interested in fighting for the Habsburg monarch – or anyone else, really: he's interested in getting through the war in one piece. His way of surviving is to obey the people with authority over him to the letter, to show up the absurdity of what they're caught up in and, of course, to avoid getting sent to the front.

The Good Soldier Schweik has inspired a film, a play by Bertolt Brecht and an opera, and it also lies behind other exposés of the surreal madness of authority in war, such as Joseph Heller's *Catch 22.*

Ivor Gurney (1890–1937)

Gurney is best known as a composer, particularly for setting some of the poems of AE Housman to music, but he was also a prolific writer, both of poetry and of letters. He was a tragic figure, mentally unstable even before the war, in which he served as a private and was badly gassed at Ypres. He made frequent suicide attempts and was eventually confined in a mental hospital.

His works reflect his love for his native Gloucestershire and the way in which the war was driving him into madness. He only came to prominence as a writer in the 1980s and 1990s when his letters and many of his poems were finally published. He's still less well known than the other war poets, though, which makes it all the more important to discover him for yourself.

Henri Barbusse (1873–1935)

Henri Barbusse was one of the best known of the French writers who were finally turned against war by their experiences of the Western Front. His most famous work was *Le Feu* (*Under Fire* in English), published in 1916, which tells both of what it was like serving in the French trenches and of the stupidity and incompetence of so many of the French generals who sent the men uselessly to their deaths.

Barbusse's work had a wide influence and it went on to win the prestigious *Prix Goncourt* literary prize. At the end of the war Barbusse emigrated to the Soviet Union, where he became an admirer of Stalin, turning a blind eye to all his hero's murderous faults. His critics suggested that Barbusse was applying double standards: he seemed to be saying that it was wrong for French generals to send thousands of men to their deaths but all right for Stalin to murder millions of Russians. Barbusse can certainly be accused of hypocrisy or naïvety, but his work was very influential and his portrayal of the callous indifference of the French generals for the lives of their men is difficult to contradict.

Vera Brittain (1893–1970)

Vera Brittain's *Testament of Youth* is one of the best memoirs to come out of the war. It tells of how Vera was rescued from a dull life as a provincial industrialist's daughter by the chance to study at Oxford. Just as she was beginning to stretch her horizons and to meet and fall in love with a handsome friend of her brother's, her world was overturned by the war. All her dreams were shattered: she had to leave Oxford to train as a nurse, while her beloved brother, his friends and her fiancé were killed in the fighting.

Brittain's book is a moving and devastating portrayal of the impact the war had on the lives of the women the young men left behind. Her story illustrates what became known as the idea of a *lost generation* of young men who died in the war and left the women of their generation alone, without their sweethearts and lovers. As the years passed, it became common to see single women of that generation, often rather scary and embittered schoolmistresses or nurses, as the 'girls left behind' by the First World War.

Historians argue about whether or not it's right to speak of a lost generation – after all, if the 1914 generation had been wiped out in the war, the succeeding generations couldn't have appeared! – but it's difficult to see what else to call it in Vera Brittain's case. Even if the idea of a lost generation is just a bit of a middle-class, romantic myth, for many individuals, such as Vera Brittain, being part of a lost generation was certainly how it *felt* to live through the First World War.

Robert Graves (1895–1985)

Robert Graves was already a poet by the time he left school, but instead of going up to Oxford to study he enlisted in the Royal Welch Fusiliers and headed for the Western Front. His war memoir, *Goodbye to All That,* is a vivid account of life in the trenches, where the average survival span of a young officer like Graves was between two and three weeks. Graves himself was so badly wounded on the Somme that he had the bizarre experience of reading his own obituary in *The Times*! He went on to be a successful writer, but many people think *Goodbye to All That* remains his masterpiece.

Erich Maria Remarque (1898–1970)

Yes, I include Remarque in this list and in the list of films in Chapter 20, but his work is important enough to feature in both. His novel *All Quiet on the Western Front,* based on his own experiences in the trenches, is probably the definitive statement of the pacifist response to the war and, given what Germany was about to unleash on the world in the 1930s, it's very important that it should've been written by a German.

The book is set on the Western Front in a quiet period at the end of the war. The central character, Paul Bäumer, and his classmates are encouraged by their schoolteacher to join the army. The book begins with Paul having survived an attack in which half his classmates were killed. The teacher stands for pre-war Germany, which had encouraged its young men to regard war as a great adventure in which it was their duty to take part. The book came out in 1929, and it struck a chord with people who never wanted to go through war again. But soon afterwards the Nazis came to power and banned the book, denouncing it as unpatriotic and anti-German.

Ernest Hemingway (1899–1961)

Ernest Hemingway was American literature's man of action. He served with an ambulance unit on the Italian front in the First World War, where he was badly wounded and decorated for bravery. He became a well-known writer between the wars, but he was always ready to launch into combat: he fought in the Spanish Civil War and, although he was supposed to be a strictly non-combatant war correspondent, he led a French resistance unit in the liberation of Paris from German occupation in 1944.

Hemingway's first literary success came in 1929 with *A Farewell to Arms,* based on his wartime experiences in Italy. This book reflects the chaotic and self-destructive state of the Italian army that fell apart at the Battle of Caporetto in 1917 (see Chapter 15 for details) and it also reflects the ups and downs of Hemingway's own stormy love life. Hemingway received the Nobel Prize for literature in 1954, making him one of the most successful, and perhaps the greatest, of the writers who came out of the First World War.

Chapter 22

Ten Enlightening Places to Visit

*I*f you really want to get to know a period of history, you need to put the books down and get out to see the places where it happened. The best way to get a feel for the First World War is to visit some of its battlefields and go to museums where you can see the soldiers' weapons and clothing and the personal things they left behind. Reading about the distance men had to cover to get to the enemy line is all very well, but you can understand it much more if you go to the spot and see the distance for yourself. And don't underestimate the power of memorials to bring home the appalling human cost of the war.

This chapter offers my own selection of places that you can visit – museums, battle sites and memorials that give you a sense of what things were like in the dark days of the war. (One important point, though: live shells, grenades and other explosives still sometimes surface on First World War battle-fields. If you find one, never touch it. Just report it immediately to the local authorities.)

The Imperial War Museum, London

The Imperial War Museum (IWM) in London, England, is *the* must-see museum for anyone interested in the First World War. It began life in 1917 with a mission to tell the story of Britain and its empire in the war – hence the name. Since 1936 it's been housed in the elegant former Bethlehem (or 'Bethlem') Hospital, the mental hospital that gave us the word 'Bedlam', a suitable setting for a museum devoted to the story of modern warfare, you might think. Nowadays the IWM is a major centre for research on the First World War with unrivalled collections of manuscripts, photographs, films and audio recordings as well as an extensive collection of exhibits. If you can't make it to anywhere else, this is the place to come.

The Military History Museum, Vienna

The assassination of the Archduke Franz Ferdinand that triggered the war still haunts people's imagination. What if the driver *hadn't* turned right? Or if Gavrilo Princip had missed his target? How different might the world have been?

You can go and contemplate these might-have-beens at Vienna's Heeresgeschichtliches Museum (that's the Military History Museum) by standing in front of the actual car the Archduke was riding in on that fateful June day in 1914. All sorts of outlandish tales get told about what happened to this car. It's supposed to have brought bad luck to its subsequent owners, to have been painted blood red and to have been destroyed by a direct hit in a Second World War bombing raid. Well, you can go and see it and when you do you'll see that it's a) still black, and b) still there.

Vienna was the vibrant cultural centre of Europe before 1914, so visiting Franz Ferdinand's car gives you a good opportunity to get a feel for the city of the Habsburg monarchy, where the First World War had its origins.

In Flanders Fields, the Cloth Hall, Ypres

The ruined medieval Cloth Hall in Ypres, Belgium, became a symbol of defiance for the British stationed in the famous salient. After the war the Cloth Hall was rebuilt and its second floor now contains a large exhibition on life in the trenches, named after John McCrae's famous poem, 'In Flanders Fields'. Ypres is also a very good base for visiting the nearby cemeteries and memorials such as Tyne Cot, Passchendaele and Messines. Make sure you catch the large German cemetery at Langemarck too, and the moving Last Post ceremony at the Menin Gate.

Gallipoli

Visit Gallipoli, and see how hopeless the Allied position really was back in 1915. Today, of course, the whole area is studded with war cemeteries and memorials, and plenty of tour companies can take you round them. Highlights include the Helles memorial at the southern end of the peninsula and the famous Beach Cemetery farther up the coast in the ANZAC section. Gallipoli, in modern-day Turkey, is sacred ground to Australians and New Zealanders, though a visit to the cemeteries reminds you that most of the Allied troops were from Britain. If you want to know what a killing ground looks like, Gallipoli gives you a very good idea.

Edith Cavell Memorial, London

Edith Cavell was a British nurse working in Brussels at the time of the German occupation. She treated Allied and German servicemen equally, but the Germans arrested and shot her for her role in helping some 200 Allied soldiers to escape. Her story was used during the war as a propaganda example of 'Hun beastliness' and memorials to her were erected all over Britain. The dignified memorial outside the National Portrait Gallery in London tells a rather different story, however. It carries the words she spoke to a priest the day before her execution: 'Patriotism is not enough; I must have no hatred or bitterness for anyone.' Not a message many wanted to hear in 1915 but a very relevant one today.

Historial de la Grande Guerre, Verdun

So taken up are the British with the Somme that they tend to forget Verdun, the epic battle that came close to draining France dry. In the forested heart of what was once a nightmare landscape stands a simple and rather beautiful 1960s building that houses the museum and study centre commemorating what for the French was the defining battle of the war. It has a large collection of artefacts from the fighting, giving a chilling view of what combat in the trenches was really like. All First World War battlefields tend to be sobering, but for sheer sacrifice and slaughter Verdun is still awe-inspiring, and many French people see visiting it as a sort of pilgrimage. It is.

Beaumont Hamel

To really understand the First World War you need to get into the open and explore the battle sites, and no tour of First World War sites is complete without a visit to the Somme battlefields of northern France. The area is studded with beautiful cemeteries such as the South African memorial at Delville Wood and the small cemetery that marks the trench where the men of the Devonshire Regiment fell on the opening day: 'The Devonshires held this trench,' runs the slogan; 'the Devonshires hold it still.'

One of the best places to get a sense of what the Battle of the Somme was like is at a place called Beaumont Hamel, where you find a memorial park dedicated to the memory of the men of Newfoundland who died there, and a large statue of a Canadian caribou greets visitors as they arrive. The park has a section of trench lines preserved including a great crater caused by a mine. It's pretty big now; just think how big it was then.

Beaumont Hamel offers the chance to get a feel for the way the fighting went in 1916 and to appreciate the sacrifice made by the men who fought and died there.

Thiepval

If you're visiting the Somme, make time for Thiepval. It's not very far from Beaumont Hamel in fact, but what earns it a separate mention here is the large, elegant memorial arch inscribed with over 72,000 names. Seventy-two *thousand*. But these aren't just the dead: these are the missing – the men whose bodies were never found and are still out there somewhere, or else they were so blown to pieces that no one could identify them. The memorial is a beautiful and dignified one, and somehow it brings the sheer scale of the losses in that terrible battle home more acutely than any other.

The Brighton Chattri

High up on the rolling Sussex Downs above Brighton you might think you're in the most typically English rural scene when suddenly you see a marble dome upheld by pillars. If you think it looks vaguely eastern, you'd be right: this is Brighton's *chattri,* which is Hindi for 'umbrella'. The chattri is where the Indian Hindu soldiers who died in the special hospital for Indians set up in Brighton's Royal Pavilion were taken to be cremated in the open air, according to Hindu custom. Nowadays the Brighton chattri is a memorial: a place to remember all those Indians – Hindu, Muslim, Parsi and Christian – who travelled halfway around the world to fight and die for Britain. Every year, British and Indian ex-servicemen and the local community stage a pilgrimage to the chattri, to honour these men. An unusual memorial, perhaps, but a very fitting tribute.

The Sleeping Soldier, Munich

Every war memorial tells a story, but few tell quite such a momentous tale as the recumbent figure on the war memorial in Munich, in south-west Germany. It shows a German soldier in full uniform lying on a slab, holding his rifle, a bit like a 20th-century equivalent of a medieval knight's tomb. But then you notice something about him: he's not dead, he's sleeping. And if your German's up to it, you'll understand the slogan, 'Siewerdenauferstehen', and give a grim smile. It means: 'They will rise again'. And, boy, did they do it.

Index

• C •

• •

• **_H_** •

• Y •

• Z •

About the Author

Dr Seán Lang is Senior Lecturer in History at Anglia Ruskin University in Cambridge, where he teaches topics from the Tudor period to the modern day. He studied history at Oxford and has taught it in schools and colleges for the past thirty years. He also lectures for the University of Cambridge Department of Continuing Education and regularly teaches on its International Summer School. He has a regular history spot on BBC local radio and has frequently appeared on television commenting on the historical aspects of current events. He chairs the Better History Forum, which advises government on issues about the history curriculum in schools and is a former Honorary Secretary of the Historical Association. He has written textbooks and resource packs for schools and colleges and has published academic articles on British India. He is also active as a playwright and has written playscripts on a wide range of historical topics, including the American War of Independence, the Australian Child Migrants and the Belgian Congo. This is his fourth *For Dummies* book: He also wrote *British History For Dummies*, *European History For Dummies* and *Twentieth Century History For Dummies*.

About Imperial War Museums

Imperial War Museums (IWM) is the world's leading authority on conflict and its impact, focusing on Britain, its former Empire and the Commonwealth, from the First World War to the present. It is dedicated to recording people's experiences of modern conflict, exploring the causes of war and its impact on people's lives. The museums' collections are made up of the everyday and the exceptional, and are drawn from people of all walks of life. They reflect the total nature of war and reveal stories of people, places, ideas and events.

IWM is a family of five museums: IWM London, the flagship branch with six floors of exhibitions and displays; IWM North, housed in an iconic award-winning building designed by Daniel Libeskind; IWM Duxford, a world-renowned aviation museum and Britain's best preserved war-time airfield; Churchill War Rooms, housed in Winston Churchill's secret headquarters below Whitehall, and the Second World War cruiser HMS *Belfast*. You can visit their website at IWM.ORG.UK.

Author's Acknowledgements

My first encounter with the First World War came from John Hawkins, the enlightened headteacher of the Sacred Heart Primary School, New Malden, who arranged a field trip to the Belgian battlefields back in 1971 and to whom I owe a lifetime's debt. Others who have helped my understanding of the conflict develop and deepen include Nicolas Kinloch, Alan Palmer and Professor Gary Sheffield. My thanks go to my ever-encouraging editor at John Wiley, Steve Edwards, and especially to my wife Lorna, to whom this book is dedicated.

Publisher's Acknowledgements

We're proud of this book; please send us your comments at http://dummies.custhelp.com. For other comments, please contact our Customer Care Department within the U.S. at 877-762-2974, outside the U.S. at (001) 317-572-3993, or fax 317-572-4002.

Some of the people who helped bring this book to market include the following:

Acquisitions, Editorial and Vertical Websites

Development Editor: Steve Edwards

Commissioning Editor: Mike Baker

Assistant Editor: Ben Kemble

Copy Editor: Charlie Wilson

Imperial War Museums Reviewer: Terry Charman (Senior Historian)

Technical Reviewers: Alex McDermott, John McManus

Proofreader: Andy Finch

Publisher: Miles Kendall

Front Cover Photos: © Imperial War Museums (Q 2756)

Back Cover Photos: © iStockphoto.com/ jaywarren79, © Imperial War Museums (Q 67524)

Special Help: Andrew Kennerley

Project Coordinator: Melissa Cossell

Take Dummies with you everywhere you go!

Whether you're excited about e-books, want more from the web, must have your mobile apps, or swept up in social media, Dummies makes everything easier .

FOR DUMMIES®

A Wiley Brand

BUSINESS

978-1-118-73077-5

978-1-118-44349-1

978-1-119-97527-4

MUSIC

978-1-119-94276-4

978-0-470-97799-6

978-0-470-49644-2

DIGITAL PHOTOGRAPHY

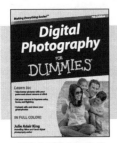

978-1-118-09203-3

978-0-470-76878-5

978-1-118-00472-2

Algebra I For Dummies
978-0-470-55964-2

Anatomy & Physiology For Dummies, 2nd Edition
978-0-470-92326-9

Asperger's Syndrome For Dummies
978-0-470-66087-4

Basic Maths For Dummies
978-1-119-97452-9

Body Language For Dummies, 2nd Edition
978-1-119-95351-7

Bookkeeping For Dummies, 3rd Edition
978-1-118-34689-1

British Sign Language For Dummies
978-0-470-69477-0

Cricket for Dummies, 2nd Edition
978-1-118-48032-8

Currency Trading For Dummies, 2nd Edition
978-1-118-01851-4

Cycling For Dummies
978-1-118-36435-2

Diabetes For Dummies, 3rd Edition
978-0-470-97711-8

eBay For Dummies, 3rd Edition
978-1-119-94122-4

Electronics For Dummies All-in-One For Dummies
978-1-118-58973-1

English Grammar For Dummies
978-0-470-05752-0

French For Dummies, 2nd Edition
978-1-118-00464-7

Guitar For Dummies, 3rd Edition
978-1-118-11554-1

IBS For Dummies
978-0-470-51737-6

Keeping Chickens For Dummies
978-1-119-99417-6

Knitting For Dummies, 3rd Edition
978-1-118-66151-2

Think you can't learn it in a day? Think again!

The *In a Day* e-book series from *For Dummies* gives you quick and easy access to learn a new skill, brush up on a hobby, or enhance your personal or professional life — all in a day. Easy!

Available as PDF, eMobi and Kindle

Printed and bound by CPI Group (UK) Ltd, Croydon, CR0 4YY